X Window Systems

Programming and Applications with Xt

Douglas A. Young

Hewlett-Packard Laboratories
Palo Alto, California

Prentice Hall, Englewood Cliffs, New Jersey 07632

Library of Congress, Cataloging-in-Publication Data

YOUNG, DOUGLAS A.

X window systems : programming and applications with Xt / Douglas A. Young.

p. cm.

Includes index.

ISBN 0-13-972167-3

1. X Window System (Computer system) 1. Title.

QA76.76.W56Y68 1989

005.4'3—dc20

Cover design: *Photo Plus Art*
Manufacturing buyer: *Bob Anderson*

Back cover line art:
courtesy of John Humphrys

Printed in the United States of America

10 9 8 7 6

ISBN 0-13-972167-3

PRENTICE-HALL INTERNATIONAL (UK) LIMITED, *LONDON*
PRENTICE-HALL OF AUSTRALIA PTY. LIMITED, *SYDNEY*
PRENTICE-HALL CANADA INC., *TORONTO*
PRENTICE-HALL HISPANOAMERICANA, S.A., *MEXICO*
PRENTICE-HALL OF INDIA PRIVATE LIMITED, *NEW DELHI*
PRENTICE-HALL OF JAPAN, INC., *TOKYO*
SIMON & SCHUSTER ASIA PTE. LTD., *SINGAPORE*
EDITORA PRENTICE-HALL DO BRASIL, LTDA., *RIO DE JANEIRO*

To Teri and D.C.

CONTENTS

PREFACE

Window-based user interfaces are becoming a common feature of most computer systems, and as a result, users have come to expect all applications to have polished user-friendly interfaces. Unfortunately, a user interface that is easy to use is seldom easy to build. Some experts estimate that as much as 90 percent of the total effort required to develop a typical window and mouse-based application goes into the user interface. The X Window System provides a standard window platform that allows application programmers to spend more time improving their programs and less time porting to new systems.

This book is intended for anyone who writes software in an environment that supports the X Window System. It should be useful to professional programmers who are beginning to develop programs using the X Window System as well as students who want to add professional quality interfaces to their projects.

This book is not intended as a reference manual. Rather, the facilities provided by X are introduced through examples. The Xlib and Xt Intrinsics reference manuals do a comprehensive job of explaining the workings of individual functions, but they don't explain how to put the pieces together to build an application. This book tries to demonstrate typical ways to combine the pieces provided by the various X layers to form working applications. It would be useful for the reader to have access to a system supporting X to experiment with the programs presented. I hope the example programs are useful as a starting point for further explorations of the X Window System, and I encourage the reader to expand, enhance, and improve them, because the easiest way to learn to program with X is to practice.

Because X has evolved into a complex system, it is often difficult to know where to start when learning to program with X. There are at least two approaches. The first approach is to follow the path by which X evolved: understand the basic X model and learn to program with Xlib, and finally explore the various higher-level toolkits. This approach has the advantage that by the time the programmer is done, he or she will thoroughly understand the lower layers of X, and have a greater appreciation of the high-level toolkits. It has the disadvantage of being time consuming and somewhat overwhelming. Programmers who follow this approach have to invest a great deal of time before building their first useful program.

This book takes a second approach, in which we briefly discuss the architectural model used by X, and then immediately use a high-level toolkit to begin to build useful programs.

The disadvantage of this approach is that the programmer may not fully understand what is happening at the lower levels and has to take many things on faith. This is more than compensated for by the fact that we can build something useful quickly, and then explore the details at our later convenience.

The programs described in this book were tested on an HP9000/350 workstation, running HP-UX and also on a Sun 3/260 running SunOS 4.0. All examples are written in the C programming language, and the book assumes at least a basic knowledge of that language. Window systems are inherently graphical in nature, and it might useful for the reader to have some familiarity with basic raster graphics, although no knowledge of graphics algorithms is needed. It would also be useful for the reader to have used X. This book does not provide a user's tutorial.

This book was composed and formatted entirely using X-based applications. The initial text was entered using a multiwindow X11-based version of Gnu-EMACS. Early drafts were formatted using troff and previewed on a version of the xdvi previewer. Final formatting, including all figures, was done on an X11 version of FrameMaker. All images of the programs in this book are screen dumps from a 4-plane color screen. The images were produced by piping the xwd window dumper through a version of Jeff Poskansker's portable bitmap programs (modified to handle gray scale) to produce PostScript. For the images in this book, the examples were linked with HP's 3-D version of the widget library.

ACKNOWLEDGMENTS

Many people contributed to this book, either directly by reviewing all or part of it, or indirectly through discussions regarding the topics in this book. Arlene Azzerello, Martin Cagan, Dan Garfinkle, Audrey Ishizaki, Phil Gust, Warren Harris, Oliver Jones, Niels Mayer, and Bob Miller all helped to improve this book with their suggestions. Steve Friedl and Rick Kelley deserve special mention for their thorough and thoughtful reviews not only of the text, but of the code as well. Their code reviews were instrumental in reducing bugs and cleaning up the examples. Many people on the xpert mailing list also contributed unknowingly, either by asking interesting questions or by providing answers. Ken Lee at Daisy Systems periodically posts a detailed X bibliography to the ba.windows.x news group. My bibliography is based in part on information he compiled. Last, but certainly not least, a special thanks must go to Teresa Stottsberry, who read more drafts of this book than she probably cares to remember, and helped me complete this book in ways too numerous to mention. I could not have finished the book without her. I would also like to thank my management at Hewlett Packard Laboratories, Jim Ambras, Martin Griss, and Alan Snyder, for their encouragement. Of course, all errors in the examples or the information in this book are my responsibility alone.

Douglas Young

1

AN INTRODUCTION TO THE X WINDOW SYSTEM

The X Window System is an industry-standard software system that allows programmers to develop portable graphical user interfaces. One of the most important features of X is its unique device-independent architecture. X allows programs to display windows containing text and graphics on any hardware that supports the X protocol without modifying, recompiling, or relinking the application. This device independence, along with X's position as an industry standard, allows X-based applications to function in a heterogeneous environment consisting of mainframes, workstations, and personal computers.

X was developed at Massachusetts Institute of Technology (MIT), with support from the Digital Equipment Corporation (DEC). The name, X, as well as some initial design ideas were derived from an earlier window system named W, developed by Brain Reid and Paul Asente at Stanford University. X was designed at MIT's Laboratory for Computer Science for Project Athena to fulfill that project's need for a distributed, hardware-independent user interface platform. Early versions of X were used primarily within MIT and DEC, but with the release of version 10, many manufacturers expressed interest in X as a commercial product. The first 10 versions of X were designed and implemented primarily by Robert Scheifler and Ron Newman from MIT and Jim Gettys from DEC, although many additional people contributed to X, Version 11. Version 11 of the X Window System is supported by a consortium of hardware and software vendors who have made a commitment to X as a standard base for user interfaces across each of their product lines. The X consortium supports and controls the standard specification of the X Window System. X is available on most UNIX systems,

Digital's VAX/VMS operating system, and also many personal computers. Many companies have also begun to produce hardware specifically designed to support the X protocol.

One important difference between X and many other window systems is that X does not define any particular user interface style. X provides *mechanisms* to support many interface styles rather than enforcing any one *policy*. Many window systems — the one used by Apple's MacIntosh, or Microsoft Windows, for example — support a particular style of user interface. In contrast, X provides a flexible set of primitive window operations, but carefully avoids dictating the look or feel of any particular application's user interface. Instead, X provides a device-independent layer that serves as a base for a variety of interface styles. Therefore, the basic X Window System does not provide user interface components such as button boxes, menus, or dialog boxes often found in other window systems. Most applications depend on higher level libraries built on top of the basic X protocol to provide these components.

The following sections introduce a few of the fundamental architectural elements of X.

1.1 THE CLIENT-SERVER MODEL

The architecture of the X Window System is based on a *client-server* model. A single process, known as the *server,* completely controls all input and output devices. The server creates and manipulates windows on the screen, produces text and graphics, and handles input devices such as a keyboard and mouse. The server provides a portable layer between all applications and the display hardware. The X server typically runs on a workstation or personal computer with a graphics display, although some vendors offer dedicated X terminals that implement the X server in hardware or firmware.

An application that uses the facilities provided by the X server is known as a *client*. A client communicates with the X server via a network connection using an asynchronous byte-stream protocol. X supports many network protocols, including TCP/IP, DECnet, and Chaos. Multiple clients can connect to a single server concurrently, and an individual client can also connect to multiple servers.

The X architecture hides most of the details of the device-dependent implementation of the server and the hardware it controls from clients. Any client can communicate with any server, provided both the client and the server obey the X protocol.

In addition to providing device independence, the distributed architecture of X allows the server and clients to run on separate machines located anywhere on a network.[1] This feature has many potential applications. For example, imagine an interactive teaching program

1. The server and client(s) often run on separate machines within a local area network. However, X can also handle not-so-local configurations transparently. I once had an interesting opportunity to use this feature to read my electronic mail during a trip to Europe. The X-based mail program (the client) ran on my workstation in Palo Alto, California, while the X server ran on a workstation in Bristol, England! Although the response of the system suffered slightly from the satellite transmission time, X worked perfectly. The mail program was completely unaware that I was interacting with it from a location several thousand miles away.

executing on a school's main computer that can display information on inexpensive personal computers located at each student's desk. In this scenario, the teaching program is a client that communicates with multiple servers, one for each student's display. Each student interacts with the program concurrently through a window on his or her local machine. The same program is also connected to another display located at the teacher's desk allowing the teacher to check the progress of any individual student or the class as a whole. While one window on each of the students' machines provides an interface to the remote teaching program, other windows on a student's machine can provide interfaces to other clients. For example, each student can use a window to interact with an electronic mail system running on a central mail server. Still another window can provide an interface to an editor running locally on each student's machine.

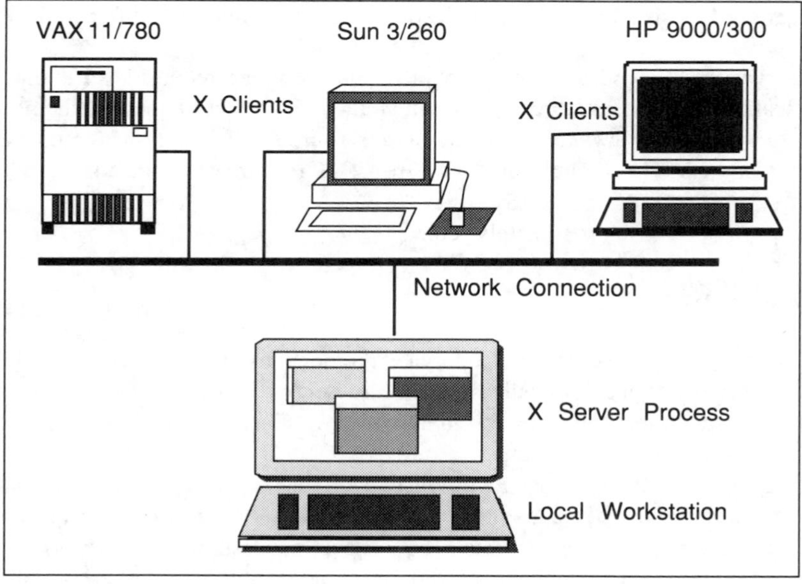

Figure 1.1 The client-server model.

1.2 DISPLAYS AND SCREENS

The terms *display* and *screen* are often used interchangeably to refer to a cathode ray tube (CRT) used by the computer to display text and/or graphics. However, X uses the term *display* to mean a single X server process, while a *screen* is a single hardware output device. A single X display can support many screens. X uses the terms *display* and *server* interchangeably. There is normally only one display per central processing unit (CPU).

Before a client can communicate with the X server it must open a connection to the server. Once a client establishes a connection to a display, it can use any of the screens controlled by the server. X provides a security mechanism that allows a server to deny clients executing on other hosts the right to connect to a display. This mechanism works on a per-host basis.

1.3 RESOURCES

The X server controls all *resources* used by the window system. Resources include windows, bitmaps, fonts, colors, and other data structures used by an application. The X server maintains these resources privately within the server, to enable clients to use and share these data structures transparently. Client programs access each resource through a *resource identifier*, usually referred to simply as an ID. A resource ID is a unique identifier assigned by the X server.

The X server usually creates and destroys resources at the request of a client. The server also automatically destroys most resources when the client that requested them exits. X allows clients to specify the *shutdown mode* of a resource. The shutdown mode controls the lifetime of a resource. The default mode destroys all resources allocated for a client when that client exits.

1.4 REQUESTS

When a client application needs to use a service provided by the X server, the client issues a *request* to the server. Clients typically request the server to create, destroy, or reconfigure windows, or to display text or graphics in a window. Clients can also request information about the current state of windows or other resources.

The X server normally runs asynchronously with respect to its clients and all client run asynchronously with respect to each other. Although the server processes requests from each particular application in the order in which they arrive, requests are not necessarily processed immediately. Requests from clients are placed in a queue until the server is able to process them, and clients do not wait for the server to respond to a request. Applications can request the server to handle requests synchronously, but this usually results in poorer performance, because each request to the server suffers a round-trip over the network connection.

1.5 BASIC WINDOW CONCEPTS

The most fundamental resource in X is the *window*. A window simply represents a rectangular section of the screen. Unlike windows in some other window systems, an X window has no title bar, scroll bar or other decorations. An X window appears as a rectangle with a background color or pattern. Each window also has a border. Applications can combine two or more windows to create scroll bars, title bars, and other higher-level user interface components.

The X server creates windows in response to requests from clients. The server stores and maintains the data structure representing a window, while clients refer to the window using the window's ID. Clients can issue requests to the server to alter the window's size, position, color, or other characteristics, and can also request the server to place text in a window or perform graphical operations on a window. Although the server creates each window at the request of a specific client, any client can request the server to manipulate the window, provided they have access to the window's ID. For example, X window managers use this feature to control the position of all windows on the screen.

1.5.1 The Window Hierarchy

X organizes windows as a hierarchy, referred to as the *window tree*. The top window in this window tree is known as the *root window*. The X server automatically creates a root window for each screen controlled it controls. The root window occupies an entire physical screen, and cannot be moved or resized. Every window except the root window has a *parent* window (also known as an *ancestor*) and can also have *children* (also known as *descendents* or *subwindows*). Windows that share the same parent are known as *siblings*.

Fig. 1.2 and Fig. 1.3 illustrate this hierarchical model and show the relationship between several windows. Fig. 1.3 illustrates how a set of windows might appear on the screen, while Fig. 1.4 shows the window tree formed by these windows. Windows A and B are children of the root window, while Windows C and E are children of Window A. Window G is a child of Window E, and Window H is a child of Window F.

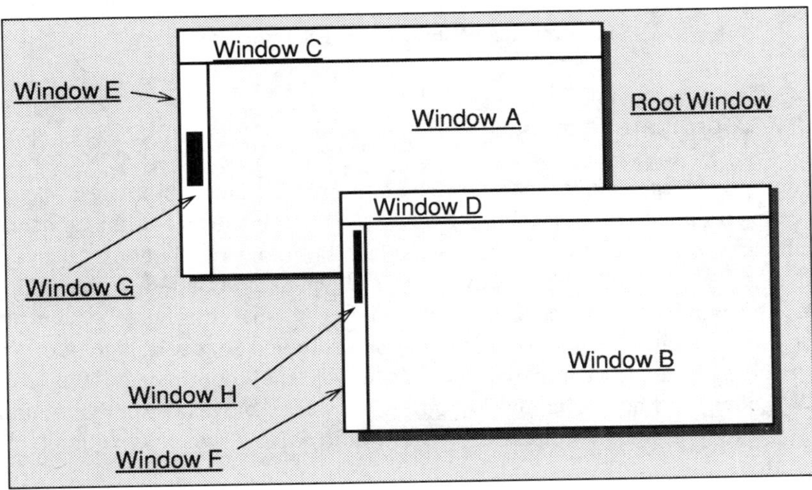

Figure 1.2 A typical window hierarchy.

X places few restrictions on the size or location of a window, but only that portion of a window that lies within the bounds of its parent is visible; the server *clips* the remaining portions to the boundaries of the parent window.

X allows windows to overlap in a way that resembles a collection of papers on a desk. The *stacking order* determines which windows or portions of windows appear to be on top (and are therefore visible). If two windows occupy the same (or overlapping) regions on the screen, the window that is higher in the stacking order completely or partially *obscures* the lower window. For example, in Fig. 1.3, Window B is higher in the stacking order than Window A. Clients can request the X server to alter a window's position in the stacking order (for example, raising a window above all other windows). A window's stacking order can only be altered relative to its siblings. Therefore, from a user's viewpoint, a window's descendants raise and lower with the window.

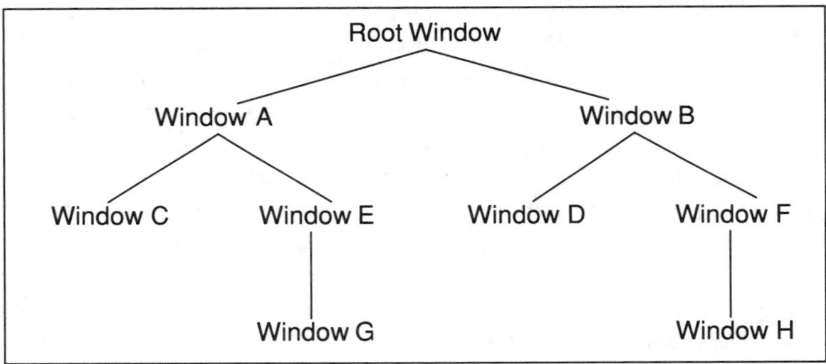

Figure 1.3 Window tree for Fig. 1.2.

1.5.2 The X Coordinate System

Each X window, including the root window, has its own integer coordinate system. The coordinate of the upper left corner of each window is *(0, 0)*. The *x* coordinate increases toward the right and the *y* coordinate increases toward the bottom. Applications always specify the coordinate of a point on the screen relative to some window. A window's position (the upper left corner of the window) is always specified relative to the coordinate system of its parent window. For example, in Fig. 1.4, Window A is positioned at coordinate *(50, 100)* relative to the coordinate system of the root window. However, the coordinate of this point is *(0, 0)* relative to Window A. Each window's coordinate system moves with the window, permitting applications to place text, graphics, or sub-windows in a window without regard to the window's location.

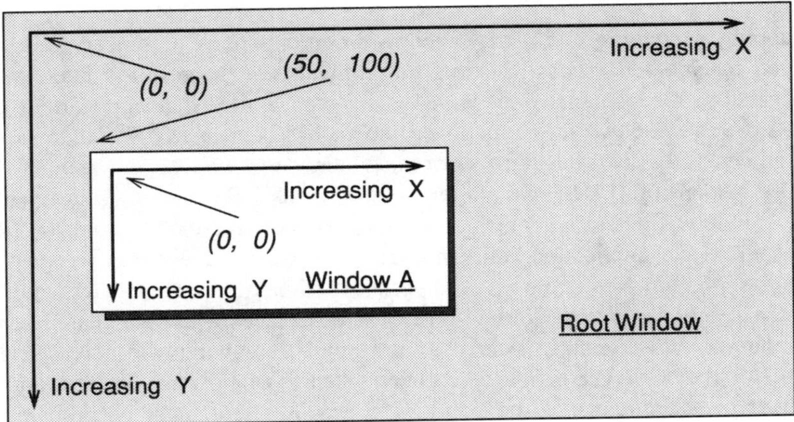

Figure 1.4 The X coordinate system.

1.5.3 Mapping and Window Visibility

Although each X window is associated with a rectangular region on the screen, all windows are not necessarily visible to the user. When the server creates a window, it allocates and initializes the data structures that represent the window within the server, but does not invoke the hardware-dependent routines that display the window on the screen. Clients can request the server to display a window by issuing a *map* request. Although a window is considered to be *mapped* if a client has issued a map request for that window, it still might not be visible for any of the following reasons:

- The window is completely *obscured* by another window on the screen. The window becomes visible only if it or the obscuring window is moved, the obscuring window is removed from the screen, or the stacking order of the two windows changes so that the obscuring window is lower in the stacking order than the other window.
- An ancestor of the window is not mapped. Before a window can appear on the screen, every ancestor of the window must be mapped. A window that is mapped, but has an ancestor that is not mapped, is said to be *unviewable*. The window automatically becomes *viewable* when all ancestors are mapped.
- The window is completely clipped by an ancestor. If a window is located completely outside the visible boundaries of any ancestor, it is not visible on the screen. The window becomes visible if the ancestor or ancestors are resized to include the region occupied by the window, or if the window is moved to lie within the visible boundaries of all ancestors.

1.5.4 Maintaining Window Contents

In an overlapping window system, each window's contents must be preserved when that window is covered by another window, so that the contents can be restored later. Many systems maintain and restore the contents of a window, in such a way that applications are unaware of the process. Such windows are sometimes known as *retained-raster* windows, because the window system generally saves the contents of the window as a *bitmap*, or *raster*.

In X, the responsibility for maintaining the contents of a windows lies with the client that uses the window. Some implementations of X support retained rasters, or *backing store* as it is known in X, but applications must not depend on this feature because there is no guarantee that all server implementations can provide this service for all windows. Saving complete raster images for every window on the screen places a huge demand on the memory resources of the server's computer system as the number of windows increases. It is usually more efficient for the X server to notify a client when a window is *exposed*, and rely on the client to redisplay the contents of the window. Every X client must be prepared to recreate the contents of its windows at any time. This places some additional burden on the application programmer, although this is seldom a problem because most applications maintain internal representations of their data anyway. The backing store feature of some X servers is best used to support compute-intensive applications that have difficulty recreating their output on demand. For servers that do not support backing store, such applications must usually resort to saving the current contents of its windows as an off-screen image.

Many X servers also support *save-unders*. A save-under is a technique of saving the image on the screen, *under* a particular window, so that the image can be restored when the window is moved to a new location or removed from the screen. This is done by taking a snapshot of an area of the screen just before this area is covered by a window. For save-unders to work, the state of the screen and all windows on the screen must be held constant between the time the snapshot is taken and the time the image is restored. Save-unders are used primarily when creating popup menus and other small transitory windows to achieve a smooth visual effect.

1.6 THE EVENT MODEL

The X server communicates with clients by sending *events* to the client applications. The server generates events as a direct or indirect result of a user action (for example, pressing a key on the keyboard, moving the mouse, or pressing a mouse button). The server also generates events to notify the client of changes in the state of its windows. For example, the server sends a client an **Expose** event when a window's contents need restored. X supports thirty-three types of events, and provides a mechanism that allows clients to define additional event types.

The server sends events to a client by placing the event on a first-in, first-out (FIFO) queue that can be read by the client. Each event consists of a data structure containing the type of event, the window in which the event occurred, and other data specific to the particular type of event.

Most X applications are completely *event-driven* and are designed to wait until an event occurs, respond to the event, and then wait for the next event. The event-driven approach provides a natural model for interactive applications. Chapter 5 discusses events and the event-driven model in detail.

1.7 INPUT DEVICES

X supports a variety of input devices. Depending on the implementation, a server can support tablets, track balls, scanners, and other data input and pointing devices. However, the most common input devices are the keyboard, used for textual input, and the mouse, which serves as both a pointing device and a selection device.

1.7.1 The Mouse

A mouse is a device that allows the user to point to locations on the screen and also to issue commands by pressing buttons. The user points to a screen location by controlling the position of an image on the screen known as a *sprite*.

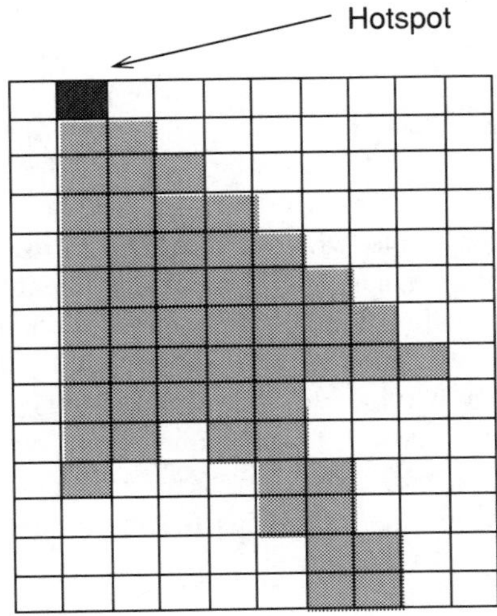

Figure 1.5 A typical mouse cursor.

The sprite is sometimes referred to as the *mouse cursor* although X usually uses the term *pointer*. The user controls the location of the sprite by moving the mouse on the user's desk.[2]

The server maintains the sprite and tracks the location of the mouse. Clients can ask the server to report events when the sprite enters or leaves a window, changes position, or when the user presses or releases a mouse button. Clients can also query the server to determine the current position of the sprite Applications can also change the size and appearance of the sprite. This feature is often used to indicate the current task or state of the application. For example, in some systems the mouse cursor assumes the shape of a diagonal arrow (see Fig. 1.5) when the user points to a location on the screen, and changes to a vertical arrow when the user uses a scroll bar.

Every mouse cursor has a *hotspot*. A hotspot is the point within the mouse cursor that defines its exact location of the sprite on the screen. The sprite is said to be *contained* by a window if the mouse cursor's hotspot is inside the visible region of the window, or one of its sub-windows. The sprite is *in* the smallest window to contain the hotspot.

1.7.2 The Keyboard

The server generates an event each time a key changes state. The information in the event structure includes a code identifying the key that was pressed or released. The client can translate this code into an ASCII character code if desired. The key code is independent of any particular keyboard arrangement to allow applications to handle a variety of keyboards made by different manufacturers.

1.8 WINDOW MANAGEMENT

A *window manager* allows the user to control the size and location of windows on the screen. In many window systems, the window manager is inseparable from the rest of the window system. In X, a window manager is an ordinary client application. However, X provides some features intended to allow window managers to control the size and placement of windows. For example, window managers can request that the X server *redirect* requests dealing with the structure of a window to the window manager rather than acting on the requests directly. If an application issues a map request for a window and a window manager has requested that such events be redirected, the X server sends a **MapRequest** event to the window manager. The window manager then has the opportunity to take some action before

2. Because of the close relationship between the motion of the mouse and the motion of the sprite on the screen, users often talk of the position of the mouse when they really mean the position of the sprite. For example, someone might say "the mouse is in the window." Of course the mouse is really on the desk; the sprite or mouse cursor is in the window. This tendency to interchange "sprite" and "'mouse" appeared in the names of some library routines in older versions of X, such as XWarpMouse(), that moved, or warped the position of the sprite (not the mouse!) to a new location. X11 consistently uses "pointer" in names of functions and macros that refer to the sprite. Thus the X10 function XWarpMouse() is known as XWarpPointer() in X11.

mapping the window, or can even refuse to map the window. Some window managers use this feature to place or resize windows according to a set of layout rules. For example, a *tiling* window manager might first rearrange or resize other windows already on the screen to ensure that no windows overlap. Many window managers use this feature to add a frame or title bar to the window before mapping it.

Window management is a complex subject that affects not only how users interact with a system, but also how applications interact with each other and with the X server. Some guidelines have been proposed to address these issues [Rosen88], although conventions are still evolving as this book is being written. In practice, these guidelines are of the most concern to those few programmers who design window managers[3] and user interface toolkits.

1.9 THE APPLICATION PROGRAMMER'S INTERFACE TO X

Although the X server protocol is defined at the level of network packets and byte-streams, programmers generally base applications on libraries that provide an interface to the base window system. One standard interface to X is the C language library known as Xlib.[4] Xlib defines an extensive set of functions that provide complete access and control over the display, windows, and input devices. Similar libraries also exist for LISP and ADA.

Although programmers can (and do) use Xlib to build applications, this library can be tedious and difficult to use correctly. Just handling the window manager conventions can require hundreds of lines of code. Many programmers prefer to use one of the higher-level toolkits designed to be used with X. In addition to the X Toolkit discussed in this book, there is InterViews (built at Stanford University), Andrew (from Carnegie Mellon), Xray (developed at Hewlett Packard), and CLUE (developed at Texas Instruments), to name just a few. Most of these toolkits are based on Xlib, but are generally easier to use and hide many implementation details from the programmer.

This book discusses a standard toolkit known as the X Toolkit. The X Toolkit consists of two parts: a layer known as the Xt Intrinsics, and a set of user interface components known as widgets. The Xt Intrinsics supports many different widget sets. The examples in this book use a typical widget set, the X widget set contributed to the X community by

3. Developing new window managers has become a popular activity among X programmers. Many programmers gained their initial understanding of X by writing new window managers. Consequently, X users have had the benefit of the many window managers that are available in the public domain. The most basic X window manager is simply named "wm". This window manager was intended only for early X11 developers, not for public use. The source to wm is kept primarily in a file named "test.c"! In spite of the implications of this file name, wm served many programmers well, and provided a model for some other window managers. Other popular X window managers include "uwm" (Ultrix Window Manager), "wm" (Ardent Window Manager), "twm" (Tom's Window Manager), and a tiled window manager, "rtl" (which takes it name from the Siemens Research Technology Laboratory).

4. The X Consortium recognizes two types of "standards," exclusive and non-exclusive. Xlib is an example of an exclusive standard. The Consortium will not recognize or adopt any other C-language interface to the underlying X protocol as a standard. Non-exclusive standards such as the Xt Intrinsics are considered part of the X Window System, but the Consortium may recognize other similar interfaces as well.

Hewlett-Packard. Other widget sets are available, and from an application programmer's viewpoint, are usually very similar to the X Widget set. A programmer who is familiar with one widget set should be able to quickly learn to use any other widget set. Both the Xt Intrinsics and the X Widget set are written in C and are built on top of Xlib. The X Widget set implements user interface components, including scroll bars, menus, and buttons, while the Xt Intrinsics provides a framework that allows the programmer to combine these components to produce a complete user interface. Fig. 1.6 shows the architecture of an application based on a widget set and the Xt Intrinsics.

The Xt Intrinsics and the X Widget set are smoothly integrated with Xlib, so applications that use the additional facilities of the higher level library can also use the functions provided by Xlib when needed. This book shows how the application programmer can use Xlib, the Xt Intrinsics, and a widget set such as the X Widget set together as a complete system for constructing user interfaces.

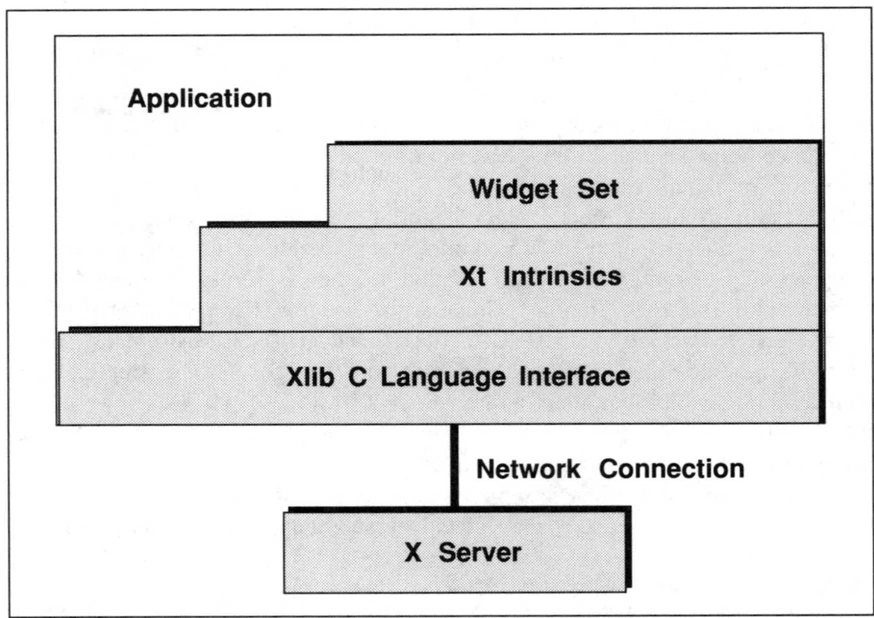

Figure 1.6 Programmer's view of the complete X Window System.

1.10 SUMMARY

This chapter presented the basic architecture of the X Window System and introduced some basic terminology. X provides a powerful platform that allows programmers to develop sophisticated user interfaces that are portable to any system that supports X. X is based on a network-transparent client-server model. The X server creates and manipulates windows in response to requests from clients, and sends events to notify clients of user input or changes in a window's state. Clients can execute anywhere on a network, making X an ideal base for distributed systems.

X does not support any particular interface style, and strives to be policy-free. Applications are free to use the X primitives to define their own type of user interface, although it is easier for an application to fit into an existing environment if the application follows a few guidelines. The easiest way for a programmer to follow these basic guidelines is to use a higher level toolkit, such as the Xt Intrinsics. As this book is being written, these guidelines are still evolving. Using a toolkit helps to partially insulate the application programmer from changes that may occur.

Many window systems refer to the entire system as a "window manager." In X, a window manager is a client, no different from any other client, that allows the user to move and manipulate windows. Users can choose from a variety of window managers, and therefore the programmer must not design an X application in such a way that it depends on a particular window manager. In fact, X applications should function properly even when there is no window manager at all.

Most programmers find it easiest to base their applications on a toolkit, such as the X Toolkit. The X Toolkit includes a layer known as the Xt Intrinsics which defines an architecture for combining user interface components known as widgets to create an application's user interface. The following chapters use Xlib, the Xt Intrinsics, and a typical widget set to build examples that demonstrate many of the features of X. Chapter 2 introduces the Xt Intrinsics and demonstrates a simple X-based application.

2

PROGRAMMING WITH THE Xt INTRINSICS

This chapter introduces the application programmer's interface to the X Window System, concentrating on the Xt Intrinsics layer of the X Toolkit. Following X philosophy, the Xt Intrinsics attempts to remain policy-free, and provides only those mechanisms that do not affect the look or feel of an application's interface. The Xt Intrinsics serves as a framework that allows programmers to create user interfaces by combining an extensible set of user interface components. These components are known as *widgets*, and include *scrollbars*, *title bars*, *menus*, and *dialog boxes*. Most widgets consist of an X window along with some procedures that operate on the window. The Intrinsics provides a small core set of widgets, and additional widgets are available from many sources.

Most programmers use a combination of Xlib, the Xt Intrinsics, and a widget set to write X-based applications. We refer to these programmers as *application programmers*. The Xt Intrinsics defines an architectural model for widgets that also allows programmers to create new types of widgets. We refer to a programmer who creates new widgets as a *widget programmer*.[1]

1. This distinction between an application programmer and a widget programmer reflects an interesting point of view that is common in the object-oriented programming community. Some programmers tend to be producers of self-contained reusable components (widgets, for example), while other programmers are consumers who use these components to build applications. Each of these activities may require a slightly different set of skills. At least in theory, the application programmer (the consumer) does not need to understand the internal implementation of a widget to use it successfully, and the widget programmer (the producer) does not need to know how any particular application will use a widget to design and build it correctly.

This book describes the Xt Intrinsics and the X Widget set based on the X11R3 version of the Xt Intrinsics, although all but a few examples work with either the R2 or R3 versions. This chapter introduces a few of the basic functions included in the Xt Intrinsics layer and presents a simple application using the Xt Intrinsics and widgets.

2.1 NAMING CONVENTIONS

Each layer of the application programmer's interface to X follows its own naming conventions. The names of all Xlib functions and user-accessible data structures begin with the capital letter **X**, and use a mixed case convention. When function names are composed of more than one word, the first letter of each word is capitalized For example,

```
XCreateWindow()
XDrawString()
```

All Xlib macros also follow this mixed case convention, but do not begin with the letter **X**. For example,

```
DisplayWidth()
ButtonPressMask
```

Xlib also follows some conventions intended to make it easier to remember the argument order used by each Xlib function. The first argument to nearly every Xlib function is a pointer to a **Display** structure. If the function requires a resource identifier as an argument, the resource ID immediately follows the display argument. *Drawable*s precede all other resources. A *drawable* is any resource that can be the object of a graphics request. In X, this can be either a window or a pixmap. Whenever a function requires both a *source* and a *destination* drawable, the source argument always precedes the destination. When the function parameters include size and location specifications, *x* always precedes *y*, *width* always precedes *height*, and the *x*, *y* pair always precedes the *width*, *height* pair. For example, consider the argument order of the following Xlib function

```
XDrawRectangle(display, drawable, gc, x, y, width, height)
```

As specified by the argument ordering conventions, the first argument to this function is a pointer to a display. The next two arguments are resources. The first of these is a drawable, and must precede the second resource (a graphics context). Finally, the *x*, *y* location precedes the **width** and **height** of the rectangle.

The Xt Intrinsics uses naming conventions similar to those used by Xlib. All functions and macros use mixed case and begin with the letters **Xt**. Unlike Xlib, the Intrinsics layer does not distinguish between functions and macros. For example,

```
XtCreateWidget()
XtSetArg()
```

The Xt Intrinsics also uses string constants to specify X resources. Defining strings as constants promotes consistency and also assists the programmer by allowing the compiler to detect spelling errors. These resource strings fall into three categories: resource *name strings*, resource *class strings*, and resource *representation strings*. Chapter 3 discusses the meaning of these terms. By convention, X defines resource name strings by adding the prefix **XtN** to the string. For example,

```
#define XtNwidth    "width"
```

Resource class strings use the prefix **XtC**:

```
#define XtCBackground    "Background"
```

A resource representation string is defined by adding the prefix **XtR** to the string, for example:

```
#define XtRCallback    "Callback"
```

Different widget sets often follow their own conventions for naming functions, types, and variables. For example, all external symbols in the X Widget set start with the letters **Xw**:

```
XwpushButtonWidgetClass
```

By convention, each widget class consists of the name of the widget class followed by the word **WidgetClass**. In addition, in the X Widget set, the first word of the widget name is usually lowercase, while following words are mixed case. Widget classes also begin with the letters **Xw**. For example,

```
XwrowColWidgetClass
XwpushButtonWidgetClass
```

Unfortunately, even within the X Widget set, not all widgets follow these conventions in a predictable way, and the programmer must usually refer to documentation to be sure of the precise capitalization of the widget names.

The first time a function is used in this book, the syntax of the function is given as it is used in a program. For example, the first time we discuss the function **XtNextEvent()** it is shown as:

```
XtNextEvent(&event)
```

To differentiate functions and variables defined by the examples presented in this book from those defined by Xlib, the Xt Intrinsics, or the X Widget set, the functions and variables defined by examples use a combination of lowercase letters and underscores. For example,

```
refresh_screen()
main_window
```

Macros defined by examples in this book follow the standard C convention of using all upper case characters. For example,

```
FONTHEIGHT()
MAX()
```

2.2 BASIC Xt INTRINSICS FUNCTIONS

Before looking at an example application, the following sections briefly discuss a few of the fundamental Intrinsics functions.

2.2.1 Initialization

All applications must call the function

```
XtInitialize(name, class, options, noptions, &argc, argv)
```

before calling any other Intrinsics function. **XtInitialize()** establishes a connection with the X server and then initializes a resource database used by the X resource manager. The first two arguments to **XtInitialize()** specify the *name* and the *class* of the top-level widget used by the application. The name is often the name of the program, for example "emacs", while the class argument indicates the more general category to which the application belongs, for example, "Editor". Although this the basic intent of names and classes, this is not precisely the convention that has evolved. By convention, the class name of an application is the name of the application, with the first letter changed to upper-case, unless the name of the application starts with the letter X, in which case the first two letters are changed to upper case. So the class name of a program named "emacs" is "Emacs", but the class name of a program named "xterm" is "XTerm".

The X resource manager uses the name and class of an application to determine the resources the program uses. It also extracts resources from the application's command-line arguments. The Intrinsics recognizes several common command-line arguments by default. These are destructively removed from the **argv[]** array and placed in a resource data base. The value of **argc** is decremented accordingly. Notice that **XtInitialize()** requires the address of **argc**. The third and fourth arguments allow an application to specify how the Intrinsics should interpret application-specific command-line arguments and are discussed in Chapter 3.

After initializing the Intrinsics layer, **XtInitialize()** creates and returns a TopLevelShell widget. This widget serves as a base for all other widgets in the calling application.

2.2.2 Creating Widgets

Rather than dealing directly with windows, applications built using the Xt Intrinsics use *widgets*. A widget is a complex data structure that combines an X window with a set of procedures that perform actions on that window. The widget structure also contains additional data need by these procedures. Chapter 12 examines the internal structure of a widget in detail. However, application programmers usually only need to understand a widget's external, public interface to use the widget in a program.

Widgets form a hierarchical structure similar to the X window tree structure, known as a *widget tree*. The root of every widget tree must be a special type of widget known as a *shell* widget. Shell widgets must have exactly one child widget. The shell widget serves as a wrapper, or shell, around its child, providing an interface between the child widget and the window manager. The window used by a shell widget is created as a child of the root window of the display.[2] **XtInitialize()** creates an initial shell widget. Applications that use multiple, independent windows must create an additional shell widget for each top-level window. The function

```
XtCreateWidget(name, class, parent, args, nargs)
```

provides the general mechanism for creating all widgets except shell widgets. The **name** argument is an arbitrary string that identifies the widget. Widget names do not need to be unique, although it is often useful if they are. (See the discussion of the resource manager in Chapter 3). The **class** argument specifies what type of widget is to be created. For example,

```
XwscrollbarWidgetClass
```

specifies a ScrollBar widget. Each widget class provides a header file that defines the widget's class. This file must be included in any application that uses the widget class. For example, an application that creates a ScrollBar widget must include the file ScrollBar.h. This file contains the declaration of **XwscrollbarWidgetClass**. The header files for the X Widgets are normally located in the directory /usr/include/Xw. The **parent** argument to **XtCreateWidget()** must be a widget that already exists. This widget can be a shell widget or any other type of widget that allows children. The arguments **args** and **nargs** specify resources used by the widget. If the application does not need to specify any widget resources, **args** can be given as NULL. **XtCreateWidget()** creates and returns a widget which must be declared as type **Widget** by the program. For example, the following function creates and returns a ScrollBar widget named "scroller" as a child of another widget.

---

2. Most X11 window managers reparent application's top-level windows so that they are no longer a direct child of the root window. However, shell widgets are initially created as children of the root window.

```
Widget create_scroll_bar(parent)
  Widget parent;
{
  Widget scroll_bar;
  scroll_bar = XtCreateWidget("scroller",
                              XwscrollbarWidgetClass,
                              parent, NULL, 0);
  return scroll_bar;
}
```

XtCreateWidget() allocates and initializes many of the data structures associated with the widget, but doesn't create the window associated with the widget. The function

```
XtRealizeWidget(widget)
```

creates a window for the widget. Once **XtRealizeWidget()** is called for a particular widget, the widget is said to be *realized*. If a widget has children, **XtRealizeWidget()** also realizes its children. Applications can use the function

```
XtIsRealized(widget)
```

to check if a widget is realized.

The function

```
XtDestroyWidget(widget)
```

destroys a widget and its children. The X server also automatically frees all resources used by an application, including the window used by each widget when the program exits.

Most Xt Intrinsics functions require a widget as the first argument. However, Xlib functions cannot deal directly with widgets, and instead require a pointer to a **Display** structure, window IDs, and so on, which are normally hidden from the programmer by the Intrinsics. The Intrinsics defines several functions that are useful when combining Xlib and Xt Intrinsics functions. These function retrieve the data structures and resource IDs required by Xlib functions from a widget. The function

```
XtDisplay(widget)
```

returns a pointer to the Xlib **Display** structure used by the widget, while

```
XtScreen(widget)
```

returns a pointer to the Xlib **Screen** structure used by the widget. The function

```
XtWindow(widget)
```

retrieves the ID of the window used by the widget.

2.2.3 Managing Widgets

Except for shell widgets, all widgets must be *managed* by a parent widget. A widget's parent manages the widget's size and location, whether or not the widget is mapped, and also controls input to the widget by controlling the input focus. For example, some widgets arrange their children into rows and columns, while others group their children in scrollable lists, and others allow the user to specify the location of each child widget.

To add a widget to its parent's managed set, the application must use the function

```
XtManageChild(widget)
```

The child widget is managed by the parent widget specified in **XtCreateWidget()**. The Intrinsics also provides a convenient function that creates a widget and then calls **XtManageChild()** automatically.

```
XtCreateManagedWidget(name, class, parent, args, nargs)
```

This function is convenient for the programmer, but is not always the best way to create widgets. When a widget is managed, its parent is notified. Often the parent widget must perform some calculation or rearrange its other children to handle the new widget properly. Many times it is more efficient to create a group of widgets first, and then manage them at the same time, using

```
XtManageChildren(widgetlist, num_widgets)
```

This reduces the work a parent widget must do, because the widget can compute the layout of all children at once rather than as each individual widget is managed.

2.2.4 Event Dispatching

When an application uses Xlib directly, it must look at each event and perform an action based on the type of the event. If the application uses multiple windows, the information in the event structure must also be examined to determine the window in which the event occurred. If an application has many windows, using a switch statement to handle events can become complicated.

The Xt Intrinsics provides a much simpler and cleaner way to handle input events. The Xt Intrinsics looks up the widget corresponding to the window in which each event occurs and looks for an *event handler*, a function registered by the application or by the widget itself to respond to a specific X event in a particular widget. If the Intrinsics finds an event handler registered with the widget in which the event occurred,[3] it invokes the function automatically. The procedure of finding the proper widget and invoking the appropriate handler for an event is known as *dispatching* the event. The function

3. Strictly speaking, an event never occurs within a widget. Events can only occur relative to a window. However, since there is normally a one-to-one correspondence between a widget and the window created and controlled by a widget, there should be no confusion if we talk about events as if they occur within a widget.

```
XtDispatchEvent(&event)
```

dispatches a single event. Applications can use the function

```
XtNextEvent(&event)
```

to obtain the next event from the X event queue. This function waits until an event is available in the application's event queue. When an event is available, the function returns after copying the event at the head of the queue into an event structure supplied by the application. **XtNextEvent()** also removes the event from the queue. Because most X applications are entirely event driven, the heart of nearly every X application is a loop that gets events from the X event queue and then uses **XtDispatchEvent()** to invoke an event handler for that event. This event loop can be written as

```
for ( ; ; ) {
  XEvent event;
  XtNextEvent(&event);
  XtDispatchEvent(&event);
}
```

Since this section of code is almost always identical in every X application, the Intrinsics provides it as a function

```
XtMainLoop()
```

Notice that there is no way to exit this loop. We must arrange another way for the application to exit.

2.2.5 Setting Widget Options

Most widgets allow the programmer to specify options and resources that affect the way the widget appears or behaves. The function **XtCreateWidget()** allows the programmer to pass an array specifying these options and resources. Options are specified using an **Arg** data structure defined as

```
typedef struct {
   String   name;
   XtArgVal value;
} Arg, *ArgList;
```

If the size of the resource stored in the **value** member is less than or equal to the size of **XtArgVal** (which is usually defined as a **long**), the value is stored directly in the structure. Otherwise the **value** member stores a pointer to the resource.

Resources are often specified using a static array of **Arg** structures. For example, the width and height of a widget can be specified by creating an argument list, such as

```
static Arg wargs[ ] = {
    { XtNwidth,  300 },
    { XtNheight, 400 },
};
```

Then, passing the **Arg** list as an argument to **XtCreateWidget()**

```
XtCreateWidget("sample", XwswindowWidgetClass,
               parent, wargs, XtNumber(wargs));
```

creates a widget 300 pixels wide and 400 pixels high. The macro **XtNumber()** determines the length of a fixed-size array. Using **XtNumber()** allows the programmer to change the arguments to the widget by simply changing the contents of the Arg array and eliminates the use of "magic numbers" in the code to indicate the length of the array. In some programs the definition of the Arg array might be placed in a separate header file, or even used in multiple places, making it difficult to keep track of a hard-coded number.

It is often more convenient for the programmer to use the macro

```
XtSetArg(arg, name, value)
```

to set a single value in an argument list. For example,

```
Arg args[10]; /* Allocate enough space for future arguments */
int n = 0;
XtSetArg(args[n], XtNwidth,  300); n++;
XtSetArg(args[n], XtNheight, 400); n++;
XtCreateWidget("sample", XwswindowWidgetClass,
               parent, args, n);
```

This approach has one primary advantage over the technique shown earlier: it places the values of the options used by a widget close to the widget definition in the program text. This often produces programs that are easier to understand because it is easier to see what options are set for each widget. On the other hand, using this approach with lengthy lists of options makes a program longer and hides the structure of a program. This book uses this style, primarily because none of the examples set more than a few options in the program. Using a consistent style for setting arguments helps to minimize mistakes when using this approach. Because **XtSetArg()** is a macro that references its first argument twice, the variable used as an index to the **Arg** array can not be auto-incremented inside **XtSetArg()**.[4]

Applications can also use the function

```
XtSetValues(widget, arglist, nargs)
```

to alter the resources used by a widget after it is created. For example, the following code segment does not provide an argument list when the widget is created. In this case,

4. If this bothers you, it is simple to define a new macro that allows the index to be auto-incremented:
#define SETARG(arg, n, v) { Arg *_tmp = &(arg) ; _tmp->name = (n) ; _tmp->value = (XtArgVal) (v) ;}

XtCreateWidget() creates the widget using defaults specified by the widget, and resources set in the user's resource files (see Chapter 3). After the widget has been created, we can use **XtSetValues()** to alter the widget's width and height.

```
Arg   args[10];
int   n = 0;
widget = XtCreateWidget("sample", XwswindowWidgetClass,
                        parent, NULL, 0);
XtSetArg(args[n], XtNwidth,  300); n++;
XtSetArg(args[n], XtNheight, 400); n++;
XtSetValues(widget, args, n);
```

The Intrinsics also allows programmers to retrieve the current value of a widget resource, using the function

```
XtGetValues(widget, arglist, num_args)
```

The argument **arglist** must be an **Arg** array that specifies pairs of resource names and addresses of variables allocated by the calling function. **XtGetValues()** retrieves the named resources from the specified widget and copies the data into the given address if the size of the resource is less than the size of **XtArgVal**. Otherwise, **XtGetValues()** stores a pointer to the resource in the variable specified by the application.

For example, the following code fragment retrieves the width and height of a widget, and also a character string kept in the widget's **XtNstring** resource.

```
Arg         args[10];
Dimension   width, height;
char       *str;
int         n = 0;
XtSetArg(args[n], XtNwidth,   &width); n++;
XtSetArg(args[n], XtNheight, &height); n++;
XtSetArg(args[n], XtNstring, &str); n++;
XtGetValues(widget, args, n);
```

When **XtGetValues()** returns, **width** and **height** contain copies of the widget's **XtNwidth** and **XtNheight** resources. Notice that width and height are declared as type **Dimension**. Declaring the wrong type is a common error that can result in subtle bugs because the Intrinsics copies the data bitwise into the provided address. The most common error is to request the width, height, or position of a widget as an **int**. The width and height of all widgets should be retrieved as type **Dimension**, while a widget's x, y position must be requested as type **Position**. A bug in the R2 Intrinsics allowed programmers to successfully retrieve resources of type **Dimension** and **Position** as type **int**. This bug was fixed in the R3 release and applications that relied on it must be fixed before they will work with the R3 and later version of the Intrinsics.

Although **width** and **height** contain copies of the widget's resources, the variable **str** contains a pointer to the widget's **XtNstring** resource. This is because the size of **Dimension** is smaller than or equal to the size of **XtArgVal**, but the size of the entire character string is greater than the size of **XtArgVal**. Instead of copying the entire string into str, **XtGetValues()** copies the *address* of the resource into **str**. If the calling application intends to modify this string, it should allocate space for the string and copy it. In all cases, the calling application is responsible for allocating and deallocating resources retrieved using **XtGetValues()**.

2.3 THE X TOOLKIT PROGRAMMING MODEL

In addition to defining an architecture for creating and combining widgets, the Xt Intrinsics provides application programmers with a specific model for their applications. Most applications that use the Xt Intrinsics follow a similar format, and every Xt application must perform several basic steps. These are:

1. **Initialize the Intrinsics.** This step establishes a connection to the X server, allocates resources, and otherwise initializes the Intrinsics layer.
2. **Create widgets.** Every program creates one or more widgets to construct the program's user interface.
3. **Register callbacks and event handlers.** Callbacks and event handlers are application-defined functions that respond to user actions within each widget.
4. **Realize all widgets.** Realizing a widget creates the X window used by the widget.
5. **Enter the event loop.** Most X applications are completely event-driven, and are designed to loop indefinitely responding to events. The event loop retrieves events from the X event queue and invokes a procedure, associated with the widget in which the event occurred, to handle the event.

Within this basic framework, the details of individual applications may vary widely, of course. However, most applications differ primarily in how they organize widgets and what callbacks and event handlers they define.

2.4 AN EXAMPLE: memo

We have now discussed enough basic functions to examine a simple X application. This first example, **memo**, is a simple program that displays any command-line arguments not recognized by the Intrinsics in a window. It is useful for displaying brief notes or memos on the screen. The example illustrates each of the steps in the Xt Intrinsics programming model discussed in the previous section, except that this example defines no event handlers or callbacks. The main body of the program is:

```
/*************************************************
 * memo.c: Display a message in a window
 *************************************************/
#include <X11/Intrinsic.h>
#include <X11/StringDefs.h>
#include <Xw/Xw.h>
#include <Xw/SText.h>

extern char    *concat_args();

main(argc, argv)
   int          argc;
   char        *argv[];
{
   Widget       toplevel, msg_widget;
   Arg          wargs[1];
   int          n;
   char        *message;
   /*
    * Initialize the Intrinsics
    */
   toplevel = XtInitialize(argv[0], "Memo", NULL, 0,
                              &argc, argv);
   /*
    * If a message is given on the command line,
    * use it as the XtNstring argument for the widget
    */
   n = 0;
   if ((message = concat_args(argc, argv)) != NULL){
     XtSetArg(wargs[n], XtNstring, message); n++;
   }
   /*
    * Create the message widget.
    */
   msg_widget = XtCreateManagedWidget("message",
                                   XwstatictextWidgetClass,
                                   toplevel, wargs, n);
   /*
    * Realize the widgets and enter the event loop.
    */
```

```
    XtRealizeWidget(toplevel);
    XtMainLoop();
}
```

All X applications must include some standard header files. Every application that uses the Intrinsics must include the file Intrinsic.h. The file StringDefs.h provides some standard string constant definitions, while, in this example, the file SText.h includes definitions required to use the StaticText widget. Applications that use the X Widget set must also include the file Xw.h before any X Widget header file.

Let's look at each step of this program. The first executable line of the main body initializes the Intrinsics, and creates a TopLevelShell widget.

```
toplevel = XtInitialize(argv[0],"Memo", NULL, 0,&argc, argv);
```

The name of the shell widget is the same as the name of the program, while the class name of this application is **Memo**. Notice that the address of **argc** is passed to **XtInitialize()**. Both **argc** and **argv** are modified by **XtInitialize()**. The function removes any command-line arguments recognized by the toolkit from **argv** and decrements **argc** accordingly.

Next, we call the application-defined function **concat_args()**. This function concatenates the command-line arguments contained in the array **argv[]** into a single string. If the command-line contains a message, the lines

```
n = 0;
if ((message = concat_args(argc, argv)) != NULL){
  XtSetArg(wargs[n], XtNstring, message); n++;
}
```

set an entry in an **ArgList** array to the string containing the message to be displayed. The **wargs** array is then used as an argument to **XtCreateManagedWidget()**.

```
msg_widget = XtCreateManagedWidget("message",
                                   XwstatictextWidgetClass,
                                   toplevel, wargs, n);
```

This statement creates a StaticText widget to display the string retrieved from the command-line. The widget class is specified as **XwstatictextWidgetClass**, and the widget's name is "**message**". The widget is a managed child of the toplevel shell widget created by **XtInitialize()**.

The next step is to realize the top level shell widget. Realizing a widget also causes the widget's children, in this case the StaticText widget, to be realized. Finally, the program enters the main event loop.

```
XtRealizeWidget(toplevel);
XtMainLoop();
```

XtMainLoop() never returns. At this point, the message window appears on the screen and the program loops endlessly, processing events. The StaticText widget automatically handles all resize and exposure events generated by the server.

This example also requires an auxiliary function, **concat_args()**, defined as:

```
/***************************************************
 * concat.c: utility function to concatenate
 *           command-line arguments into a string.
 ***************************************************/
#include <stdio.h>
char * concat_args(n, words)
    int   n;
    char *words[];
{
  char *buffer;
  int   i, len = 0;
  /*
   * If there are no arguments other than the program
   * name, just return an empty string.
   */
  if (n <= 1)
    return ("");
  /*
   * Figure out the total length of the string.  We
   * need to include one space between each word too.
   */
  for (i = 1; i < n; i++)
    len += strlen(words[i]);
  len += (n - 1);     /* One space between each word */
  /*
   * Allocate the buffer and initialize.  Die if
   * memory is not available.
   */
  buffer = (char *) malloc(len + 1);/* For the NULL*/
  if (buffer == NULL) {
    fprintf(stderr, "Out of memory in concat_args()\n");
    exit(1);
  }
  buffer[0] = '\0';
  /*
   * Put each word in the buffer, putting a
   * space between each one.
   */
```

```
    for (i = 1; i < n; i++)   {
      if (i > 1)
        strcat(buffer, " ");
      strcat (buffer, words[i]);
    }
    return (buffer);
}
```

Fig. 2.1 shows the widget tree formed by the **memo** example. The figure shows each widget's name above its class name (shown in italics). Most, but not all, widget trees directly correspond to the X window tree created by the application. This widget tree is very simple, but we will see widget trees that are much more complex in later examples.

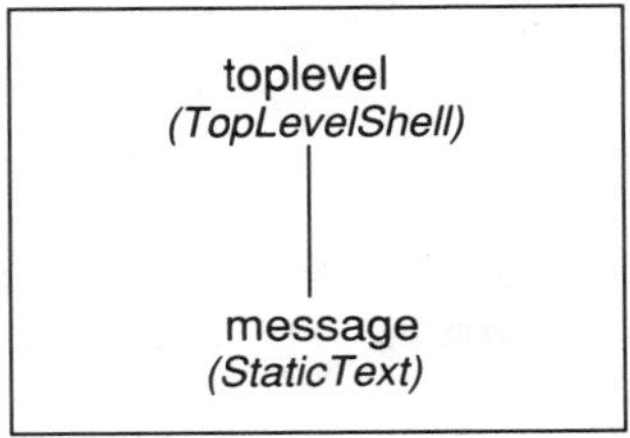

Figure 2.1 The widget tree created by memo.

2.4.1 Building and Using memo

The **memo** example can be compiled and linked with the X libraries with the UNIX shell command

```
cc -o memo memo.c concat.c -lXw -lXt11 -lX11
```

This compiles the files memo.c and concat.c and links the Xlib, Xt Intrinsics, and widget libraries with the program The ordering of the libraries is significant. All widget libraries must precede the Intrinsics library, which must precede the Xlib library.

In addition, it is important to be sure the version of the widget library matches that of the Intrinsics library. R2 widgets cannot be used with the R3 Intrinsics nor vice-versa. This example will work with either the R2 or R3 versions of the StaticText widget, as long as the versions of both the widget and the Xt Intrinsics library are the same.

We can now invoke **memo** from a UNIX shell in an X terminal emulator, for example:

```
memo Hello World
```

This produces the message window shown in Fig. 2.2.

Figure 2.2 memo's message window.

Depending on the window manager you use, **memo** might appear complete with a title bar and other decorations added by the window manager. Fig. 2.3 shows the **memo** window with a title bar and several other gadgets added by a window manager.

Figure 2.3 memo's window with window manager decorations.

One practical application of **memo** is to invoke it from a makefile. A makefile is a script used by the UNIX **make** utility, which manages compilation of applications. For example, consider a basic makefile that can be used to build **memo** itself:

```
################################
# Makefile for memo.c
################################
memo:memo.o
    cc -o memo memo.c concat.c -lXw -lXt -lX11
    memo Program Compiled Successfully
```

Now, the shell command

```
make memo
```

builds **memo** and make uses **memo** itself to announce the successful compilation.

One obvious problem with **memo** is that there is no way to exit the program. The rest of this chapter discusses several ways to solve this problem including event handlers, callbacks, and actions.

2.4.2 Creating a Utilities Library

As we demonstrate different parts of X, this book occasionally presents functions or utilities that are useful in more than one program. Some of these functions combine widgets to perform some higher level task, while others have little to do with X, but are useful nevertheless. For example, the function **concat_args()** is a simple, self-contained procedure that we will use again in other examples. It is convenient to group these functions together in a library where applications can use them by linking the library to the program. Libraries are useful for grouping collections of small functions into a single module that can be linked to any program needing any of the functions. A library also serves a useful purpose in this book, by reducing the number of times a simple function used by multiple examples must be presented. The first time such a reusable function is defined, we will add it to our library. Then, when we discuss examples that use the same function, we can simply refer to the library. We can start a library used by nearly all examples in this book with the function **concat_args()**. We will name this library libXs. The letters "Xs" stand for "X-sample library", a pun on "example". The library consists of an archive file that stores the relocatable compiled functions, and a header file containing external definitions. At this point the file libXs.h contains only the following lines

```
/***********************************************
 * libXs.h: Header file for X-sample library
 ***********************************************/
 extern char * concat_args();
```

We add to this library throughout this book, as we find other useful functions. Refer to Appendix F for a complete listing of the libXs library functions used in this book.
We can create a library containing **concat_args()** with the commands

```
cc -c concat.c
ar ruv libXs.a concat.o
```

These commands compile concat.c into an object file, and then archive the file into the library file libXs.a. It is common practice to place library files in some standard location such as

```
/usr/lib
/usr/local/lib
```

where they can be found by the linker. Then we can build **memo** with the command

```
cc -o memo memo.c -lXs -lXw -lXt -lX11
```

This command compiles the file memo.c and links it with the libXs library as well as the X libraries.

2.4.3 Event Handlers

An event handler is a procedure invoked by the Intrinsics when a specific type of event occurs within a widget. The widget programmer can define event handlers to handle some, all, or none of the X events. The application programmer can also use the function

```
XtAddEventHandler(widget, eventmask, nonmaskable,
                  handler, client_data)
```

to register additional event handlers for events that occur in a widget. This function registers an application-defined function specified in the argument **handler** as an event handler for the event or events specified in the **eventmask**. The argument **eventmask** must be one of the standard X event masks defined in the file X.h. The event handler can also be registered for more than one event by specifying the inclusive-OR of two or more event masks. The Xt Intrinsics automatically invokes the function when the event specified by **eventmask** occurs within the widget's window. Applications can register multiple event handlers for the same event and the same widget. When an event occurs, each event handler registered for that event is called. However, the Intrinsics does not define the order in which multiple event handlers are invoked. Applications can use the argument **client_data** to specify some data to be passed as a parameter to the event handler. This argument can be given as **NULL** if the event handler does not require any application-specific data.

Some X events that applications need to handle have no event mask. These events are said to be *nonmaskable* because they are sent to all applications whether an application selects them or not.[5] To register an event handler for a nonmaskable event, the argument **nonmaskable** must be set to **TRUE**. Since nonmaskable events have no event mask, the **mask** argument must be specified as **NoEventMask**. The form of every event handler is

```
void handler(w, client_data, event)
  Widget   w;
  caddr_t  client_data;
  XEvent  *event;
```

Every event handler is called with three arguments. The first argument is the widget in whose window the event occurred. The second argument contains the client data specified by the application when it registers the event handler. The event handler usually coerces this argument to the expected data type.[6] In C, this can be done by simply declaring the **client_data** argument to be the expected type in the definition of the event handler. The last argument is a pointer to the X event structure that caused this function to be invoked. Event handlers never return a useful value, and should be declared to be of type **void**.

We can use an event handler to provide a way to exit from the **memo** program. First we must define an event handler that simply exits when it is called.

---

5. The nonmaskable event types are ClientMessage, SelectionNotify, SelectionClear, and SelectionRequest. These events are used for interclient communication, and are discussed in Chapter 11.

6. The Xt Intrinsics uses the type caddr_t to indicate an untyped pointer. On most systems, caddr_t is defined as:

    typedef caddr_t char *

   In the proposed X3J11 ANSI C standard, a generic pointer is specified by "void *".

```
void quit(w, client_data, event)
  Widget    w;
  caddr_t   client_data;
  XEvent   *event;
{
   exit(0);
}
```

Then we must register the event handler so that it is called when some event occurs. For example, let's redesign the **memo** program to exit when the user presses a mouse button in the message window. The new version of **memo** simply adds the line

```
XtAddEventHandler(msg_widget, ButtonPressMask, FALSE,
                  quit, NULL);
```

to register the **quit()** event handler for **ButtonPress** events. Notice that this version of **memo** includes the header file libXs.h (see Section 2.4.2) and must be linked with the libXs library which contains the **concat_args()** function. The new version of **memo** can be written as:

```
/*************************************************************
 * memo.c: Adding an event handler
 ************************************************/
#include <X11/Intrinsic.h>
#include <X11/StringDefs.h>
#include <Xw/Xw.h>
#include <Xw/SText.h>
#include "libXs.h"

extern void quit();

main(argc, argv)
   int              argc;
   char            *argv[];
{
   Widget           toplevel, msg_widget;
   Arg              wargs[1];
   int              n;
   char            *message;
   /*
    * Initialize the Intrinsics
    */
   toplevel = XtInitialize(argv[0], "Memo", NULL, 0,
                           &argc, argv);
```

```
    /*
     * If a message is given on the command-line,
     * use it as the XtNstring argument for the widget
     */
    n = 0;
    if ((message = concat_args(argc, argv)) != NULL){
      XtSetArg(wargs[n], XtNstring, message); n++;
    }
    /*
     * Create the message widget.
     */
    msg_widget = XtCreateManagedWidget("message",
                                       XwstatictextWidgetClass,
                                       toplevel, wargs, n);
    /*
     * Register the event handler to be called when
     * a button is pressed
     */
    XtAddEventHandler(msg_widget, ButtonPressMask, FALSE,
                      quit, NULL);
    /*
     * Realize the widgets and enter the event loop.
     */
    XtRealizeWidget(toplevel);
    XtMainLoop();
}
```

2.4.4 Callback Functions

Some widgets provide hooks that allow applications to define procedures to be called when some widget-specific condition occurs. These hooks are known as *callback lists* and the application's procedures are known as *callback functions*, or simply *callbacks*, because the widget makes a "call back" to the application-defined function. Each widget maintains a callback list for each type of callback it supports. For example, every widget supports a **XtNdestroyCallback** callback list. Each callback on a widget's **XtNdestroyCallback** callback list is invoked before the widget is destroyed. The names of the callback lists supported by each widget are specified in the widget's public header file, and are usually explained in the widget's documentation. Callbacks are different than event handlers because they are invoked by the widget rather that the Intrinsics, and are not necessarily tied to any particular event. Applications can add a callback to a callback list with the function

```
XtAddCallback(widget, callback_name, procedure, client_data)
```

The argument, **callback_name**, specifies the callback list to which **procedure** is to be added. The application can use **client_data** to specify some application-defined data to be passed to the callback procedure by the Intrinsics when the callback is invoked.

The form of a callback procedure is

```
void CallbackProcedure(widget, client_data, call_data)
        Widget  widget;
        caddr_t client_data;
        caddr_t call_data;
```

The first argument to every callback function is the widget for which the callback is registered. The second parameter is the **client_data** specified by the application in the call to **XtAddCallback()**. The last argument contains data provided by the widget. The type and purpose of this data can be determined by checking the documentation for the specific widget. Like event handlers, callbacks do not return any useful value, and should be declared as type **void**.

The **memo** example in Section 2.4.3 uses an event handler to exit the application when a **ButtonPress** event occurs. Another way to do this is to use a callback procedure. The StaticText widget used in **memo** supports the callback lists

XtNdestroyCallback	**XtNselect**	**XtNrelease**
XtNenter		**XtNleave**

When a StaticText widget is selected, the widget invokes the functions on its **XtNselect** callback list. Selection is an abstract concept and is not necessarily tied to any particular X event. By default, the user selects a StaticText widget by pressing the left mouse button in the window. Therefore, we can use the **XtNselect** callback in **memo** to perform the same task as the event handler in Section 2.4.3.

We only need to change a few lines of code. First, we must change the definition of **quit()** to the form used by a callback function.

```
void quit(w, client_data, call_data)
   Widget w;
   caddr_t client_data, call_data;
{
   exit(0);
}
```

Then we must replace the line

```
XtAddEventHandler(msg_widget,ButtonPressMask, FALSE,
                  quit, NULL);
```

from the previous version with the line

```
XtAddCallback(msg_widget, XtNselect, quit, NULL);
```

With these changes, the widget calls all functions on its **XtNselect** callback list, including **quit()**, when the user presses a mouse button in the message window. The difference between using the event handler and a callback may seem to be insignificant, since we accomplished the same task using both. However, there is at least one important advantage to using callbacks functions. With callbacks, the method used to destroy the message window is no longer tied directly to a specific X event, but instead is tied to a more abstract *action*, in this case the action of selecting the window. Further, the user can use the *translation manager* facility provided by the Xt Intrinsics to customize the action that selects a widget. The next section discusses the translation manager, and shows yet another way that we can make **memo** respond to user actions.

2.4.5 Using The Translation Manager

The Xt Intrinsics's translation manager provides a mechanism that allows the user to specify the mapping between user actions and functions provided by a widget or an application. For example, the user can use the translation manager to alter the action that causes the **memo** program from the previous section to exit. Adding the line

```
memo*StaticText*translations:<Key>Q:    select()
```

to the user's .Xdefaults file specifies that the select action occurs when the user presses the key **Q**.

In its most basic form, a translation table consists of a list of expressions. Each expression has a left side and a right side, separated by a colon. The left side specifies the user action that invokes the widget action given on the right side. The action can specify modifier keys and also sequences of events. For example, we could select the message window of the **memo** program with a double click of the mouse, by specifying

```
*StaticText*translations: <Btn1Down>,<Btn1Down>:  select()
```

The translation manager also provides a shorthand notation for multiple clicks:

```
*StaticText*translations: <Btn1Up>(2):    select()
```

The expression **<Btn1Up>**(2) is a shorthand for

```
<Btn1Down>, <Btn1Up>, <Btn1Down>, <Btn1Up>
```

We can specify that a modifier key must also be held down. For example,

```
*StaticText*translations: Ctrl <Btn1Down>:    select()
```

The combinations can be arbitrarily complex. However, the more complex the translation table, the more difficult it is to determine just what is specified. More specific events should always precede less specific events. For example, in the specification

```
# WRONG
*StaticText*translations:  <Btn1Down>:      select() \n\
                           Meta <Btn1Down>: release()
```

the second button action overrides the first, because specifying no modifier keys is the same as specifying all modifier keys. The correct way to do this is

```
# CORRECT
*StaticText*translations:  Meta <Btn1Down>: release() \n\
                           <Btn1Down>:      select()
```

When multiple translations are given, each specification must be separated by a newline character ('**\n**'). It is often convenient to use a backslash to break the translations across multiple lines.

These examples show how the translation manager maps between each user event and a corresponding procedure defined by a widget. However, applications can also define new action procedures, using the function

```
XtAddActions(actions, num_actions)
```

The **actions** argument must be an array of type **ActionsRec**. This structure consists of a string that names an action and a pointer to a procedure that performs the action. For example, we can register an action procedure named **quit()** for the **memo** program as

```
static XtActionsRec actionsTable [] ={
                  {"quit",   quit},
                  };
```

The action procedure **quit()**, which must be declared before referencing it, takes four arguments, a widget, an X event, a parameter list, and the length of the parameter list. It is defined as

```
static void quit(w, event, params, num_params)
     Widget  w;
     XEvent *event;
     String *params;
     int     num_params;
{
  exit(0);
}
```

The first argument specifies the widget that caused this action procedure to be called, while **event** is the event that caused the procedure to be invoked. The **params** argument is an array of strings containing any arguments specified in the translation, while **num_params** indicates the length of this array. If we use **XtAddActions()** to register this action list with the translation manager, the user can define a translation for the **quit** action in the .Xdefaults file. For example,

```
memo*StaticText*translations: Ctrl <Key> Q:    quit()
```

Programmers often need to specify translations for specific widgets in a program. This can be done using the function

```
XtAugmentTranslations(widget, translation_table)
```

or

```
XtOverrideTranslations(widget, translation_table)
```

Both of these functions attach a translation table to a particular widget. **XtAugmentTranslations()** merges a list of translations with the list of current translations. It does not override existing translations specified by the widget or the user. **XtOverrideTranslations()** destructively replaces existing translations with the new translation list.

A translation table is a structure of type **XtTranslations**. The function

```
XtParseTranslations(source)
```

compiles a string containing a translation specification into a **XtTranslations** structure. For example, we can programmatically define translations for **memo** as

```
static char defaultTranslations[] =  "<Key>Q:  quit()";
```

In the body of the program, we must call **XtParseTranslations()** to compile the string. For example,

```
trans_table = XtParseTranslationTable(defaultTranslations);
```

Then we must add the translations to the existing translations for the message widget with

```
XtAugmentTranslations(msg_widget, trans_table);
```

This new version of **memo** is defined as:

```
/***********************************************************
 * memo.c: Defining application actions and translations
 **********************************************************/

#include <X11/Intrinsic.h>
#include <X11/StringDefs.h>
#include <Xw/Xw.h>
#include <Xw/SText.h>
#include "libXs.h"
```

```
static void quit();
static XtActionsRec actionsTable [] = {
  {"quit",   quit},
};
static char defaultTranslations[] =  "<Key>Q:  quit()";
static void quit(w, event, params, num_params)
     Widget  w;
     XEvent *event;
     String *params;
     int     num_params;
{
  exit(0);
}

main(argc, argv)
   int              argc;
   char            *argv[];
{
   Widget           toplevel, msg_widget;
   Arg              wargs[1];
   int              n;
   char            *message;
   XtTranslations   trans_table;
   /*
    * Initialize Intrinsics
    */
   toplevel = XtInitialize(argv[0], "Memo", NULL, 0,
                                 &argc, argv);
   /*
    * Register the new actions, and compile
    * translations table
    */
   XtAddActions(actionsTable, XtNumber(actionsTable));
   trans_table =
      XtParseTranslationTable(defaultTranslations);
   /*
    * If a message is given on the command-line,
    * use it as the XtNstring argument for the widget
    */
   n = 0;
   if ((message = concat_args(argc, argv)) != NULL){
     XtSetArg(wargs[n], XtNstring, message); n++;
```

```
    }
    /*
     * Create the message widget.
     */
    msg_widget = XtCreateManagedWidget("message",
                                       XwstatictextWidgetClass,
                                       toplevel, wargs, n);
    /*
     * Merge the program-defined translations with
     * existing translations.
     */
    XtAugmentTranslations(msg_widget, trans_table);
    /*
     * Realize all widgets and enter the event loop.
     */
    XtRealizeWidget(toplevel);
    XtMainLoop();
}
```

Using the translation manager to map between action procedures and events provides a flexible way for programmers to design customizable applications. It also provides a way for the application programmer to define additional behavior for any widget.

2.5 APPLICATION CONTEXTS

The R3 version of the Xt Intrinsics supports the notion of an *application context*. An application context allows multiple logical applications to exist in a single address space. Each context corresponds to a logical application that has its own independent event loop and connection to the X server. This use is limited, for the most part, to systems that support multiple threads within a single process. Application contexts also allow applications to use multiple displays. Each application context maintains a list of displays opened by **XtOpenDisplay()**.

Most of the Xt Intrinsics functions described in this chapter are convenience routines that use a default context. These functions are adequate for most applications and also are compatible with the R2 Intrinsics. Applications can create a unique application context using the function

```
XtCreateApplicationContext()
```

This function returns a context that is used as the first argument to many other Intrinsics function with the context. Every application must have at least one application context. Applications that use the convenience functions described in this chapter use a default context created by the Intrinsics.

The programmer can destroy an application context using the function:

```
XtDestroyApplicationContext(app_context)
```

This function destroys the context and closes the connection to the X server used by the context.

The initialization function **XtInitialize()** is a convenience function that calls three other Intrinsics functions. These are:

```
XtToolkitInitialize()

XtOpenDisplay(app_context, display_name, app_name,
              app_class,options, noption, &argc, argv)

XtAppCreateShell(app_context, classname, class, display,
                 args, nargs)
```

XtToolkitInitialize() initializes the internals of the Xt Intrinsics. Unlike **XtInitialize()**, it does not open a connection to the server, nor create an initial shell widget. **XtOpenDisplay()** opens a new connection to the X server using the given application context. If a NULL context is specified, **XtOpenDisplay()** uses the default application context. **XtAppCreateShell()** creates a top-level shell for the application. Applications that use application contexts should call these function directly rather than using **XtInitialize()**. Fig. 2.4 shows the functions that require application contexts and the corresponding versions that use the default application context.

Convenience Routine	Context Routine
XtMainLoop()	**XtAppMainLoop()**
XtNextEvent()	**XtAppNextEvent()**
XtProcessEvent()	**XtAppProcessEvent()**
XtPeekEvent()	**XtAppPeekEvent()**
XtPending()	**XtAppPending()**
XtAddInput()	**XtAppAddInput()**
XtAddTimeOut()	**XtAppAddTimeOut()**
XtAddWorkProc()	**XtAppAddWorkProc()**
XtCreateApplicationShell()	**XtAppCreateShell()**
XtInitialize()	**XtToolkitInitialize()**

Figure 2.4 Xt Intrinsics convenience functions.

Let's look at the skeleton of the **memo** example, this time using application contexts:

```
/*****************************************************
 * memo.c: Skeleton Using Application Contexts, R3 Only
 *****************************************************/
/*
 * Includes and global declarations......
 */

main(argc, argv)
   int              argc;
   char            *argv[];
{
  XtAppContext    app;
  Display        *dpy;
  /*
   * Other declarations .....
   */

  /*
   * Initialize the Intrinsics
   */
  XtToolkitInitialize();
  /*
   * Create a context.
   */
  app = XtCreateApplicationContext();
  /*
   * Open the display.
   */
  dpy = XtOpenDisplay(app, "", argv[0], "Memo", NULL, 0,
                      &argc, argv)
  /*
   * Create a toplevel shell.
   */
  toplevel = XtAppCreateShell(app, "Memo",
                              applicationShellWidgetClass,
                              dpy, NULL, 0);
  /*
   * Extract message and Create message widget here .....
   */
  XtRealizeWidget(toplevel);
  XtAppMainLoop();
}
```

2.6 SUMMARY

This chapter briefly introduced the key concepts of the Xt Intrinsics layer. We learned how to create and display a widget on the screen, explored four implementations of a simple X application, including examples that used event handlers, callbacks, and actions. Using the Xt Intrinsics and a widget set has many advantages over using Xlib directly:

- The higher level libraries reduce the amount of code that must be written by the application programmer, and helps make an application easier to understand and modify.
- The customization facilities provided by the Xt Intrinsics allow the end user to modify the behavior of applications in a consistent way.
- Standard widgets that provide essential components needed by many applications are available, eliminating the need for each programmer to re-implement these components for each application.
- Using the Xt Intrinsics and a widget set allows the application programmer can spend more time on the problems of the specific application, and less time on the user interface.
- A project with unique user interface requirements can create new widgets that can be used alone or mixed with an existing widget set. When many applications need to work together, using a common set of widgets is an excellent way to ensure consistency across all applications.

One major advantage of the Xt Intrinsics is the degree to which it is integrated with Xlib. Using the Intrinsics and the X Widget set does not prevent the programmer from calling Xlib function directly. Most applications use a combination of the Xt Intrinsics framework, a set of widgets, and Xlib functions. Whenever an appropriate widget set is available, it is generally better to use these higher level facilities than to program directly with Xlib. However, when writing application-specific callbacks and event handlers, the programmer often needs to use Xlib functions as well.

The following chapter introduces the X resource manager, a facility that provides a simple and consistent way for users to customize applications. Chapter 4 introduces the X Widget set and shows how to combine widgets to create more complex interfaces.

3

THE X RESOURCE MANAGER

Managing resources is an important part of programming with X. It is difficult to write or even use any significant X application without understanding the X resource management facilities. This chapter explains what resources are and shows how both the programmer and the user can use the resource manager to customize applications.

3.1 WHAT IS A RESOURCE?

X programmers often use the word *resource* to mean different things, depending on the context in which they use the word. For example, the Xlib documentation often refers to windows, graphics contexts, and fonts as resources. Xlib resources are maintained by the X server and accessed by clients through a resource ID. Widget programmers generally refer to any internal data required by the widget as a resource. To application programmers, a resource is any data required by the application. In this broader sense, resources include window IDs, colors, fonts, images, text, names of windows or widgets, positions and sizes of windows, or any option that affects the behavior of the application.

By convention, X applications allow the end user to specify most or all resources used by an application. Application programmers should always provide reasonable defaults for all resources required by a program, but should allow the end user to override these defaults whenever possible. It is important to allow the user to customize an application because no matter how well the programmer tries to anticipate the needs of the end user, there is always someone who wishes to alter the behavior of a program.

The X resource manager facility encourages programmers to write customizable applications by providing an easy-to-use mechanism for determining user customizations and specifying defaults. The basic resource manager facilities provided by Xlib allow applications to store and retrieve information from a resource database. The Xt Intrinsics provides a higher level interface, built on the Xlib resource manager, that makes it easy for the application programmer to access the user's options and blend them with the program-defined defaults.

3.2 SPECIFYING RESOURCES

Traditional databases contain information that is completely and precisely specified. Users of such a database search for information by making imprecise queries. You might, for example, query a bibliographical database for books about the X Window System by requesting information on "windows." This query would return a possibly large list of books about "windows," (some of which might actually be about computer window systems).

The X resource manager uses a slightly different model. In X, the database contains general information, usually specified by the user, about the resources used by applications. For example, a user can specify that "All buttons should be red," or "All terminal-emulator windows should be 24 characters high and 80 characters wide." Applications query the database to determine the value of a specific resource for a specific application: "What color should the quit button be?" or "How wide should the command window be?"

3.2.1 Names and Classes

The resource manager requires that every application and resource in X have both a name and a class. The class indicates the general category to which each of these entities belongs, while the name identifies the specific entity. For example, a program named "emacs" might belong to the class "Editor". Similarly, the resource "destroyCallback" names a specific callback list. The class name of this resource, "Callback", identifies all callback lists. Both resource names and resource classes are strings. The header file, StringDefs.h, contains a set of commonly used resource names, and programmers can define additional resource names as needed. However, programmers should not create new resource names unnecessarily. Programmers should choose standard resource names whenever they apply, to promote consistency between applications. By convention, resource names generally begin with a lowercase letter, while class names begin with a capital letter. Resource names are often identical to the corresponding resource classes, except for the capitalization. For example, the resource name used to specify a foreground color is "foreground" and the resource class is "Foreground". A widget's class name can be an arbitrary string, but is usually related to its function within the application. The class name of every widget is determined by the widget programmer who designs the widget, although the application programmer determines the widget's name. For example, the class name of the widget used to display a string in the previous chapter is "StaticText". The memo program specified the widget's name as "message".

As we noted earlier, an application queries the resource database using a complete specification of the desired resource. Resources are completely specified by two strings that together uniquely identify a resource for a particular window or widget. The first string consists of the name of the application, followed by the names of each widget in the applications widget tree between the top widget and the widget using the resource, followed by the name of the resource. Each name in the string is separated by a dot ("."). The second string is similar except that it uses class names instead of the resource names of the application and each widget. Together, these strings (sometimes referred to a resource lists) specify a unique path through the application's widget tree.

Fig. 3.1 and Fig. 3.2 show the widget layout and hierarchy of a hypothetical graphics editor named "draw." According to convention, the programmer has chosen the class name of the application as "Draw". Fig. 3.2 shows the name of each widget in Fig. 3.1 with its class name in parentheses below the name. We can specify the foreground color of the widget named **button1** in the upper portion of the window with a string containing the resource names[1]

```
draw.panel.commands.button1.foreground
```

and a string containing the resource classes

```
Draw.BulletinBoard.RowCol.PushButton.Foreground
```

Notice that the resource name string uniquely identifies **button1**, differentiating it from the other children of the **commands** widget, and also from any other button with the same name but in a different widget hierarchy (such as the **button1** in the **options** widget). The class string, however, specifies all buttons that have the same class ancestry. In this example, the class string specifies the foreground color of widget's **button1**, **button2** and **button3** in both the **commands** widget and the **options** widget. This class string also applies to buttons in any other application that contains this exact widget tree.

A resource database consists of a set of associations between resource names or class names and the value of a resource. The user can specify these associations in a resource file, such as the .Xdefaults file. Each association consists of strings containing resource names or class names, followed by a colon, one or more spaces, and a value. For example, we can specify that the foreground color of **button1** in the **commands** panel should be red by adding the line

```
draw.panel.commands.button1.foreground: red
```

to a resource file (typically the user's .Xdefaults file). We can specify the color of all buttons in the application with the line

```
Draw.BulletinBoard.RowCol.PushButton.Foreground: red
```

1. Notice that the top-level shell does not appear in the resource specification. This is correct for R3, but not R2. In the R2 version of the Intrinsics, the top-level shell must be included as well.

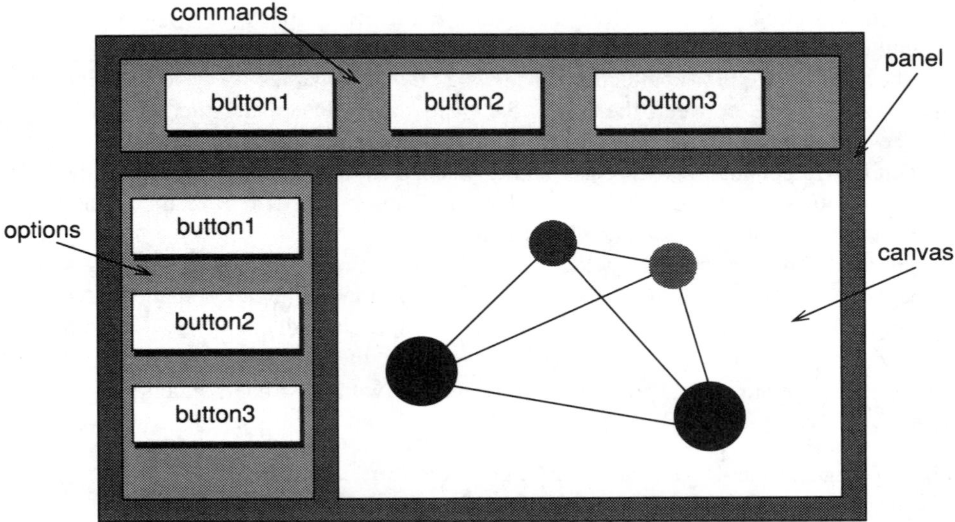

Figure 3.1 An example application.

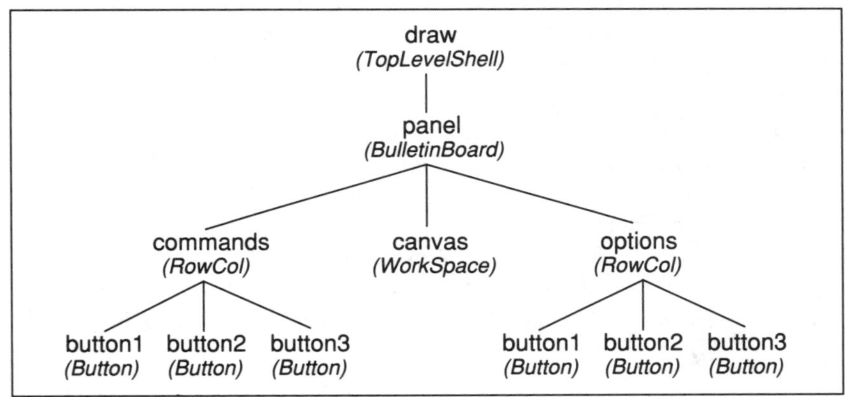

Figure 3.2 Widget tree for Fig. 3.1.

Although this example specifies resources relative to widgets, we can use the same mechanism to specify resources unrelated to any particular widget or window by using the program name and the resource name. For example

```
draw.bufsize:     100
```

specifies the value of some resource named "bufsize" used by the application.

3.2.2 The Resource Manager's Matching Algorithm

It is often inconvenient to specify the value of every resource using the complete name or class list as in the previous examples. Instead, the resource manager allows us to use an asterisk "*" as a wild card character to represent any number of resource names or class names. For example, continuing to use the widget tree in Fig 3.1 and Fig. 3.2, we can specify the foreground color of a button named **button1** with

```
draw*button1*foreground:      red
```

Notice however, that there are two buttons in this example named **button1**. This resource specification applies to both buttons, because the asterisk matches both **options** and **commands**. We can be more specific and indicate the foreground color of **button1** in the **commands** widget with

```
draw*commands*button1*foreground:      red
```

We can also be more general, and specify all foreground colors used by the application with

```
draw*foreground:      red
```

or we can specify the foreground color of the **options** widget and all its children with

```
draw*options*foreground:      red
```

Partial resource specifications can also consist of any combination of resource names and class name. For example, we can specify that the foreground color of all widgets belonging to class PushButton should be green, regardless of the application, with the line

```
*PushButton.foreground:      green
```

Although the user can specify resources using incomplete name and class lists, applications must query the database using both the complete name list and the complete class list. At the lowest level, the Xlib function

```
XrmGetResource(db, name, class, &type, &value)
```

is used to query the database. It returns the value and type of the resource that best matches the complete resource name and class name specification. The resource manager uses a matching algorithm to determine if any entry in the resource database matches the requested resource and returns a type and a value for the query. If no match is found, the returned value is NULL.

The matching algorithm uses several precedence rules to arbitrate between multiple matching entries in the resource database. These rules are:

1. Either the resource name or the class name of each item in the query must match the corresponding item in the database entry. For example, a query for the foreground color of **button1**, using the resource name and class name specifications

```
draw.panel.commands.button1.foreground
Draw.BulletinBoard.RowCol.PushButton.Foreground
```

matches the resource database entry

```
draw.BulletinBoard.commands.button1.Foreground: Blue
```

but not

```
draw.BulletinBoard.commands.button1.Highlight:  Yes
```

because the class name **Foreground**, specified in the query, does not match the class name, **Highlight**, in the database.

2. Entries in the database prefixed by a dot (".") are more specific than (and therefore have precedence over), those prefixed by an asterisk ("*"). Therefore, the database entry

   *commands.Background: green

   has precedence over

   ```
   *commands*Background:    red
   ```

   If these specifications are both in the user's resource database, the **commands** widget will have a green background. However, all children of the **commands** widget (here, **button1**, **button2**, and **button3**) will have a red background.

3. Resource names always have precedence over class names. Therefore

   ```
   *button1.Foreground:    red
   ```

   has precedence over

   ```
   *PushButton.Foreground:    green
   ```

   because the name **button1** is more specific than the class PushButton.

4. A resource name or a class name has precedence over an asterisk. So

   ```
   Draw*BulletinBoard*PushButton*Foreground: red
   ```

   has precedence over

   ```
   Draw*BulletinBoard*foreground: green
   ```

   because the first entry more completely identifies the path through the widget tree, because the PushButton class name is present.

5. The resource manager compares database entries left to right, and the first items in a resource specification have precedence over successive items. For example,

   ```
   draw*BulletinBoard*foreground: green
   ```

   has precedence over

```
draw*PushButton*foreground: red
```

Specifying resources takes practice and is often a matter of trial and error, particularly as the size of the user's resource files grows.

3.3 MANAGING APPLICATION RESOURCES

Individual widgets usually manage their own resources and require no action from the application programmer. However, programmers often need to obtain application level resources that have nothing to do with widgets and perhaps little to do with the application's user interface. The resource manager provides the programmer with a consistent mechanism for retrieving all options and resources used by applications. Although Xlib provides the basic resource manager facilities, the Xt Intrinsics provides a higher level interface that is much easier to use. This section discusses and demonstrates how the application programmer uses the resource manager facilities provided by the Xt Intrinsics.

3.3.1 Loading the Resource Database

Every application must call **XtInitialize()** before calling any other Xt Intrinsics function. This procedure automatically creates and initializes a resource database, and also loads the user's resource files. **XtInitialize()** also extracts all options specified on the command line and adds them to the resource database. Because the command-line arguments are added last, they override the corresponding values specified in all resource files. X applications usually do not need to parse the command-line arguments directly, but instead use the resource manager interface to obtain command-line arguments.

XtInitialize() loads the resource database from several different places. Fig. 3.3 summarizes the order in which the resource manager loads these files. **XtInitialize()** first searches for the file

/usr/lib/X11/app-defaults/<class>

where <class> is the class name given to **XtInitialize()**. If this file exists, the resource manager loads it into the resource database. Next, if the UNIX environment variable **XAPPLRESDIR** is set, it is expected to specify a directory containing application-specific resource files. The resource manager appends the class of the program to the value of the **XAPPLRESDIR** variable and tries to load the file named by the result. Next, if the root window has a **RESOURCE_MANAGER** property, the resource manager assumes that this property contains additional options. If this property doesn't exist, the resources in the file named .Xdefaults in the user's home directory are merged into the database. Finally, the environment variable **XENVIRONMENT** can contain the name of a resource file. If this environment variable is defined, the resource manager loads the contents of the file. If no such environment variable exists, the resource manager loads the file .Xdefaults-<*host*>, where <*host*> is the name of the user's machine. We will refer to any of these files used to hold user-defined options as *resource files*. All resource files use the same format as the .Xdefaults file.

1. Load /usr/lib/X11/app-defaults/<class>
   where <class> is the class of the application.
2. Load $**XAPPRESDIR**/<lass>
   where <class> is the class of the application.
3. Load data in **RESOURCE_MANAGER** property
4. If **RESOURCE_MANAGER** property does not exist,
   Load $HOME/.Xdefaults
5. Load file specified by $**XENVIRONMENT**
6. If $**XENVIRONMENT** is not set,
   Load $HOME/.Xdefaults-<host>
   where <host> is the machine where the client is running.
7. Load command-line options

Figure 3.3 Algorithm for loading the resource database.

After processing all resource files, **XtInitialize()** also merges any recognized options from the application's command line into the resource database. **XtInitialize()** removes all recognized options from argv and leaves unrecognized options for the application to process. The contents of the resource database are accessible through the resource manager to every widget used by the application. The Xt Intrinsics supports a standard set of options to ensure that all applications recognize the same basic options. Fig. 3.4 lists the standard command-line options along with the corresponding resource name used to set the option in a resource file.

A few of the command-line options have different forms for compatibility with applications built using earlier versions of X. For example, a user can specify that the **memo** example from the previous chapter should use the font **6x13** by placing the line

```
memo*font:   6x13
```

in a resource file. A font can also be specified on the command line using either

```
memo -fn 6x13 Just Testing
```

or

```
memo -font 6x13 Testing Again
```

Each application can also define additional options, which are passed in the **option** argument to **XtInitialize()**. Section 3.3.3 discusses the format of these options.

Command-Line Option	Resource Name
+rv	reverseVideo
+synchronous	synchronous
-background	background
-bd	borderColor
-bordercolor	borderColor
-bg	background
-borderwidth	TopLevelShell.borderWidth
-bw	TopLevelShell.borderWidth
-display	display
-fg	foreground
-foreground	foreground
-fn	font
-font	font
-geometry	TopLevelShell.geometry
-iconic	TopLevelShell.iconic
-name	name
-reverse	reverseVideo
-rv	reverseVideo
-selectionTimeout	selectionTimeout
-synchronous	synchronous
-title	TopLevelShell.title
=	TopLevelShell.geometry
-xrm	NULL

Figure 3.4 Standard command-line options.

3.3.2 Retrieving Application Resources From The Database

Applications can use an **XtResource** structure to specify the resources to be retrieved from the database. This structure is defined in the header file /usr/include/X11/Xresource.h as

```
typedef struct _XtResource {
  String     resource_name;   /* Resource name          */
  String     resource_class;  /* Resource class         */
  String     resource_type;   /* Desired type           */
  Cardinal   resource_size;   /* Size in bytes          */
  Cardinal   resource_offset; /* Offset from base       */
```

```
    String      default_type;    /* Type of specified default  */
    caddr_t     default_addr;    /* Address of default resource*/
  } XtResource;
```

The **resource_name** member is a string that specifies the resource name of the resource being retrieved. For example, to retrieve a foreground color, an application uses the string "**foreground**". Whenever possible, the constants defined in the header file Stringdefs.h should be used. This not only encourages consistency between applications, but also allows the compiler to catch spelling errors. For example, StringDefs.h defines the string "foreground" as the constant **XtNforeground**.

The **resource_class** member specifies the class of the resource, and is used by the resource manager's matching algorithm. For a foreground color, the class name is "**Foreground**", or the predefined constant **XtCForeground**. The **resource_type** specifies the desired type of the resource. The type can be any valid C language data type as well as any application-defined type. For example, an application might reasonably ask for a color by name (a string) or ask for the pixel value (an integer) that represents the color. The file StringDefs.h also contains definitions of common resource types. By convention, a resource type consists of the name of the type preceded by the letters **XtR**, for example **XtRString** or **XtRPixel**. The **resource_size** member indicates the size, in bytes, of the resource to be retrieved. Applications can determine the size of a resource using the C library function **sizeof()**. The **resource_offset** member of the **XtResource** structure indicates a relative address where the resource value should be placed. The Xt Intrinsics provide a utility macro

```
XtOffset(type *, field)
```

that determines the byte offset of a member of a C struct.[2] The last members of the **XtResource** structure specify a default value for the resource and the type of the default value. The resource manager uses this default if it does not find a match in the user's resource database. This provides a simple way for the application programmer to specify default values for all resources.

Applications can use the function

---

2. The type argument to this macro must be defined as a pointer to the structure. Therefore, by convention, structures are often defined with both a type and a pointer type. For example, we can define a structure representing a coordinate as:

```
typedef struct {
    int    x, y;
} Coord, *CoordPtr;
```

This allows the byte offset of the y member of a Coord structure to be determined using

```
XtOffset(CoordPtr, y);
```

although the statement

```
XtOffset(Coord *, y);
```

achieves the same result. The proposed ANSI C standard includes a similar macro, offsetof().

```
XtGetApplicationResources(widget, base, resources,
                          nresources, args, nargs)
```

to retrieve the resources specified in a **XtResource** list from the database. The **widget** argument should specify the top-level Shell widget that identifies the name and class of the application. The **base** argument specifies the base address of a data structure where the resource manager is to store the retrieved values. If the offsets specified in the **XtResource** list are not relative addresses, the **base** argument must be specified as zero. The next argument, **resources**, is an **XtResource** list, while **nresources** indicates the length of the **resource** list. The last arguments, **args** and **nargs** provide a way for the application to override values in the database. The **args** parameter must be a list of resource names and values while **nargs** indicates the length of the list.

Let's look at an example of how an application uses this mechanism. A simple test program, named **rmtest**, retrieves and prints the value of four parameters. The program supplies default values for these resources, but the user can also use the resource manager to customize the parameters. The four parameters are: **foreground** (color), **background** (color), a **delay** parameter, and **verbose** flag. First we must include the header files Intrinsic.h and StringDefs.h.

```
/***********************************************
 * rmtest.c: simple test of the resource manager
 ***********************************************/
#include <X11/Intrinsic.h>
#include <X11/StringDefs.h>
```

Next, we define a single global data structure to store the four parameters:

```
typedef struct {
   Pixel    fg, bg;
   int      delay;
   Boolean  verbose;
} ApplicationData, *ApplicationDataPtr;
```

Then we define an **XtResource** array that specifies how the resource manager should retrieve these resources from the database.

```
static XtResource resources[] = {
 { XtNforeground, XtCForeground, XtRPixel, sizeof (Pixel),
   XtOffset(ApplicationDataPtr, fg), XtRString, "Black"     },
 { XtNbackground, XtCBackground, XtRPixel, sizeof (Pixel),
   XtOffset(ApplicationDataPtr, bg), XtRString, "White"     },
 { "delay", "Delay", XtRInt, sizeof (int),
   XtOffset(ApplicationDataPtr, delay), XtRString, "2"      },
```

```
  { "verbose", "Verbose", XtRBoolean, sizeof (Boolean),
    XtOffset(ApplicationDataPtr, verbose), XtRString, "False"},
};
```

The first line of this declaration specifies that the value of a resource with name **XtNforeground** and class **XtCForeground** should be retrieved from the resource database. The function **XtOffset()** determines the offset from some base address where the resource manager is to store the retrieved value. This line also specifies that the value should be retrieved as type **XtRPixel**. If the value in the resource database is some type other than **XtRPixel**, the resource manager automatically converts the data to the requested type (See Section 3.3.4). If the resource database does not contain a foreground color specification, the resource manager uses the default value, "Black".[3] Similarly, this resource list specifies that the background color should be retrieved as type **XtPixel**, **delay** as type **XtRInt**, and the flag **verbose** as a **XtRBoolean**.

The body of **rmtest** uses **XtGetApplicationResources()** to retrieve the resources and then prints each value before exiting: Notice that this example specifies the address of the **ApplicationData** structure, **data**, as the base address in the call to **XtGetApplicationResources()**.

```
main(argc, argv)
  int    argc;
  char  *argv[];
{
  Widget           toplevel;
  ApplicationData data;

  toplevel = XtInitialize(argv[0], "Rmtest", NULL, 0,
                          &argc, argv);
  /*
   * Retrieve the application resources.
   */
  XtGetApplicationResources(toplevel, &data, resources,
                            XtNumber(resources), NULL, 0);
  /*
```

3. Notice that all the specified defaults in this example are given as strings. This is not necessary; any type can be specified as the default. However, the default resource must be a pointer, so we cannot use an integer constant directly, for example. To specify the default value of the delay resource in this example, we could use:

```
int two = 2;
static XtResource resources[] = {
  { "delay", "Delay", XtRInt, sizeof (int),
    XtOffset(ApplicationDataPtr, delay), XtRInt, &two },
};
```

It is usually simpler to specify defaults as strings and let the resource manager do the work of converting the data.

```
     * Print the results.
     */
    printf("fg = %d, bg = %d, delay = %d, verbose = %d\n",
            data.fg, data.bg, data.delay, data.verbose);
}
```

If none of the resources in the application's resource list are specified in the user's resource files, the resource manager uses the default values in the **XtResource** list. So, with no matching entries in any resource file, running the program gives the following output.

```
% rmtest
fg = 0, bg = 1, delay = 2, verbose = 0
```

Notice that the resource manager converts the foreground and background values from the colors named "Black" and "White" to the pixel values one and zero. These are pixel indexes used by X graphics functions that correspond to the named colors. Chapter 6 discusses the color model used by X. Also notice that the resource manager converts the value of **verbose** from the string "False" to the boolean value zero used by convention in C to mean **False**.

Since the class name of this program is "Rmtest", resources can be specified in the class resource file, /usr/lib/X11/app-defaults/Rmtest. Let's create a class resource file containing the following lines:

```
*foreground: Red
*delay:      10
*verbose:    True
```

Now, if we run the program rmtest from a shell, we should see

```
% rmtest
fg = 9, bg = 1, delay = 10,verbose = 1
```

Again, the printed values of the foreground and background colors may vary because of X's color model. However, it should be clear that, in this case, the resource manager obtained the values of **foreground**, **delay**, and **verbose** from the class resource file rather than from the application-defined defaults. However, the background color still reflects the default value specified by the application, because the class resource file does not specify a background color.

Class resource files are generally used to define resources that apply to all applications in the class. This file is often used by a systems integrator to define resources for all users of the system. For example, a systems integrator might decide for some reason that all applications that belong to the class "Rmtest" should default to verbose mode. This could be done by setting the **verbose** resource to **True** in the class resource file. The class resource file also serves as a good place to document the options that can be set for each application. Comments can be inserted in the file after a "#" character.

End users of an application can selectively override any or all resource specifications in their own .Xdefaults file. Suppose we place the lines

```
*background: Blue
*delay:      20
```

in the file $HOME/.Xdefaults. Now, if we run this program we should see:

```
% rmtest
fg = 9, bg = 13, delay = 20, verbose = 1
```

In this example, the resource manager obtains the values for foreground and verbose from the class resource file, while the retrieving values of delay and background from the user's .Xdefaults file.

3.3.3 Specifying Resources on the Command Line

It is often more convenient to specify options using resource files than using the conventional UNIX command-line argument mechanism, because resource files allow defaults to be specified once in a file rather than each time the application is run. Also, resource files allow users to specify general defaults to be used by all applications rather than specifying every option to every program on the command line. In addition, in a window-based environment, applications are less likely to be invoked from a UNIX command shell. In spite of this, there are many cases where it is convenient to specify arguments on a command line. Often, the user needs to specify options on a per-process basis. For example, a user cannot use a resource file to run one **xterm** (an X terminal emulator program) with a red foreground and another **xterm** with a blue foreground. As one solution to this problem, Xlib and the Xt Intrinsics provide mechanisms for parsing the command-line arguments and placing the contents into the resource database. This allows applications to use the same retrieval mechanism discussed in the previous section to determine the value of command-line arguments.

As discussed in Section 3.3.1, the Xt Intrinsics automatically recognizes many common command-line options. Applications can also use the **options** argument to **XtInitialize()** to define additional command-line arguments. The options argument, which must be an array of type **XrmOptionDescList**, specifies how additional command-line arguments should be parsed and loaded into the resource database. The **XrmOptionDescList** structure is defined as

```
typedef struct {
    char          *option;       /* argv abbreviation */
    char          *specifier;    /* Resource specifier*/
```

```
      XrmOptionKind    argKind;          /* Style of option    */
      caddr_t          value;            /* Default Value      */
   } XrmOptionDescRec, *XrmOptionDescList;
```

The **option** member is the name by which the option is recognized on the command line, while the **specifier** is the name by which the resource is known in the resource database. The field **argKind** specifies how the command-line arguments should be parsed, and must be one of the values shown in Fig. 3.5.

Argument Style	Meaning
XrmoptionNoArg	Value is specified in **OptionDescRec**.value
XrmoptionIsArg	Value is the option string itself
XrmoptionStickyArg	Value is characters immediately following option
XrmoptionSepArg	Value is next argument in **argv**
XrmoptionResArg	Resource and value in next argument in argv
XrmoptionSkipArg	Ignore this option and the next argument in **argv**
XrmoptionSkipLine	Ignore this option and the rest of **argv**

Figure 3.5 Command-line parsing options.

Let's see how this works by adding some command-line arguments to the **rmtest** program from the previous section. We can define a command-line flag corresponding to each of the four resources used by the program. The command-line options -fg and -bg are predefined by the Xt Intrinsics (see Section 3.3.1) so they are recognized automatically. We can specify command-line arguments corresponding to the other resources with

```
XrmOptionDescRec options[] = {
  {"-verbose", "*verbose", XrmoptionNoArg, "True"},
  {"-delay", "*delay", XrmoptionStickyArg,  NULL }
};
```

The **verbose** resource is parsed as type **XrmoptionNoArg**, which means the command-line flag is itself the value of the argument. The Intrinsics will extract the **delay** resource from the command line as type **XrmoptionStickyArg**, which means that the value of the resource immediately follows the command-line flag, with no spaces.

We must add these lines to the file rmtest.c and also change the first line of the program to

```
toplevel = XtInitialize(argv[0], "Rmtest", options,
                        XtNumber(options), &argc, argv);
```

After making these changes to the **rmtest** program, we can try the new command-line options. Let's assume the contents of the class resource file and .Xdefaults file are the same as at the end of the previous section. We can now override the resource values in the resource files using command-line arguments. For example,

```
% rmtest -fg green -delay15
fg = 14, bg = 13, delay = 15, verbose = 1
```

Now the resource manager retrieves the value of **verbose** from the class resource file and the value of **background** from the .Xdefaults file. However, the values of **foreground** and **delay** are specified by the command-line arguments.

Occasionally a programmer needs to override the values in the resource database, possibly because of a calculated condition that makes that option invalid. The resources obtained using **XtGetApplicationResources()** can be overridden by specifying a list of resource names and values as the **args** argument to the function.

3.3.4 Type Conversion

In each of the previous examples, the resource manager automatically converted the requested resources from one data type to another. The resource manager performs these conversions using functions known as *type-converters*. The most common type-converters convert from a string to some other data type, because resource files specify resources as strings. However, type-converters can be used to convert between any two data types, including application-defined types. Fig. 3.6 lists the standard type-converter conversions supported defined by the Xt Intrinsics for converting between data types.

From	To
String	Boolean
String	Bool
String	short
String	unsigned char
String	Font
String	LongBoolean
String	Fontstruct
String	Cursor
String	int
String	Display
String	Pixel
String	File
Color	Pixel
int	Boolean
int	Bool
int	Short
int	Pixel
int	Pixmap
int	Font

Figure 3.6 Type converters defined by the Xt Intrinsics.

Applications can define additional type conversions by writing a type-converter function and registering it with the resource manager. A type converter is a procedure that has the form:

```
void Converter(args, nargs, from, to)
      XrmValue   *args;
      Cardinal    nargs;
      XrmValue   *from;
      XrmValue   *to;
```

The **args** parameter is used to pass additional arguments to the type converter, when they are needed. The arguments are given in an array of type **XrmValue**, defined as

```
typedef struct {
  unsigned int  size;
  caddr_t       *addr;
} XrmValue, *XrmValuePtr;
```

This structure holds a pointer to a value, and the size of the value. The type converter's second argument indicates the number of arguments contained in **args**. Since many converter functions require no additional parameters, **args** is often given as NULL, and **nargs** as zero. The last two parameters provide a pointer to an **XrmValue** structure containing the original data, and a location to store the converted value.

Let's see how this works by writing an example type converter. One useful type converter that the Xt Intrinsics does not provide is a function to convert a string to a floating point number. We can define this function as

```
/**************************************************
 * str2flt.c: Convert a string to a float.
 **************************************************/
#include <X11/Intrinsic.h>
#include <X11/StringDefs.h>

void CvtStringToFloat(args, nargs, fromVal, toVal)
     XrmValuePtr args, fromVal, toVal;
     int         *nargs;
{
  static float result;
  /*
   * Make sure the number of args is correct.
   */
  if (*nargs != 0)
   XtWarning("String to Float conversion needs no arguments");
  /*
   * Convert the string in the fromVal to a floating pt.
```

```
     */
    if (sscanf((char *)fromVal->addr, "%f", &result) == 1) {
      /*
       * Make the toVal point to the result.
       */
      toVal->size = sizeof (float);
      toVal->addr = (caddr_t) &result;
    }
    else
    /*
     * If sscanf fails, issue a warning that something is wrong.
     */
     XtStringConversionWarning((char *) fromVal->addr, "Float");
}
```

This type converter first checks how many **args** were given as parameters. Since no additional parameters are needed, the function uses the utility function

```
XtWarning(message)
```

to print a warning if the number of arguments is not equal to zero. The type converter uses **sscanf()** to convert the string representation to a floating point value. The **toVal** structure is then filled in with the size of a float and the address of the variable **result**. If **sscanf()** fails, the function

```
XtStringConversionWarning(from, to);
```

is used to issue a warning. This function takes two arguments indicating the two data types involved in the conversion.

Notice that the variable **result**, which contains the value returned by the type converter, is declared as static. This is important because otherwise the address of **result** would be invalid after the function returns. Functions that call type converters must copy the returned value immediately, because the type converter reuses the same address each time it is called.

Before the resource manager can use a type converter, the function must be registered with the resource manager. The function

```
XtAddConverter(from_type, to_type, converter, args, nargs)
```

registers a type converter with the resource manager. The arguments **from_type** and **to_type** must be strings indicating the data types. Whenever appropriate, the standard names defined in StringDefs.h should be used for consistency. The **converter** argument specifies the address of new type-converter function, while **args** and **nargs** specify any additional arguments that should be passed to the type-converter when it is called.

The **CvtStringToFloat** type-converter is a useful function to add to the libXs library and we will use it again in later chapters.

We can test the string-to-float function by modifying the **rmtest** program from Section 3.3.2. The example now defines the **delay** member of the **ApplicationData** structure as a floating point number, rather than an integer as in the earlier version. We must also change the **XtResource** array to specify that the value of **delay** should be retrieved as type **XtRFloat**. The Intrinsics does not define **XtRFloat**, but we can easily add it to the libXs header file, defined as

```
#define XtRFloat  "Float"
```

The main difference in this version of **rmtest** is that the main body of the test application registers the type-converter function before retrieving the application resources.

```
/**********************************************************
 * rmtest3.c: floating point version.
 **********************************************************/

#include <X11/Intrinsic.h>
#include <X11/StringDefs.h>
#include "libXs.h"

typedef struct {
   Pixel     fg, bg;
   float     delay;
   Boolean   verbose;
} ApplicationData, *ApplicationDataPtr;

static XtResource resources[] = {
  { XtNforeground, XtCForeground, XtRPixel, sizeof (Pixel),
    XtOffset(ApplicationDataPtr, fg), XtRString, "Black"    },
  { XtNbackground, XtCBackground, XtRPixel, sizeof (Pixel),
    XtOffset(ApplicationDataPtr, bg), XtRString, "White"    },
  { "delay", "Delay", XtRFloat, sizeof (float),
    XtOffset(ApplicationDataPtr, delay), XtRString,"2.5"    },
  { "verbose", "Verbose", XtRBoolean, sizeof (Boolean),
    XtOffset(ApplicationDataPtr,verbose), XtRString, "False"},
  };

XrmOptionDescRec options[] = {
 {"-verbose", "*verbose", XrmoptionNoArg, "True"},
 {"-delay", "*delay", XrmoptionStickyArg,  NULL}
};
```

```
main(argc, argv)
    int   argc;
    char *argv[];
 {
  Widget toplevel;
  ApplicationData data;
  toplevel = XtInitialize(argv[0], "Rmtest", options,
                          XtNumber(options), &argc, argv);
  /*
   *   Add the string to float type-converter.
   */
  XtAddConverter(XtRString, XtRFloat, CvtStringToFloat,
                 NULL,0);
  /*
   *  Retrieve the resources.
   */
  XtGetApplicationResources(toplevel, &data, resources,
                            XtNumber(resources), NULL, 0);
  /*
   * Print the result.
   */
  printf("fg = %d, bg = %d, delay = %f, verbose = %d\n",
         data.fg, data.bg, data.delay, data.verbose);
 }
```

We can test this version of **rmtest** using the following class resource file.

```
########################################
# Rmtest: resource file for rmtest.c
########################################
*foreground:     Red
*background:     Blue
*verbose:        False
*delay:          23.54
```

Now, if we run this version of **rmtest** from a shell, we should see something like

```
% rmtest
fg = 9, bg = 1, delay = 23.54, verbose = 0
```

3.4 SUMMARY

The resource manager provides a simple and powerful mechanism that allows the application programmer to create customizable applications easily. This chapter examined the basic principles of the Xlib resource manager and showed how applications can use the Xt Intrinsics resource facilities to manage application resources. The Intrinsics encourages consistency between all applications by providing a standard set of resource names recognized by all applications. The Intrinsics also assists the programmer by providing an easy-to-use mechanism for handling user-defined resources, command-line options, and programmer-defined defaults.

We have now discussed the general architecture of X, the architecture of the Xt Intrinsics, and the resource manager. The following chapter introduces the widgets provided by the Xt Intrinsics and the X Widgets, and begins to put these pieces together as we explore more complex applications.

4

PROGRAMMING WITH WIDGETS

Chapter 2 introduced the Xt Intrinsics, a framework that allows programmers to combine user interface components known as widgets to create complete applications. Widgets are simply an X window along with some procedures that manipulate the window.[1] Each widget also maintains a data structure that stores information used by the widget's procedures. This chapter examines widgets more closely. We will explore the basic widgets provided by the Xt Intrinsics, discuss a few representative widgets from HP's X Widget set and show how we can combine widgets to create a complete user interface for an application.

As this book is being written, the X Consortium has not recognized any widget set as a standard. However, at least three sets of widgets are freely available as contributed software. These are: Hewlett Packard's X Widget set, Sony's Xsw widget set, and the Athena widget set developed by M.I.T.'s Project Athena. The examples in this book use the X Widget set, contributed to the X community by Hewlett-Packard, as a representative widget set. Like Xlib and the Xt Intrinsics, the X Widget set is available as part of the standard distribution of the X Window System, in the "contrib" directory. Many vendors also sell their own proprietary widget sets. Hewlett-Packard sells a proprietary version of the X Widget set which is programmatically compatible with the contributed version described in this book. HP's proprietary version, known as the Common X Interface, features a three-dimensional appearance. Digital Equipment Corporation supplies a proprietary widget set as part of

1. The X11 R3 version of the Intrinsics supports another user interface component known as a "gadget." A gadget is similar to a widget, except that a gadget does not have a window associated with it. Gadgets are often more efficient than widgets. As this book goes to press, the X Consortium has not yet accepted the gadget mechanism as a standard part of the definition of the Xt Intrinsics. However, the OSF/MOTIF widget set is expected to rely heavily on gadgets, and gadgets will most likely be a standard part of the Intrinsics in the future.

their DECWindows system and AT&T markets a widget set that implements the OpenLook interface. The Open Software Foundation (OSF) is developing a widget set named Motif which is based on the features of both Hewlett-Packard's Common X Interface and Digital Equipment Corporation's DECWindows widget set. The screen images in this book were generated using the Hewlett-Packard Common X Interface widget set, which shows a "look and feel" similar to that of the OSF widget set. The X Consortium is also designing yet another widget set, known as the "Core Components" widget set.

Each of these widget sets provide a different appearance or style of interaction, and offers somewhat different functionality, but from the application programmer's viewpoint they should be similar to the widgets used in this book.

While an in-depth look at every available widget is beyond the scope of this book, we can discuss general features of widgets by dividing them into several functional categories. This chapter looks at a few widgets belonging to each category, and provides examples of how they can be used in typical applications. The X Widget set used in the examples is freely distributed along with the X Window System, and source is available for little or no cost. Other widget sets offer slightly different features, but usually are similar enough to the X Widget set so that a programmer who understands a few basic principles can use any widget set easily.

4.1 WIDGET CLASSES

The Xt Intrinsics defines an object-oriented architecture that organizes widgets into *classes*.[2] In general, a class is a set of things that have similar characteristics. Individual things (objects) are always *instances* of some class. For example, an object-oriented drawing program might define a class named Rectangle. This class could define various attributes common to all rectangles: color, width, height, position, and so on. To display a particular rectangle on the screen, the program *instantiates* (creates an instance of) a rectangle. This rectangle has specific values for all its attributes, for example: color: red, width: 10, height: 20, x: 200, y: 325. In the Xt Intrinsics, the function **`XtCreateWidget()`** creates an instance of the widget class given as the **`class`** argument. In the example in Chapter 2, the message window was an instance of the StaticText widget class.

Inheritance is another useful object-oriented concept supported by the Xt Intrinsics. In most object-oriented systems, a class can inherit some or all the characteristics of another class, in much the same way that people inherit characteristics from their parents. For example, the drawing program we discussed above could define a class named GraphicalObject that defines the attributes common to all objects that can be displayed on the screen. GraphicalObject might define position and color attributes. Next, we can define *subclasses* of

2. Object-oriented programming is a programming style that organizes systems according to the objects in the system, rather than the functions the system performs. An object is an abstraction that combines data and the operations that can be performed on that data in a single package.

GraphicalObject, such as Circle and Rectangle. The Circle class inherits the position and color attributes from its *superclass*, GraphicalObject and adds another attribute: radius. The Rectangle class also inherits the position and color attributes, but adds two more attributes: width and height.

The widget programmer (a programmer who designs new widgets) needs to understand these concepts to create new widget classes. Chapters 12, 13, and 14 discuss how the Xt Intrinsics implements classes and uses the architecture of the Xt Intrinsics to create several new widget classes. However the application programmer should also understand these concepts because it is possible to characterize the behavior of a widget by knowing its class and its superclasses. For example, the X Widget set defines a Button widget class and subclass of the Button widget class, the PushButton class. Because PushButton is a subclass of Button, it is safe to assume that the PushButton widget class is similar to the Button widget class. For example, the PushButton recognizes many of the same options and uses the same resource names as the Button widget class.

The characteristics that each widget class inherits from its superclass include all user-customizable resources and all callback lists. For example, all widget classes are subclasses of the Core widget class provided by the Xt Intrinsics. Therefore, because the Core widget class provides a **XtNdestroy** callback list, all widget classes also support the **XtNdestroy** callback list. A widget can also inherit the procedures that define the widgets behavior, including the action list used by the translation manager.

Each widget class has a *class name* used by the resource manager to retrieve resources, and also defines a pointer to a structure known as a *widget class*. The widget class is used as an argument to **XtCreateWidget()**. For example, the widget class for the Core widget is defined in Core.h as

```
WidgetClass widgetClass;
```

Therefore,

```
XtCreateWidget("core", widgetClass, parent, NULL, 0);
```

creates an instance of a widget belonging to the Core class.

4.2 WIDGET RESOURCE CONVENTIONS

Widgets use the resource manager to retrieve the resources specified by the user when the widget is created. Applications can also set the value of a widget resource by passing an argument list to **XtCreateWidget()** or by using **XtSetValues()** to change the value of a resource after the widget is created. Because the options specified by the programmer are applied *after* the user-specified resources are retrieved from the resource data base, they override the user's chosen options. It is sometimes difficult to determine when a widget resource should be set by an application programmer or when it should be left for the end user. The convention used in this book is as follows:

Application programmers should avoid specifying widget resource values in the program except where necessary to ensure that the application works correctly.

Application programmers should think carefully whenever they are tempted to hard code resource values into an application. Whenever possible, the programmer should leave decisions regarding widget layout, fonts, labels, colors, and so on, to the end user. Applications that are customizable by the end user tend to be more portable. For example, the labels displayed by Button widgets can be set by the user. A programmer could probably justify hard coding the button labels for important functions to prevent the user from using the resource manager to mis-labeling them. But what if the labels are programmed in English, and the user reads only French? Labels that can be set in a resource data base can be changed easily and without access to source code.

Unfortunately, it is difficult to design a program to be customizable by the end user and still ensure that it works correctly. For example, if command labels can be redefined by the end user, there is nothing to prevent the labels of the buttons from being altered in a misleading way. Imagine a situation where the user has inadvertently switched the labels of the "Delete" and "Save" command buttons of an editor. The results could be disastrous. Documenting software that can be radically customized by the end user is also an enormous problem. Therefore the approach advocated here is not without flaws.

One way to make programs customizable, while still providing useful defaults, is to provide a class resource file for every program. The programmer can use the class resource file to specify default resources that the user can override in the .Xdefaults file, if desired. The class resource file also provides a useful public place to document the resources and options recognized by an application.

Even when it is necessary to hard code some resources into a program, using a resource file while developing the application makes it easier for the application programmer to determine the best value for a resource. Rather than recompiling an application every time a resource needs to be changed, the programmer can simply change the appropriate entries in the resource file and run the program again until the proper value is determined. The examples in this book specify few resources in the source code, and many examples are accompanied by a class resource file containing the default resources used by the example.

4.3 INTRINSIC WIDGET CLASSES

The Xt Intrinsics defines several basic widget classes that serve as superclasses for other widgets. These widget classes define the architecture used by all other widgets, and also provide some fundamental characteristics inherited by all other widget classes. The following sections discuss the fundamental widget classes provided by the Intrinsics.

4.3.1 The Core Widget Class

The Core widget class is the most fundamental widget, and serves as the superclass for all other widget classes. The Core widget's class name is Core and its class is **widgetClass**.[3] The Core widget class provides resources inherited by all widgets.

The Core widget class is an example of a *meta-class*. In the Xt Intrinsics, a meta-class is a class that serves only as a superclass to other widgets.[4] Meta-classes are never used directly in applications In spite of its intended purpose, the Core widget class *can* be instantiated, as illustrated by the following program:

```
/*****************************************************
 * generic.c: Test the Core widget class
 *****************************************************/

#include <X11/Intrinsic.h>

main(argc, argv)
  int   argc;
  char *argv[];
{
  Widget toplevel;
  /*
   * Initialize the Intrinsics.
   */
  toplevel = XtInitialize(argv[0], "Generic", NULL, 0,
                          &argc, argv);
  /*
   * Create a Core widget.
   */
  XtCreateManagedWidget("widget", widgetClass,
                        toplevel, NULL, 0);
  XtRealizeWidget(toplevel);
  XtRealizeWidget(toplevel);
  XtMainLoop();
}
```

3. The remainder of this book simply refers to widgets by their class name, thereby avoiding any more statements like "the Core widget's class name is Core." Appendix B lists the class and class names for the widgets in the X Widget set.

4. One of the difficulties that we face when discussing object-oriented techniques is that few people agree on basic terminology. In some object-oriented languages, the term meta-class refers to a class that is instantiated to create another class. In other words, every class is itself an object, an instance of a meta-class. It would probably be more accurate to refer to the Core widget class as an abstract class.

This program simply creates an empty window. The application does nothing useful, but does obey all conventions of the X Window System. The program interacts correctly with window managers, and allows the end user to customize all resources supported by the Core widget class. Applications that need a basic window for displaying text or graphics can use the Core widget, although the X Widget set provides another widget, the WorkSpace widget, specifically for this purpose.

4.3.2 The Composite Widget Class

The Composite widget class is a subclass of the Core widget class, and is also a meta-class. All subclasses of the Composite widget class are also known as composite widgets. Composite widgets serve primarily as containers for other widgets, and any widget that has children must be a subclass of the Composite widget class. A composite widget manages its children, which means that composite widgets are responsible for:

- Determining the physical layout of all managed children. Each composite widget has a geometry manager that controls the location of each child widget according to its management policy.
- Deallocating the memory used by all children when the composite widget is destroyed. When a composite widget is destroyed, all children are destroyed first.
- Mapping and unmapping children. By default, a widget's window is mapped when it is managed, and unmapped when it is unmanaged. This behavior can be altered by setting the widget's **`XtNMappedWhenManaged`** resource to **`False`**.
- Controlling which child has the keyboard input focus. For example, a multiple field forms editor might shift the input focus from one field to the next when the <RETURN> key is entered.

4.3.3 The Constraint Widget Class

The Constraint widget class is a subclass of the Composite widget class, and therefore can also manage children. Constraint widgets manage their children based on some type of constraint associated with each child. For example, children can be constrained to some minimum or maximum size, or they can be constrained to a particular location relative to another widget. The Constraint widget class is also a meta-class and is never instantiated directly. Section 4.4.6.3 discusses an example constraint widget.

4.3.4 The Shell Widget Class

The Shell widget class is a subclass of the Composite widget class, but can have only one child. Shell widgets are special purpose widgets that provide an interface between other widgets and the window manager. A Shell widget negotiates the geometry of the application's top level window with the window manager, sets the properties required by the window manager, and generally handles the window manager protocol for the application. The following sections discuss several subclasses of the Shell widget class.

4.3.4.1 Top-Level Shells

The TopLevelShell widget class is a subclass of Shell. **XtInitialize()** creates a TopLevelShell widget that applications usually use as their main top-level window. Applications that use multiple top-level windows can use the function

```
XtCreateApplicationShell(name, class, args, nargs)
```

to create additional TopLevelShell widgets.

The following program is a modified version of the example from Section 4.3.1 that creates two independent top-level windows. Both windows can be manipulated independently, although both are created by the same client. Notice that applications must realize each top-level Shell individually.

```
/**************************************************************
 *
 * twoshells.c: Example of two independent top-level shells
 **************************************************************/
#include <X11/Intrinsic.h>
#include <X11/Shell.h>

main(argc, argv)
    int   argc;
    char *argv[];
{
  Widget toplevel, shell2;
  /*
   * Initialize the Intrinsics, create one TopLevelShell.
   */
  toplevel = XtInitialize(argv[0], "Generic", NULL, 0,
                          &argc, argv);
  /*
   * Create a second TopLevelShell widget.
   */
   shell2= XtCreateApplicationShell("Window2",
                                   topLevelShellWidgetClass,
                                   NULL, 0);
  /*
   * Create a Core widget as a child of each shell.
   */
  XtCreateManagedWidget("Widget", widgetClass,
```

```
                              toplevel, NULL, 0);
  XtCreateManagedWidget("Widget2", widgetClass,
                              shell2, NULL, 0);
  /*
   * Realize both shell widgets.
   */
   XtRealizeWidget(toplevel);
  XtRealizeWidget(shell2);
  XtMainLoop();
}
```

4.3.4.2 Transient Shells

Transient shells are similar to TopLevelShells except in the way they interact with window managers. Transient shells cannot be iconified separately. If an application's top-level window is iconified, the window manager should also iconify all Transient shells created by that application. Applications can create a transient shell by specifying the widget class **transientShellWidgetClass** as an argument to **XtCreateApplicationShell()**.

4.4 THE X WIDGET CLASSES

The X Widget set contains many components, including scroll bars, title bars, menus, buttons, and so on that can be combined to create user interfaces. We can divide the widget classes that implement these components into several categories based on the general functionality they offer. For example some widgets display information, while others allow the user to edit text or graphical images. Still others allow widgets to be grouped together in various combinations. The following sections describe a few examples of each of these categories.

4.4.1 X Widget Meta-Classes

The X widget set contains several additional meta-classes. The most basic of these is the Primitive widget class, which is a subclass of the Core widget class. The Primitive widget class is never instantiated, and serves only to define some standard resources inherited by its subclasses, including a foreground color and several callback lists. The Manager widget class is another X Widget meta-class. It is a subclass of the Constraint widget class, and defines basic resources used by all composite and constraint widgets in the X Widget set.

4.4.2 Display Widgets

Many applications need to display text or graphical images. The X Widget set contains two display widgets, one for text and the other for raster images.

The StaticText widget displays a string in a window. The text is called static because the string cannot be edited. The StaticText widget is a subclass of the Primitive widget class and therefore inherits the resources and callback lists of both the Primitive widget class and the Core widget class. The StaticText widget's class is **`XwstatictextWidgetClass`**. The memo program in Chapter 2 provides an example using the StaticText widget.

The StaticRaster widget displays a static raster image. This widget, whose class is **`XwstaticrasterWidgetClass`**, is also a subclass of the Primitive widget class. Chapter 7 demonstrates the StaticRaster widget.

4.4.3 Editing

Applications also often need to allow the user to edit text or graphics. The TextEdit widget is a subclass of the Primitive widget class that provides basic text editing capability. The TextEdit widget is a complex widget and provides many public functions for programmatically inserting, deleting, and otherwise manipulating the text displayed by the widget.

It is often useful to be able to edit a single line of text. The TextEdit widget is a multiline editor, but it can be set to a height that allows only a single line of text to be seen at once. Unfortunately, the height of a single line of text depends on the font used, and there is no convenient way to specify that the widget height should correspond to the height of a single character. However, we can write a utility function that creates a single line TextEdit widget and put it in our libXs library for future use. This function takes a name, a parent widget, and a resource list and creates a TextEdit widget. Once the widget is created, the function retrieves the height of the font using **`XtGetValues()`**.

Once the font used by the TextEdit widget is retrieved, our utility function uses **`XtSetValues()`** to force the height of the widget to be six pixels greater than the height of the font. The extra space is necessary to allow room for the editing cursor.

Notice that in this example, it seems justifiable to set a widget's size in the program. The function of the widget in the application is to edit a single line of text. However, the user can still specify the font and all other widget resources. A less friendly approach would be to hard code the font used by the widget and then set the widget's height to a specific pixel value.

Forcing the height of the widget to be the same as the height of one character makes the TextEdit widget appear to be a single-line editor. However, the user can still type a <RETURN> to move to the next line. Fortunately, we can use the translation manager to disable this feature. First we define an action procedure named **`beep()`** that rings the terminal bell when it is called. Then we can use the translation manager to override the key translations that normally move to a new line, so that they call **`beep()`** instead.

```
/*********************************************************
 * one_line.c: Create a single line editable text field
 *********************************************************/
#include <X11/StringDefs.h>
#include <X11/Intrinsic.h>
#include <Xw/Xw.h>
#include <Xw/TextEdit.h>
#include "libXs.h"
/*
 * Just ring the terminal bell.
 */
static void beep(w, event, params, num_params)
     Widget w;
     XEvent *event;
     String *params;
     int    num_params;
{
  XBell(XtDisplay(w), 100);
}
/*
 * Associate the action "beep" with the function.
 */
static XtActionsRec actionsTable [] = {
  {"beep",   beep},
};
/*
 * Override all translations that enter a newline.
 */
static char defaultTranslations[] =
  "Ctrl<Key>J:           beep() \n\
   Ctrl<Key>O:           beep() \n\
   Ctrl<Key>M:           beep() \n\
   <Key> Return:         beep()";

Widget create_one_line_text_widget(name, parent, args, nargs)
     char   *name;
     Widget parent;
     Arg    args[];
     int    nargs;
{
  XFontStruct   *font;
  Widget         w;
```

```
  Arg            wargs[1];
  XtTranslations trans_table;
  /*
   * Add the actions and compile the translations.
   */
  XtAddActions(actionsTable, XtNumber(actionsTable));
  trans_table = XtParseTranslationTable(defaultTranslations);
  /*
   * Create a TextEdit widget.
   */
  w = XtCreateManagedWidget(name, XwtexteditWidgetClass,
                            parent, args, nargs);
  /*
   * Install our translations.
   */
  XtOverrideTranslations(w, trans_table);
  /*
   * Get the font used by the widget.
   */
  XtSetArg(wargs[0], XtNfont, &font);
  XtGetValues(w, wargs, 1);
  /*
   * Set the widget height according to the font height.
   */
  XtSetArg(wargs[0], XtNheight, FONTHEIGHT(font) + 6 );
  XtSetValues(w, wargs, 1);
  return (w);
}
```

FONTHEIGHT() is a macro that extracts the maximum character height of the font. We can define it in libXs.h as

```
#define FONTHEIGHT(f) ((f)->max_bounds.ascent + \
                        (f)->max_bounds.descent)
```

Let's test this function with a simple program that displays a single text edit widget. The program places the TextEdit widget in **XwtextEdit** mode to allow the user to edit the contents of the widget. The other possible modes are **XwtextRead** (read-only mode) and **XwtextAppend** (append mode).

```
/************************************************************
 * singleline.c: Test a single line text editor
 ************************************************************/
#include <X11/Intrinsic.h>
```

```
#include <Xw/Xw.h>
#include <Xw/TextEdit.h>
#include "libXs.h"
main(argc, argv)
     int   argc;
     char *argv[];
{
  Widget toplevel;
  Arg    wargs[1];

  toplevel = XtInitialize(argv[0], "Edit", NULL, 0 ,
                               &argc, argv);
  /*
   * Create a one line TextEdit widget, set to "edit" mode.
   */
  XtSetArg(wargs[0], XtNeditType, XwtextEdit);
  create_one_line_text_widget("edit", toplevel, wargs, 1);

  XtRealizeWidget(toplevel);
  XtMainLoop();
}
```

The TextEdit widget is a complex widget with many customizable resources. The interested reader should refer to the X Widget documentation for more details. We will discuss more of this widget's features when we use the TextEdit widget again later in this book.

4.4.4 Utility Widgets

The X Widget set provides many widgets that perform simple but often needed functions. These include a Valuator widget that allows the user to select a value interactively by positioning a slider with the mouse and an Arrow widget that displays an image of an arrow pointing up, down, left, or right. Applications can use these simple widgets by themselves, although other widgets often combine them to create more complex widgets. For example, the Scrollbar widget combines two Arrow widgets with a Valuator widget to provide vertical and horizontal scroll bars.

The Arrow widget is a subclass of the Primitive widget class. The Arrow widget's **XtNdirection** resource determines the arrow's direction. Fig. 4.1 shows four Arrow widgets, one in each of the possible directions.

Figure 4.1 Arrow widgets.

The Valuator widget class is also a subclass of the Primitive widget class. In addition to allowing the user to control the position of the slider, the Valuator widget is useful as an analog dial. Its position can be set programmatically or by the user. Fig. 4.2 shows two Arrow widgets combined with a Valuator widget to form a ScrollBar.

Figure 4.2 A ScrollBar widget.

4.4.5 Button Widgets

Many applications allow the user to issue simple commands or set options interactively. One common way to do this is to provide buttons that the user can "press" by clicking a mouse button while the sprite is in the button widget's window. The X Widget set provides several types of buttons. Each type is a subclass of the Button meta-class. The Button class is a subclass of the Primitive widget class that serves as a superclass for the PushButton, Toggle, and MenuButton widget classes.

All button widgets recognize "**select()**" and "**release()**" actions, and provide **XtNselect** and **XtNrelease** callback lists. The following example creates a PushButton widget that executes commands when the user selects and releases the button.

```
/**********************************************************
 * buttontest.c: Test the X Widget pushbutton widget.
 **********************************************************/
#include <X11/Intrinsic.h>
```

```
#include <Xw/Xw.h>
#include <Xw/PButton.h>
/*
 * Define callbacks.
 */
void select_button(w, client_data, call_data)
   Widget   w;
   caddr_t  client_data;
   caddr_t  call_data;
{
  printf("Button selected\n");
}
void release_button(w, client_data, call_data)
   Widget   w;
   caddr_t  client_data;
   caddr_t  call_data;
{
  printf("Button released\n");
}

main(argc, argv)
    int   argc;
    char *argv[];
{
  Widget toplevel, button;

  toplevel = XtInitialize(argv[0], "Buttontest", NULL, 0,
                          &argc, argv);
  /*
   * Create the pushbutton widget.
   */
  button = XtCreateManagedWidget("button",
                                 XwpushButtonWidgetClass,
                                 toplevel, NULL, 0);

  /*
   * Add select and release callbacks.
   */
  XtAddCallback(button, XtNselect, select_button, NULL);
  XtAddCallback(button, XtNrelease, release_button, NULL);

  XtRealizeWidget(toplevel);
  XtMainLoop();
}
```

Fig. 4.3 shows the PushButton widget created by this example. The user can specify the button label in a resource file by setting the **XtNlabel** resource. If no label is given, the widget displays the name specified when the widget was created. The label in Fig. 4.3 is produced by the following line in the user's .Xdefaults file.

```
*Buttontest*button*label:  Push Here
```

Figure 4.3 A PushButton widget.

A PushButton widget provides a convenient way to issue a command. For example, we could have designed the **memo** example in Chapter 2 with a "quit" button rather than having the user click the mouse on the message window. Since many applications need such a button, let's use a PushButton widget to write a simple routine for the libXs library that causes an application to exit when the user clicks on the button with the mouse. This function takes two arguments: the parent widget of the button, and a label for the button. The function simply adds a PushButton widget to its parent widget and registers a single callback function to exit when the button is released.

```
/*****************************************************
 * quit.c: A utility function that adds a quit button
 *****************************************************/
#include <X11/Intrinsic.h>
#include <X11/StringDefs.h>
#include <Xw/Xw.h>
#include <Xw/PButton.h>
/*
 * Define a callback to exit(). Make it static - no need
 * to make it known outside this file.
 */
static void quit_callback(w, client_data, call_data)
     Widget     w;
     caddr_t    client_data;
     caddr_t    call_data;
{
```

```
    exit(0);
}
/*
 * Function to add a quit button to any composite widget.
 */
Widget create_quit_button(label, parent)
     char   *label;
     Widget  parent;
{
  Arg    wargs[1];
  Widget w;
  XtSetArg(wargs[0], XtNlabel, label);
  w = XtCreateManagedWidget("quit", XwpushButtonWidgetClass,
                                   parent, wargs, 1);
  /*
   * Quit on the release (button up), so the application can
   * do something on the select (button down) if needed.
   */
  XtAddCallback(w, XtNrelease, quit_callback, NULL);
  return (w);
}
```

To add this function to the libXs library, we also need to add the line

```
extern Widget create_quit_button();
```

to the file libXs.h. Notice that this function assigns the quit callback to the **XtNrelease** callback list. This allows applications that use this quit button to register callbacks for the **XtNselect** callback list to perform some application-specific action before exiting.

4.4.6 Layout Widgets

So far, every example program in this chapter has created a single widget that occupies the entire top-level window of the application. Because most applications require a more complex interface, the X Widget set provides many composite widgets used to combine other widgets. These widgets allow endless combinations of buttons, scroll bars, text panes, and so on, to be grouped together in an application. Widgets that control the layout of multiple children must be subclasses of the Composite widget class. In the X Widget set, most widgets that control the layout of other widgets are also a subclass of the meta-class Manager. The Manager widget is a subclass of the Constraint widget class. The following sections discuss several subclasses of the Manager widget class.

4.4.6.1 The BulletinBoard Widget

The BulletinBoard widget class is one of the simplest examples of a Composite widget. The BulletinBoard widget allows children to be placed at absolute *(x, y)* coordinates within the widget. If no coordinates are provided for children of the BulletinBoard widget, the Bulletin-Board widget places them all at location *(0, 0)*. The BulletinBoard widget supports three different layout policies that can be specified using the **XtNlayout** resource inherited from the Manager widget class:

- **Xw_MINIMIZE**. When this policy is specified, the BulletinBoard widget is created just large enough to hold all children and ignores its width and height resources. The widget grows, shrinks, or resizes in response to widgets being moved, added, or deleted. This is the default layout policy.
- **Xw_MAXIMIZE**. When the **Xw_MAXIMIZE** layout style is chosen, the BulletinBoard widget grows in response to widgets being added or moved, but does not give up unused space.
- **Xw_IGNORE**. When this layout style is chosen, the BulletinBoard widget obeys its given width and height, and ignores the space needs of its children.

The following example demonstrates a BulletinBoard widget managing three single-line TextEdit widgets and three PushButton widgets. The example allows the user to type text into any of the TextEdit fields. Each PushButton widget has an **XtNselect** callback defined that retrieves the contents of the corresponding TextEdit widget when the user selects the button. For this simple example, the callback function simply prints the contents of the corresponding TextEdit widget to the standard output.

```
/************************************************************
 * formedit.c: Simple example of multiple edit fields managed
 *             by a BulletinBoard widget.
 ************************************************************/
#include <X11/Intrinsic.h>
#include <Xw/Xw.h>
#include <Xw/TextEdit.h>
#include <Xw/PButton.h>
#include <Xw/BBoard.h>
#include "libXs.h"

void get_text();
char *buttons[] = {"button1", "button2", "button3"};
char *editors[] = {"field1", "field2", "field3"};

main(argc, argv)
     int   argc;
     char *argv[];
```

```
{
  Widget toplevel, bb;
  Arg    wargs[1];
  int    i;

  toplevel = XtInitialize(argv[0], "Formedit", NULL, 0 ,
                          &argc, argv);
  /*
   * Create the BulletinBoard widget that manages
   * the edit fields.
   */
  bb = XtCreateManagedWidget("board",  XwbulletinWidgetClass,
                             toplevel, NULL, 0);
  /*
   * Create three single line edit widgets
   * and associate a button with each text edit widget.
   * Assign a XtNselect callback to each button.
   */
  XtSetArg(wargs[0], XtNeditType, XwtextEdit);
  for(i=0; i < XtNumber(buttons); i++){
    Widget editor, button;
    editor = create_one_line_text_widget(editors[i], bb,
                                         wargs, 1);
    button = XtCreateManagedWidget(buttons[i],
                                   XwpushButtonWidgetClass,
                                   bb, NULL, 0);
    XtAddCallback(button, XtNselect, get_text, editor);
  }
  XtRealizeWidget(toplevel);
  XtMainLoop();
}
```

This example creates a more interesting widget tree than earlier examples. Fig. 4.4 shows the widget tree formed by the TopLevelShell widget along with the BulletinBoard widget and its children.

The **XtNselect** callback procedure, **get_text()**, retrieves the contents of the TextEdit widget passed to the callback procedure as client data and prints the string. The function **XwTextCopyBuffer()**, a public function defined by the TextEdit widget, returns the entire contents of the TextEdit buffer.

```
void get_text(w, textwidget, call_data)
   Widget   w;
   Widget   textwidget;
```

```
    caddr_t  call_data;
  {
   printf("retrieving text:%s\n",XwTextCopyBuffer(textwidget));
  }
```

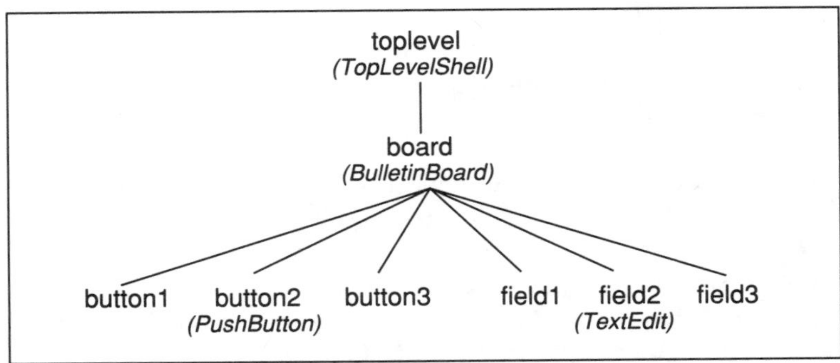

Figure 4.4 The widget tree created by formedit.

The BulletinBoard widget does not control the position of its children. Since this example also does not specify any sizes or locations for the widgets, they will all appear at *(0,0)*, unless we specify the placement in a resource file. The following class resource file defines the widget layout shown in Fig. 4.5.

```
#############################################################
# Formedit: Class resource file for the formedit example
#############################################################
#
# Specify labels for each button.
#
Formedit*button1*label:    Name:
Formedit*button2*label:    Phone:
Formedit*button3*label:    Address:
#
# Specify positions for each widget.
#
Formedit*TextEdit*x:        100
Formedit*field1*y:           10
Formedit*field2*y:           40
Formedit*field3*y:           70
Formedit*PushButton*x:       10
```

```
Formedit*button1*y:          10
Formedit*button2*y:          40
Formedit*button3*y:          70
```

Figure 4.5 A BulletinBoard widget.

4.4.6.2 The Row Column Manager

The RowCol widget is a subclass of the Manager widget class that organizes its children as rows and columns. The RowCol widget provides several resources that determine how it arranges its children. The **XtNlayoutType** resource controls how children are managed, and can be one of:

- **XwREQUESTED_COLUMNS** specifies that children should be arranged in the number of columns requested by the **XtNcolumns** resource. The children are laid out row by row, and each column is as wide as its widest element. This is the default.
- **XwMAXIMUM_COLUMNS** specifies that children should be arranged in as many columns as fit in the RowCol widget, based on the size of the Row widget. Each column is as wide as its widest element.
- **XwMAXIMUM_UNALIGNED** specifies that each row should contain as many widgets as possible. The columns are not aligned.

If the **XtNlayoutType** is set to **XwREQUEST_COLUMNS**, the number of columns can be set using **XtNcolumns**. When **XtNlayoutType** is set to either of the other values, the resource **XtNsingleRow** can also be set to **True** to specify that the widgets should all be kept in one row.

The RowCol widget also supports three different layout policies that determine its size. These policies also interact to some extent with the **XtNlayoutType** to determine the position of its managed children. The **XtNlayout** resource, inherited from the Manager widget class, determines the RowCol widget's layout policy. The possible policies are **Xw_MINIMIZE**, **Xw_MAXIMIZE**, and **Xw_IGNORE**, and have nearly the same meaning as the corresponding policies in the BulletinBoard widget. When **XtNlayout** is set to maximize, any additional space is used as padding between the managed children.

Often, a RowCol widget manages widgets that are intended to be selected by the user. The RowCol manager supports a selection mode resource, **XtNmode**, that controls how its children are selected. There are two selection modes, **n_of_many** (the default) or **one_of_many**. The default behavior does not interfere with the normal behavior of the managed children. However, if **one_of_many** mode is specified, only one child widget can be selected at once. The RowCol manager keeps track of each selected child and invokes the functions on the child's **XtNrelease** callback list when another widget is selected.

Let's look at an example that demonstrates these different policies. The following example program creates a row column manager that manages six PushButton widgets.

```
/**********************************************************
 * rowtest.c: An example of a row column manager
 **********************************************************/
#include <X11/StringDefs.h>
#include <X11/Intrinsic.h>
#include <Xw/Xw.h>
#include <Xw/RCManager.h>
#include <Xw/PButton.h>
char * buttons[] = {"button1", "button2", "button3",
                    "button4", "button5", "button6"};
main(argc, argv)
    int    argc;
    char  *argv[];
{
  Widget toplevel, rowcol;
  int    i;
  toplevel = XtInitialize(argv[0], "Rowtest", NULL, 0,
                          &argc, argv);
  /*
   * Create a RowCol widget.
   */
  rowcol = XtCreateManagedWidget("rowcol",
                                 XwrowColWidgetClass,
                                 toplevel, NULL, 0);
  /*
   * Create six children of the RowCol widget.
   */
  for(i=0;i< XtNumber(buttons); i++)
   XtCreateManagedWidget(buttons[i], XwpushButtonWidgetClass,
                         rowcol, NULL, 0);
```

```
    XtRealizeWidget(toplevel);
    XtMainLoop();
}
```

The buttons in this example can be arranged in many different ways. For example, Fig. 4.6 shows the layout corresponding to the class resource file.

```
###################################################
# Rowtest: Class Resources for rowtest.c
###################################################
#
# Request buttons in 3 columns.
#
*Rowtest*rowcol.columns:    3
#
# Specify labels for all buttons.
#
*Rowtest*button1.label:     Button One
*Rowtest*button2.label:     Button Two
*Rowtest*button3.label:     Button Three
*Rowtest*button4.label:     Button Four
*Rowtest*button5.label:     Button Five
*Rowtest*button6.label:     Button Six
```

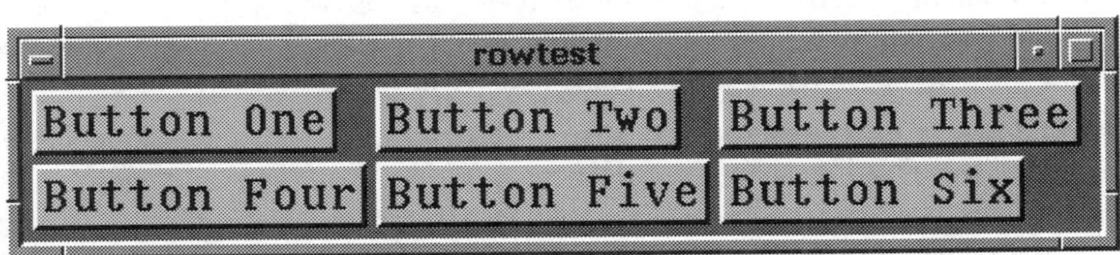

Figure 4.6 A RowCol widget managing three columns.

This resource file uses the **XtNcolumns** resource to arrange the buttons into three columns. It is also easy to specify that all widgets should be placed in a single row, by adding the lines

```
*Rowtest*rowcol*singleRow:  TRUE
*Rowtest*rowcol*layoutType: maximum_columns
```

The **XtNlayoutType** resource specifies that the buttons should occupy as many columns as fit in the Row widget, while the **XtNsingleRow** resource causes the Row to be large enough to place all button widgets in one row.

By default, each PushButton widget highlights when it is selected and unhighlights when it is released. We can change this behavior by setting the **XtNmode** resource of the RowCol manager to **n_of_many**. For example

```
rowtest*RowCol*mode:                one_of_many
rowtest*PushButton*translations: <Btn1Down>:      select()
```

When the RowCol manager is in **one_of_many** mode, it allows only one PushButton widget to be selected at any one time. In addition, because the PushButton widget now has only a single translation, "**select()**", the PushButton is no longer unselected, and therefore unhighlighted, when the user releases the mouse button. The RowCol widget releases each button when another button is selected, producing a toggling effect.

4.4.6.3 The Form Widget

The Form widget class is a subclass of the Manager widget class that manages its children based on constraints that specify the position of each widget relative to another widget, known as a reference widget. Each widget can have a reference widget for the horizontal direction and another for the vertical direction. The Form widget retains these relative positions when it is resized, when new children are added or deleted, or when one of its children is resized. The Form widget attaches additional resources to each managed child that allow the programmer or the user to specify the constraints for each widget.

These resources include:

- **XtNxRefWidget**, **XtNyRefWidget**. These resources specify the reference widget in the *x* and *y* directions. Because these resources must refer to a widget pointer, they can only be used by an application, and cannot be set by the end user in a resource file. In each case, the default reference widget is the parent Form widget.
- **XtNxRefName**, **XtNyRefName**. These resources serve the same function as **XtNxRefWidget** and **XtNyRefWidget** but allow the reference widget to be specified by name. Therefore, users can use these resources to specify the reference widget in a resource file. The default value in each case is the parent Form widget.
- **XtNxOffset**, **XtNyOffset**. These specify the *x* and *y* distances in pixels between the origin of the widget and the origin of the reference widget. The default values are zero.
- **XtNxAddWidth**, **XtNyAddHeight**. These resources determine whether or not the Form widget adds the width and height of the reference widget to the **XtNoffset** distance. The default values are **False**.
- **XtNxVaryOffset**, **XtNyVaryOffset**. These options specify whether the Form widget should view the *x* and *y* offsets as rigid, or whether the Form widget can vary the offsets slightly. The default values are **False**.
- **XtNxResizable**, **XtNyResizable**. These options indicate whether or not the Form widget can resize the child to satisfy its constraints. The default values are **False**.

- **XtNxAttachRight**, **XtNyAttachBottom**. A widget can be attached to the right side or the bottom side of the Form widget, by setting these resources to **True**. The defaults are **False**.
- **XtNxAttachOffset**, **XtNyAttachOffset**. If a widget is attached to the right or bottom side of its parent Form widget, this resource specifies an offset, in pixels, from the right or bottom side of the parent widget. The default values are zero.

The easiest way to understand these constraints is by looking at an example. The following simple program creates a Form widget that manages three MenuButton widgets.

```
/*****************************************************
 * formtest.c: Test the constraints of the Form Widget
 *****************************************************/

#include <X11/Intrinsic.h>
#include <Xw/Xw.h>
#include <Xw/Form.h>
#include <Xw/PButton.h>

char * buttons[] = {"button1", "button2", "button3"};

main(argc, argv)
     int   argc;
     char *argv[];
{
  Widget toplevel, form;
  int    i;
  toplevel = XtInitialize(argv[0], "Formtest", NULL, 0,
                          &argc, argv);
  /*
   * Create a Form manager widget
   */
  form = XtCreateManagedWidget("form", XwformWidgetClass,
                               toplevel, NULL,0);
  /*
   * Add three PushButton widgets to the Form Widget.
   */
  for(i=0;i< XtNumber(buttons); i++)
    XtCreateManagedWidget(buttons[i],
                          XwpushButtonWidgetClass,
                          form, NULL,0);
```

```
  XtRealizeWidget(toplevel);
  XtMainLoop();
}
```

Now we can see how each constraint affects the layout by experimenting with different resource values. Fig. 4.7 shows the initial layout produced by the following class resource file:

```
##########################################################
# Formtest: Constraint One for formtest program
##########################################################
#
# Specify labels for all buttons.
#
Formtest*button1*label:              Button One
Formtest*button2*label:              Button Two
Formtest*button3*label:              Button Three
#
# Make all buttons resizable.
#
Formtest*PushButton*xResizable:    TRUE
Formtest*PushButton*yResizable:    TRUE
#
# Make the Form widget the x reference widget for all buttons
# and attach all buttons to the right side of the Form widget.
#
Formtest*PushButton*xRefName:      form
Formtest*PushButton*xAttachRight: TRUE
#
# Attach button2 to the bottom of button1.
#
Formtest*button2*yRefName:           button1
Formtest*button2*yAddHeight:         TRUE
#
# Attach button3 to the bottom of button3
# and also the bottom of the Form widget.
#
Formtest*button3*yRefName:           button2
Formtest*button3*yAddHeight:         TRUE
Formtest*button3*yAttachBottom:      TRUE
```

This set of constraints declares all buttons to be resizable in both the *x* and *y* directions. In addition, we have declared the Form widget to be the reference widget along the *x* axis for all button widgets. The right side of each button widget is attached to the reference widget, specifying that each button spans the entire form widget regardless of its size. The remaining declarations indicate that **button2** should be positioned relative to **button1** along the *y* axis, offset by the height of **button1**. Similarly, **button3** is positioned relative to **button2** along the *y* axis and offset by the height of **button2**. Finally, **button3** is attached to the bottom of the Form widget. Fig. 4.7 shows the initial layout produced by these resources, while Fig. 4.8 shows the layout after resizing the Form widget.

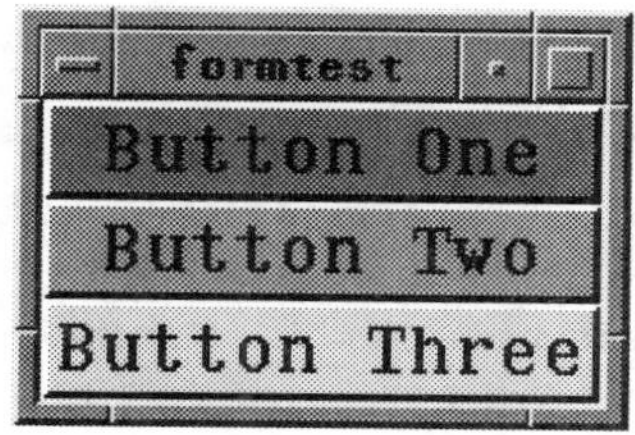

Figure 4.7 A Form widget using constraint one.

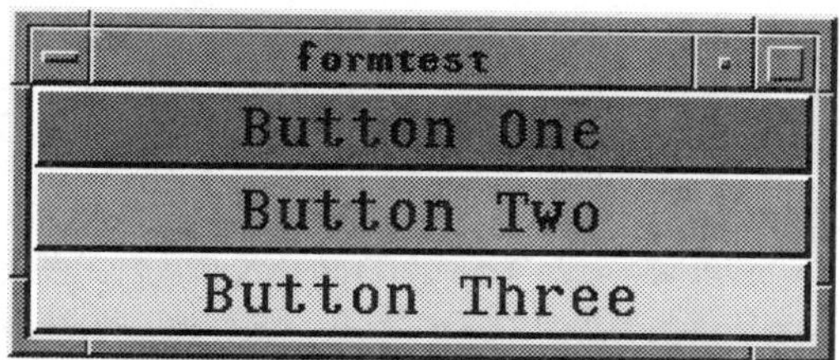

Figure 4.8 Resized Form widget using constraint one.

Now let's define a completely different layout.

```
###########################################################
# Formtest: Constraint Two for formtest program
###########################################################
#
# Specify labels for all buttons.
#
Formtest*button1*label:              Button One
Formtest*button2*label:              Button Two
Formtest*button3*label:              Button Three
#
# Make all buttons resizable.
#
Formtest*PushButton*xResizable:      TRUE
```

```
Formtest*PushButton*yResizable:    TRUE
#
# Make the Form widget the x and y reference widget for all
# buttons. Attach all buttons to the right side of the Form
# widget.
#
Formtest*PushButton*xRefName:      form
Formtest*PushButton*yRefName:      form
Formtest*PushButton*xAttachRight:  TRUE
#
# Attach button2 to the right side of button1.
#
Formtest*button2*xRefName:         button1
Formtest*button2*xAddWidth:        TRUE
#
# Attach button3 to the bottom of button3
# and also the bottom of the Form widget.
#
Formtest*button3*yRefName:         button2
Formtest*button3*yAddHeight:       TRUE
Formtest*button3*yAttachBottom:    TRUE
```

This constraint specification is nearly the same as the previous one, except that **button2** now uses the Form widget as its *y* axis reference widget and **button1** as its reference widget along the *x* axis. Fig. 4.9 shows the result.

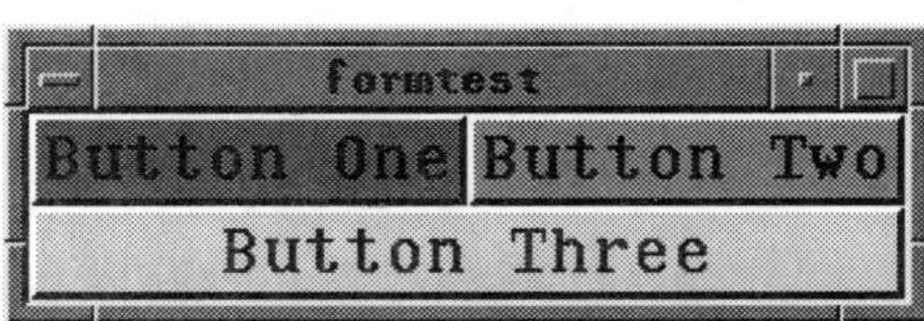

Figure 4.9 Form Widget using constraint two.

Still other layouts are possible. For example, consider the following constraints, which specify that all three buttons line up horizontally, as shown in Fig. 4.10.

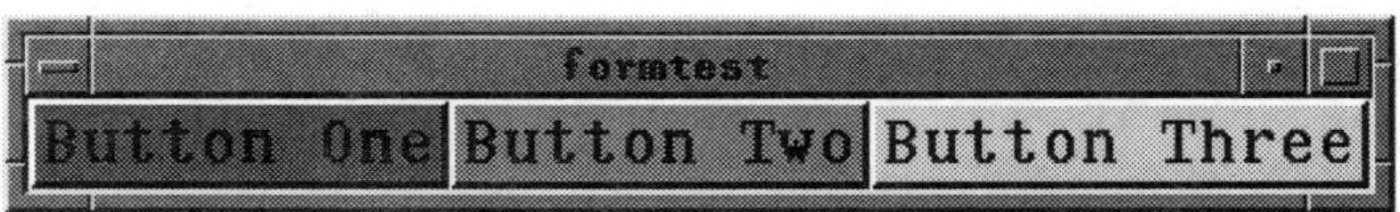

Figure 4.10 Form widget using constraint three.

```
##############################################################
# Formtest: Constraints Three for formtest program
##############################################################
#
# Specify labels for all buttons.
#
Formtest*button1*label:              Button One
Formtest*button2*label:              Button Two
Formtest*button3*label:              Button Three
#
# Make all buttons resizable.
#
Formtest*MenuButton*xResizable:     TRUE
Formtest*MenuButton*yResizable:     TRUE
#
# Make the Form widget the x and y reference widget for all
# buttons and attach all buttons to the bottom of the Form
# widget.
#
Formtest*MenuButton*xRefName:            form
Formtest*MenuButton*yRefName:            form
Formtest*MenuButton*yAttachBottom:       TRUE
#
# Attach button2 to the right side of button1.
#
Formtest*button2*xRefName:               button1
Formtest*button2*xAddWidth:              TRUE
#
# Attach button3 to the right side of button2
# and to the right side of the Form widget.
#
Formtest*button3*xRefName:               button2
Formtest*button3*xAddWidth:              TRUE
Formtest*button3*xAttachRight:           TRUE
```

4.4.7 Menu Widgets

The X Widget set provides a versatile set of widgets that allow applications to create popup menus. Menus use a widget tree whose root is a popup Shell widget. This Shell widget manages a PopupMgr widget. The PopupMgr widget class, a subclass of the MenuMgr widget class, is a composite widget that manages one or more menu panes. Each menu pane consists of yet another popup Shell that contains a Cascade widget. The Cascade widget is also a composite widget and manages one or more MenuButton widgets that correspond to each item in the menu. Fig. 4.11 shows the widget tree for a typical menu. Most widget trees created by applications correspond directly to a similar X window tree. That is, each widget's window is usually a sub-window of the window belonging to the widget's parent. However, the pop-up Shell widgets used to create a menu break the window hierarchy. Fig. 4.12 shows the X window tree that corresponds to the widget tree in Fig. 4.11.

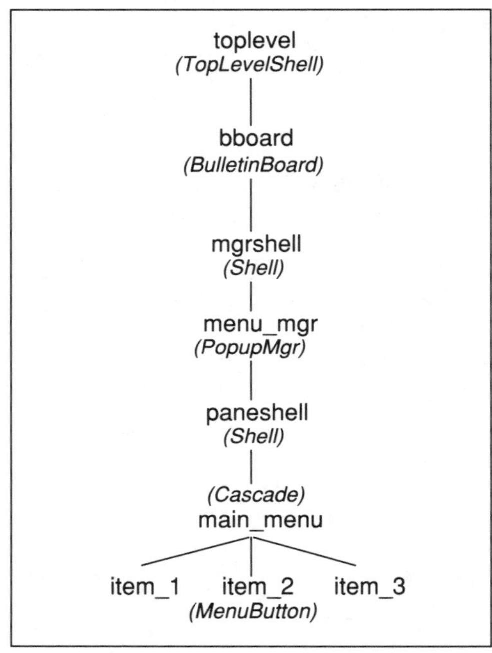

Figure 4.11 A menu widget tree.

This may seem confusing and rather complicated, but menus are easy to use in practice. Before we build a menu, let's look briefly at each of the components of a popup menu:

- The MenuMgr widget class is a meta-class for all menu manager classes. It is a subclass of the Manager widget class, and defines basic resources used by all menu panes.
- The PopupMgr widget class is a subclass of the MenuMgr widget class. Each popup menu creates a PopupMgr as a child of a popup Shell widget.
- The MenuPane widget class is a meta-class. It is a subclass of the Manager widget class and provides basic resources use by its subclasses.
- The Cascade widget class is a subclass of the MenuPane widget class. It manages a single column of menu buttons.

- The MenuButton widget class is a subclass of the Button widget class. A MenuButton widget has three main areas. The first is a mark area that can be used to display an image. This image defaults to a check mark. The second is a label area. This area can display a string or an image and displays the name or icon of the menu. The third area is known as a cascade area, and is used to show that the menu has a cascading submenu.

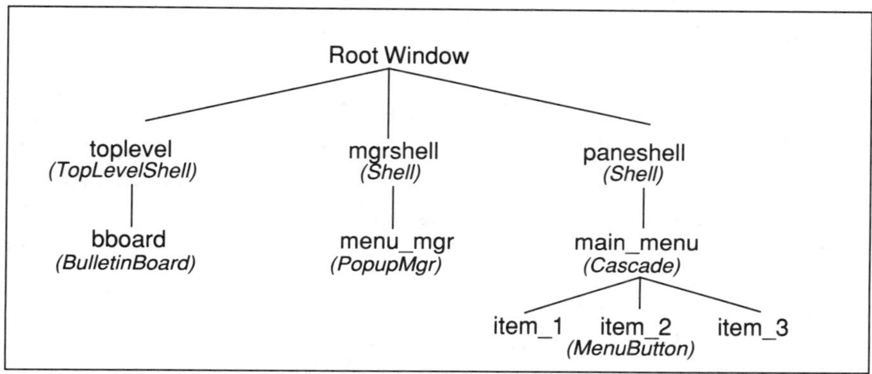

Figure 4.12 A menu window tree.

4.4.7.1 Creating Menus

Creating a menu requires five basic steps.

1. Create a popup Shell widget as the root of the menu tree. This popup Shell must be created as a child of a widget with which the menu is to be associated. The Intrinsics function

   ```
   XtCreatePopupShell(name,widget_class,parent,args,num_args)
   ```

   creates a popup Shell. Notice that the widget's parent must be specified. However, the popup Shell widget's window is a child of the root window of the screen. Applications should not realize this widget, as it is used only as a Shell wrapper for the PopupMgr widget created in step 2.

2. Create a PopupMgr widget as a child of the popup Shell widget created in step 1. Applications should not realize this widget because the PopupMgr widget does not have a window associated with it.

3. Create another popup Shell widget as a child of the PopupMgr created in step 2. The programmer does not need to realize this widget or its children because the PopupMgr handles this automatically.

4. Create a Cascade widget as a child of the popup Shell widget created in step 3. This widget must be attached to the PopupMgr widget, using the Cascade widget resource **XtNattachTo**. New panes can also be attached to menu buttons to create cascading menu trees.
5. Create MenuButton widgets as children of the Cascade widget created in step 4. These represent each entry in the menu. Applications can define callback functions for the buttons in the menu to define what happens when each button is selected.

Applications can create additional menu panes by repeating steps 3, 4, and 5 as needed.

Let's build an example menu. The following program creates a single menu pane and attaches it to a BulletinBoard widget.

```
/************************************************************
 * menu.c: First pop up menu example
 ************************************************************/

#include <X11/StringDefs.h>
#include <X11/Intrinsic.h>
#include <X11/Shell.h>
#include <Xw/Xw.h>
#include <Xw/MenuBtn.h>
#include <Xw/PopupMgr.h>
#include <Xw/Cascade.h>
#include <Xw/BBoard.h>
/*
 * Define callbacks for each menu entry.
 */
void do_item1(w, textwidget, call_data)
     Widget    w;
     Widget    textwidget;
     caddr_t   call_data;
{
  printf("Item one selected\n");
}
void do_item2(w, textwidget, call_data)
     Widget    w;
     Widget    textwidget;
     caddr_t   call_data;
{
  printf("Item two selected\n");
}
void do_item3(w, textwidget, call_data)
     Widget    w;
     Widget    textwidget;
```

```
     caddr_t  call_data;
{
  printf("Item three selected\n");
}
main(argc, argv)
     int   argc;
     char *argv[];
{
  Widget toplevel, bboard,
         mgr_shell, menu_mgr, pane_shell, main_menu_pane,
         button1, button2, button3, button4;
  Arg    wargs[1];
  /*
   * Initialize the Intrinsics and create a BulletinBoard
   * widget to be the primary widget in the program.
   */
  toplevel = XtInitialize (argv[0], "MenuTest", NULL, 0,
                           &argc, argv);
  bboard = XtCreateManagedWidget("bboard",
                                 XwbulletinWidgetClass,
                                 toplevel, NULL, 0);
  /*
   * Create a popup shell to be used by the menu manager.
   */
  mgr_shell = XtCreatePopupShell("mgrshell", shellWidgetClass,
                                 bboard, NULL, 0);
  /*
   * Create a popup menu manager as a child of
   * the popup shell.
   */
  menu_mgr = XtCreateManagedWidget("menu_mgr",
                                   XwpopupmgrWidgetClass,
                                   mgr_shell, NULL, 0);
  /*
   * Create a popup shell for the menu pane.
   */
  pane_shell = XtCreatePopupShell("paneshell",
                                  shellWidgetClass,
                                  menu_mgr, NULL, 0);
  /*
   * Create a Cascade menu pane and attach it to the
   * menu manager.
```

```
   */
  XtSetArg(wargs[0], XtNattachTo, (XtArgVal) "menu_mgr");
  main_menu_pane = XtCreateManagedWidget("Main Menu",
                                         XwcascadeWidgetClass,
                                         pane_shell, wargs,1);
  /*
   * Add buttons to the menu pane.
   */
  button1 = XtCreateManagedWidget("Item_1",
                                  XwmenubuttonWidgetClass,
                                  main_menu_pane, NULL, 0);
  XtAddCallback (button1, XtNselect, do_item1, NULL);

  button2 = XtCreateManagedWidget("Item_2",
                                  XwmenubuttonWidgetClass,
                                  main_menu_pane, NULL, 0);
  XtAddCallback (button2, XtNselect, do_item2, NULL);

  button3 = XtCreateManagedWidget("Item_3",
                                  XwmenubuttonWidgetClass,
                                  main_menu_pane, NULL, 0);
  XtAddCallback (button3, XtNselect, do_item3, NULL);

  XtRealizeWidget (toplevel);
  XtMainLoop();
}
```

Fig. 4.13 shows the menu created by this example. The PopupMgr's **XtNmenuPost** resource determines the user action that displays (*posts*) the menu. By default this action is **Button1Down**, so pressing mouse button one while the sprite is in the application's top--level window pops up the menu. When the user releases the mouse button, the menu disappears.

Some applications have many large menus, and creating each menu as in the previous example can be tedious, although the approach allows maximum flexibility in configuring menus and setting the resources of each individual pane and menu button. However, it is often easier to wrap the steps of the menu creation in some higher level functions. Let's define a higher level interface to the menu widgets that we can add to the libXs library. We can separate the menu creation into two functions. The first, **create_menu_manager()**, creates the popup Shell and PopupMgr that manages the widget. The function's arguments specify the menu's parent widget and the name of the menu manager. The function returns the menu manager widget.

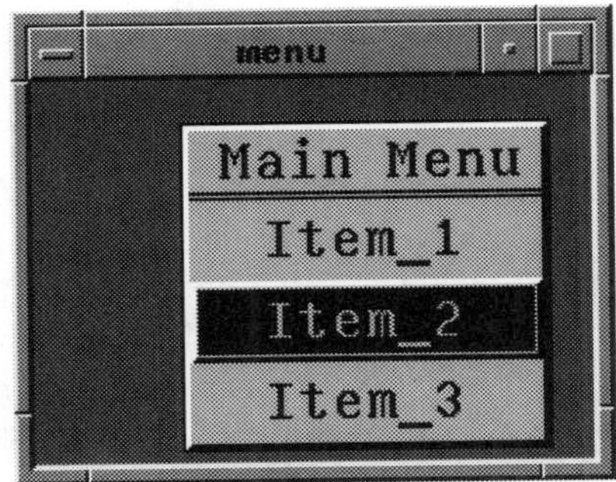

Figure 4.13 A popup menu.

```
/**********************************************************
 * menus.c: Simple menu package
 **********************************************************/
#include <X11/StringDefs.h>
#include <X11/Intrinsic.h>
#include <X11/Shell.h>
#include <Xw/Xw.h>
#include <Xw/MenuBtn.h>
#include <Xw/Cascade.h>
#include <Xw/PopupMgr.h>
#include "libXs.h"
Widget create_menu_manager(parent, mgrname)
   Widget  parent;
   char   *mgrname;
{
  Widget shell = XtCreatePopupShell(mgrname, shellWidgetClass,
                                    parent, NULL, 0);
  Widget menu_mgr=XtCreateManagedWidget(mgrname,
                                    XwpopupmgrWidgetClass,
                                    shell, NULL, 0);

  return (menu_mgr);
}
```

The second function, **create_panel()**, creates a menu pane based on the contents of a structure defining the contents of each item in the pane. This structure contains a name, a pointer to a callback function, and a pointer to some client-defined data. To add this menu package to libXs, we need to place the definition of this function in the file libXs.h.

```
typedef struct {
   char*       name;
   void        (*func)();
   caddr_t     data;
 } menu_struct;
```

The function **create_pane()** takes five arguments. The first specifies the PopupMgr widget that manages this pane. The second specifies the name of the widget to which the pane is to be attached, while the third is the name of the menu pane. The last two arguments specify an array of type **menu_struct** and the size of the **menu_struct** array. The function creates a popup Shell widget and a Cascade menu widget that together make up a menu pane. It then loops through the **menu_struct** list, creating a menu button for each entry.

```
create_pane(mgr, mgrname, name, menulist, nitems)
     Widget        mgr;
     char          *name, *mgrname;
     menu_struct   *menulist;
     int           nitems;
{
  Arg          wargs[1];
  Widget       menupane, pane_shell;
  int          i;
  WidgetList buttons;
  /*
   * Allocate a widget list to hold all
   * button widgets.
   */
  buttons = (WidgetList) XtMalloc(nitems * sizeof(Widget));
  /*
   * Create a popup shell to hold this pane.
   */
  pane_shell=XtCreatePopupShell("pane_shell",shellWidgetClass,
                                    mgr, NULL, 0);
  /*
   * Create a Cascade menu pane, and attach
   * it to the given menu manager.
   */
  XtSetArg(wargs[0], XtNattachTo, (XtArgVal) mgrname);
  menupane = XtCreateManagedWidget(name, XwcascadeWidgetClass,
                                       pane_shell, wargs, 1);
  /*
   * Create a menu button for each item in the menu.
   */
```

```
  for(i=0;i<nitems;i++){
    buttons[i] = XtCreateWidget(menulist[i].name,
                                XwmenubuttonWidgetClass,
                                menupane, NULL, 0);
    XtAddCallback (buttons[i], XtNselect,
                   menulist[i].func, menulist[i].data);
  }
  /*
   * Manage all button widgets.
   */
  XtManageChildren(buttons, nitems);
}
```

The menu example we built earlier is much simpler when we use these functions. The callbacks assigned to each menu button can be defined similar to those in the previous example, and are not shown.

```
/***************************************************************
 * menu2.c: Menu example using libXs menu wrapper
 ***************************************************************/
#include <X11/StringDefs.h>
#include <X11/Intrinsic.h>
#include <Xw/Xw.h>
#include <Xw/BBoard.h>
#include "libXs.h"
/*
 * Declare callbacks for each menu entry
 */
extern void do_item1();
extern void do_item2();
extern void do_item3();
/*
 * Create the list of menu items for one pane.
 */
static menu_struct Menu[] = {
  {"Item 1" , do_item1,  NULL},
  {"Item 2" , do_item2,  NULL},
  {"Item 3" , do_item3,  NULL},
};

main(argc, argv)
     int   argc;
     char *argv[];
```

```
{
  Widget toplevel, bboard, menu_mgr;
  /*
   * Initialize the Intrinsics and create a
   * Bulletin Board widget as a base.
   */
  toplevel = XtInitialize (argv[0], "Menu", NULL, 0,
                           &argc, argv);
  bboard = XtCreateManagedWidget("bboard",
                                 XwbulletinWidgetClass,
                                 toplevel, NULL, 0);
  /*
   * Create the menu manager.
   */
  menu_mgr = create_menu_manager(bboard, "menu_mgr")  ;
  /*
   * Create the menu pane.
   */
  create_pane(menu_mgr, "menu_mgr", "Main Menu",
              Menu, XtNumber(Menu));
  XtRealizeWidget (toplevel);
  XtMainLoop();
}
```

4.4.7.2 Cascading Menu Panes

We can create a cascading menu by attaching a menu pane to a button in another menu pane. We can do this easily using the menu functions built in the previous section. The following example creates two additional **menu_struct** arrays and attaches them to the first and third menu buttons of the main menu pane. The definitions of the various callback functions are not shown.

```
/**************************************************************
 * menu3.c: Example of cascading menus
 **************************************************************/
#include <X11/StringDefs.h>
#include <X11/Intrinsic.h>
#include <Xw/Xw.h>
#include <Xw/BBoard.h>
#include "libXs.h"

extern void do_item1();
extern void do_item2();
```

```
extern void do_item3();
extern void do_itema();
extern void do_itemb();
extern void do_itemc();
extern void do_itemd();

static menu_struct Menu[] = {
  {"Item 1" , do_item1,  NULL},
  {"Item 2" , do_item2,  NULL},
  {"Item 3" , do_item3,  NULL},
};
static menu_struct SubMenuA[] = {
  {"Item A" , do_itema,  NULL},
  {"Item B" , do_itemb,  NULL},
};
static menu_struct SubMenuB[] = {
  {"Item C" , do_itemc,  NULL},
  {"Item D" , do_itemd,  NULL},
};

main(argc, argv)
     int   argc;
     char *argv[];
{
  Widget toplevel, bboard, menu_mgr;
  /*
   * Initialize the Intrinsics and create a
   * BulletinBoard widget as a base.
   */
  toplevel = XtInitialize (argv[0], "Menu", NULL, 0,
                           &argc, argv);
  bboard = XtCreateManagedWidget("bboard",
                                 XwbulletinWidgetClass,
                                 toplevel, NULL, 0);

  /*
   * Create the menu manager.
   */
  menu_mgr = create_menu_manager(bboard, "menu_mgr")  ;
  /*
   * Create the Main menu pane.
   */
  create_pane(menu_mgr, "menu_mgr", "Main Menu", Menu, 4);
```

```
    /*
     * Create two sub menus for the first and third items on
     * the main menu.
     */
    create_pane(menu_mgr, "Item 1", "Sub Menu A", SubMenuA, 2);
    create_pane(menu_mgr, "Item 3", "Sub Menu B", SubMenuB, 2);

    XtRealizeWidget (toplevel);
    XtMainLoop();
}
```

Fig. 4.14 shows the cascading menu pane created by this example.

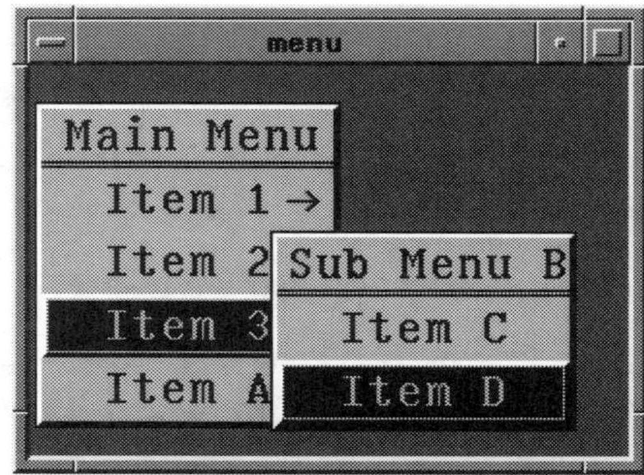

Figure 4.14 A cascading popup menu.

4.5 USING POPUP WIDGETS

Often we want to display a temporary window to request the user to enter some information, or to display a message. The Xt Intrinsics supports several types of *popups* that allow the programmer to do this. The popup menu widgets discussed in the previous section are an example of a popup widget. However, sometimes the application programmer needs to create a custom popup. This section discusses the Xt Intrinsics function for handling popups and shows an example of a popup dialog box.

All popups must have their own shell, usually created using **XtCreatePopupShell()**. A popup Shell and its children can be displayed using the function

```
XtPopup(shell, grab_mode)
```

The **shell** argument must be a popup Shell. Applications do not need to realize popup shells, because **XtPopup()** does it automatically. Sometimes popup shells pop up other shells, creating a cascade of popup shells. The cascading menu in the previous section is one example. The **grab_mode** argument allows the programmer to specify how events are dispatched within a cascade of popups. If **XtNgrabNone** is specified, events are processed normally. If the **grab_mode** is **XtNGrabNonExclusive**, device events are sent to any widget in the popup cascade. If the grab mode is **XtNGrabExclusive**, all device events are sent only to the last popup in the cascade.

A popup widget can be popped down using the function

```
XtPopDown(popup_shell)
```

Because these functions are often used inside callback functions, the Xt Intrinsics provides several callback function as a convenience. The functions are **XtCallbackNone()**, **XtCallbackNonexclusive()**, and **XtCallbackExclusive()**. Each of these calls **XtPopup()** with the corresponding grab mode. These callbacks also disable the sensitivity of the widget from which the popup was invoked.

Popup shells that are popped up from within one of these callback functions should be popped down using the callback function **XtCallbackPopupdown()**. This callback function expects to be passed a pointer to a structure of type **XtPopdownIDRec** as client data. This structure must contain the Shell widget to be popped down, and optionally the widget that initiated the popup. The **XtPopdownIDRec** is defined as

```
typedef struct{
    Widget shell_widget;
    Widget enable_widget;
} XtPopdownIDRec, *XtPopdownID
```

Let's look at a simple example that uses these callbacks to pop up a dialog box. The dialog box is similar to the BulletinBoard widget example from Section 4.4.6.1. The main part of the program creates a PushButton widget and calls a function **build_popup()** to create a popup dialog box. The dialog box pops up when the user selects the button, and pops down when the user selects a "done" button on the dialog box.

```
/************************************************
 * popup.c: popup a simple dialog box.
 ************************************************/
#include <X11/Intrinsic.h>
#include <X11/Shell.h>
#include <Xw/Xw.h>
#include <Xw/BBoard.h>
#include <Xw/PButton.h>
#include <Xw/TextEdit.h>
#include <Xw/SText.h>
```

```
#include "libXs.h"
Widget build_popup();

main(argc, argv)
     int   argc;
     char *argv[];
{
  Widget toplevel, button, popup;
  Arg wargs[2];

  toplevel = XtInitialize(argv[0], "Popup", NULL, 0,
                          &argc, argv);
  /*
   * Create a pushbutton widget to trigger the popup.
   */
   XtSetArg(wargs[0], XtNlabel, "Push to pop up Dialog Box");
   button =  XtCreateManagedWidget("button",
                                   XwpushButtonWidgetClass,
                                   toplevel, wargs, 1);
  /*
   * Create the popup widget and add a popup callback.
   */
   popup = build_popup(toplevel, button);
   XtAddCallback(button, XtNrelease, XtCallbackNone, popup);

   XtRealizeWidget(toplevel);
   XtMainLoop();
}

static char * fields[] = {"field1", "field2", "field3"};
static char * labels[] = {"label1", "label2", "label3"};

Widget build_popup(parent, enable)
    Widget parent, enable;
{
  Widget bb, popup, button;
  static XtPopdownIDRec pdrec;
  Arg    wargs[2];
  int    i;
  /*
   * Create a popup shell to hold the dialog box.
   */
```

```
  popup =  XtCreatePopupShell("popup", shellWidgetClass,
                                 parent, NULL, 0);
 /*
  * Create a BulletinBoard widget to hold the fields.
  */
  bb = XtCreateManagedWidget("board",  XwbulletinWidgetClass,
                                 popup, NULL, 0);
  /*
   * Create a "done" button and register a popdown callback.
   */
  button = XtCreateManagedWidget("done",
                                     XwpushButtonWidgetClass,
                                     bb, NULL, 0);
  pdrec.shell_widget  = popup;
  pdrec.enable_widget = enable;
  XtAddCallback(button, XtNrelease,
                  XtCallbackPopdown, &pdrec);
  /*
   * Create labels and TextEdit widgets for the dialog box
   */
  XtSetArg(wargs[0], XtNeditType, XwtextEdit);
  for(i=0;i< XtNumber(fields); i++)
     create_one_line_text_widget(fields[i], bb, wargs, 1);
  for(i=0;i< XtNumber(labels); i++)
     XtCreateManagedWidget(labels[i], XwstatictextWidgetClass,
                               bb, NULL, 0);
  return popup;
}
```

One possible class resource file for this example creates a name, phone, and address dialog box similar to the one from the BulletinBoard example in Section 4.4.6.1.

```
/###############################################
 # Popup: Class resource file for popup
 ###############################################
#
# Set location of edit fields
#
*popup*TextEdit*x: 120
*popup*field1*y:    40
*popup*field2*y:    70
*popup*field3*y:   100
#
```

```
# Set locations of "done" button
#
*popup*PushButton*x:        10
*popup*PushButton*y:        10
*popup*PushButton*width: 100
#
# Set location of labels
#
*popup*label1*y:  40
*popup*label2*y:  70
*popup*label3*y: 100
#
# Specify labels
#
*popup*label1*string: Name:
*popup*label2*string: Phone:
*popup*label3*string: Address:
```

It is important to notice the model used in this example to pop up the dialog box. The dialog box is popped up in response to an action and stays up until it is popped down. Often programmers want to call a function which pops up a dialog box and blocks until the user responds. Then the function returns some value. This is *not* the model used here. This example continues to use the event-driven model supported by the Xt Intrinsics. Creating a function that blocks is a more difficult task.

4.6 SUMMARY

This chapter demonstrated how applications can use various widgets as to create a user interface. Widgets provide basic user interface components such as scroll bars, buttons, and menus. Applications can use composite and constraint widgets to group simple widgets together to form complex user interfaces.

The widgets in the X Widget set are powerful enough to meet most of the user interfaces needs of typical applications. These widgets allow the programmer to display and edit text and graphics, pop up dialog boxes and menus, and display a variety of selection devices, such as buttons. For those applications that need functionality not addressed by existing widgets, the application programmer has two choices:

- Use a primitive widget class, such as the WorkSpace widget class, as a window in which to display output. Such applications must use Xlib text and graphics functions to draw the contents of the window, handle refreshing the widget's window, and use event handlers to manage input. The following chapter discusses events and event handlers, while the Xlib text and graphics functions are discussed beginning with Chapter 9.

- Write a new widget to provide the needed function. This is a reasonable option, although it requires a good understanding of the widget architecture. Chapters 12, 13, and 14 show how a programmer can write new widgets.

The next chapter discusses the events generated by the X server and shows examples of how applications can handle events.

5

HANDLING EVENTS

The X server communicates with clients by sending events. The architecture of the Xt Intrinsics allows individual widgets to handle most common events automatically. For example, most widgets handle the **Expose** events sent by the server when the contents of a widget's window needs refreshed, and also handle configuration events generated by the server a window is resized. In addition, most widgets use the translation manager to handle keyboard and mouse input. In spite of this, most programmers still find occasions when they must handle events directly, even when using widgets. Having a good understanding of the events generated by the X server also helps the programmer understand and use the Xt Intrinsics and widgets more effectively.

Chapter 2 provided a brief introduction to events and event handlers. This chapter examines events in more detail and provides examples that use features of the Intrinsics to handle events. We begin by examining the events and event structures provided by X and Xlib and then look at the event-handling mechanisms built on top of Xlib by the Xt Intrinsics. We also examine some applications that depend on input from sources other than X events. Events used for interclient communication are discussed in Chapter 11.

5.1 WHAT IS AN EVENT?

An *event* is a notification, sent by the X server to a client, that some condition has changed. The X server generates events as a result of some user input, or as a side effect of a request to the X server. The server sends each event to interested clients, who determine what type of event occurred by looking at the *type* of the event. Applications do not receive events automatically. They must specifically request the X server to send the events in which they are interested. Fig. 5.1 lists the types of events supported by X. Events always occur relative to a window, known as the *source window* of the event. If no client has requested the event for the source window, the server propagates the event up the X window hierarchy until it finds a window for which some client has requested the event, or it finds a window that prohibits the event propagation. The server only propagates *device events* generated as a result of a key, mouse button, or sprite motion. If the server reaches the root of the window tree without finding a client interested in the event, the event is discarded. The window to which the server finally reports the event is known as the *event window*.

The X server places all events in an event queue. Clients usually remove events from the event queue using the Xt Intrinsics function, **`XtNextEvent()`**. These functions fill in an **`XEvent`** structure allocated by the client. Each event type is defined as a C struct. The XEvent structure is a C union of all event types. Fig. 5.1 shows the union member corresponding to each event type.

Event Type	Union Member	Event Type	Union Member
Any Type	xany	CreateNotify	xcreatewindow
ButtonPress	xbutton	ButtonRelease	xbutton
MotionNotify	xmotion	MapNotify	xmap
EnterNotify	xcrossing	FocusIn	xfocus
LeaveNotify	xcrossing	FocusOut	xfocus
Expose	xexpose	GraphicsExpose	xgraphicsexpose
NoExpose	xnoexpose	VisibilityNotify	xvisibility
KeyPress	xkey	DestroyNotify	xdestroywindow
UnmapNotify	xunmap	MapRequest	xmaprequest
ReparentNotify	xreparent	ResizeRequest	xresizerequest
ConfigureNotify	xconfigure	GravityNotify	xgravity
CirculateNotify	xcirculate	CirculateRequest	xcirculaterequest
PropertyNotify	xproperty	SelectionClear	xselectionclear
KeymapNotify	xkeymap	SelectionNotify	xselection
ColormapNotify	xcolormap	ClientMessage	xclient
MappingNotify	xmapping	SelectionRequest	xselectionrequest
KeyRelease	xkey	ConfigureRequest	xconfigurerequest

Figure 5.1 X event types.

All events contain a core set of basic information, contained in the first five members of every event structure. This information specifies

- the **`type`** of the event,
- the **`display`** where the event occurred,
- the event **`window`**,

- the **serial** number of the last request processed by server,
- and a **send_event** flag that indicates if this event was generated by the server or if the event was sent by another client.

The structure **XAnyEvent** is defined to allow access to those members that are common to all event types. Clients can access this basic information in any event using the **xany** member of the **XEvent** union, for example,

```
event.xany.window
```

The type of every event can also be accessed directly using

```
event.type
```

Each event contains additional information, specific to the type of the event, that must be accessed using the member of the union corresponding to that event type. For example, the width of a window can be extracted from an **XConfigureNotify** event with

```
event.xconfigure.width
```

5.2 EVENT MASKS

An Xlib application must request the event types it wishes the server to report for each window by passing an *event mask* to the Xlib function **XSelectInput()**, or the registering an event handler for the event using the Xt Intrinsics function **XtAddEventHandler()**. For example, the statement

```
XSelectInput(display, window,
             ButtonPressMask | ButtonReleaseMask);
```

requests the server to generate events when a mouse button is pressed or released in the given window. Fig. 5.2 shows the X event masks defined in X.h. Notice that the names of these masks are not the same as the names of the event types listed in Fig. 5.1.

EventMask	**KeyPressMask**
KeyReleaseMask	**ButtonPressMask**
ButtonReleaseMask	**EnterWindowMask**
LeaveWindowMask	**PointerMotionMask**
PointerMotionHintMask	**Button1MotionMask**
Button2MotionMask	**Button3MotionMask**
Button4MotionMask	**Button5MotionMask**
ButtonMotionMask	**KeymapStateMask**
ExposureMask	**VisibilityChangeMask**
StructureNotifyMask	**ResizeRedirectMask**

SubstructureNotifyMask	**SubstructureRedirectMask**
FocusChangeMask	**PropertyChangeMask**
ColormapChangeMask	**OwnerGrabButtonMask**

Figure 5.2 Event masks used to select X events.

There is not always a direct correlation between the masks clients use to select events and the types of events reported by the server. For example, when a client selects events with **ExposureMask** the server sends the events **Expose**, **GraphicsExpose**, and **NoExpose**. On the other hand, clients requesting events using **PointerMotionMask** or **ButtonMotionMask** receive a **MotionNotify** event when either type of event occurs. The correspondence between event masks, event types, and event structures is shown in Appendix E.

5.3 EVENT TYPES

We can group the events supported by X into several general categories. The following sections discuss each event category and examine the information contained in some common event types.

5.3.1 Keyboard Events

The server generates a **KeyPress** event whenever a key is pressed and generates a **KeyRelease** event when the key is released. All keys, including modifier keys, (the <SHIFT> key, for example) generate events. A client can request **KeyPress** events by specifying **KeyPressMask** as the event mask when calling **XSelectInput()** or when defining an event handler. Clients request **KeyRelease** events using **KeyReleaseMask**. The server reports both **KeyRelease** and **KeyPress** events using an **XKeyEvent** structure. In addition to the members common to all X events, the **XKeyEvent** structure contains some additional information.

```
Window          root;
Window          subwindow;
Time            time;
int             x, y;
int             x_root, y_root;
unsigned int    state;
unsigned int    keycode;
Bool            same_screen;
```

The **root** member contains the ID of the root window of the screen where the event occurred. If the source window is a descendent of the event window, the **subwindow** member contains the ID of the immediate child of the event window that lies between the event window and the source window. For example, assume that a window named BaseWindow has a child named ScrollBar, and that ScrollBar has a child name Slider, as shown in Fig. 5.3 and Fig. 5.4. Also assume that only window BaseWindow has selected **KeyPress** events. If a **KeyPress** event occurs in Slider, the event propagates to **BaseWindow**. The source window is **Slider**. The event received by BaseWindow indicates BaseWindow as the event window. The **subwindow** member of the event contains the ID of the ScrollBar window.

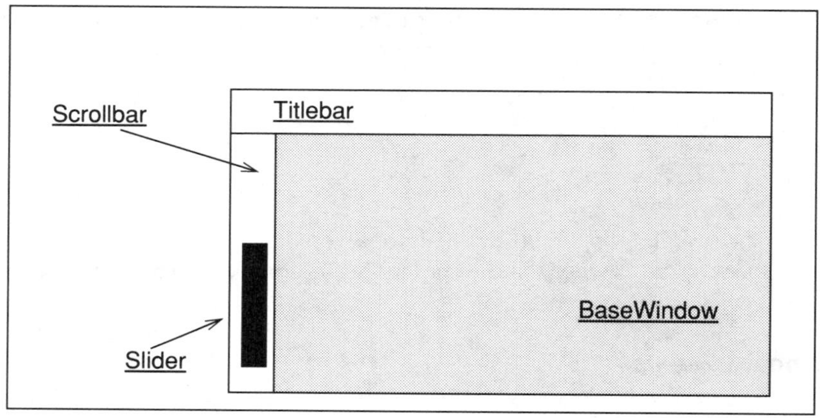

Figure 5.3 Event propagation.

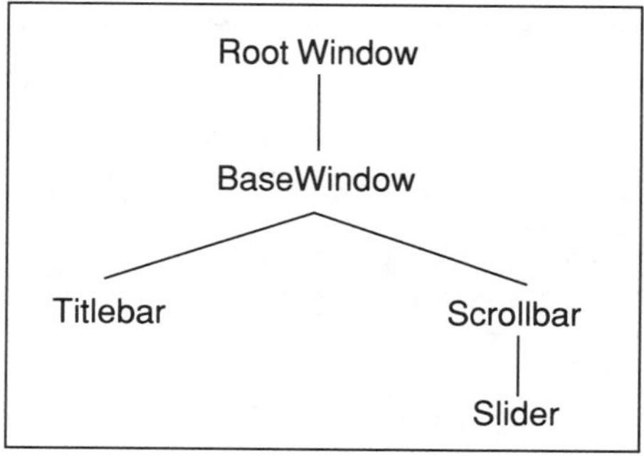

Figure 5.4 Window tree for Fig. 5.3.

The **time** member indicates the time in milliseconds since the server reset. This information is useful in preventing race conditions that can arise because the X server and its clients run asynchronously with respect to each other.

The **XKeyEvent** structure also contains the coordinates of the sprite relative to both the event window and the root window, as long as the event window is on the same screen as the root window. If this is not the case, the event reports the coordinates of the sprite as *(0, 0)*, relative to the root window.

The **XKeyEvent** structure also contains a keycode that uniquely identifies the key that caused the event. Applications can use the Xlib function **XLookupString()** to map this keycode to the character it represents. The Intrinsics also includes several function for manipulating keycodes.

The **state** member of the event contains a mask indicating which, if any, modifier keys were depressed when this key was pressed. X supports many modifier keys including **<SHIFT>**, **<SHIFTLOCK>**, **<CONTROL>**, as well as up to five additional system-dependent modifier keys.

5.3.2 Pointer Events

The server generates the pointer events **ButtonPress**, **ButtonRelease**, and **MotionNotify** when the user presses or releases a mouse button or moves the sprite. The source window for pointer events is always the smallest window containing the sprite, unless some client has *grabbed* the pointer. When the pointer is grabbed, the server reports all pointer events to the window that initiated the grab. The server reports **ButtonPress** and **ButtonRelease** events using an **XButtonEvent** structure. This event structure is similar to the **KeyPress** event structure, but instead of a key code, the **XButtonEvent** structure contains a **button** member that indicates which mouse button was pressed or released. X supports up to five mouse buttons, defined in the file X.h as **Button1**, **Button2**, **Button3**, **Button4**, and **Button5**. The mouse buttons can also be combined with a modifier key, such as the **<SHIFT>** or **<META>** key. The state of all modifier keys when the event occurred is indicated by the **state** member.

The server reports pointer motion events using an **XMotionEvent** structure. Clients can request the server to generate motion events whenever the user moves the sprite, or only when the user moves the sprite while holding down a particular button or combination of buttons. However, the server reports all motion events as type **MotionNotify**, using the **XMotionEvent** structure. Clients can determine the state of the mouse buttons (which buttons are up and which are down) by looking at the **state** member of the event.

By default, the server reports motion events continuously as the pointer moves. Clients can also request the server to *compress* motion events and generate events only when the pointer starts or stops moving. Most applications do not need continuous motion events and should request the server to compress pointer motion into *hints*, by requesting motion events with **PointerMotionHintMask**. The **is_hint** member of the **XMotionEvent** structure indicates whether an event indicates continuous motion or a hint. Other members of the event structure report the *(x, y)* position of the sprite relative to both the event window and the root window. The members of the **XMotionEvent** event include

```
Window          root;
Window          subwindow;
Time            time;
int             x, y;
int             x_root, y_root;
unsigned int    state;
char            is_hint;
Bool            same_screen;
```

5.3.3 Crossing Events

The server generates crossing events whenever the sprite crosses the boundary of a window. The server sends an **EnterNotify** event to the window the sprite enters and a **LeaveNotify** event to the window the sprite leaves. The server also generates crossing events when the sprite enters a window because of a change in the window hierarchy. For example, if a window containing the sprite is lowered to the bottom of the window stack, so that the sprite is now in another window, the first window receives a **LeaveNotify** event and the second window receives a **EnterNotify** event. Clients must request **EnterNotify** events using the mask **EnterWindowMask** and **LeaveNotify** events using the mask **LeaveWindowMask**. Both crossing events use the **XCrossingEvent** structure, which includes the members

```
Window          root;
Window          subwindow;
Time            time;
int             x, y;
int             x_root, y_root;
int             mode;
int             detail;
Bool            same_screen;
Bool            focus;
unsigned int    state;
```

The **XCrossingEvent** structure always contains the final *(x, y)* coordinate of the sprite relative to both the event window and the root window. The state member of the event structure indicates the state of the mouse buttons immediately preceding the event.

Applications often need to determine the hierarchical relationship of the windows involved in a crossing event. For example, suppose we wish to write a program that highlights the border of its top-level window whenever the window contains the sprite. Highlighting the window border whenever the client receives an **EnterNotify** event, and unhighlighting the border whenever the client receives an **LeaveNotify** event works correctly unless the window has subwindows. When the sprite enters a subwindow, the top-level window receives a **LeaveNotify** event, even though the sprite is still within the bounds of the window. In addition, if the application has not requested **EnterNotify** events for the subwindow, the server propagates the **EnterNotify** event to the top-level window, producing an annoying flashing effect as the user moves the sprite in and out of subwindows. To do this correctly, we must inspect the detail member of the event structure. The server sets this member to one of the constants **NotifyAncestor**, **NotifyVirtual**, **NotifyInferior**, **NotifyNonlinear**, or **NotifyNonlinearVirtual**, signifying the different types of window crossings that can occur.

Fig. 5.5 through Fig. 5.8 show five windows, the root window, and two children, Window A and Window B. Window A and Window B have subwindows Window C and Window D respectively. The arrow in each figure represents a sprite movement starting in one window and ending in the window containing the arrow head. The text at the beginning and end of each line indicates the type of event generated in that window, with the value of the detail member of the event structure shown in parenthesis. Fig. 5.5 illustrates the sprite moving from the root window into a child, Window B. The root window receives a **LeaveNotify** event with the **detail** member of the event set to **NotifyInferior**, while Window B receives an **EnterNotify** event, with **detail** set to **NotifyAncestor**.

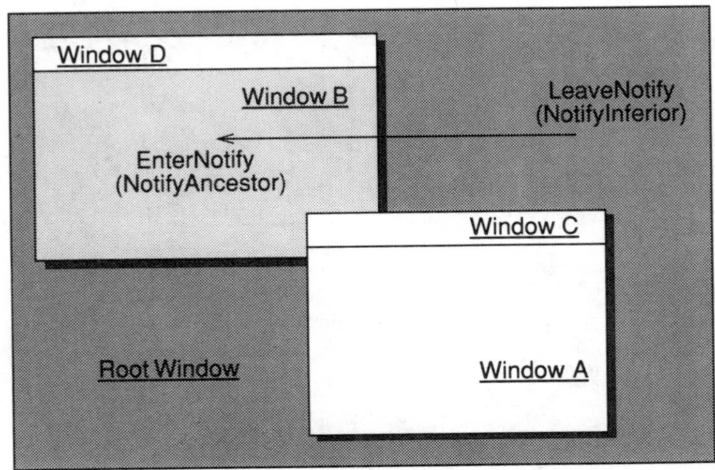

Figure 5.5 Crossing events.

Fig. 5.6 illustrates the opposite situation, where the sprite moves from a window into the window's parent.

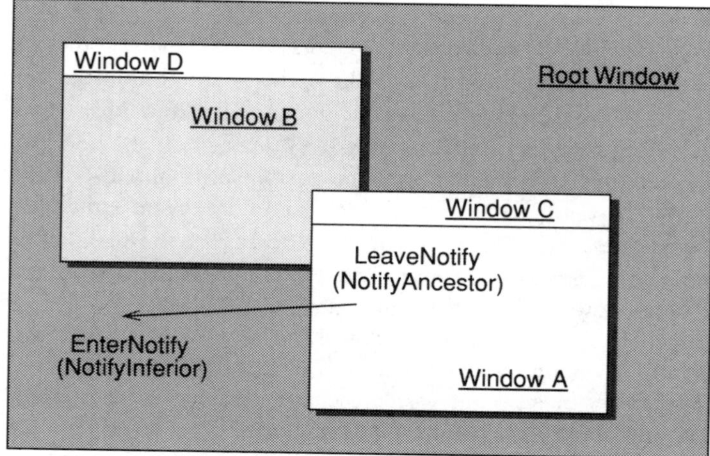

Figure 5.6 Crossing events.

Fig. 5.7 illustrates movement of the sprite between two siblings. In this case, the server sets the **`detail`** member of each event to **`NotifyNonlinear`**.

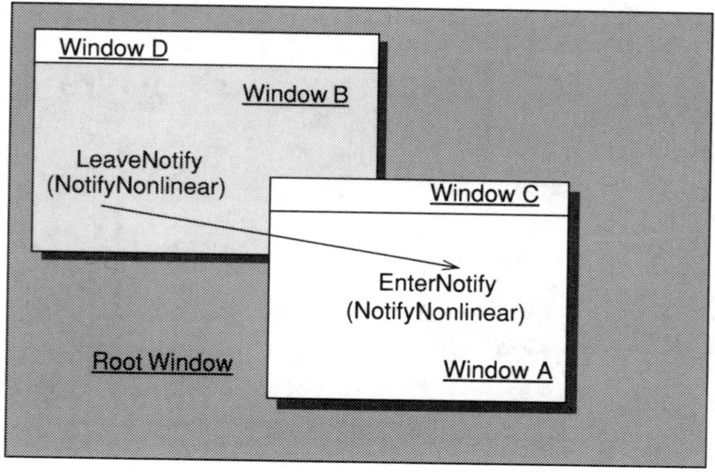

Figure 5.7 Crossing events.

Fig. 5.8 shows the most complex situation, in which the sprite moves between two windows that are more than one level apart in the window hierarchy. In this case, Window C receives a **LeaveNotify** event and Window B receives an **EnterNotify** event. The **detail** member in both events is **NotifyNonlinear**. However, Window A also receives a **LeaveNotify** event, with the **detail** member set to **NotifyNonlinearVirtual**.

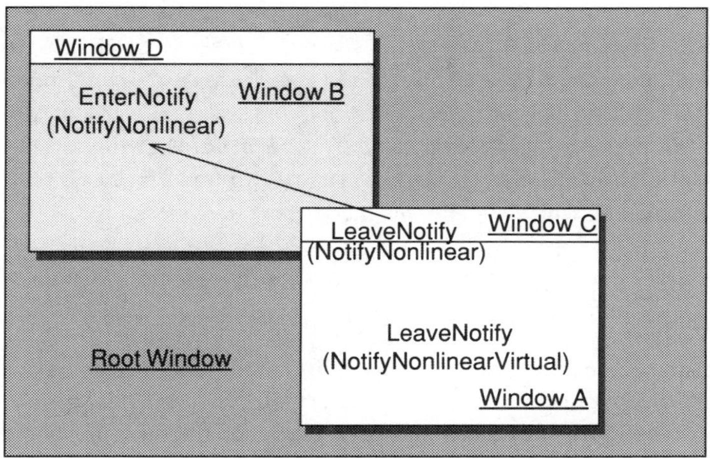

Figure 5.8 Crossing events.

The server also generates crossing events when an application grabs or ungrabs the pointer. When an application grabs the pointer, the server sends the window containing the sprite a **LeaveNotify** event with the mode member set to the constant **NotifyGrab**. When the grabbing application ungrabs the pointer the server sends the window containing the sprite an **EnterNotify** event with the **mode** member set to **UngrabNotify**. If the crossing event is not a result of a grab, the server sets the **mode** member of the event to **NormalNotify**.

5.3.4 Focus Events

The window to which the X server sends keyboard events is known as the focus window. The server generates **FocusIn** and **FocusOut** events whenever the focus window changes. Applications wishing to receive these events must select them using **FocusChangeMask** as an argument to **XtAddEventHandler()**. Focus events are similar to **EnterNotify** and **LeaveNotify** events but are even more complex, because the sprite is not necessarily in any of the windows involved in the change of focus. Most applications that use the Xt Intrinsics do not need to handle focus events directly, because focus is handled by manager widgets.

5.3.5 Exposure Events

The server generates exposure events when a window or a portion of a window becomes visible. Clients must request exposure events using the **ExposureMask** event mask. There are three types of exposure events. The most common type, **Expose**, is generated when the contents of a region of a window are lost for any reason. The server sends a **GraphicsExpose** event when a client attempts to use **XCopyArea()** to copy an obscured region of a window. **NoExpose** events can also be generated when copying areas between drawables. The server generates this event when an application requests **GraphicsExpose** events but no regions are exposed when **XCopyArea()** is called. The server reports **Expose** events using an **XExposeEvent** structure, which includes the members

```
int     x, y;
int     width, height;
int     count;
```

The **XExposeEvent** structure contains the x and y coordinates relative to the upper left corner of the window and the width and height of the rectangular region of the window that has been exposed. The event also contains a **count** member that indicates how many **Expose** events are still pending. If **count** is zero, there are no more **Expose** events pending for this window. However, if the **count** member is non-zero, then *at least* this many events are still pending. Multiple **Expose** events occur primarily when an exposed region consists of more than one rectangular region. Applications that are not capable of redrawing arbitrary regions of windows can ignore **Expose** events with a non-zero **count** member, and redraw the entire contents of the window when the server generates an event whose **count** member is zero. The Xt Intrinsics allows widgets to request that multiple exposure events be *compressed* into a single **Expose** event. The Intrinsics automatically accumulates all **Expose** events until an event with **count** set to zero is received. The Intrinsics then replaces the region in this last **Expose** event with the bounding box of the regions in all previous **Expose** events and invokes the widget's **Expose** event handler with the single **Expose** event.

5.3.6 Structure Control

The server reports structure control events to clients that ask for requests to be *redirected*. Window managers generally use event redirection to exercise more control over windows. For example, if a window manager requests events using the mask **ResizeRedirectMask**, the X server ignores all requests from other applications to resize windows and instead sends a **ResizeRequest** event to the window manager. The window manager then has the opportunity to act on the request according to its screen management policy. Requests that circulate a window's position in the stacking order, configure the window in any way, or map the window can also be redirected. If a window manager requests events using **Substructure-**

RedirectMask, the X server generates **CirculateRequest**, **ConfigureRequest**, and **MapRequest** events instead of acting directly on these requests. Only one application can request the server to redirect events at any one time.

5.3.7 State Notification

Some applications need to be informed when its windows are reconfigured in any way. Clients can use the **StructureNotifyMask** event mask to request events when a window's configuration changes, or **SubstructureNotifyMask** to request notification of changes to a window's subwindows.

Clients that request **StructureNotify** events can receive many different types of events, depending one what changes occur. When a window's position in the stacking order changes because of a call to the Xlib functions **XCirculateSubwindows()**, **XCirculateSubwindowsUp()**, or **XCirculateSubwindowsDown()**, the server generates a **CirculateNotify** event, which uses an **XCirculateEvent** structure. The **event** member of this structure indicates the event window. The **window** member is set to the ID of the window that was restacked. This window ID is not necessarily the same as the event window. The server also sets the **place** member of this event to the constant **PlaceOnBottom**, indicating the window is below all siblings, or the constant **PlaceOnTop**, indicating that the window is above all siblings.

The server generates **ConfigureNotify** events whenever a window's size, position, or border width changes. The server reports this event using an **XConfigureEvent** structure. **ConfigureNotify** events are also generated when a window's position in the stacking order changes because of a call to the Xlib functions **XLowerWindow()**, **XRaiseWindow()**, **XRestackWindow()**, or **XRestackWindows()**. The **event** member of the **XConfigureEvent** structure indicates the event window while the **window** member indicates the window that has changed. The **above** member contains the ID of the sibling window just below the window whose position in the stacking order has changed. If the window is on the bottom of the stacking order, the **above** member of the **XConfigureNotify** event is set to **None**. The members in the **XConfigureEvent** structure include

```
Window  event;
Window  window;
int     x, y;
int     width, height;
int     border_width;
Window  above;
Bool    override_redirect;
```

The server generates **CreateNotify** and **DestroyNotify** events whenever a window is created or destroyed, respectively. Clients that wish to receive these events must request events for the window's parent using **SubstructureNotifyMask**. The event structure of the **CreateNotify** event contains the ID of the parent of the new window, and also the size and location of the window. The **DestroyNotify** event structure contains only the event window and the ID of the destroyed window.

Other structure-notification events include **GravityNotify**, **MapNotify**, **MappingNotify**, **ReparentNotify**, **UnmapNotify**, and Visibi**lityNotify**. The applications programmer seldom needs to deal with these events directly, because the Intrinsics normally handles them automatically.

5.3.8 Colormap Notification

Applications that need to know when a new color map is installed can request Co**lormapNotify** events using the mask **ColormapChangeMask**. Color maps determine the colors available to an application, and are discussed in Chapter 6.

5.3.9 Communication Events

X also supports events that allow direct communication between applications, and events that provide a mechanism for exchanging and sharing data between applications. **ClientMessage** events can be used by applications to define additional event types that can be sent between applications using the Xlib function

```
XSendEvent(display, window, propagate, mask, event)
```

Applications cannot specifically request **ClientMessage** events. The server always sends **ClientMessage** events to the destination window. Chapter 11 discusses **ClientMessage** events and shows some examples of direct inter-client communication.

The server generates **PropertyNotify** events when the value of a window *property* is modified. Applications interested in receiving **PropertyNotify** events must select the event using **PropertyChangeMask** as an argument to **XSelectInput()** or **XtAddEventHandler()**. Properties and **PropertyNotify** events are discussed in Chapter 11.

SelectionClear, **SelectionNotify**, and **SelectionRequest** events are used by the X *selection* mechanism for exchanging data between applications. Like **ClientMessage** events, selection events cannot be specifically selected by an application. Selections are also discussed in Chapter 11.

5.4 HANDLING EVENTS WITH THE Xt INTRINSICS

The Xt Intrinsics hides many of the details of handing events from the programmer and allows widgets to handle many of the common X events automatically. As a result, many applications built using the X Toolkit do not need to deal directly with events at all. However, the Xt Intrinsics does provide facilities that allow applications to receive and handle events if needed. Applications can request a specific type of event by defining a handler for that event. The memo example in Chapter 2 introduced the use of event handlers. That chapter also demonstrated the value of using callbacks and the translation manager instead of handling the events directly. There are situations, however, where applications need to handle events directly. The following sections explore some ways to use events and event handlers.

5.4.1 Using Event Handlers

This section presents two examples that use event handlers to handle **MotionNotify** events, **ButtonPress** events, and crossing events. The examples illustrate accessing and using the information in the event structures. Later examples demonstrate dynamically installing and removing event handlers.

The first example creates a module that tracks and reports the position of the sprite in an arbitrary widget. We will refer to this module as a *mouse tracker*. For purposes of demonstration, the mouse tracker displays the current position of the sprite in a StaticText widget, but you can probably imagine more practical uses for such a function. Let's first examine the body of a simple driver program to test the mouse tracker, named **mousetracks**.

```
/*************************************************************
 * mousetracks.c: Driver to test the mouse tracker module
 *************************************************************/
#include <X11/StringDefs.h>
#include <X11/Intrinsic.h>
#include <Xw/Xw.h>
#include <Xw/VPW.h>
#include <Xw/RCManager.h>
#include <Xw/WorkSpace.h>
#include <Xw/SText.h>
#include "libXs.h"

main(argc, argv)
   int             argc;
   char           *argv[];
{
   Widget          toplevel, panel, command, target;
  /*
   * Initialize the Intrinsics.
   */
   toplevel = XtInitialize(argv[0], "Mousetracks", NULL, 0,
                                &argc, argv);
   /*
```

```
    * Create a vertical paned widget, to hold
    * all the other widgets.
    */
   panel = XtCreateManagedWidget("panel", XwvPanedWidgetClass,
                                  toplevel, NULL, 0);
   /*
    * Create a command widget to hold both a quit button
    * and the mouse tracker display.
    */
    command = XtCreateManagedWidget("command",
                                     XwrowColWidgetClass,
                                     panel, NULL, 0);
    /*
     *  Add a quit button.
     */
    create_quit_button("Quit", command);
    /*
     *  Create the widget in which we track the
     *  motion of the sprite.
     */
    target = XtCreateManagedWidget("target",
                                    XwworkSpaceWidgetClass,
                                    panel, NULL, 0);
    /*
     * Create the mouse tracker.
     */
    create_mouse_tracker(command, target);
    XtRealizeWidget(toplevel);
    XtMainLoop();
}
```

This test driver initializes the Intrinsics and then creates a VPanedWindow widget that manages two children, a RowCol widget and a Workspace widget. The VPanedWindow widget is a composite widget that creates a pane for each widget it manages. The user can adjust the vertical size and position of each pane by using the mouse to move a small control (really a widget) known as a *Sash*. The Workspace widget provides an empty window, used in this example as the window in which the sprite motion is tracked. The RowCol widget manages a quit button (created by the libXs function defined in Chapter 4) and also a StaticText widget created by the mouse tracker. Fig. 5.9 shows the widget tree formed by the widgets in this example.

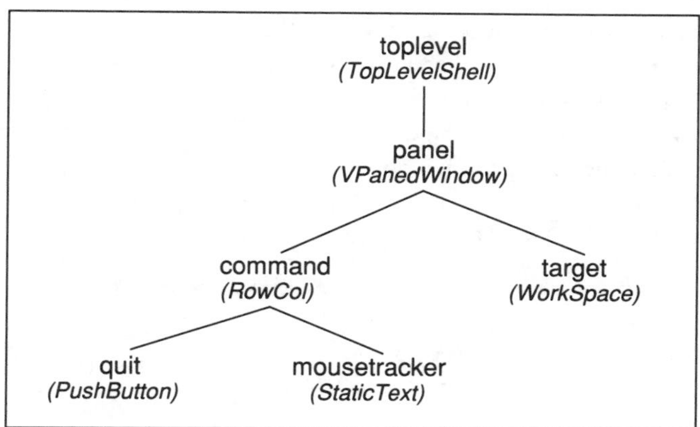

Figure 5.9 The mousetracks widget tree.

The function **create_mouse_tracker()** creates the mouse tracker module, and takes two arguments. The first indicates a parent widget that manages the StaticText widget created by the mouse tracker. The second specifies the widget in which the sprite position is to be tracked. The mouse tracker only reports the sprite position when the sprite is in this target widget. The function **create_mouse_tracker()** is defined as

```
create_mouse_tracker(parent, target)
    Widget             parent, target;
{
    extern void  clear_tracker();
    extern void  track_mouse_position();
    Widget    tracker;
    /*
     * Create the tracker widget and register event
     * handlers for the target widget.
     */
    tracker = XtCreateManagedWidget("mousetracker",
                                      XwstatictextWidgetClass,
                                      parent, NULL, 0);
    XtAddEventHandler(target, LeaveWindowMask, FALSE,
                       clear_tracker, tracker);
    XtAddEventHandler(target, PointerMotionMask, FALSE,
                       track_mouse_position, tracker);
}
```

This function creates a StaticText widget, **tracker**, as a child of the given parent widget and then registers two event handlers for the **target** widget. The first handles **PointerMotion** events while the other handles **LeaveNotify** events. The **tracker** widget is given as client data for both event handlers.

The Intrinsics invokes the event handler **track_mouse_motion()** whenever the user moves the sprite within the **target** window. This function extracts the current sprite location from the event structure and converts it to a string, which is then displayed in the tracker widget using **XtSetValues()**. This event handler is defined as

```
void track_mouse_position(w, tracker, event)
    Widget          w;
    Widget          tracker;
    XEvent         *event;
{
    char            str[100];
    Arg             wargs[1];
    /*
     * Extract the position of the sprite from the event
     * and display it in the tracker widget.
     */
    sprintf(str, "X: %04d, Y: %04d", event->xmotion.x,
                                      event->xmotion.y);
    XtSetArg(wargs[0], XtNstring, str);
    XtSetValues(tracker, wargs, 1);
}
```

It is usually a bad idea to display status information when it is no longer valid, such as when the sprite is no longer in the target window. The **clear_tracker()** event handler clears the contents of the **tracker** widget when the sprite leaves the **target** widget's window.

```
void clear_tracker(w, tracker, event)
    Widget          w;
    Widget          tracker;
    XEvent         *event;
{
    Arg     wargs[1];
    int     n = 0;
    /*
     * Display an empty string in the tracker widget.
     */
```

```
        XtSetArg(wargs[n], XtNstring, ""); n++;
        XtSetValues(tracker, wargs, n);
    }
```

The mouse tracker could be added to nearly any application without interfering with the normal operation of the program. The Intrinsics allows applications to define multiple event handlers for each event, so the event handlers added by **create_mouse_tracker()** are invoked in addition to any other handlers registered with the target widget for the same events.

This example uses event handlers in a very straight forward way, but we can create more complex variations of this example. For example, let's modify the mouse tracker to report the position of the sprite only while a mouse button is pressed. To do this, we first need to redefine the **create_mouse_tracker()** function.

```
create_mouse_tracker(parent, target)
      Widget           parent, target;
{
  extern void  clear_tracker();
  extern void  track_mouse_position();
  extern void  show_mouse_position();

  Widget           tracker;
  /*
   * Create the tracker widget.
   */
  tracker = XtCreateManagedWidget("mousetracker",
                                  XwstatictextWidgetClass,
                                  parent, NULL, 0);
  /*
   * Set up event handlers on target widget.
   */
  XtAddEventHandler(target, ButtonPressMask, FALSE,
                    show_mouse_position, tracker);
  XtAddEventHandler(target, ButtonMotionMask, FALSE,
                    track_mouse_position, tracker);
  XtAddEventHandler(target,
                    ButtonReleaseMask | LeaveWindowMask,
                    FALSE, clear_tracker, tracker);
}
```

This variation registers three event handlers for the **target** widget. The function **track_mouse_position()** (defined exactly as before) is registered for **MotionNotify** events using the **ButtonMotionMask** instead of the **PointerMotionMask** event mask. This function is only invoked if the user moves the sprite while holding down a mouse button. This version of the mouse tracker registers a new event handler, **show_mouse_position()**, for **ButtonPress** events. This function is defined as

```
void show_mouse_position(w, tracker, event)
    Widget          w;
    Widget          tracker;
    XEvent         *event;
{
    char            str[100];
    Arg             wargs[1];
    /*
     * Extract the position of the sprite from the event
     * and display it in the tracker widget.
     */
    sprintf(str, "X: %04d, Y: %04d", event->xbutton.x,
                                     event->xbutton.y);
    XtSetArg(wargs[0], XtNstring, str);
    XtSetValues(tracker, wargs, 1);
}
```

This function is nearly the same as **track_mouse_position()**, except that it extracts the position of the sprite from the **ButtonPressedEvent** structure, using the **xbutton** member of the **XEvent** union rather than **xmotion**. We could use the same function to handle both of these events, because the definition of the **XButtonEvent** and **XMotionEvent** event structures are identical, except for the names. The expressions

```
event->xbutton.x
```

and

```
event->xmotion.x
```

both access the same member in the event structure. However it is not good programming practice to rely on such implementation-dependent details.

In this version of **create_mouse_tracker()**, the function **clear_tracker()** (also defined exactly as in the earlier version) is registered as an event handler for both **LeaveNotify** and **ButtonRelease** events by passing the inclusive-OR of both event masks to **XtAddEventHandler()**. When a single function handles multiple types of events, the event handler can check the type member of the event to determine the event type. In this example, **clear_tracker()** performs the same action in either case.

5.5 MANAGING THE EVENT QUEUE

Most applications use the function **XtMainLoop()** to remove events from the event queue and dispatch them to the appropriate widgets. However, occasionally an application needs to have more control over this process. Xlib provides many functions for examining and manipulating the event queue. These are seldom needed by applications that use the Intrinsics and widgets, although they can be used if needed. The Xt Intrinsics layer provides its own versions of the most common functions for examining the event queue

```
XtPending()
```

and

```
XtPeekEvent(&event)
```

XtPending() returns the total number of events pending in the event queue and returns zero if the event queue is empty. **XtPeekEvent()** copies the event at the top of the event queue into the application-supplied event structure, but does not remove the event from the event queue. **XtPending()** is useful when an application needs to do other tasks whenever there are no events in the event queue. For example, we could write an application's main event loop as

```
if(XtPending()){
   XtNextEvent(&event);
   XtDispatchEvent (&event)
}
else{
  /* Do something else for a while */
}
```

Notice that this can result in many wasted CPU cycles because the application continuously polls for events. To prevent this, the loop should block for some length of time after the task has completed. This can be done easily using the UNIX function **select()** to watch for input from the X file descriptor.

```
while(TRUE){
  if(XtPending()){  /* If an event is pending, get it and */
     XEvent event;  /* process it normally.               */
     XtNextEvent(&event);
     XtDispatchEvent (&event);
  }
  else{             /* Otherwise do a "background" task */
    struct timeval timeout;
    int readfds = 0;  /* Initialize arguments to select() */
    int maxfds = 1 + ConnectionNumber(XtDisplay(toplevel));
```

```
            timeout.tv_sec = 1; /* Set timeout for 1 second. */
            timeout.tv_usec = 0;
            /*
             * Do something else for a while - insert code here.
             */
            readfds = 1 << ConnectionNumber(XtDisplay(toplevel));
            /*
             * Block for tv.sec or until input is pending from X
             */
            if (select(maxfds, &readfds, NULL, NULL, &timeout) == -1){
              if (EINTR != errno)
                  exit(1);
            }
        }
    }
```

This approach assumes the task being performed when no events are available is short, so that the loop returns to process events in a reasonable time period. Section 5.7 describes a slightly different approach to doing this.

5.6 HANDLING TIMEOUTS

Although many useful X applications only process events from the user, some applications need to perform other tasks as well. The next few sections explore facilities provided by the Xt Intrinsics that extend Xlib's notion of events to allow applications to use the event dispatching mechanism to perform these tasks. One such feature provides the ability to invoke a callback procedure when a specified interval has elapsed. Applications can register use the function

```
XtAddTimeOut(interval, proc, data)
```

to register a timeout callback and specify the time delay before it is invoked. **XtAddTimeOut()** returns an ID of type **XtIntervalId** that uniquely identifies this timeout event. The arguments specify the time interval, in milliseconds, until the Intrinsics invokes the callback function **proc**, and also some client data to be passed to the timeout callback function. The form of a timeout callback is

```
void proc(data, id)
   caddr_t        data;
   XtIntervalId   *id;
```

where **data** is the client data specified in the call to **XtAddTimeOut()** and **id** is a pointer to the **XtIntervalId** identifier of the timeout event. When a timeout event occurs, Intrinsics invokes the corresponding callback and then automatically removes the callback. Therefore, timeout events are only invoked once. Clients can use the function

```
XtRemoveTimeOut(id)
```

to remove a timeout callback before the timeout occurs. The argument, **id**, must be the **XtIntervalId** of the timer event to be removed.

5.6.1 Using Timeouts as Alarms

Timeout events are basically alarms that can be set to go off some time in the future. This section uses an alarm to improve the original version of the mouse tracker example from Section 5.4.1.

One problem with tracking and reporting all **MotionNotify** events is that both the X server and clients generally have trouble keeping up with the large number of events that can be generated. Moving the sprite across the mouse tracker's target window can slow the entire system, because of the overhead involved in generating continuous motion events. This might be acceptable to someone actually using the mouse tracker, but what if the sprite just happens to cross the mouse tracker's target window on the way to another application's window? It can be frustrating to have the sprite slow down while it passes through the target area, when we are not really interested in the sprite position in the window.

We can solve this problem by using **XtAddTimeOut()** to set an alarm whenever the sprite enters the target window. We can then redesign the mouse tracker so that the position of the sprite is not reported (and no events are generated) until the alarm goes off. By setting the alarm interval appropriately, we can keep the mouse tracker from being activated when the sprite passes quickly through the target window.

In addition to demonstrating the use of timeout events, this version of the mouse tracker also demonstrates several other techniques for using event handlers. The previous examples defined and installed event handlers when the program began. This example dynamically adds and removes event handlers and callbacks within other event handlers. In addition, this example exploits the ability to pass client defined data to event handlers and callbacks to allow all event handlers access to some common data without resorting to global data structures.

In this example, all data used by the mouse tracker and its event handlers is kept in a single data structure, defined as

```
typedef struct {
    Widget        tracker;
    Widget        target;
    XtIntervalId  id;
    int           delay;
} track_data, *track_data_ptr;
```

The **tracker** member contains the tracker's StaticText widget, while the **target** member indicates the ID of the target widget. The **id** member of this data structure contains the **XtIntervalId** identifier for the timeout event, and **delay** specifies the time, in milliseconds, that the sprite must remain in the target window before the sprite position is reported. In this example, this delay is set to one second. The function **create_mouse_tracker()** allocates and initializes this structure and then registers a single event handler for the target widget.

```
#define DEFAULT_DELAY 1000

create_mouse_tracker(parent, target)
     Widget          parent, target;
{
  extern void        enter_window_handler();
  static track_data data;

  data.delay = DEFAULT_DELAY;
  /*
   * Store the target and tracker widgets in the data.
   */
  data.target = target;
  data.tracker =
          XtCreateManagedWidget("mousetracker",
                                 XwstatictextWidgetClass,
                                 parent, NULL, 0);
  /*
   * Start with a single event handler.
   */
  XtAddEventHandler(data.target, EnterWindowMask, FALSE,
                    enter_window_handler, &data);
}
```

The Intrinsics invokes **enter_window_handler()** when an **EnterNotify** event occurs. The client data for this event handler is a pointer to the **track_data** structure, containing both the tracker and the target widgets, allocated and initialized in the **create_mouse_tracker()** routine. This event handler does two things: first, it registers a new event handler, **disable_alarm()**. The Intrinsics calls this event handler when the sprite leaves the target window. Second, it adds a timeout callback, **start_tracking()**, to be invoked after the time specified by the **delay** member of **data**. Notice that **data** is also given as the client data argument for the timeout callback.

```
static void enter_window_handler(w, data, event)
    Widget          w;
    track_data     *data;
    XEvent         *event;
{
   extern void  start_tracking();
   extern void  disable_alarm();
   /*
    * When the sprite enters the window, install
    * a timeout callback, and start the count-down.
    */
   XtAddEventHandler(data->target, LeaveWindowMask, FALSE,
                     disable_alarm, data);
   data->id = XtAddTimeOut(data->delay, start_tracking, data);
}
```

So, what happens when the sprite quickly passes through the target window? First, the Intrinsics invokes the function **enter_window_handler()**. This function sets an alarm that causes the function **start_tracking()** to be invoked after the specified delay. However, if the sprite leaves the target window before the timeout event occurs, the event handler **disable_alarm()** is called. This event handler is defined as

```
static void disable_alarm(w, data, event)
   Widget          w;
   track_data     *data;
   XEvent         *event;
{
   /*
    * Remove the timeout callback and then remove
    * ourself as an event handler.
    */
   XtRemoveTimeOut(data->id);
   XtRemoveEventHandler(data->target, LeaveWindowMask, FALSE,
                        disable_alarm, data);
}
```

This function uses **XtRemoveTimeOut()** to remove the timeout callback before it is invoked. The function **disable_alarm()** also uses **XtRemoveEventHandler()** to remove itself as an event handler. At this point, the mouse tracker is in the same state as before the sprite entered the window, and the only event handler registered is the **enter_window_handler()** function. Notice that in this scenario, no **MotionNotify** events are generated because the mouse tracker never requests motion events.

Now suppose the sprite is still within the target window when the timeout event occurs. In this case, the Intrinsics invokes the timeout callback **start_tracking()**. This callback does three things. First, it removes the **disable_alarm()** event handler, which is no longer needed because the Intrinsics removes timeout callbacks automatically when the timeout occurs. Next, it registers the function **show_mouse_position()** as an event handler for **MotionNotify** events, and last, it registers **leave_window_handler()** as an event handler for **LeaveNotify** events. This sets up the event handlers in the same way as the original example in Section 5.4.1.

```
static void start_tracking(data, id)
    track_data      *data;
    XtIntervalId     id;
{
    extern void  disable_alarm();
    extern void  leave_window_handler();
    extern void  show_mouse_position();
    /*
     * If this function was called, the alarm must have
     * gone off, so remove the disable_alarm event handler.
     */
    XtRemoveEventHandler(data->target, LeaveWindowMask,
                         FALSE, disable_alarm, data);
    /*
     * Now add event handlers to track the sprite motion
     * and clear the tracker when we leave the target window.
     */
    XtAddEventHandler(data->target, PointerMotionMask,
                      FALSE, show_mouse_position, data);
    XtAddEventHandler(data->target, LeaveWindowMask,
                      FALSE, leave_window_handler, data);
}
```

The function **show_mouse_position()** is similar to the previous version in Section 5.4.1, but extracts the tracker widget from the **track_data** structure passed as client data.

```
static void show_mouse_position(w, data, event)
    Widget          w;
    track_data     *data;
    XEvent         *event;
{
    char            str[100];
    Arg             wargs[1];
    /*
```

```
       * Extract the position of the sprite from the event
       * and display it in the tracker widget.
       */
      sprintf(str, "X: %04d, Y: %04d", event->xmotion.x,
                                        event->xmotion.y);
      XtSetArg(wargs[0], XtNstring, str);
      XtSetValues(data->tracker, wargs, 1);
}
```

As long as the sprite remains in the target widget, the tracker widget displays the current position of the sprite. When the sprite leaves the target widget, the Intrinsics invokes the event handler **leave_window_handler()**. This function resets the mouse tracker to its initial state by removing the **show_mouse_position()** event handler, clearing the mouse tracker's display widget, and finally removing itself as an event handler.

```
static void leave_window_handler(w, data, event)
   Widget          w;
   track_data     *data;
   XEvent         *event;
{
  Arg             wargs[1];
  extern void  show_mouse_position();
  /*
   * Clear the tracker widget display.
   */
  XtSetArg(wargs[0], XtNstring, "");
  XtSetValues(data->tracker, wargs, 1);
  /*
   * Remove the dynamically installed event handlers.
   */
  XtRemoveEventHandler(data->target, PointerMotionMask, FALSE,
                       show_mouse_position, data);
  XtRemoveEventHandler(data->target, LeaveWindowMask, FALSE,
                       leave_window_handler, data);
}
```

5.6.2 Cyclic Timeouts

Applications often need to perform some action repeatedly at designated intervals. Although the Xt Intrinsics automatically removes timeout callbacks when the timeout event occurs, applications can arrange for timeout callbacks to be invoked at regular intervals by designing the callback to re-install itself each time it is called. An obvious application of this technique is a clock. We can write a digital clock easily using a StaticText widget and a single timeout callback. The body of the clock program is

```
/**************************************************
 * xclock.c : A simple digital clock
 **************************************************/

#include <X11/Intrinsic.h>
#include <X11/StringDefs.h>
#include <Xw/Xw.h>
#include <Xw/SText.h>
#include <time.h>

void update_time();

main(argc, argv)
   int              argc;
   char            *argv[];
{
   Widget           toplevel, clock;
   /*
    * Create the widgets.
    */
   toplevel = XtInitialize(argv[0], "Clock", NULL, 0,
                           &argc, argv);
   clock = XtCreateManagedWidget("face",
                                 XwstatictextWidgetClass,
                                 toplevel, NULL, 0);
   /*
    * Get the initial time.
    */
   update_time(clock, NULL);
   XtRealizeWidget(toplevel);
   XtMainLoop();
}
```

Before entering the main loop, the program calls the function **update_time()** to display the initial time in the widget. This function uses the UNIX system call **time()** to determine the current time in seconds since 00:00:00 GMT (Greenwich Mean Time), Jan 1, 1970. After rounding the time to the nearest minute, the function calls the UNIX library routine **ctime()** to convert this value to a string representing the current time and date. **XtSetValues()** then updates the string displayed in the StaticText widget, and finally re-registers itself as a timeout callback. The delay until the next timeout event is calculated to occur on the next full minute, to keep the clock reasonably accurate. The **update_time()** function is defined as

```
void update_time(w, id)
    Widget          w;
    XtIntervalId    id;
{
    Arg    wargs[1];
    long   tloc, rounded_tloc, next_minute;
    char  *str;
    int    n = 0;
   /*
    * Ask Unix for the time.
    */
    time(&tloc);
    /*
     * Convert the time to a string and display it,
     * after rounding it down to the last minute.
     */
    rounded_tloc = tloc / 60 * 60;
    str = ctime(&rounded_tloc);
    XtSetArg(wargs[n], XtNstring, str);n++;
    XtSetValues(w, wargs, n);
    /*
     * Adjust the time to reflect the time till
     * the next round minute.
     */
    next_minute = (60 - tloc % 60) * 1000;
    /*
     * The Intrinsics removes timeouts when they occur,
     * so put ourselves back.
     */
    XtAddTimeOut(next_minute, update_time, w);
}
```

Fig. 5.10 shows the digital clock created by this example.

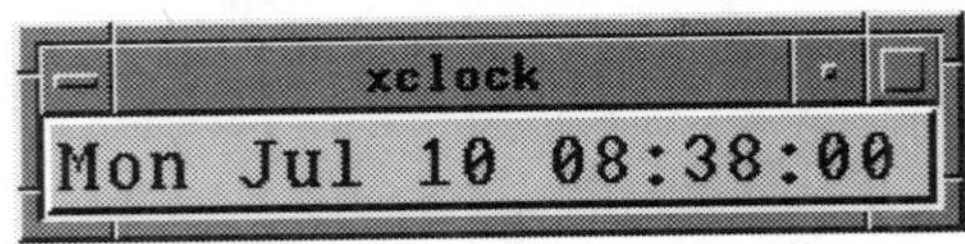

Figure 5.10 xclock: A digital clock.

5.7 USING WORKPROCS

The R3 Intrinsics includes a facility for handling a limited form of background processing. This facility works in much the same way as the example using **select()** in Section 5.5. However, WorkProcs allow the programmer to register a callback and hides the details of the event processing from the programmer. A WorkProc is a callback that is invoked by the Intrinsics whenever there are no events pending. A WorkProc takes only a single argument, which is client-defined data. The procedure is expected return **True** if it should be removed, and **False** otherwise. Applications can register a WorkProc using the function

XtAddWorkProc(proc, client_data)

This function returns an ID that identifies the WorkProc. WorkProcs can be removed by calling the function

XtRemoveWorkProc(id)

where **id** is the identifier returned by **XtAddWorkProc()**. We can use WorkProcs to write a "stopwatch" variation on the clock program from the previous section that updates the time continuously. This example shows how WorkProcs allow a mixture of background processing and event handling. In addition to a StaticText widget in which time is continuously displayed, there are three PushButton widgets. One starts the time, another stops the time, while the third is a quit button. The main body of the program creates the PushButton and StaticText widgets and sets up several callbacks.

```
/*****************************************************
 * stopwatch.c: A digital stopwatch using workprocs.
 *              NOTE, This example only works with R3
 *                    or later widgets and Intrinsics.
 *****************************************************/

#include <X11/Intrinsic.h>
#include <X11/StringDefs.h>
#include <Xw/Xw.h>
#include <Xw/SText.h>
#include <Xw/RCManager.h>
#include <Xw/PButton.h>
#include <time.h>
#include "libXs.h"

Boolean update_time();
void start_timing();
void stop_timing();
```

```
static  long  start_time, current_time;
static XtWorkProcId work_proc_id = NULL;


main(argc, argv)
   int       argc;
   char     *argv[];
{
   Widget   toplevel, panel, commands, start, stop, timer;

   toplevel = XtInitialize(argv[0], "Stopwatch", NULL, 0,
                           &argc, argv);
   /*
    * Create a RowCol widget to hold everything.
    */
   panel = XtCreateManagedWidget("panel",
                                 XwrowColWidgetClass,
                                 toplevel, NULL, 0);
    /*
     * A StaticText widget shows the current time.
     */
   timer = XtCreateManagedWidget("timer",
                                 XwstatictextWidgetClass,
                                 panel, NULL, 0);
    /*
     * Add a start and stop button and register callbacks.
     */
   commands = XtCreateManagedWidget("commands",
                                    XwrowColWidgetClass,
                                    panel, NULL, 0);
   start = XtCreateManagedWidget("start",
                                 XwpushButtonWidgetClass,
                                 commands, NULL, 0);
   XtAddCallback(start, XtNrelease, start_timing, timer);
   stop = XtCreateManagedWidget("stop",
                                XwpushButtonWidgetClass,
                                commands, NULL, 0);
   XtAddCallback(stop, XtNrelease, stop_timing, timer);
   create_quit_button("Quit", commands);
```

```
    XtRealizeWidget(toplevel);
    XtMainLoop();
}
```

The **start_timing()** callback function determines the initial time and registers a WorkProc with the Intrinsics to update the stopwatch display. It uses **time()** to get the current time in seconds since 00:00:00 GMT, Jan 1, 1970. Next, in case the user presses the start button multiple times, the function removes any previous WorkProc before registering the function **update_time()** as a WorkProc.

```
void start_timing(w, timer, call_data)
   Widget       w, timer;
   caddr_t      call_data;
{
  /*
   * Get the initial time, and save it in a global.
   */
  time(&start_time);
  /*
   * If a WorkProc has already been added, remove it.
   */
  if(work_proc_id)
    XtRemoveWorkProc(work_proc_id);
  /*
   * Register update_time() as a WorkProc.
   */
  work_proc_id = XtAddWorkProc(update_time, timer);
}
```

The **stop_timing()** callback function simply removes the WorkProc, if one exists.

```
void stop_timing(w, timer, call_data)
   Widget        w, timer;
   caddr_t       call_data;
{
  if(work_proc_id)
    XtRemoveWorkProc(work_proc_id);
  work_proc_id = NULL;
}
```

The stopwatch display is updated by the WorkProc, **update_time()**, which is called whenever no events are pending. The client data for this function specifies the StaticText widget in which the time is displayed. The function **update_time()** subtracts the initial time from the current time to obtain the elapsed time in seconds since the user pressed the start button. The function converts the time to minutes and seconds before displaying the elapsed time. Because WorkProcs are called whenever there are no events pending, **update_time()** can be called more often than necessary. Therefore it remembers the elapsed time each time the display is updated, and if at least one second has not elapsed, it simply returns. Otherwise the StaticText widget would be updated so often that an annoying flashing effect would occur.

```
Boolean update_time(w)
      Widget   w;
{
  static long elapsed_time, last_time = -1;
  int minutes, seconds;
  /*
   * Retrieve the current time and calculate the elapsed time.
   */
  time(&current_time);
  elapsed_time = current_time - start_time;
  /*
   * WorkProcs are irregularly called; don't update the
   * display if it's been less than a second since the last
   * time it was updated.
   */
  if(last_time ==  elapsed_time)
    return FALSE;
  /*
   * If one or more seconds has elasped, remember this time,
   * and convert the elapsed time to minutes and seconds.
   */
  last_time = elapsed_time;
  minutes = elapsed_time / 60;
  seconds = elapsed_time % 60;
  /*
   * Display the time as minutes and seconds.
   */
  wprintf(w, "%02d : %02d", minutes, seconds);
  /*
   * Return FALSE so this WorkProc keeps getting called.
   */
  return FALSE;
}
```

The function **wprintf()** is a useful function that uses **XtSetValues()** to change the string displayed in a static text widget. The function has a form similar to the C library function **fprintf()**, except that it displays its output in a StaticText widget. This function is useful enough to place in the libXs library. The function uses the utility macros found in the UNIX header file /usr/include/varargs.h in combination with **vsprintf()** to handle a variable number of arguments.

```
/************************************************************
 * wprintf: fprintf-like function for StaticText
 ************************************************************/
#include <varargs.h>
#include <stdio.h>
#include <X11/Intrinsic.h>
#include <X11/StringDefs.h>
#include <Xw/Xw.h>
#include <Xw/SText.h>

void wprintf(va_alist)
     va_dcl
{
  Widget    w;
  char     *format;
  va_list   args;
  char      str[1000];
  Arg       wargs[1];
  /*
    * Init the variable length args list.
    */
  va_start(args);
 /*
   * Extract the destination widget.
   * Make sure it is a StaticText widget.
   */
  w = va_arg(args, Widget);
  if(XtClass(w) != XwstatictextWidgetClass)
     XtError("wprintf() requires a Static Text Widget");
  /*
   * Extract the format to be used.
   */
  format = va_arg(args, char *);
  /*
   * Use vsprintf to format the string to be displayed
   * in the StaticText widget.
   */
  vsprintf(str, format, args);
```

```
    XtSetArg(wargs[0], XtNstring, str);
    XtSetValues(w, wargs, 1);
    va_end(args);
}
```

The layout for the stopwatch program shown in Fig. 5.11 can be specified using the resources

```
stopwatch*panel*columns:          1
stopwatch*panel*commands*columns: 3
```

Figure 5.11 The stopwatch program.

5.8 HANDLING OTHER INPUT SOURCES

Many X applications require input from sources other than the X event queue. The Xt Intrinsics provides a simple way to handle additional input sources. Applications can define input callbacks to be invoked when input is available from a specified file descriptor. The function

```
XtAddInput(source, condition, proc, client_data)
```

registers an input callback with the Intrinsics. The argument **source** must be a UNIX file number, while condition indicates under what circumstances the input callback should be invoked. The **condition** must be one of the constants

```
XtInputNoneMask
XtInputReadMask
XtInputWriteMask
XtInputExceptMask
```

When the given condition occurs, the Intrinsics invokes the callback function specified by proc. The **client_data** argument allows the application to provide some data to be passed to the callback function when it is called. **XtAddInput()** returns an identifier of type XtIn**putId** that uniquely identifies this callback.

Input callback functions have the form

```
void io_callback(client_data, source, id)
    caddr_t      client_data;
    int         *source;
    XtInputId   *id;
```

When the Intrinsics invokes an input callback, it passes the **client_data** provided by the application along with a pointer to the file number of the input source where input is available. It also provides a pointer to the **XtInputId** associated with this callback.

Input callbacks that are no longer needed can be removed using

```
XtRemoveInput(id)
```

The argument, **id**, must be the **XtInputId** identifier for the input callback to be removed.

5.8.1 Using Input Callbacks

This section looks at an example that uses an input callback to read input from a UNIX *pipe*. Pipes provide a way to connect the output of one UNIX program to the input of another. This example uses pipes to add a mouse-driven interface to a standard UNIX utility without modifying the code of the original application in any way. The example builds a simple interface for the UNIX calculator program **bc** that allows the user to input commands using the mouse and displays the results in a window. The resulting "desktop calculator," named **xbc**, communicates with **bc** using UNIX pipes. To keep this example simple, **xbc** provides only a few basic arithmetic functions, although it could easily be extended to take advantage of more advanced features of **bc**. Fig. 5.12 shows the calculator interface to **bc**.

Figure 5.12 xbc: A mouse-driven calculator.

The body of the calculator program creates the widgets used as a keypad and the calculator display panel.

```
/*****************************************************
 * xbc.c: An X interface to bc
 *****************************************************/
#include <stdio.h>
#include <ctype.h>
#include <X11/StringDefs.h>
#include <X11/Intrinsic.h>
#include <Xw/Xw.h>
#include <Xw/PButton.h>
#include <Xw/VPW.h>
#include <Xw/RCManager.h>
#include <Xw/TextEdit.h>
#include "libXs.h"

Widget      display;
Widget      create_button();
void        quit_bc();
void        get_from_bc();
void        send_to_bc();

main(argc, argv)
  int        argc;
  char      *argv[];
{
  Widget     toplevel, panel, keyboard, qbutton;
  Arg        wargs[2];
  int        n;
  toplevel = XtInitialize(argv[0], "Xbc", NULL, 0,
                               &argc, argv);
  /*
   * Create a vertical paned widget as a base for the
   * rest of the calculator.
   */
  panel = XtCreateManagedWidget("panel",
                                    XwvPanedWidgetClass,
                                    toplevel, NULL, 0);
  /*
   * Create the calculator display.
   */
  n = 0;
```

```
XtSetArg(wargs[n], XtNstring, "X Calculator");n++;
XtSetArg(wargs[n], XtNeditType, XwtextEdit);n++;
display = create_one_line_text_widget("display", panel,
                                       wargs, n);
/*
 * Make the keyboard, that manages 4 columns of button
 */
XtSetArg(wargs[0], XtNcolumns, 4);
keyboard = XtCreateManagedWidget("keyboard",
                                  XwrowColWidgetClass,
                                  panel, wargs, 1);
/*
 * Create the keyboard buttons. This order makes it
 * look like a typical desktop calculator.
 */
create_button("1", keyboard);
create_button("2", keyboard);
create_button("3", keyboard);
create_button("+", keyboard);
create_button("4", keyboard);
create_button("5", keyboard);
create_button("6", keyboard);
create_button("-", keyboard);
create_button("7", keyboard);
create_button("8", keyboard);
create_button("9", keyboard);
create_button("*", keyboard);
create_button("0", keyboard);
create_button(".", keyboard);
create_button("=", keyboard);
create_button("/", keyboard);
/*
 *  Create a quit button and add a callback that
 *  tells bc to exit.
 */
qbutton = create_quit_button("Q", keyboard);
XtAddCallback(qbutton, XtNselect, quit_bc, NULL);
/*
 * Add callback get_from_bc() --  invoked when input
 * is available from stdin.
 */
XtAddInput(fileno(stdin), XtInputReadMask,
```

```
                  get_from_bc, display);
    /*
     * Exec the program "bc" and set up pipes
     * between it and us.
     */
    talkto("bc");

    XtRealizeWidget(toplevel);
    XtMainLoop();
  }
```

Fig. 5.13 shows the widget tree created by **xbc**. The calculator consists of a display area (a TextEdit widget) and a keyboard area (a RowCol widget). Both of these widgets are managed by a VPanedWindow widget. The RowCol widget manages four columns of buttons used for input to the calculator.

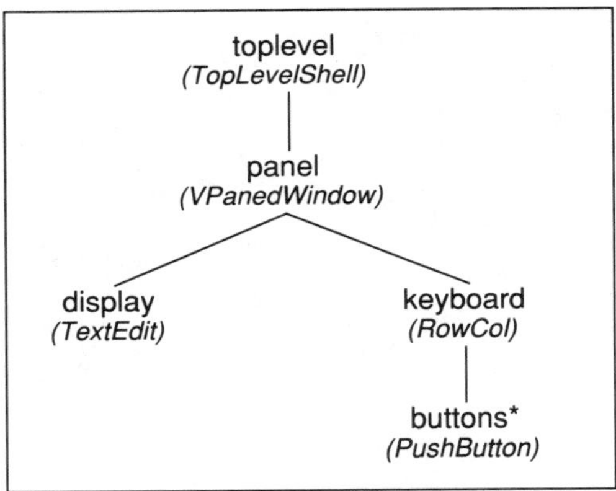

Figure 5.13 The xbc widget tree.[1]

The function **create_button()** takes two arguments, a label for the calculator key and the parent widget of the button. The function creates a single PushButton widget and adds the callback **send_to_bc()** to the **XtNselect** callback list. The name of the widget is also given as client data to be used as a string that is sent to **bc** when the user selects the button. This function is defined as

```
Widget create_button(name, parent)
  char    *name;
  Widget   parent;
```

1.The asterisk after the button widget in this figure signifies many button widgets.

```
{
  extern void send_to_bc();
  Widget      button;
  /*
   * Create a single button and attach a select callback.
   */
  button = XtCreateManagedWidget(name,
                                 XwpushButtonWidgetClass,
                                 parent, NULL, 0);
  XtAddCallback(button, XtNselect, send_to_bc, name);
  return (button);
}
```

The main program also creates a quit button, using the libXs function defined in Chapter 4, and registers a **XtNselect** callback. This callback prints the string "**quit**" when the user selects the button, causing the **bc** process to exit before **xbc**.

```
void quit_bc(w, client_data, event)
     Widget    w;
     caddr_t   client_data;
     XEvent   *event;
{
   /*
    * Tell bc to quit.
    */
   fprintf(stdout, "quit\n");
}
```

The line

```
XtAddInput(fileno(stdin),XtInputReadMask,get_from_bc,display);
```

in the main program registers an input callback. Whenever input is pending from **stdin**, the Intrinsics calls the function **get_from_bc()** with the StaticText widget display as client data. We will look at this function shortly, but first we must discuss how **xbc** communicates with **bc**.

Before entering **XtMainLoop()**, **xbc** calls the function **talkto()**. This function starts up the program **bc** and establishes a two-way connection between **bc** and **xbc**, by creating two pipes that connect the **stdin** and **stdout** of the parent process (**xbc**) and the child process (**bc**). This function can be used to establish similar pipes between any two programs.

```
/*****************************************************
 * talkto.c: set up two way pipes
 *****************************************************/
#include <stdio.h>
void talkto(cmd)
   char   *cmd;
{
  int   to_child[2], /* pipe descriptors from parent->child */
        to_parent[2];/* pipe descriptors from child->parent */
  int   pid;

  pipe(to_child);
  pipe(to_parent);
  if (pid = fork(), pid == 0){       /* in the child   */
     close(0);                       /* redirect stdin */
     dup(to_child[0]);
     close(1);                       /* redirect stdout*/
     dup(to_parent[1]);
     close(to_child[0]);             /* close pipes    */
     close(to_child[1]);
     close(to_parent[0]);
     close(to_parent[1]);
     execlp(cmd, cmd, NULL);         /* exec the new cmd */
   }
   else if (pid > 0){                /* in the parent  */
      close(0);                      /* redirect stdin */
      dup(to_parent[0]);
      close(1);                      /* redirect stdout  */
      dup(to_child[1]);
      setbuf(stdout, NULL);          /* no buffered output */
      close(to_child[0]);            /* close pipes */
      close(to_child[1]);
      close(to_parent[0]);
      close(to_parent[1]);
    }
    else {                           /* error!        */
      fprintf(stderr,"Couldn't fork process %s\n", cmd);
      exit(1);
    }
}
```

Initially, **talkto()** creates two pipes and *forks* a new process. The **fork()** command is a UNIX system call that creates a duplicate of the calling process, and returns the *process* *id* of the newly created process to the parent. Both processes have access to the pipes created earlier. The calling process closes its **stdin** and **stdout** file descriptors and replaces them, using **dup()**, with one end of each pipe. Similarly, the forked process closes its input and output files and replaces them by the other end of the same pipes. Finally the forked process is overlaid by **cmd** by calling **execlp()**. For a thorough explanation of UNIX pipes, see [Roch85].

The UNIX standard I/O (stdio) package normally buffers its output. The function **setbuf()** turns off buffering so that all output from the parent process is sent to the child process immediately. Unfortunately, we can only unbuffer the output in the parent process. To avoid problems, both processes should used unbuffered output, but we do not have access to the child process.

After calling **talkto()**, when **xbc** reads from **stdin**, it is really reading from the pipe connected to the output of b**c**. Whe**n xbc** writes to **stdout** it is actually writing to a pipe connected to the input of **bc**. Notice that **bc** does not have to be modified in any way. As far as **bc** is concerned, it is reading from **stdin** and writing to **stdout**.

This approach can be used to create window-based interfaces to many UNIX applications. However, it is not always as simple as we might wish, partially because of inconsistencies in the output of UNIX commands. In spite of UNIX conventions that encourage small applications that can be piped together in various combinations, the output of many UNIX applications is often inconsistent. For example, many applications add headers at the top of each page. Others produce different output formats depending on the options specified on the command line. The same utility may also behave differently on different machines. Therefore, one of the difficulties in using existing UNIX applications this way is sending the correct input to the application and parsing the results.

The pipe mechanism itself can also cause other problems. Handling all the exceptions and error conditions that can occur when using two-way pipes can be difficult. For example, this version of **talkto()** neglects the problems that can arise when either process exits unexpectedly, and also does not attempt to do any signal handling. Problems can also occur if the maximum buffer size of a pipe is exceeded. This is usually not a problem for **xbc** because only a few digits cross the pipes at any time.

The callback function **send_to_bc()**, invoked each time an **xbc** button is selected, sends a command to **bc**. As a first pass, we could define this function as

```
/* INCOMPLETE VERSION */
void send_to_bc(w, buffer, call_data)
   Widget      w;
   char       *buffer;
   caddr_t     call_data;
{
  fprintf(stdout, "%s", buffer);  /* Not Good Enough! */
  XwTextInsert(display, buffer);
}
```

This simplified function prints the characters given as client data to **stdout**, (now attached to the input of **bc**), and calls **XwTextInsert()**, a public function provided by the TextEdit widget, to insert the characters in the display. Although this function shows the general idea, we must write a slightly more complex function to make **xbc** act like a real calculator and also send correct input to **bc**. The complete **send_to_bc()** function is

```
void send_to_bc(w, buffer, event)
  Widget    w;
  char     *buffer;
  XEvent   *event;
{
  static int  start_new_entry = TRUE;
  /*
   * If this is the beginning of a new operand,
   * clear the display.
   */
  if(start_new_entry){
    reset_display();
    start_new_entry = FALSE;
  }
  switch (buffer[0]) {
  /*
   * If the user entered and '=', send bc a newline, clear
   * the display, and get ready for a new operand.
   */
  case '=':
    fprintf(stdout, "%s", XwTextCopyBuffer(display));
    fprintf(stdout, "\n");
    reset_display();
    start_new_entry = TRUE;
    break;
  /*
   * If this is an operator, get the previous operand
   * from the display buffer, and send it to bc before
   * sending the operand.
   */
  case '-':
  case '+':
  case '/':
  case '*':
  case '^':
    fprintf(stdout, "%s", XwTextCopyBuffer(display));
    fprintf(stdout, "%s", buffer);
```

```
      reset_display();
      break;
    /*
     * Anything else must be a digit, so append it to the
     * display buffer.
     */
    default:
      XwTextInsert(display, buffer);
    }
    fflush(stdout);
}
```

This function creates an interface between the input **bc** expects and the behavior we expect from a desktop calculator. A flag, **start_new_entry**, indicates when one calculation sequence has been completed and another one is beginning. If this flag is **True**, the calculator display is cleared and reset using the function **reset_display()**.

Normally, a calculator displays the results of a calculation when the user presses the "=" key. However, **bc** evaluates an expression when a newline character is entered. The first case ('=') in the switch statement uses the function **XwTextCopyBuffer()** to retrieve the contents of the display widget, sends it to **bc** by printing it to **stdout**, and then prints a newline character to get **bc** to evaluate the expression. It also sets the flag **start_new_entry** to **True** to signal the end of a calculation sequence, and calls **reset_display()** to clear the **display** widget.

Calculators display numbers as they are entered, but do not usually display math operators. Therefore, all operators are sent to **bc**, but not displayed. When an operator is selected, **send_to_bc()** prints the current contents of the **display** widget, followed by the operator. It then clears the **display** widget to prepare for the next operand.

The default case handles all digits and simply calls **XwTextInsert()** to insert the digit at the current position in the **display** widget. The digit is not sent to **bc** until the user presses an operator or the "=" key.

The input callback **get_from_bc()** handles output from **bc**. This function reads from stdin, and, after adding a NULL to the end of the buffer, calls **XwTextInsert()** to display the string.

```
void get_from_bc(w, fid, id)
  Widget       w;
  int         *fid;
  XtInputId   *id;
{
  char         buf[BUFSIZ];
  int          nbytes;
  /*
```

```
     * Get all pending input and append it to the display
     * widget. Discard lines that begin with a newline.
     */
    nbytes = read(*fid, buf, BUFSIZ);
    if (nbytes && buf[0] != '\n') {
    /*
     * Null terminate the string at the first newline,
     * or at the end of the bytes read.
     */
     for(i=0;i<nbytes;i++)
       if(buf[i] == '\n')
           buf[i] = '\0';
       buf[nbytes] = '\0';
       XwTextInsert(w, buf);
    }
}
```

The only complication is that this function must handle the newline characters that **bc** prints after each result, by ignoring the data if the first character is a newline character and by stripping off any other newlines that appear in the buffer.

The last function, **reset_display()**, simply clears the **display** widget and sets the current insert position to zero.

```
reset_display()
{
   /*
    * Clear the text buffer and go to position 1.
    */
   XwTextClearBuffer(display);
   XwTextSetInsertPos(display, 0);
}
```

5.9 SUMMARY

This chapter examined many of the events supported by the X Window System and discussed the use of the event-handling mechanisms provided by the Xt Intrinsics. Xlib reports events whenever any aspect of a window's environment changes. The Intrinsics provide a higher level interface to the X event mechanism and also adds the ability to handle input from sources other than the X server using a similar event handling mechanism. Timeout events provide a useful way to performing tasks not directly related to user input.

This chapter did not discuss some of the most powerful and interesting events provided by X, communication events, which are discussed in Chapter 11. The following chapter examines X's color model.

6

USING COLOR

Previous chapters demonstrated some simple applications using the Xt Intrinsics and the X Widgets. In these programs, the widgets completely controlled how they displayed the information specified by an application. The next few chapters discuss Xlib facilities that allow applications to display text and graphics directly in windows. Discussing these facilities gives us a better understanding of X and allows us to write applications that cannot be built from existing widgets. Before discussing the use of text and graphics we need to understand the color model used by X. This chapter discusses how X uses color, and presents a simple color editor as an example.

6.1 THE X COLOR MODEL

X uses a flexible color model that provides a common interface to many different types of display hardware. The color model allows a properly designed application to run equally well on a variety of monochrome and color screens.

It is particularly difficult to design a color model for a window system that supports multiple processes, because most color screens support a limited number of colors. For example, a typical color screen with four bit planes of display memory supports only 16 colors at one time. Often, these 16 colors can be chosen from a large palette of available colors. One common configuration provides a palette of nearly 16 million different colors; however, on a screen with four bit planes, only 16 of these colors can be displayed at any given time.

This might not be a serious problem for systems where one graphics application controls the entire screen. However, in a multiprocess window-based system, many applications are present on the screen at once, and therefore each application competes for the limited number of colors available.

One way to solve this problem is to support only a fixed set of colors used by all applications. Some low-cost personal computers use this approach by providing a basic set of colors: red, green, blue, magenta, yellow, and so on. All applications must chose from one of these preset colors. Using a fixed palette of colors is not an acceptable solution for X, because portability between many architectures was a basic design goal of X.

Instead, X uses a unique approach that allows each application to use as many colors as it needs, but also encourages applications to share colors. The approach used by X is based on an allocation scheme, in which applications request the server to allocate the colors needed by the application. Applications usually request colors by name, so that if two applications request the color "blue," the server gives each application a pointer to the same color cell.

6.1.1 Colormaps

The X color model uses a *colormap*. A colormap, sometimes called a color lookup table, is an array of colors. Applications refer to colors using an index into the colormap. The colormap provides a level of indirection between the color index used by an application and the color displayed on the screen. Most displays provide a hardware colormap. To draw a point on the screen, applications place a value in the appropriate location of the display's *frame buffer*. A frame buffer is a large contiguous area of memory. The frame buffer must contain at least one bit for each screen location (pixel) on the screen. The amount of memory corresponding to one bit per pixel is known as a *bit plane*. The number of colors that a screen can display at one time is determined by the number of bit planes in the frame buffer, according to the relation $colors = 2^{planes}$. For example, a frame buffer with four color planes can indicate 16 different colors. Fig. 6.1 shows how a typical hardware display uses the colormap to convert a value in the frame buffer to a color on the screen. This figure illustrates a display with a 4 plane frame buffer. The hardware scans each cell, or pixel, in the frame buffer, and uses the combined value of all planes as an index to the colormap. The contents of this location in the colormap is then converted to an intensity on the screen. Fig. 6.1 shows a 4 bit colormap for a monochrome display. A display with a single, 4 bit colormap can display 16 levels of a single color.

Each X window has a virtual colormap associated with it. Before the colors in this colormap are reflected on the screen, the colormap must be *installed* into the hardware colormap. Some hardware displays allow multiple colormaps to be installed at once, but many support only one colormap at a time. By convention, X window managers install the colormap of the current focus window, allowing the application using this window to be displayed using correct colors. However, when this approach is used, other applications on the screen are unlikely to be displayed in their true colors, because the colors stored in the hardware color map change, but the indexes used by applications do not.

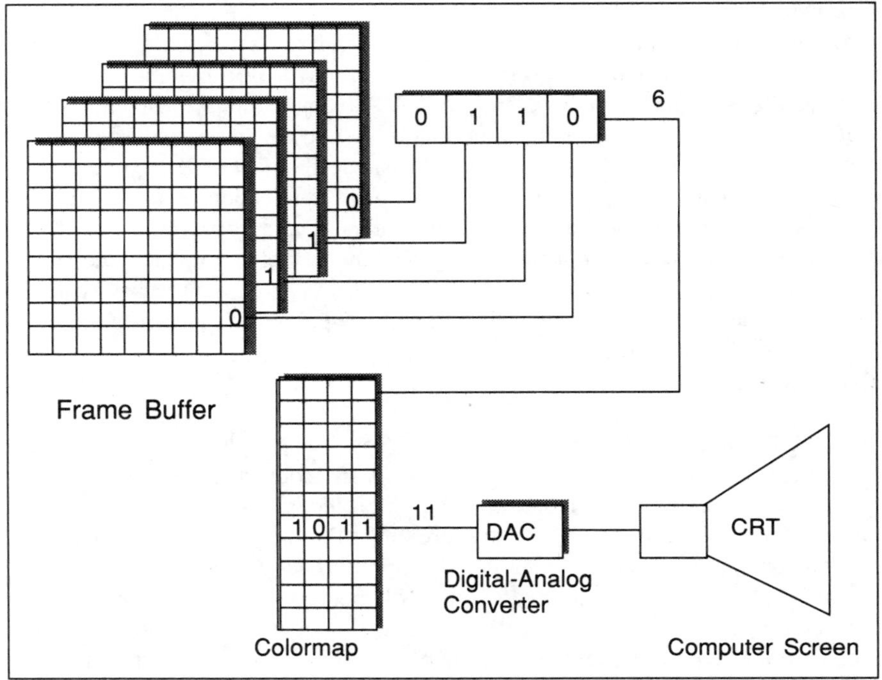

Figure 6.1 A Typical Colormap Architecture.

Applications can often share the same colormap. By default, windows inherit the colormap of their parent, and most applications can use the default colormap of the root window. Applications can use the macro

```
DefaultColormap(display, screen)
```

to access the default colormap of any screen. This default colormap is installed by the X server when the server starts up. The server normally allocates two colors, black and white, from the default colormap. All other color cells can be allocated by clients. (See Section 6.1.3). Applications can also create their own colormaps. A programmer might consider creating a new colormap when an application needs many colors, requires colors to be placed in particular locations in the colormap, or needs to alter the contents of the colormap dynamically. Applications can use the function

```
XCreateColormap(display, window, visual, alloc)
```

to create a colormap. The function returns a unique ID for the new colormap. **XCreateColormap()** uses the **window** argument only to determine the screen where the colormap is used, so this window does not need to be the window associated with the colormap. This function also requires the programmer to specify the *visual type* of the screen. Every screen supports one or more visual types. A visual type is represented by a structure, **XVisual**, defined in the header file Xlib.h. This structure contains information about the screen, including how many colormap entries it supports, whether it supports monochrome, color, gray scale only, and so on. It is possible for a screen to support more than one visual type, although it is currently more common for the hardware to support only one. The previous discussion of colormaps applies most directly to a screen whose visual type is **PseudoColor**. The visual types recognized by X are:

- **PseudoColor**. On a **PseudoColor** screen, pixel values index a colormap to produce independent, dynamically changeable red, green, and blue values.
- **StaticColor**. This type is similar to **PseudoColor**, except that the colormap contains predefined (fixed) values.
- **GrayScale**. This type is similar to **PseudoColor**, except only a single primary color (usually gray) is available.
- **StaticGray**. Screens with a **StaticGray** visual type have a fixed, predetermined monochrome colormap.
- **DirectColor**. Screens that support **DirectColor** decompose the pixel values into separate red, green, and blue fields. Each component is then used as an index into a separate color lookup table.
- **TrueColor**. This visual type is similar to **DirectColor** except that the colormap contains pre-defined, fixed values.

The default visual structure for a particular screen can be obtained using the Xlib macro

```
DefaultVisual(display, screen)
```

Colormaps contain no colors when first created. Before an application can store colors in a colormap, it must *allocate* color cells. The last argument to **XCreateColormap()** specifies how many entries in the colormap should be allocated initially. This argument must be one of the constants **AllocNone** or **AllocAll**. The correct value depends on the visual type supported by the screen. The value **AllocNone** must be used for screens with a static visual type.

The function

```
XInstallColormap(display, cmap)
```

installs a colormap as the current colormap used by the display. When a colormap is installed, the screen instantly reflects the colors in the new colormap, and the server sends a **ColormapNotify** event to all windows associated with the newly installed colormap. By default, a window inherits its parent's colormap. The function

```
XSetWindowColormap(display, window, cmap)
```

associates a colormap with a window. Applications can use the function

```
XFreeColormap(display, id)
```

to free a colormap when it is no longer needed. The **id** argument must specify a resource ID of a colormap.

6.1.2 Standard Colormaps

X supports the concept of *standard colormaps*. Colormaps may be stored in a property (see Chapter 11) in the X server, where they can be retrieved by any application that wishes to use them. Xlib defines the property names for several standard colormaps, including **RGB_DEFAULT_MAP**, **RGB_BEST_MAP**, and **RGB_GRAY_MAP**. Notice that only the *names* of these colormaps are defined. The colormaps, as well as the exact organization of the colormaps, are not precisely defined. These colormaps exist only if some application (most often a window manager) defines them and stores them in the server.

A standard colormap can be stored in the server using the Xlib function

```
XSetStandardColormap(display, window, cmap, property)
```

Once a standard colormap has been stored in the server, applications can use the Xlib function

```
XGetStandardColormap(display, window, &cmap, property)
```

to retrieve a standard colormap from the server.

6.1.3 Allocating Colors

Once an application has access to a colormap, it can allocate colors in that colormap. The Xlib functions that allocate colors make use of an **XColor** structure. This structure includes the members

```
unsigned long  pixel;
unsigned short red, green, blue;
char           flags;
```

Colors are specified by the intensity of each of their red, green, and blue (RGB) components. The values of these components can range from 0 to 65535, where 0 corresponds the lowest intensity of a color component, and 65535 corresponds to the highest intensity. For example, we can create an **XColor** structure representing bright white with:

```
XColor color;
color.red   = 65535;
color.green = 65535;
color.blue  = 65535;
```

or create a bright red color structure with

```
XColor color;
color.red   = 65535;
color.green = 0;
color.blue  = 0;
```

The X server scales these values to the range of color intensities supported by the screen. Color cells of a colormap can be *read-only* or *read-write*. The color components in a read-only cell can not be altered, and therefore can be shared between all applications that use the same colormap. Attempts to change the value of a read-only cell generate an error. A read-write cell cannot be shared between applications, because the application that allocated the cell can change it at any time.

The Xlib function

```
XAllocColor(display, cmap, &color)
```

allocates a read-only entry in a colormap. This function requires an **XColor** structure containing the RGB components of the color to be allocated. If some other application has already allocated the same color as a read-only cell, the same cell is reused and the **pixel** member of the **XColor** structure is set to the value of the existing colormap cell. Otherwise, **XAllocColor()** attempts to store the given color components in the next available cell of the colormap **cmap**. If successful, the function fills in the **pixel** member of the **XColor** structure to the newly allocated color cell and returns a status of **True**.

To see how this function is used, let's write a function named **get_pixel()** that allocates a color cell from the default colormap and loads it with a color. The function takes a widget and the red, green, and blue components of the desired color as input. It returns a pixel index that refers to the specified color.

```
get_pixel(w, red, green, blue)
   Widget  w;
   int     red, green, blue;
{
   Display *dpy =  XtDisplay(w);
   int      scr =  DefaultScreen(dpy);
   Colormap cmap = DefaultColormap(dpy, scr);
   XColor   color;
   /*
    * Fill in the color structure.
    */
   color.red   = red;
   color.green = green;
   color.blue  = blue;
   /*
    * Try to allocate the color.
    */
```

```
    if(XAllocColor(dpy, cmap, &color))
       return (color.pixel);
    else {
       printf("Warning: Couldn't allocate requested color\n");
       return (BlackPixel(dpy, scr));
    }
}
```

Whenever color allocation fails, applications should always be prepared to use one of the default values, usually black or white, available in all visual types. Applications can use the macros

```
BlackPixel(display, screen)
WhitePixel(display, screen)
```

to access the default pixels representing black and white on a particular screen.

Because new colors are allocated in the next available cell of the colormap, applications must not assume that the index representing a particular color in a shared colormap is the same each time the application runs. The exact index used to refer to a particular color depends on the order in which all applications request the colors.

Applications sometimes need to know the color components stored in any pixel index of a colormap. The function

```
XQueryColor(display, cmap, &color)
```

fills in the RGB components of the **color** structure corresponding to the **pixel** member of that structure. The function

```
XQueryColors(display, cmap, colors, ncolors)
```

fills in the RGB components of an array of colors.

Sometimes applications need to set up the colormap in a specific way, controlling the colors in each cell. Such applications should first allocate the number of color cells needed, using the function

```
XAllocColorCells(display, cmap, contig, &plane_masks,
                      nplanes, cells, ncells)
```

This function allocates $ncells * 2^{nplanes}$ read-write color cells. Applications that do not need to control the bit planes of the screen can specify **nplanes** as zero.[1]

XAllocColorCells() allocates read-write color cells. If the application requires the color cells to be contiguous, it must set **contig** argument to **True**, otherwise the

1. A common mistake is to attempt to allocate all planes and all color cells. This generates more colors than the screen supports. For example, on a screen with 4 bit-planes (and therefore 16 colors), a request such as

```
XAllocColorCells(display, cmap, TRUE, &planes, 4, &cells, 16);
```

attempts to allocate $16 * 2^4$, or 256 colors.

planes and cells are allocated from wherever they are available. **XAllocColorCells()** fails and returns a status of **False** it cannot allocate the exact number of planes and cells. If the function is able to allocate the requested number of colors, it returns the allocated color cells in **cells**, which must be an integer array created by the application. If the application requested one or more planes, each bit set in the **plane_mask** argument represents one of the allocated planes.

Once color cells are allocated, applications can use the function

```
XStoreColor(display, cmap, &color)
```

to alter the values stored in each cell of the colormap. The **color** argument must be an **XColor** structure containing both the **pixel** value and the **red, green** and **blue** values to store in that cell. Let's see how this works by defining a function, **load_rgb()**, that loads the colors red, green, and blue into three consecutive color cells of the default colormap. The pixel indexes are assigned to the parameters **red**, **green**, and **blue**.

```
load_rgb(w, red, green, blue)
   Widget  w;
   int     *red, *green, *blue;
{
   Display *dpy  = XtDisplay(w);
   int      scr  = DefaultScreen(dpy);
   Colormap cmap = DefaultColormap(dpy, scr);
   XColor   color;
   int      cells[3];
  /*
   *  Try to allocate three consecutive color cells.
   */
  if(XAllocColorCells(dpy, cmap, True,
                          NULL, 0, cells, 3)){
    /*
    *  If successful, create a red color struct, and store
     *  it in the first allocated cell.
     */
    color.red = 65535;
    color.green = color.blue = 0;
    *red = color.pixel = cells[0];
    XStoreColor(dpy, cmap, &color);
    /*
     *  Store Green in the second cell.
     */
    color.green = 65535;
    color.red =  color.blue = 0;
```

```
        *green = color.pixel = cells[1];
        XStoreColor(dpy, cmap, &color);
        /*
         * Store Blue in the second cell.
         */
        color.blue = 65535;
        color.red = color.green = 0;
        *blue = color.pixel = cells[2];
        XStoreColor(dpy, cmap, &color);
      }
      else{
        printf("Warning:Couldn't allocate color cells\n");
        *blue = *red = *green = BlackPixel(dpy, scr);
      }
    }
```

The function

```
XStoreColors(display, colormap, colors, ncolors)
```

stores multiple colors with a single request. The colors argument must be an array of XColor structures and ncolors indicates the number of colors in the array.

Xlib also provides functions that allow applications to refer to colors by their symbolic names. Color names are stored in a database along with their RGB components. The location and format of this database is operating-system-dependent. On UNIX systems the color database files can be found in the directory /usr/lib/X11/. The file rgb.txt contains a human-readable version of the database.

The color database distributed with X defines many common colors, and users can add additional colors. The function

```
XLookupColor(display, cmap, name, &color, &exact)
```

returns the color components corresponding to a named color in the color database. If the color exists in the database, **XLookupColor()** fills in the **red**, **green**, and **blue** members of the **XColor** structures color and exact. The **color** argument contains the closest color supported by the screen, while **exact** indicates the precise value of color components specified in the color database. The **cmap** argument must specify a colormap ID. **XLookupColor()** uses this colormap only to determine the visual type of the screen on which the color is used. This function does not allocate or store the color in the colormap.

Applications can also allocate colors by name, using the function

```
XAllocNamedColor(display, cmap, name, &color, &exact)
```

This function is similar to **XAllocColor()**, except that the color is specified by name. Let's use **XAllocNamedColor()** to write a function called **get_pixel_by_name()**.

This function is similar to the **get_pixel()** function described earlier, but it returns a pixel index for a named color.

```
get_pixel_by_name(w, colorname)
   Widget w;
   char   *colorname;
{
  Display *dpy   = XtDisplay(w);
  int      scr   = DefaultScreen(dpy);
  Colormap cmap = DefaultColormap(dpy, scr);
  XColor   color, ignore;
  /*
   * Allocate the named color.
   */
  if(XAllocNamedColor(dpy, cmap, colorname, &color, &ignore))
    return (color.pixel);
  else{
    printf("Warning: Couldn't allocate color %s\n",colorname);
    return (BlackPixel(dpy, scr));
  }
}
```

6.2 EXAMPLE: A COLORMAP EDITOR

This section demonstrates how these Xlib color functions are used in a program named **coloredit** that allows the user to edit a colormap interactively. The color editor allocates color cells in the default colormap and allows the user to alter the red, green, and blue components stored in each cell. This program allows the user to change the colors used by other applications by installing a new colormap which duplicates the default colormap of the screen.

Fig. 6.2 shows the window layout of the **coloredit** program. The top row of buttons displays the colors available for editing. The user chooses a color cell for editing by selecting one of these buttons using the mouse. The color of the currently selected button can then be edited using the three sliders located below the buttons. Each slider allows the user to set the intensity of one component of the current color. A StaticText widget also displays the numeric values of the red, green, and blue components of the current color, scaled to the range 0-255. Although the X server supports colors in the range of 0-65535, the rgb.txt file distributed with X specifies colors in the range of 0-255. A program named rgb compiles the colors into the 0-65535 range. Since the user must enter colors into the rgb.txt file in the narrower range it is more useful for the coloredit program to scale colors to the same range.

When the user selects a color button, each of the three sliders moves to the position corresponding to the red, green, and blue values of the button's current color.

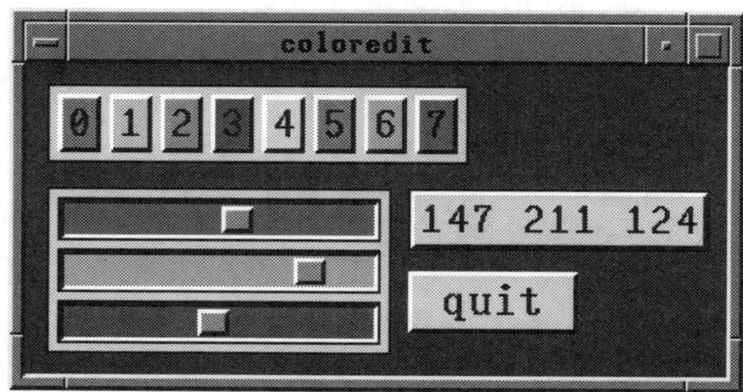

Figure 6.2 The coloredit Program.

6.2.1 The Header File: coloredit.h

The file coloredit.h includes the Xt Intrinsics and X Widget header files for the widgets used by coloredit, declares several callbacks, and defines the resources and global parameters used in the example

```
/*****************************************************
 * coloredit.h: Header file for coloredit
 *****************************************************/

#include <X11/StringDefs.h>
#include <X11/Intrinsic.h>
#include <Xw/Xw.h>
#include <Xw/BBoard.h>
#include <Xw/Valuator.h>
#include <Xw/RCManager.h>
#include <Xw/SText.h>
#include <Xw/PButton.h>

#define MAXCOLORS   256

Display    *dpy;
Colormap    edit_colormap;
XColor      current_color;
int         ncolors;
```

```
Widget          red_slider,
                blue_slider,
                green_slider,
                color_display_panel;

void            slider_selected();
void            slider_moved();
void            set_current_pixel();
Widget          make_slider();
```

The global variable, **ncolors**, stores the total number of colors available to be edited. **MAXCOLORS** determines the maximum number of colors the program can edit. The variable **edit_colormap** stores the ID of an editable colormap, while **current_color** is an **XColor** structure used to set a color cell.

6.2.2 The Source File, coloredit.c

The file coloredit.c contains the main body of the **coloredit** program. The program first uses the Xlib macro **DisplayCells()** to determine the number of colors the screen supports and gets the ID of the default colormap. It then initializes an array of **XColor** structures to represent each color cell in the colormap. The color components in each cell of the colormap are loaded into the **XColor** array using **XQueryColors()**. Then, the program makes a copy of the default colormap by creating a new color map and storing the colors from the default colormap. Finally the new colormap is installed as the current colormap.[2] This allows the editor to change the colors of the colormap including those used by other applications.

After setting up the colormap, coloredit creates the widgets and installs the event handlers and callbacks used to edit the colormap.

```
/*****************************************************
 * coloredit.c: A simple color editor.
 *****************************************************/

#include "coloredit.h"

main(argc, argv)
  int    argc;
  char  *argv[];
{
```

2. Caution! Some window managers will not allow an application to install a new colormap. You may have to try this program with no window manager or experiment with different window managers.

```
  Widget     toplevel, bb, controls;
  Colormap   def_colormap;
  XColor     Colors[MAXCOLORS];
  int        i;
 /*
  * Initialize Intrinsics and save pointer to the display.
  */
  toplevel = XtInitialize(argv[0], "Coloredit", options,
                          XtNumber(options), &argc, argv);
  dpy = XtDisplay(toplevel);
  /*
   * Get the number of colors to be edited from
   * the resource database.
   */
  ncolors = DisplayCells(dpy, DefaultScreen(dpy));
  /*
   * Get the ID of the default colormap.
   */
  def_colormap = DefaultColormap(dpy, DefaultScreen(dpy));
  /*
   * Initialize the Colors array to indicate each
   * available pixel.
   */
  for( i = 0; i < DisplayCells(dpy,0); i++ ) {
     Colors[i].pixel = i;
     Colors[i].flags = DoRed|DoGreen|DoBlue;
  }
  /*
   * Fetch the RGB colors for each cell in the def_olormap.
   */
  XQueryColors( dpy, def_colormap, Colors, ncolors);
  /*
   * Create a new colormap with all cells allocated, and
   * store the colors retrieved from the default colormap
   * in the new colormap.
   */
  edit_colormap =
     XCreateColormap(dpy, DefaultRootWindow(dpy),
                     DefaultVisual(dpy, DefaultScreen(dpy)),
                     AllocAll);
  XStoreColors( dpy, edit_colormap, Colors, ncolors);
  /*
```

```
 * Install the new colormap.
 */
XInstallColormap( dpy, edit_colormap);
/*
 * Initialize the pixel member of the global color struct
 * To the first editable color cell.
 */
current_color.pixel = 0;
/*
 * Create a base for the sliders and color buttons.
 */
bb = XtCreateManagedWidget("base",
                           XwbulletinWidgetClass,
                           toplevel, NULL, 0);

/*
 * Create a static text to display the current rgb values.
 */
color_display_panel =
          XtCreateManagedWidget("display",
                                XwstatictextWidgetClass,
                                bb, NULL,0);

/*
 * Create a row column widget containing three sliders,
 * one for each color component.
 */
controls = XtCreateManagedWidget("sliderpanel",
                                 XwrowColWidgetClass,
                                 bb, NULL, 0);
red_slider   = make_slider("red",  controls);
green_slider = make_slider("green",controls);
blue_slider  = make_slider("blue", controls);
/*
 * Create a row of buttons, one for each
 * color to be edited.
 */
create_color_bar(bb);
/*
 * Add a quit button.
 */
create_quit_button("quit", bb);
```

```
    XtRealizeWidget(toplevel);
    XtMainLoop();
}
```

Fig. 6.3 shows the widget tree created by the **coloredit** program.

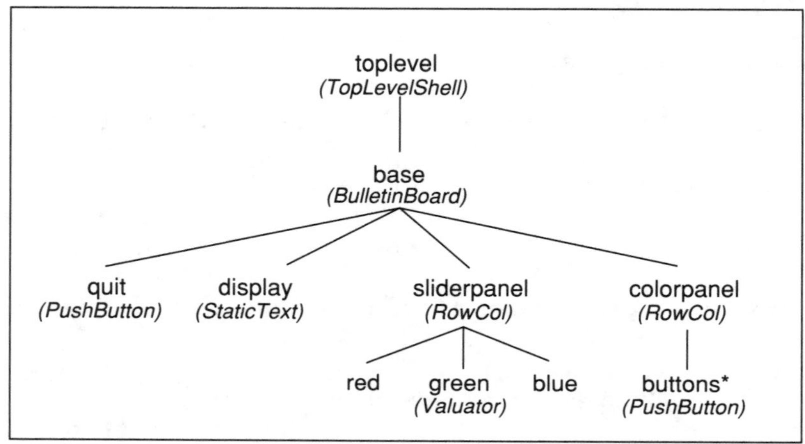

Figure 6.3 The coloredit widget tree.

The function **make_slider()** creates a Valuator widget used to control one color component and assigns the associated callbacks. The range between the minimum and maximum values of the slider allows us to map directly between the position of a slider and the color component (scaled from 0 to 255) controlled by the slider. The minimum value of the slider, zero, corresponds to zero contribution from that color component, while the maximum valuator position (255 plus the extent of the movable slider bar) corresponds to a one hundred percent contribution of the color.

```
Widget make_slider(name, parent)
  char   *name;
  Widget parent;
{
  Widget  w;
  int     n, max, slider_size;
  Arg     wargs[1];

  /*
   * Create a Valuator widget.
   */
  w = XtCreateManagedWidget(name, XwvaluatorWidgetClass,
```

```
                                    parent, NULL, 0);
  /*
   * Add callbacks to be invoked when the slider moves.
   */
  XtAddCallback(w, XtNsliderMoved, slider_moved,    NULL);
  XtAddCallback(w, XtNareaSelected, slider_selected, NULL);
  /*
   * Get the size of the slider, which may have
   * been set by the user.
   */
  n = 0;
  XtSetArg(wargs[n], XtNsliderExtent, &slider_size); n++;
  XtGetValues(w, wargs, n);
  /*
   * Set the valuator to range between zero and
   * 255 + the slider size.
   */
  n = 0;
  max = 255 + slider_size;
  XtSetArg(wargs[n], XtNsliderMin, 0); n++;
  XtSetArg(wargs[n], XtNsliderMax, max); n++;
  XtSetValues(w, wargs, n);

  return (w);
}
```

The function **create_colorbar()** creates a row of buttons, one button for each color to be edited, managed by a RowCol widget. This function sets the background color of each button to one of the pixel values allocated for editing.

```
create_color_bar(parent)
  Widget parent;
{
  Widget  panel, button;
  int     i, n;
  char    name[10];
  Arg     wargs[1];

  /*
   * Create the row column manager to hold all
   * color buttons.
   */
  panel = XtCreateManagedWidget("colorpanel",
```

```
                                        XwrowColWidgetClass,
                                        parent, NULL, 0);
  /*
   * Create ncolors buttons. Use the color
   * cell number as the name of each button. Add a
   * XtNselect callback for each button with the color
   * index as client_data.
   */
  for(i=0;i<ncolors;i++){
   n = 0;
   XtSetArg(wargs[n], XtNbackground, i); n++;
   sprintf(name, "%d", i);
   button = XtCreateManagedWidget(name,
                                   XwpushButtonWidgetClass,
                                   panel, wargs, n);
   XtAddCallback(button, XtNselect, set_current_pixel, i);
  }
}
```

Whenever the user moves a slider, the Intrinsics invokes the callback function **slider_moved()**. This function sets the corresponding member of global **XColor** structure, **current_color**, to the value indicated by the current position of the valuator, provided by the Valuator widget as call data. This color structure is used to update the color of the button corresponding to the color currently being edited and always contains the current value of each color component. When the user selects a color button, the function **set_current_pixel()** sets the **pixel** member of **current_color**. Before the **slider_moved()** callback returns, the function **update_color()** is called to update the color components displayed in the StaticText widget.

```
void slider_moved(w, client_data, sliderpos)
     Widget   w;
     caddr_t  client_data;
     int      sliderpos;
{
 /*
  * Set the appropriate color components of  the global
  * current_color structure, depending on which color
  * slider has moved.
  */
  if(w == red_slider){
    current_color.red = sliderpos * 256;
  }
  else
```

```
     if(w == green_slider){
      current_color.green = sliderpos * 256;
     }
     else
       if(w == blue_slider){
         current_color.blue = sliderpos * 256;
       }
   /*
    * Update the digital rgb display and the current
    * color button.
    */
   update_color();
 }
```

The callback **slider_selected()** moves the valuator slider to the spot where the user clicked the mouse and then calls the **XtNsliderMoved** callbacks to perform the actions that correspond to moving the slider. The function

```
XtCallCallbacks(widget, callback_list, call_data)
```

invokes all callbacks registered with the specified widget for the given callback list. The last argument specifies the data passed to each callback function as call data.

```
void slider_selected(w, ignore, sliderpos)
     Widget   w;
     caddr_t  ignore;
     int      sliderpos;
{
  Arg wargs[1];
  /*
   * Move the slider bar to the selected point.
   */
  XtSetArg(wargs[0], XtNsliderOrigin, sliderpos);
  XtSetValues(w, wargs, 1);
  /*
   * Call the callback list for XtNsliderMoved to
   * alter the colors appropriately.
   */
  XtCallCallbacks(w, XtNsliderMoved, sliderpos);
}
```

This is a commonly needed function and so we can place it in the libXs library, where it can be reused by other examples.

The function **update_color()** scales the values in the global **current_color** structure, and prints the resulting values into a string that is then displayed in the Static-

Text widget. The scaling is necessary because the colors components range from 0 to 65535 and we want to display them in the range between 0 to 255.

```
update_color()
{
  Arg  wargs[1];
  char str[25];

  /*
   * Update the digital display.
   */
  sprintf(str, "%3d %3d %3d", current_color.red   / 256,
                              current_color.green / 256 ,
                              current_color.blue  / 256);
  XtSetArg(wargs[0], XtNstring, str);
  XtSetValues(color_display_panel, wargs, 1);
  /*
   * Update the current color button.
   */
  XStoreColor(dpy, edit_colormap, &current_color);
}
```

The callback **set_current_pixel()** is invoked when the user selects a button in the color bar. This function sets the pixel member of the global **XColor** structure **current_color** to the pixel corresponding to the selected button. The **flags** member of the color structure is also set to the mask **DoRed|DoGreen|DoBlue**. The Xlib function **XQueryColor()** is used to initialize the **red**, **green**, and **blue** members of **current_color** to the components currently shown by the selected button. **XQueryColor()** fills in the existing RGB blue components of an **XColor** structure, given a pixel index. Finally, **set_current_pixel()** invokes the functions on the **XtNareaSelected** callback list of each slider, using the components of the current color as the call data, to move each slider to the appropriate position.

```
void set_current_pixel(w, number, call_data)
  Widget   w;
  int      number;
  caddr_t  call_data;
{
  current_color.flags = DoRed | DoGreen | DoBlue;
  /*
   * Get the current color components of the selected button.
   */
  current_color.pixel = number;
```

```
    XQueryColor(dpy, edit_colormap, &current_color);
    /*
     * Use each color component to as the new
     * position of the corresponding slider.
     */
    XtCallCallbacks(red_slider, XtNareaSelected,
                    current_color.red / 256);
    XtCallCallbacks(green_slider, XtNareaSelected,
                    current_color.green / 256);
    XtCallCallbacks(blue_slider, XtNareaSelected,
                    current_color.blue / 256);
}
```

6.2.3 The Class Resource File: Coloredit

Because the color editor uses the BulletinBoard widget to manage the buttons and sliders used to edit colors, we need to specify the position of each widget in a resource files. The class resource file, Coloredit, corresponding to the layout shown in Fig. 6.2 contains:

```
#########################################################
# Coloredit: Resources for the coloredit program
#########################################################
#
*base.geometry:                  =400x400
#
# Set the location of the digital display
#
*display*x:                      180
*display*y:                       60
*display*height:                  30
*display*width:                  140
#
# Set the location of color buttons
#
*colorpanel*x:                    10
*colorpanel*y:                    10
*colorpanel*singleRow:           True
*colorpanel*layoutType:          maximum_columns
#
# Position the color controls
#
*sliderpanel.x:                   10
```

```
*sliderpanel.y:                   60
*sliderpanel.columns:              1
*sliderpanel*singleRow:          False
*sliderpanel*layoutType:         requested_columns
#
# Specify the valuator orientation and size
#
*Valuator*slideOrientation: horizontal
*Valuator*width:                 150
#
# Place the quit button.
*quit*x:                         180
*quit*y:                         100
```

Notice that the widgets in this program are organized so that the user can specify the location of functionally related groups of widgets, but cannot separate widgets that belong together. For example, all buttons used to select colors are grouped in a RowCol widget. The user can specify the location of this color bar, and also control whether the buttons are arranged vertically in a single column, horizontally in a single row, or in a matrix. Similarly, the Valuator widgets can be oriented horizontally or vertically, in rows or columns, anywhere within the application window. However, they cannot be completely separated. This is one way the programmer can allow the user to achieve drastically different layouts, while maintaining some control over the appearance of the program. It is also easier for the user to customize such a configuration than if each widget had to be placed individually.

6.3 SUMMARY

This chapter introduced the use of color in the X Window System. X provides a uniform color model that supports the design of portable applications across many types of displays, from monochrome to "true color" displays. It is important for programmers to be aware of the X color model and use it correctly so that their applications function properly on as many display type as possible.

The number of colors available, and also how colors can be used, depends on the visual type of the hardware. One common screen type is **PseudoColor**, which allows applications to display a large number of colors, although only a subset of the available colors can be used at once.

X associates a colormap with each window. A colormap contains the colors potentially available to an application. At any given time, one or more colormaps are installed into the hardware, so that the colors can be displayed. Applications specify colors in the color map using an index, or pixel. The server maintains the contents of each colormap. Applications can request the serve to allocate sharable, read/write color cells in a colormap, or private, read-only cells. Xlib provides many functions for allocating and manipulating the colors in a colormap.

7

MANIPULATING RASTER IMAGES

X provides many functions for creating and manipulating images that are stored in off-screen memory in addition to those displayed on the screen. These images fall into three categories: *pixmaps, bitmaps*, and *images*. This chapter introduces the Xlib functions for creating and manipulating these images and briefly describes how they are used.

7.1 PIXMAPS

A pixmap is a chunk of memory similar to a rectangular region of the screen, except that pixmaps are stored in *off-screen memory* and therefore are not visible to the user. Pixmaps have a depth, which is often, but not necessarily, the same as the depth of the screen with which it is associated. The function

```
XCreatePixmap(display, drawable, width, height, depth)
```

creates a pixmap of **width** by **height** pixels. Each pixel contains **depth** bits. The new pixmap is associated with the same screen as the specified **drawable**. The pixmap can be used only on this screen, or on a screen with the same visual type. Applications can deallocate pixmaps when they are no longer needed using the Xlib function

```
XFreePixmap(display, pixmap)
```

Pixmaps are drawables and can be used as destinations for text and graphics operations the same as windows. Because data can also be copied between drawables, pixmaps can be used to store off-screen representations of windows. Pixmaps can be used to specify clipping regions for graphics operations and can also be combined with other graphics operations to create patterns used by many Xlib graphics primitives.

7.2 BITMAPS

A pixmap with a depth of one is referred to as a bitmap. Applications can create a bitmap by specifying a depth of one in the function **XCreatePixmap()**. However, Xlib also provides functions used specifically to create bitmaps. The function

```
XCreateBitmapFromData(display, drawable, data, width, height)
```

creates a bitmap of **width** by **height** from the specified **data**, which must be a series of bits that represent the value of each pixel in the bitmap. One easy way to generate the data for a bitmap is to create it interactively using the standard editor, **bitmap**, usually distributed with X. This program creates a file that can be included directly in a program. The directory

```
/usr/include/X11/bitmaps/
```

also contains some predefined bitmap files. For example, the file

```
/usr/include/X11/bitmaps/xlogo64
```

defines the data for a bitmap of the X logo shown in Fig. 7.1.

Figure 7.1 A bitmap of the X logo.

7.3 COPYING BETWEEN DRAWABLES

The contents of a drawable (a window or a pixmap) may be copied to any other drawable that has the same depth using the function

```
XCopyArea(display, src, dest, gc, src_x, src_y,
          width, height, dest_x, dest_y)
```

XCopyArea() copies the rectangular region of size **width** by **height**, starting at coordinate **(src_x, src_y)** in the **src** drawable, to **(dest_x, dest_y)** in the **dest** drawable. The graphics context, **gc**, controls how the bits from the source drawable are combined with the bits in the destination drawable. If the source and destination drawables do not have the same depth, the server generates a **BadMatch** error.

Applications can use the function

```
XCopyPlane(display, src, dest, gc, src_x, src_y,
           width, height, dest_x, dest_y, plane)
```

to copy data between drawables of different depths. **XCopyPlane()** copies the contents of a single plane of the specified region in the source drawable to the destination drawable. The graphics context determines the foreground and background color of the pattern in the destination drawable.

Let's examine a simple program named **xlogo** that uses bitmaps and pixmaps to display the X logo shown in Fig. 7.1. The header portion of the program includes the widget header files, the xlogo64 bitmap file, and declares a bitmap, a pixmap, and a graphics context used by the program. The body of the program creates a WorkSpace widget in which to display the pixmap and registers the function **redisplay()** as a callback to be invoked when the widget's window needs to be refreshed. It then calls the function **create_logo()** to create and initialize a pixmap containing the X logo.

```
/**********************************************
 * xlogo.c: Display the X logo
 **********************************************/

#include <X11/StringDefs.h>
#include <X11/Intrinsic.h>
#include <Xw/Xw.h>
#include <Xw/WorkSpace.h>
#include <X11/Xutil.h>
#include "xlogo64"
Pixmap   Xpix;
Pixmap   Xbits;
GC       gc;
```

```
void     redisplay();

main(argc, argv)
  int   argc;
  char *argv[];
{
  Widget toplevel, canvas;

  toplevel = XtInitialize(argv[0], "Xlogo", NULL, 0,
                          &argc, argv);
  /*
   * Create a widget in which to display the logo.
   */
  canvas = XtCreateManagedWidget("canvas",
                                 XwworkSpaceWidgetClass,
                                 toplevel, NULL, 0);
  XtAddCallback(canvas, XtNexpose, redisplay, NULL);
  /*
   * Realize the widget before creating the pixmap,
   * because create_logo needs the window to exist.
   */
  XtRealizeWidget(toplevel);
  /*
   * Generate the logo.
   */
  create_logo(canvas);
  XtMainLoop();
}
```

The function **create_logo()** creates a pixmap containing the X logo. The widget passed to **create_logo()** must already be realized, because the function uses the widget's window ID. First, the function uses **XCreateBitmapFromData()** to create a bitmap from the data declared in the header file xlogo64. **XCreatePixmap()** creates a pixmap of the same width and height as the bitmap, but with the default depth of the screen. After creating a graphics context using the colors of the WorkSpace widget, **XCopyPlane()** copies the logo from the single plane of the bitmap to the pixmap.[1] The graphics context determines the foreground and background colors of the pixmap. Since the bitmap is no longer needed, we can use **XFreePixmap()** to free it.

---

1. This is an example of an area where many programmers introduce portability problems into their programs. A programmer using a single-plane system (black-and-white screen) can use XCopyArea() to copy the bitmap to the pixmap, or to a window, because both the bitmap and the destination drawable have the same depth. However, such a program will fail when run on a multiplane system.

```
 create_logo(w)
   Widget   w;
{
  Arg       wargs[2];
  int       n;
  XGCValues values;
  /*
   * Play it safe. Make sure the widget's window exists.
   */
  if(!XtIsRealized(w))
    XtError("Can't display a pixmap in an unrealized widget");
  /*
   * Create a bitmap from the data.
   */
  Xbits = XCreateBitmapFromData(XtDisplay(w), XtWindow(w),
                                xlogo64_bits, xlogo64_width,
                                xlogo64_height);

  /*
   * Create a pixmap of the same depth as the default screen.
   */
  Xpix = XCreatePixmap(XtDisplay(w), XtWindow(w),
                       xlogo64_width, xlogo64_height,
                       DefaultDepthOfScreen(XtScreen(w)));
  /*
   * Use the foreground and background colors
   * of the widget to create a graphics context.
   */
  n = 0;
  XtSetArg(wargs[n], XtNforeground, &values.foreground);n++;
  XtSetArg(wargs[n], XtNbackground, &values.background);n++;
  XtGetValues(w, wargs, n);
  gc = XtGetGC(w, GCForeground | GCBackground, &values);
  /*
   * Copy the contents of plane 1 of the bitmap to the
   * pixmap, using the widget's colors.
   */
  XCopyPlane(XtDisplay(w), Xbits, Xpix, gc, 0, 0,
             xlogo64_width, xlogo64_height, 0, 0, 1);
  /*
   * We don't need the bitmap anymore, so free it.
```

```
    */
   XFreePixmap(XtDisplay(w), Xbits);
 }
```

The function **redisplay()** is registered as an **XtNexpose** callback function.. The WorkSpace widget calls all callback functions on this list when the widget's window needs to be redrawn. The **redisplay()** callback function checks the current width and height of the widget and then uses **XCopyArea()** to transfer the contents of the pixmap to the center of the WorkSpace widget's window.

```
void redisplay (w, data, region)
     Widget     w;
     caddr_t    data;
     Region     region;
{
  Arg wargs[2];
  Dimension widget_width, widget_height;
  /*
   * Get the current size of the widget window.
   */
  XtSetArg(wargs[0], XtNwidth,  &widget_width);
  XtSetArg(wargs[1], XtNheight, &widget_height);
  XtGetValues(w, wargs,2);
  /*
   * Copy the contents of the pixmap to the
   * center of the window.
   */
  XCopyArea(XtDisplay(w), Xpix, XtWindow(w), gc, 0, 0,
            xlogo64_width, xlogo64_height,
            (widget_width  - xlogo64_width) / 2,
            (widget_height - xlogo64_height) / 2);
}
```

This example illustrates many of the Xlib functions that create and initialize bitmaps and pixmaps, and also shows how data can be transferred between bitmaps, pixmaps, and windows. However, you may have noticed that one step in this example is unnecessary. The **redisplay()** callback could use **XCopyPlane()** to copy directly between the bitmap and the widget window, completely eliminating the need for the pixmap. Using this approach, we can define **create_logo()** as

```
create_logo(w)
  Widget w;
{
  Arg          wargs[2];
```

```
    XGCValues values;
    /*
     * Make sure the widget's window exists.
     */
    if(!XtIsRealized(w))
      XtError("Create logo requires a realized widget\n");
    /*
     * Create a bitmap containing the logo.
     */
    Xbits = XCreateBitmapFromData(XtDisplay(w),
                                  XtWindow(w),
                                  xlogo64_bits, xlogo64_width,
                                  xlogo64_height);
    /*
     * Create a graphics context using the foreground
     * and background colors of the widget.
     */
    XtSetArg(wargs[0], XtNforeground, &values.foreground);
    XtSetArg(wargs[1], XtNbackground, &values.background);
    XtGetValues(w, wargs, 2);
    gc = XtGetGC(w, GCForeground | GCBackground, &values);
  }
```

Now, we can write the **redisplay()** callback as

```
  void redisplay (w, data, region)
       Widget    w;
       caddr_t   data;
       Region    region;
  {
    Arg wargs[2];
    Dimension widget_width, widget_height;
    /*
     * Get the current size of the widget window.
     */
    XtSetArg(wargs[0], XtNwidth,  &widget_width);
    XtSetArg(wargs[1], XtNheight, &widget_height);
    XtGetValues(w, wargs,2);
    /*
     * Copy plane 1 of the bitmap to the center
     * of the window, using the widget's foreground
     * and background color.
     */
```

```
    XCopyPlane(XtDisplay(w), Xbits, XtWindow(w), gc, 0, 0,
               xlogo64_width, xlogo64_height,
               (widget_width - xlogo64_width)/ 2,
               (widget_height - xlogo64_height)/ 2, 1);
}
```

7.4 TILES

A *tile* is another name for a pixmap. Pixmaps are usually referred to as tiles when they are used to generate a repeating pattern in a window. Such pixmaps are often small (16 pixels wide by 16 pixels high, for example) and are usually used to produce a repeating pattern.

The X Widget library includes a function that provides an easy way for applications to create some common tiling patterns. The function

```
XwCreateTile (screen, foreground, background, pattern)
```

returns a pixmap with the depth of the specified screen, using the given foreground and background colors. The function creates a tile that is 16 pixels wide and also 16 pixels high. The possible pixmap patterns are defined as constants in the file Xw.h. These constants are

XwFOREGROUND	**XwBACKGROUND**	**Xw25_FOREGROUND**
Xw50_FOREGROUND	**Xw75_FOREGROUND**	**XwVERTICAL_TILE**
XwHORIZONTAL_TILE	**XwSLANT_RIGHT**	**XwSLANT_LEFT**

XwCreateTile() caches the tile for efficiency, and therefore applications should treat them as read only. Fig. 7.2 shows the patterns provided by **XwCreateTile()**.

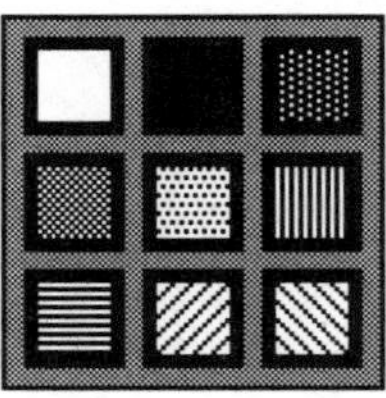

Figure 7.2 Pixmap patterns provided by the HP X widget set.

7.5 IMAGES

X provides a way to transfer images between applications and the server using an **XImage** data structure. This structure stores data in a device-dependent format; therefore applications should never access the data directly. Because the image is stored in the server, the server handles byte swapping and other data transformations that are sometimes necessary between clients running on different machines. The **XImage** data structure contains the pixel data representing the image as well as information about the format of the image.

7.5.1 Creating Images

Applications can allocate an **XImage** data structure using the function

```
XCreateImage(display, visual, depth, format, offset, data,
                width, height, bitmap_pad, bytes_per_line)
```

This function requires a pointer to the **Visual** structure used by the display. The **data** argument must specify an array of bits representing the image. The size of this data is specified by the **width, height** and **depth**. The **format** specifies the byte order of the data and must be one of the constants **XYPixmap** or **ZPixmap**. In **XYPixmap** format each byte of data specifies the values of 8 pixels along one plane of a raster, with one bit of the data going to each pixel. **ZPixmap** format specifies the data *depth-first.* For example, in **XYPixmap** format, on a display with eight bit planes, each byte of data represents one pixel. The argument **bytes_per_line** specifies the number of bytes in one raster and must be a multiple of 8, 16, or 32 bits.

Images may also be extracted from a drawable using the function

```
XGetImage(display, drawable, x, y, width, height,
            plane_mask, format)
```

XGetImage() creates an **XImage** structure, copies a rectangular region of a drawable into the image, and returns a pointer to the **XImage** structure. The argument **plane_mask** determines which planes in the drawable are included in the image, while the **format** argument determines whether the image is created in **XYPixmap** or **ZPixmap** format.

X also provides several other functions for manipulating images, including:

- **XSubImage()** creates a new image and copies the contents of a rectangular sub-region of an old image into the new image.
- **XDestroyImage()** frees an image.
- **XPutPixel()** sets the pixel value of an *(x, y)* location in an **XImage**.
- **XGetPixel()** retrieves the value of a pixel at a particular *(x, y)* location with an **XImage**.
- **XPutImage()** transfers an image to a drawable.

The X Widget set also includes a RasterEdit widget that allows users to create and edit **XImage** structures interactively.

7.5.2 Displaying Images

The X Widget set contains a widget that displays an **XImage** in a selectable window. Fig. 7.2 shows a row of StaticRaster widgets displaying the nine tile patterns provided by the X Widget set. The figure was created by the function **create_raster_widgets()**, which uses a RowCol widget to manage a row of StaticRaster widgets.

```
create_raster_widgets(parent)
   Widget parent;
{
  Widget panel;

  panel = XtCreateManagedWidget("panel", XwrowColWidgetClass,
                                    parent, NULL, 0);
  create_raster(panel, XwFOREGROUND);
  create_raster(panel, XwBACKGROUND);
  create_raster(panel, Xw25_FOREGROUND);
  create_raster(panel, Xw50_FOREGROUND);
  create_raster(panel, Xw75_FOREGROUND);
  create_raster(panel, XwVERTICAL_TILE);
  create_raster(panel, XwHORIZONTAL_TILE);
  create_raster(panel, XwSLANT_RIGHT);
  create_raster(panel, XwSLANT_LEFT);
}
```

The function **create_raster()** creates a StaticRaster widget for a particular tile pattern. This function starts by calling **XwCreateTile()** to create a pixmap. The contents of the pixmap are then copied to an **XImage** structure using **XGetImage()**. The resulting **image** is then displayed by the StaticRaster widget.

```
create_raster(parent, pattern)
     Widget  parent;
     int     pattern;
{
  Display *dpy = XtDisplay(parent);
  int      scr = DefaultScreen(dpy);
  Pixel    white = WhitePixel(dpy, scr);
  Pixel    black = BlackPixel(dpy, scr);
  Pixmap   tile, bitmap;
  XImage  *raster;
  Arg      wargs[5];
  /*
   * Get the indicated tile pattern in black and white.
```

```
     */
    tile = XwCreateTile(XtScreen(parent), white, black,pattern);
    /*
     * Create an XImage containing the contents of the tile.
     */
    raster = XGetImage(dpy, tile, 0, 0, 16, 16,
                       AllPlanes, XYPixmap);
    /*
     * Create a StaticRaster widget to display the image.
     */
    XtSetArg(wargs[0], XtNsRimage,  raster);
    XtCreateManagedWidget("button", XwsrasterWidgetClass,
                          parent, wargs, 1);
}
```

7.6 SUMMARY

This chapter introduced Xlib functions that manipulate raster images. X supports several types of image formats, bitmaps, pixmaps, and **XImage** structures. Pixmaps are drawables, and can be used as destinations for Xlib graphics operations. Pixmaps are stored in off-screen memory, and are useful for storing and manipulating raster images without displaying them on the screen. A bitmap is simply a single-plane pixmap. Tile is another name for pixmap, usually used to refer to a pixmap containing a repeating pattern.

Applications can store images in the server using the Xlib **XImage** structure and its related functions. The primary reason for using **XImages** is to allow images to be transferred between clients running on different machines. Different machines sometimes store data in different formats, and the X server handles the byte swapping required to move images from one machine to another.

The following chapter discusses graphics contexts, a resource that controls how X graphics operations are performed. Graphics contexts affect how images are transferred between drawables such as pixmaps and bitmaps, and pixmaps and bitmaps can also be used by a graphics contexts as patterns to be combined with a drawing operation.

8

GRAPHICS CONTEXTS

All graphics operations use attributes that determine the width of lines, foreground and background colors, fill patterns, fonts to be used when displaying text, and so on. X stores these attributes in an internal data structure known as a *graphics context*, often abbreviated as GC. This chapter discusses the attributes of GCs as well as the Xlib and Intrinsics functions that create and manipulate them. Chapters 9 and 10 show how to use graphics contexts with the X text and graphics functions.

8.1 CREATING GRAPHICS CONTEXTS

The Xlib function

```
XCreateGC(display, drawable, mask, &values)
```

creates a graphics context and returns a resource identifier that applications can use to refer to the GC. The X server maintains the data associated with the graphics context, and all clients must reference the graphics context by its ID. Graphics contexts are associated with a specific drawable, but can be used with any drawable of the same depth on a screen with the same visual type.

Applications can specify the initial value of each component of a graphics context in the **values** argument when calling **XCreateGC()**. This argument must be an **XGCValues** structure, which includes the following members:

```
int           function;     /* logical operation          */
unsigned long plane_mask;   /* plane mask                 */
unsigned long foreground;   /* foreground pixel           */
unsigned long background;   /* background pixel           */
int           line_width;   /* line width (in pixels)     */
int           line_style;   /* LineSolid,
                               LineOnOffDash, or
                               LineDoubleDash             */
int           cap_style;    /* CapNotLast, CapButt,
                               CapRound, CapProjecting    */
int           join_style;   /* JoinMiter, JoinRound,
                               or JoinBevel               */
int           fill_style;   /* FillSolid, FillTiled,
                               FillStippled,
                               or FillOpaqueStippled      */
int           fill_rule;    /* EvenOddRule, WindingRule   */
int           arc_mode;     /* ArcChord, ArcPieSlice      */
Pixmap        tile;         /* tile pixmap for tiling     */
Pixmap        stipple;      /* stipple 1 plane pixmap     */
int           ts_x_origin;/* tile and stipple offset    */
int           ts_y_origin;
Font          font;         /* default text font          */
int     subwindow_mode;     /* ClipByChildren, or
                               IncludeInferiors           */
Bool    graphics_exposures;/*report graphics exposures? */
int     clip_x_origin;      /* clipping origin            */
int     clip_y_origin;
Pixmap  clip_mask;          /* bitmap clipping            */
int     dash_offset;        /* line information           */
char    dashes;
```

The **mask** argument to **XCreateGC()** specifies which members of the **XGCValues** structure contain valid information. If this mask is zero, the GC will be created with default values for all attributes. To override the default value for a particular field, the mask must include a constant corresponding to that fields. Fig. 8.1 lists the GC attribute masks, along with the default values of each attribute.

Mask	Default Value of GC
GCFunction	GXCopy
GCPlaneMask	AllPlanes
GCForeground	0
GCBackground	1
GCLineWidth	0
GCLineStyle	LineSolid

GCCapStyle	CapButt
GCJoinStyle	JoinMiter
GCFillStyle	FillSolid
GCFillRule	EvenOddRule
GCTile	Foreground
GCStipple	0
GCTileStipXOrigin	0
GCTileStipYOrigin	1
GCFont	Implementation-Dependent
GCSubwindowMode	ClipByChildren
GCGraphicsExposures	True
GCClipXOrigin	0
GCClipYOrigin	0
GCClipMask	None
GCDashOffset	0
GCDashList	4
GCArcMode	ArcPieSlice

Figure 8.1 Masks used with graphics contexts.

For example, the following code segment creates a graphics context, specifying the foreground pixel, background pixel, and line style.

```
XGCValues gcv;
GC        gc;
gcv.foreground = 1;
gcv.background = 2;
gcv.line_style = LineOnOffDash;
gc = XCreateGC(display, window,
               GCForeground | GCBackground | GCLineStyle,
               &gcv);
```

The Xt Intrinsics also provides a function for creating graphics contexts

```
XtGetGC(widget, mask, values)
```

This function caches graphics contexts to allow sharing of GCs within an application. Therefore applications must not modify GCs created with **XGetGC()**.

8.2 MANIPULATING GRAPHICS CONTEXTS

After a GC is created, applications can use the function

```
XChangeGC(display, gc, mask, &values)
```

to modify any of the GCs attributes. The **mask** and **values** arguments serve the same function here as they do in **XCreateGC()**. Xlib also provides many convenience functions for modifying individual GC attributes. The following sections introduce many of these functions as we discuss the purpose of each of the attributes of a graphics context.

8.2.1 Display Functions

A graphics context's **GCFunction** attribute specifies a logical display function that determines how each pixel of a new image is combined with the current contents of a destination drawable. The new image, referred to as the *source*, could be copied from another drawable, or be generated by a graphics request. For example, when this attribute is set to **GXcopy**, the source image completely replaces the current contents of the affected region of the drawable. On the other hand, if the same figure is drawn using the **GXor** display function, the bits of the affected region of the drawable are set to the logical OR of the source and the previous contents of the destination. Fig. 8.2 shows the display functions defined in Xlib.h, along with their corresponding logical operations. The **src** parameter represents the bits being written and the **dst** parameter represents the current state of the bits in the drawable.

Mask	Display Function
GXclear	0
GXand	src AND dst
GXandReverse	src AND NOT dst
GXcopy	src
GXandInverted	(NOT src) AND dst
GXnoop	dst
GXxor	src XOR dst
GXor	src OR dst
GXnor	NOT (src OR dst)
GXequiv	(NOT src) XOR dst
GXinvert	NOT dst
GXorReverse	src OR (NOT dst)
GXcopyInverted	NOT src
GXorInverted	(NOT src) OR dst
GXnand	NOT (src AND dst)
GXset	1

Figure 8.2 Display functions.

On color screens, these logical operations are performed bit-wise on each pixel within the affected area. For example, let's see what happens if we draw a line using the **GXand** drawing function and a pixel index of 3 for the foreground color. If we draw the line in a drawable whose background color is pixel 10 on a display with 4 bit planes, the resulting line color is the represented by the pixel 2. This is easier to see if we examine the binary representation of these numbers:

$$3_{10} \text{ AND } 10_{10} = 2_{10}$$
$$0011_2 \text{ AND } 1010_2 = 0010_2$$

The *exclusive-OR* (XOR) function, specified by the constant **GXxor** is a commonly used display function. The **XOR** function has the interesting property that drawing a figure twice in XOR mode restores the screen to its original state. This allows us to erase an image drawn in XOR mode simply by drawing it a second time. (Contrast this with erasing an object on the screen by drawing the object in the background color of the screen). In the latter case, the application must redraw the previous contents of the screen. When an image is redrawn in XOR mode, the original contents of the screen is restored to its previous state, as long as nothing else on the screen has changed. The most common use of the **XOR** display function is for *rubber banding* operations, where an object, often a line or rectangle, on the screen is moved and stretched in response to mouse motion. The **XOR** mode allows the rubber band object to move across other objects on the screen without disturbing them. Chapter 10 presents an example that illustrates rubber banding.

The function

```
XSetFunction(display, gc, function)
```

provides an easy way for applications to alter a graphics context's display function. The default value is **GXcopy**.

8.2.2 Plane Mask

The value of the **GCPlaneMask** attribute determines which bit planes of a drawable are affected by a graphics operation. The plane mask contains a one in each bit that can be modified. The function

```
XSetPlaneMask(display, gc, mask)
```

sets the plane mask of a graphics context. For example, a line drawn with foreground pixel 6 would normally affect bit planes 2 and 3 ($6_{10} = 0110_2$). However, if the plane mask of the graphics context is set to 5_{10} (0101_2), drawing a line with a foreground pixel 6 affects only plane 3, and the resulting line is displayed in the color indicated by the pixel index 4. Applications can use a macro

```
AllPlanes
```

to indicate 1's for all planes supported by a screen. The default value of the **GCPlaneMask** attribute is **AllPlanes**.

8.2.3 Foreground and Background

The **GCForeground** and **GCBackground** attributes of a graphics context indicate the pixels used as foreground and background colors for graphics operations. The pixel index must be an integer between zero and $n - 1$, where n is the number of colors supported by the display. This index is usually obtained using the color allocation functions discussed in Chapter 6. The function

```
XSetForeground(display, gc, pixel)
```

sets the **GCForeground** attribute and the function

```
XSetBackground(display, gc, pixel)
```

sets the **GCBackground** attribute. The default value of **GCForeground** is 0 and the default value of **GCBackground** is 1.

8.2.4 Line Attributes

Several attributes determine how a line is drawn. The **GCLineWidth** controls the width, in pixels, of the line. The default width is 0. The server draws zero width lines one pixel wide using an implementation-dependent algorithm. On displays that have hardware support for line drawing, this is often the fastest way to draw lines. The **GCLineStyle** attribute can be one of the constants

```
LineSolid
LineOnOffDash
LineDoubleDash
```

Fig. 8.3 shows each of these styles. The default value is **LineSolid**.

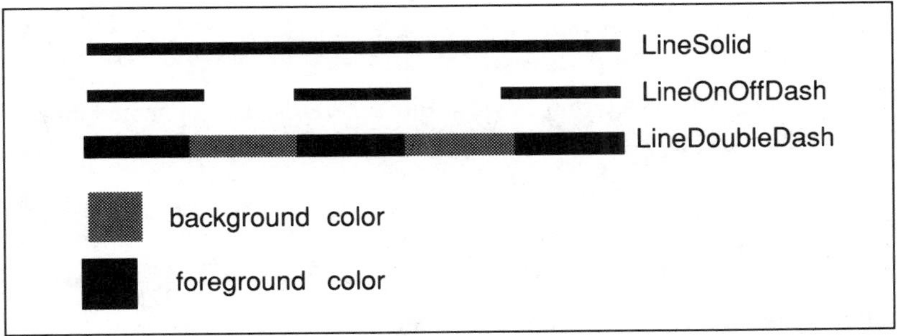

Figure 8.3 Line styles.

Graphics contexts also control how the server draws the ends of wide lines. The **GCCapStyle** of a line can be one of the constants

CapNotLast
CapButt
CapRound
CapProjecting

The default value is **CapButt**. Fig. 8.4 shows how X draws each of these styles.

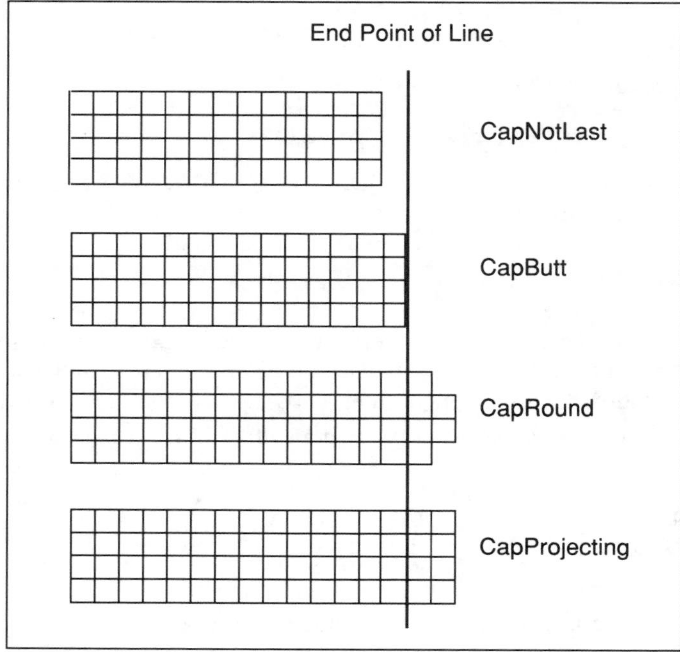

Figure 8.4 Line cap styles.

The graphics context also determines how the server draws connected lines. The style is determined by the **GCJoinStyle** attribute and can be one of the constants

JoinMiter
JoinRound
JoinBevel

Fig. 8.5 illustrates each of these styles. The default style is **JoinMiter**.

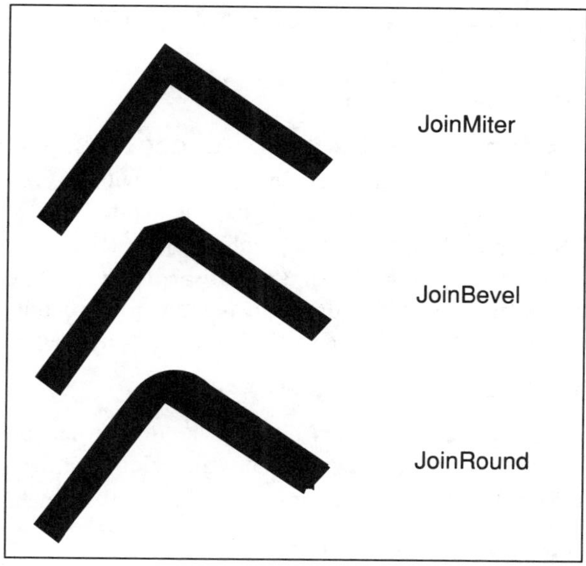

Figure 8.5 Line join styles.

The function

```
XSetLineAttributes(display, gc, width, style,
                   cap_style, join_style)
```

sets a GC's line attributes.

8.2.5 Fill Styles

X allows graphics figures to be *filled* by some color or pattern. The **GCFillStyle** attribute determines how figures are filled and must be one of the constants

```
FillSolid
FillTiled
FillStippled
FillOpaqueStippled
```

Applications can use the function

```
XSetFillStyle(display, gc, style)
```

to set the fill style of a graphics context. The default fill style, **FillSolid**, specifies that figures are to be filled with the current foreground color. The **FillTiled** style indicates that figures are to be filled with the pixmap specified in the **tile** attribute. This pixmap must have the same depth as the drawable with which the graphics context is used. The function

```
XSetTile(display, gc, tile)
```

sets a graphics context's **GCTile** attribute Setting the **GCFillStyle** to **FillStippled** or **FillOpaqueStippled** specifies that regions be filled with a *stipple.* A stipple is a repeating pattern produced by using a bitmap (a pixmap of depth 1) as a mask in the drawing operation. When **FillStippled** is specified, graphics operations only operate on those bits of the stipple pattern that are set to 1. When **FillOpaqueStippled** is specified, bits in the stipple pattern that contain a one are drawn using the foreground color of the graphics context and those that contain a zero are drawn using the background color. The function

```
XSetStipple(display, gc, stipple)
```

sets a **GC**'s stipple pattern. Graphics contexts also use a fill rule attribute, **GCFillRule**, to determine the algorithm used to fill a region. The fill rule must be one of the constants **EvenOddRule** or **WindingRule**. The function

```
XSetFillRule(display, gc, rule)
```

sets the fill rule for a graphics context. Fig. 8.6 shows how the fill rule affects the appearance of a filled polygon. If **EvenOddRule** is specified, the server sets a pixel at a particular point if an imaginary line drawn between the point and the outside of the figure crosses the figure an odd number of times. If **WindingRule** is specified, the server determines whether a point should be filled using an imaginary line between the point and a vertex of the figure. The line is rotated about the point so that it touches each vertex of the figure, in order, until it returns to the original position. If the line makes one or more complete rotations, the point is considered to be inside the figure, and the point is filled.

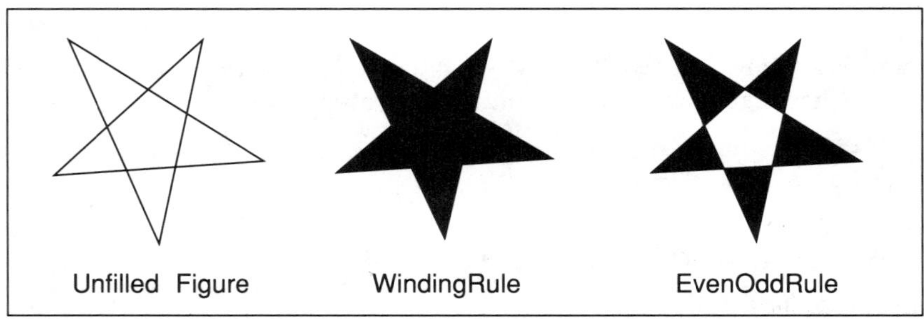

Figure 8.6 Comparison of EvenOddRule and WindingRule.

8.2.6 Fonts

The **GCFont** attribute of a graphics context determines the font used for all text operations. The function

```
XSetFont(display, gc, font_id)
```

sets a graphics context's font attribute. The default font is implementation dependent. Chapter 9 discusses what fonts are and how they are used to display text in a window.

8.2.7 Clip Masks

The **GCClipMask** attribute specifies a bitmap as a clip mask for all drawing operations. If a graphics context has a clip mask, drawing operations affect only those pixels in the drawable that correspond to a 1 in the clip mask. The function

```
XSetClipMask(display, gc, bitmap)
```

sets the bitmap used as a clip mask. The default value is **None**, in which case no clipping is performed. The function

```
XSetClipOrigon(display, gc, x, y)
```

alters the location of the clipmask relative to the origin of the drawable. A clipping region can also be specified as a list of rectangular areas, using the function

```
XSetClipRectangles(display, gc, xoffset, yoffset,
                   rect, nrect, ordering)
```

The arguments **xoffset** and **yoffset** indicate the position of all rectangles relative to the origin of the drawable. The argument **rect** must be an array of **XRectangle** structures. This structure has the members

```
short          x, y;
unsigned short width, height;
```

If the list of rectangles is given as **None**, no clipping is performed. Some X servers can perform clipping more efficiently if they know the order of the rectangles. The **order** argument must specify one of the constants **Unsorted, YSorted, YXSorted,** or **YXBanded** to indicate the order of the rectangles within the array.

8.3 GRAPHICS EXPOSURES

The server generates **GraphicsExpose** events when an **XCopyArea()** or **XCopyPlane()** function is unable to copy an area because the area is occluded by a window. The function

```
XSetGraphicsExposures(display, gc, flag)
```

enables or disables generation of these events for graphics operations that use the graphics context. **GraphicsExpose** events are enabled when **flag** is set to **True**. The default value is **True**.

8.4 REGIONS

X provides a set of utility routines for representing and manipulating non-rectangular areas. For example, applications often need to determine whether an exposed area intersects with the area occupied by a particular object on the screen. To deal with such situations, X provides an *opaque*[1] data type known as a **Region** and a set of functions that operate on regions. Internally, a **Region** consists of an array of rectangles. Applications cannot access the **Region** data structure directly, but must use functions provided by Xlib to manipulate **Region**s. Functions that manipulate regions do not make requests to the server; all calculations are done locally in the client.

Some widgets use regions when reporting exposure events. The **Workspace** widget, for example, provides an **XtNexpose** callback that consolidates the areas contained in all expose events into a single region. This widget passes a **Region** to the application as the **call_data** argument to all **XtNexpose** callback functions. Applications that use **Region**s must include the header file Xutil.h.

The function

```
XCreateRegion()
```

creates and returns a new, empty **Region**. The function

```
XPolygonRegion(points_array, npoints, fill_rule)
```

creates a **Region** representing the polygonal area defined by an array of **XPoint** structures. This structure contains the members

```
short x, y;
```

The function

```
XDestroyRegion(region)
```

destroys a **Region** and frees the memory used by the **Region**. The function

```
XEqualRegion(r1, r2)
```

1. An opaque data structure is one whose true definition is hidden using data abstraction techniques. The public definition of the function is a pointer to a "bogus" structure. The true definition and the procedures that operate on the data are kept in a private file. This same technique is used by the Xt Intrinsics to hide the implementation of widgets, and is discussed in more detail in Chapter 12.

compares two Regions and returns True if they are equal, or False if they are not.

The function

```
XEmptyRegion(region)
```

returns **True** if the given **Region** is empty. A new **Region** defined by the intersection of two **Regions** can obtained using the function:

```
XIntersectRegion(region1, region2, result)
```

For example, we can use **XIntersectRegion()** to write a simple function that determines if two regions intersect

```
does_intersect(region1, region2)
   Region region1, region2;
{
   Region intersection;
   int is_empty;
   /*
    * Get the intersection of the two regions.
    */
   XIntersectRegion(region1, region2, intersection);
   /*
    * Check whether the result is an empty region.
    */
   is_empty = XEmptyRegion(intersection));
   /*
    * Free the region we created before returning the result.
   XDestroyRegion(intersection);
   return (!is_empty);
}
```

The function

```
XPointInRegion(region, x, y)
```

returns **True** if the given (*x*, *y*) point lies within the bounds of the region, while the function

```
XRectInRegion(region, x, y, width, height)
```

determines whether a rectangular area intersects a region. **XRectInRegion()** returns the constant **RectangleIn** if the rectangle is totally contained within the region, **RectangleOut** if the rectangle lies completely outside the region, and **RectanglePart** if the rectangle partially intersects the Region.

The smallest enclosing rectangle of a region can be obtained using the function:

```
XClipBox(region, &rect)
```

When this function returns, the **XRectangle** structure **rect** contains the bounding box of the specified region.

Applications can also use a **Region** as a clip mask in a graphics context. The function

```
XSetRegion(display, gc, region)
```

sets the clip mask of a graphics context. Xlib also includes many other useful functions that operate on **Region**s. These include functions that find the union of two regions, subtract regions, move regions, and so on.

8.5 SUMMARY

This chapter discussed graphics contexts and regions. Graphics contexts control color, style and other attributes used by the Xlib text and graphics primitives. Graphics contexts are maintained by the server and accessed by applications through a resource ID. Xlib provides functions to control the attributes of a graphics context, and the Xt Intrinsics provides a way to cache graphics contexts, so they can be shared within an application.

This chapter also discussed regions, which are often used by graphics to define clipping areas. Regions allow non-rectangular areas to be represented, compared, and manipulated.

The following two chapters show how the topics discussed in this and the previous chapters (graphics contexts, raster images, regions, and color) are used in conjunction with the Xlib text and graphics operations.

9

TEXT AND FONTS

Xlib provides a set of primitive functions for drawing text in a window or pixmap. X draws characters on the screen using bitmaps that represent each character. A *font* is a collection of bitmapped characters. This chapter discusses fonts and presents the Xlib functions that draw text in a window. The chapter also presents examples that combine the elements of the last few chapters with the Xlib text-drawing functions.

9.1 FONTS

A font is a collection of *glyphs*, which are rectangular bitmaps representing an image. Although a glyph may contain any bit pattern, fonts usually contain textual characters.[1] Before an application can use a font, it must load the font into the server. The function

```
XLoadFont(display, font_name)
```

finds and loads the named font, and returns a resource ID that refers to the font. It is common, but not necessary, for fonts to be kept in a file. However, this is an implementation-dependent detail that application programmers do not need to be concerned with.

The function

```
XQueryFont(display, font_ID)
```

1. In addition to English-language alpha-numeric fonts, the X11R2 font set includes a set of chess pieces, fonts for the game "rogue", a set of mouse cursors, and fonts for several different languages. The X11R3 distribution includes font sets contributed by Adobe and Bitstream. The X Consortium does not currently recognize any font set as a standard.

returns an **XFontStruct** structure that contains detailed information about the font. The function

```
XLoadQueryFont(display, name)
```

performs the equivalent of an **XLoadFont()** followed by an **XQueryFont()** and returns the **XFontStruct** information with a single server request. The information in the **XFontStruct** structure includes:

- **fid**: The resource ID used to refer to the font.
- **direction**: A flag that indicates whether the characters in the font are defined left to right or right to left. X supports only horizontally drawn text.
- **min_bounds**: An **XCharStruct** structure that contains the bounding box of the smallest character in the font.
- **max_bounds**: An **XCharStruct** structure that contains the bounding box of the largest character in the font.
- **ascent**: An integer that indicates how far the font extends above the baseline.
- **descent**: An integer that indicates how far the font extends below the baseline.
- **per_char**: An array of **XCharStruct** structures for each character in the font. X fonts can be *mono-spaced* (having the same width) or *proportional* (varying widths between characters).

The **XCharStruct** structure is defined in Xlib.h and contains the following information:

```
short          lbearing;
short          rbearing;
short          width;
short          ascent;
short          descent;
unsigned short attributes;
```

This structure contains information about the size and location of a single character relative to the origin, as shown in Figure 9.1. When specifying the location of a character, the character's origin is the lower left corner of the bounding box.

Xlib provides functions that calculate the size, in pixels, of character strings based on the font used. The function

```
XTextWidth(fontstruct, string, string_length)
```

calculates the pixel length of a character string for a particular font. The function

```
XTextExtents(font, string, string_length, &direction,
             &ascent, &descent, &overall)
```

provides additional information. In addition to the ascent and descent, this function returns the **direction**, **ascent**, and **descent** for the entire string, and also returns an

XCharStruct, **overall**, containing the width, left bearing, and right bearing of the entire string.

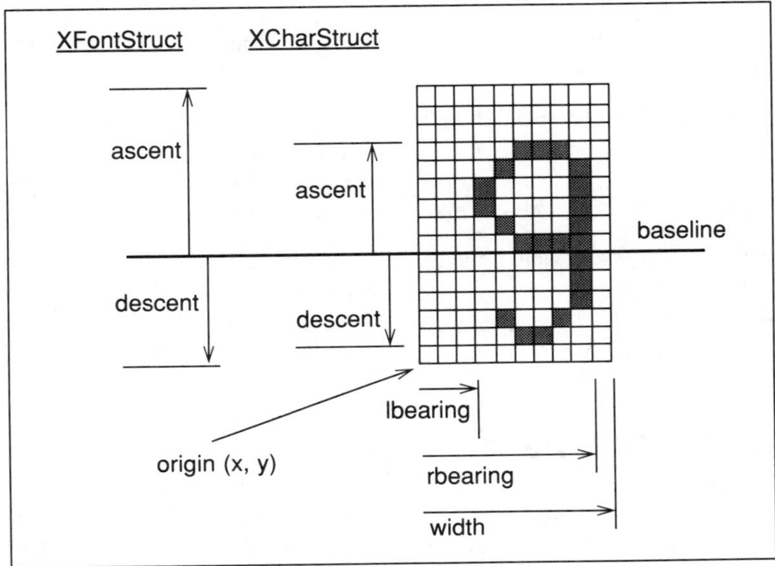

Figure 9.1 Bounding box of a character.

9.2 TEXT OPERATIONS

X displays text in a drawable by performing a fill operation on a region using the text font as a mask. Xlib provides two simple functions for displaying strings:

```
XDrawString(display, drawable, gc, x, y, str, length)
```

and

```
XDrawImageString(display, drawable, gc, x, y, str, length)
```

Both functions draw a string in a drawable starting at the given position. The graphics context determines the foreground color, background color, the display function, the font, and the fill style. The graphics context also determines the stipple or tile pattern and clipping region used. **XDrawString()** draws only the foreground component of the text, while **XDrawImageText()** also fills the background region within each character's bounding box.

Xlib also includes drawing functions that draw lines of text using multiple fonts in a single operation. The function

```
XDrawText(display, drawable, gc, x, y, items, nitems)
```

draws **nitems** of text as specified in an array of type **XTextItem**. This structure contains the following members:

```
char  *chars;     /* pointer to string            */
int    nchars;    /* number of characters in string */
int    delta;     /* distance from previous string  */
Font   font;      /* Font for this string or None   */
```

XDrawText() processes each item in the array. If an entry in the array specifies the font as **None**, **XDrawText()** uses the font used by the previous item. The **delta** member of the structure specifies the distance along the *x* axis between the start of the current item and the end of the previous item.

9.3 EXAMPLE: A FILE VIEWER

This section uses some of the text and font functions discussed in the previous section to build a simple file viewer, called **fileview**. The viewer allows the user to view and scroll through the contents of a UNIX text file in a window. The example uses a WorkSpace widget as a drawing surface on which to display the text, and demonstrates how the Xlib drawing functions can be used with the Xt Intrinsics and X Widgets.[2]

The header of the **fileview** program includes the widget header files used by the program and defines the global variables and data structures used by the program.

```
/***********************************************************
 * fileview.h: declarations for fileview program
 ***********************************************/
#include <stdio.h>
#include <X11/Intrinsic.h>
#include <X11/StringDefs.h>
#include <X11/Xutil.h>
#include <Xw/Xw.h>
#include <Xw/Form.h>
#include <Xw/WorkSpace.h>
#include <Xw/ScrollBar.h>
```

2. The approach used in this example is hardly the easiest way to write a file viewer. The most straightforward approach would simply combine a TextEdit or StaticText widget and a ScrolledWindow widget. The entire program would fit on a single page. However the point of this section is to demonstrate the Xlib text functions, so that we can use these functions when necessary (when writing a new widget that displays text, for example).

```
#include "libXs.h"

#define MAXLINESIZE  300
#define MAXLINES    2000
#define MIN(a,b)      (((a) < (b)) ? (a) : (b))
#define MARGIN         5

typedef struct {
  char          *chars[MAXLINES];   /* Lines of text           */
  int            ll[MAXLINES];      /* Length of each line     */
  int            rbearing[MAXLINES];/* right bearing of line */
  int            descent;           /* descent below baseline*/
  int            foreground,        /* Color used for text     */
                 background;
  XFontStruct   *font;              /* The font struct         */
  GC             gc;                /* A read/write GC         */
  GC             gcread;            /* A read-only GC          */
  Widget         scrollbar;
  Widget         canvas;
  Dimension      canvas_height;     /* canvas dimensions       */
  Dimension      canvas_width;
  int            fontheight;        /* descent + ascent        */
  int            nitems;            /* number of text lines    */
  int            top;               /* line at top of window */
  } text_data, *text_data_ptr;

text_data  data;
void        handle_exposures();
void        slider_selected ();
void        scroll_bar_moved ();
void        resize ();

static XtResource resources[] = {
 {XtNfont, XtCFont, XtRFontStruct, sizeof (XFontStruct *),
    XtOffset(text_data_ptr, font), XtRString, "Fixed"      },
 {XtNforeground, XtCForeground, XtRPixel, sizeof (int),
    XtOffset(text_data_ptr, foreground), XtRString, "Black"},
 {XtNbackground, XtCBackground, XtRPixel, sizeof (int),
    XtOffset(text_data_ptr, background), XtRString, "White"}
};
```

This example limits the size of the file to 2000 lines, as defined by the constant **MAXLINES**; a more realistic implementation would allocate space based on the size of the file. The **text_data** structure contains two arrays. The **chars** member is an array of character strings, while **ll** is an array that caches the length of each line of the file. The **nitems** member records the number of lines in the file, and **top** contains the index of the line at the top of the window. The structure also contains other useful information that needs to be passed to the event handlers and callbacks in this example, including the foreground color, background color, font, graphics context used to draw the text, and the widgets used by the application.

The **resource** structure is used by the resource manager to load the font and color information into the buffer data structure.

The file viewer window contains both a Workspace widget, used as a drawing surface, and a scroll bar that scrolls the text in the Workspace widget. These widgets are managed by a Form widget. The main body of the program creates these widgets, and calls other functions to load the file into the text buffer and initialize the global data structures defined in the header file.

```
/*********************************************************
 * fileview.c: a file viewer
 *********************************************************/
#include "fileview.h"

main (argc, argv)
  int                argc;
  char             **argv;
{
  Widget             toplevel, frame;

  toplevel = XtInitialize (argv[0], "Fileview",
                           NULL, 0, &argc, argv);
  XtGetApplicationResources (toplevel, &data, resources,
                  XtNumber (resources), NULL, 0);
  /*
   * Read the file specified in argv[1] into the
   * text buffer.
   */
  load_file (&data, (argc == 2) ? argv[1] : NULL);
  /*
   * Create a Form widget as a base to allow children to be
   * resize easily.
   */
  frame = XtCreateManagedWidget ("framework",
                                 XwformWidgetClass,
                                 toplevel, NULL, 0);
  create_scrollbar (frame, &data);
```

```
    /*
     * Create the drawing surface.
     */
    data.canvas = XtCreateManagedWidget ("canvas",
                                         XwworkSpaceWidgetClass,
                                         frame, NULL, 0);
    XtAddCallback (data.canvas, XtNexpose,
                   handle_exposures, &data);
    XtAddCallback (data.canvas, XtNresize, resize, &data);
    XtRealizeWidget (toplevel);
    /*
     * Create the graphics contexts after realizing the widgets
     * because create_gcs requires a valid window ID.
     */
    create_gcs (&data);
    XtMainLoop ();
  }
```

After calling **XtInitialize()**, the program retrieves the application resources that specify the font and color used to display the text. The function **load_file()** then reads the file into the text buffer. After creating the ScrollBar and WorkSpace widgets, the program registers two callback functions with the Workspace widget. The **XtNresize** callback updates the data in the text buffer when the widget is resized, while the **XtNexpose** callback function redraws the text when necessary. The function **create_gcs()** creates the graphics contexts used by the program. Notice that the graphics contexts are not created until after the widgets have been realized. This is because we need to create a modifiable graphics context using the Xlib function **XCreateGC()**, which requires a valid window ID.

The function **load_file()** attempts to open a file. If successful, the function uses **fgets()** to read each line of the file and load it into the text buffer. Because the content of the buffer cannot change once the file has been read, we can use **XTextExtents()** to calculate the bounding box of each line of the file as it is read, and store this information with the text buffer. When the entire file has been read, the function stores the number of lines in the file and initializes the line at the top of the window to zero.

```
  load_file (data, filename)
    text_data     *data;
    char          *filename;
  {
    int            foreground, background, i, dir, ascent, desc;
    XCharStruct    char_info;
    FILE          *fp, *fopen ();
    char           buf[MAXLINESIZE];
    /*
```

```
     * Open the file.
     */
    if ((fp = fopen (filename, "r")) == NULL) {
      fprintf (stderr, "Unable to open %s\n", filename);
      exit (1);
    }
    /*
     * Read each line of the file into the buffer,
     * calculating and caching the extents of
     * each line.
     */
    i = 0;
    while ((fgets (buf, MAXLINESIZE, fp)) != NULL &&
            i < MAXLINES) {
      data->chars[i] = XtMalloc (strlen (buf) + 1);
      buf[strlen (buf) - 1] = '\0';
      strcpy (data->chars[i], buf);
      data->ll[i] = strlen (data->chars[i]);
      XTextExtents(data->font, data->chars[i],
                   data->ll[i], &dir, &ascent,
                   &desc, &char_info);
      data->rbearing[i] = char_info.rbearing;
      data->descent     = desc;
      data->fontheight  = ascent + desc;
      i++;
    }
    /*
     * Close the file.
     */
    fclose(fp);
    /*
     * Remember the number of lines, and initialize the
     * current line number to be 0.
     */
    data->nitems = i;
    data->top = 0;
  }
```

The function **create_scrollbar()** creates a ScrollBar widget and defines callbacks for the scroll bar's **XtNsliderMoved** and **XtNareaSelected** callback lists. This function also sets the minimum position of the ScrollBar widget to zero and the maximum position to the number of lines in the file. This allows the current position of the scroll bar to correspond directly to the line number of the first line of text in the window.

```
create_scrollbar (parent, data)
  Widget          parent;
  text_data      *data;
{
  Arg             wargs[2];
  int             n = 0;
  data->scrollbar =
          XtCreateManagedWidget ("scrollbar",
                                 XwscrollbarWidgetClass,
                                 parent, NULL, 0);
  XtAddCallback (data->scrollbar, XtNsliderMoved,
                 scroll_bar_moved, data);
  XtAddCallback (data->scrollbar, XtNareaSelected,
                 slider_selected, data);
  /*
   * Set the scrollbar so that movements are
   * reported in terms of lines of text.
   */
  XtSetArg (wargs[n], XtNsliderMin, 0);  n++;
  XtSetArg (wargs[n], XtNsliderMax, data->nitems);  n++;
  XtSetValues (data->scrollbar, wargs, n);
}
```

The function **create_gcs()** creates the graphics contexts from the foreground and background colors retrieved from the resource data base. The **handle_exposures()** procedure uses the modifiable graphics context to set a clipping region before redrawing the text.

```
create_gcs (data)
  text_data      *data;
{
  XGCValues       gcv;
  Display *dpy  = XtDisplay(data->canvas);
  Window   w    = XtWindow(data->canvas);
  int      mask = GCFont | GCForeground | GCBackground;
  int      read_only_mask = GCForeground | GCBackground;
  /*
   * Create two graphics contexts. One is
   * modifiable, the other is read only.
   */
  gcv.foreground = data->foreground;
  gcv.background = data->background;
  gcv.font       = data->font->fid;
```

```
    data->gc      = XCreateGC (dpy, w, mask, &gcv);
    data->gcread = XtGetGC (data->canvas, read_only_mask, &gcv);
}
```

The callback **handle_exposures()** draws as many lines of text as the WorkSpace widget's window can hold. This function uses the region given as the **call_data** argument to set the clip mask of the graphics context before redrawing the text. This eliminates redrawing areas of the window outside the exposed region.

Next, **handle_exposures()** draws each line in the text buffer, beginning with the line indexed by **data->top**, and continuing until either the text line lies outside the extent of the window, or the last line in the buffer has been drawn. The variable **yloc**, which determines the current *y* coordinate of the next line of text, is incremented by the height of the text each time through the while loop. Notice that **yloc** is incremented *before* each line is drawn, because **XDrawImageString()** draws text relative to the *lower* left corner of the bounding box. Therefore, the first line is drawn at **data>fontheight**.

Although setting the clipping region in the graphics contexts allows the server to clip the text to the region that needs to be redrawn, it is also somewhat inefficient to send the server requests for every line in the window, when only a few may need to be redrawn. A smart application should be able to redraw only those lines or portions of lines that are required, instead of relying on the server to do the clipping. The **fileview** example does this is a crude way, by using **XRectInRegion()** to determine whether or not each line intersects with the exposed region. By redrawing a line of text only if it intersects the exposed region, we can reduce the number of server requests and thereby improve the performance of the program. In this example, the performance gain is probably too small to be measured, but the technique is applicable to more complex examples as well.

```
void handle_exposures (w, data, region)
  Widget      w;
  text_data  *data;
  Region      region;
{
  int         yloc = 0, index = data->top;
  /*
   * Set the clip mask of the GC.
   */
  XSetRegion (XtDisplay (w), data->gc, region);
  /*
   * Loop through each line until the bottom of the
   * window is reached, or we run out of lines. Redraw any
   * lines that intersect the exposed region.
   */
  while (index < data->nitems && yloc < data->canvas_height) {
    yloc += data->fontheight;
```

```
      if(XRectInRegion(region, 0, yloc - data->fontheight,
                       data->canvas_width,
                       data->fontheight) != RectangleOut)
        XDrawImageString (XtDisplay (w), XtWindow (w),
                          data->gc, MARGIN, yloc,
                          data->chars[index], data->ll[index]);

      index++;
    }
}
```

To scroll the text in the window, all we have to do is change the value of **data->top** and redraw the entire buffer. The callback **scroll_bar_moved()** sets **data->top** to the current position of the scroll bar and then calls **redraw_window()** to redraw an entire window of text.

```
void scroll_bar_moved (w, data, sliderpos)
  Widget          w;
  text_data      *data;
  int             sliderpos;
{
  data->top = sliderpos;
  redraw_window (data->canvas, data);
}
```

The function **redraw_window()** uses the read-only GC because the function always redraws the entire window. This function clears the window before redrawing it.

```
redraw_window (w, data)
  Widget      w;
  text_data  *data;
{
  int  yloc = 0, index = data->top;
  /*
   * Clear the entire window.
   */
  XClearWindow (XtDisplay (w), XtWindow (w));
  /*
   * Redraw each line until the bottom of the
   * window is reached, or we run out of lines.
   */
  while (index < data->nitems && yloc < data->canvas_height) {
    yloc += data->fontheight;
    XDrawImageString (XtDisplay (w), XtWindow (w),
                      data->gcread, MARGIN, yloc,
```

```
                                data->chars[index], data->ll[index]);
        index++;
      }
    }
```

The last function to discuss is the **resize()** callback function. This function simply updates the width and height information stored in the text buffer. Because the server generates an **Expose** event after a resizing a window, no further action is required.

```
void resize (w, data, call_data)
  Widget          w;
  text_data      *data;
  caddr_t         call_data;
{
  Arg             wargs[2];

  XtSetArg (wargs[0], XtNheight, &data->canvas_height);
  XtSetArg (wargs[1], XtNwidth,  &data->canvas_width);
  XtGetValues (w, wargs, 2);
}
```

9.3.1 The Resource File: Fileview

The **fileview** program's class resource file specifies the constraints that control the layout of the ScrollBar and WorkSpace widgets. Both the Workspace widget and the ScrollBar widget must be resizable in the vertical direction and attached to the bottom of the window. In addition, the canvas widget is resizable in the horizontal direction and is attached to the right side of the scroll bar and to the left side of the Form widget. This allows the text pane to stretch in the vertical and horizontal directions, but keeps the scrollbar a fixed width.

```
##################################################################
# Fileview: Class Resource File for fileview program
##########################################################

Fileview*yResizable:            True
Fileview*yAttachBottom:         True

Fileview*canvas.xRefName:       scrollbar
Fileview*canvas.xResizable:     True
Fileview*canvas.xAddWidth:      True
Fileview*canvas.xAttachRight:   True
Fileview*canvas.yAttachTop:     True
```

Figure 9.2 shows the layout created by these constraints. Because these resources are essential to the proper layout of the file viewer, it would probably be a good idea to set them in the program.

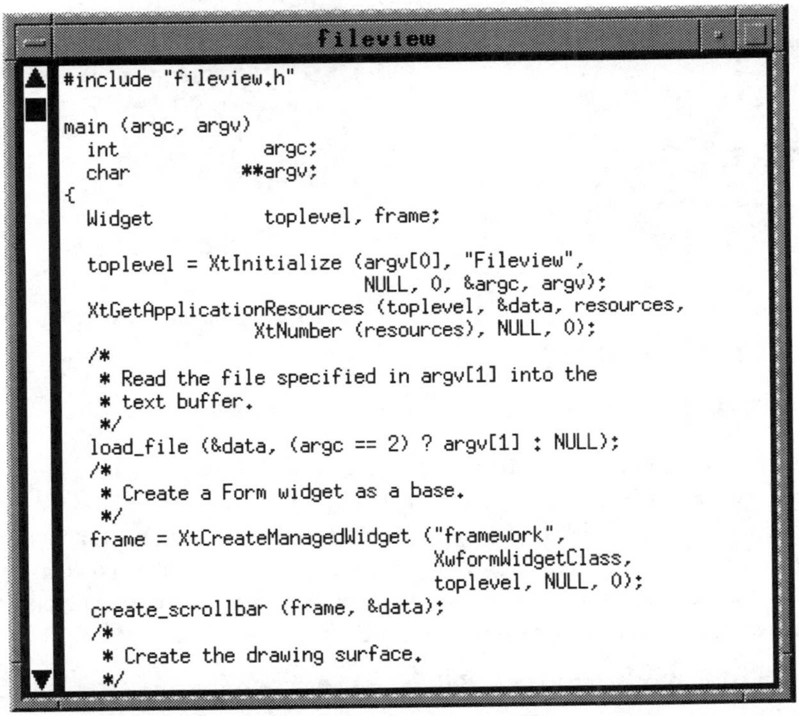

fileview

```
#include "fileview.h"

main (argc, argv)
  int            argc;
  char         **argv;
{
  Widget         toplevel, frame;

  toplevel = XtInitialize (argv[0], "Fileview",
                           NULL, 0, &argc, argv);
  XtGetApplicationResources (toplevel, &data, resources,
                 XtNumber (resources), NULL, 0);
  /*
   * Read the file specified in argv[1] into the
   * text buffer.
   */
  load_file (&data, (argc == 2) ? argv[1] : NULL);
  /*
   * Create a Form widget as a base.
   */
  frame = XtCreateManagedWidget ("framework",
                                 XwformWidgetClass,
                                 toplevel, NULL, 0);
  create_scrollbar (frame, &data);
  /*
   * Create the drawing surface.
   */
```

Figure 9.2 The file viewer.

9.3.2 Adding Smooth Scrolling

There are many optimizations and improvements that we can make to the file viewer example. For example, in the version in the previous section, each time the text is scrolled by even a single line, the entire window of text is redrawn. It is often better to copy the bitmapped image of some of the lines to their new location, and redraw only a few lines. Figure 9.3 illustrates this approach, which produces a smooth scrolling effect.

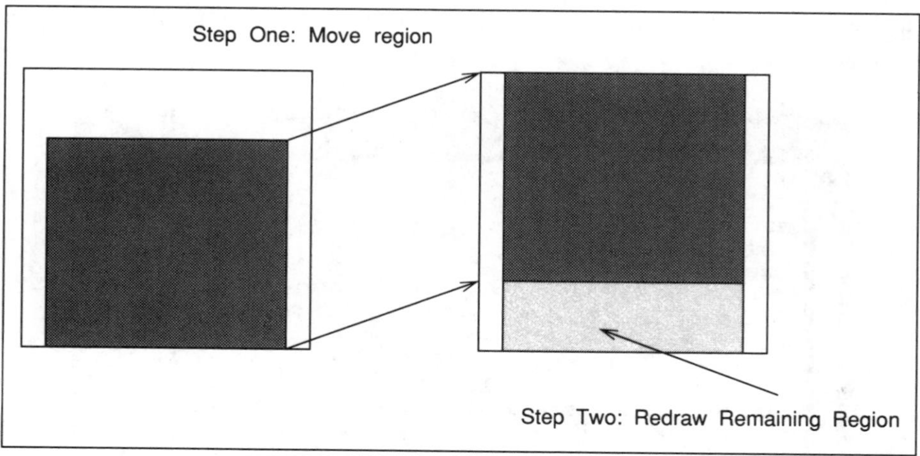

Figure 9.3 Using **`XCopyArea()`** to scroll the contents of a window.

To achieve a smooth scrolling effect, all we need to do is redesign the **`scroll_bar_moved()`** callback function. All other parts of the program can remain the same, although we no longer need the **`redraw_window()`** function. The new **`scroll_bar_moved()`** function uses **`XCopyArea()`** to move as much text as possible. It also calculates the remaining region of the window that must be redrawn, clears that area, and then invokes the **`handle_exposures()`** callback to redraw the area.

```
void scroll_bar_moved(w, data, sliderpos)
   Widget     w;
   text_data *data;
   int        sliderpos;
{
  XPoint points[4];
  Region region;
  int    xsrc, ysrc, xdest, ydest;
  /*
   * These points are the same for both cases,
   * so set them here.
   */
  points[0].x = points[3].x = 0;
  points[1].x = points[2].x = data->canvas_width;
  xsrc  = xdest = 0;

  if(sliderpos < data->top){ /* If we are scrolling down... */
```

```
  ysrc  =  0;
  /*
   * Convert the slider's position (rows) to pixels.
   */
  ydest = (data->top - sliderpos) * data->fontheight;
  /*
   * Limit the destination to the window height.
   */
  if(ydest > data->canvas_height)
      ydest = data -> canvas_height;
  /*
   * Fill in the points array with the bounding box
   * of the area that needs to be redrawn - that is,
   * the area that is not copied.
   */
  points[1].y = points[0].y = 0;
  points[3].y = points[2].y = ydest +  data->fontheight;
}
else{                    /* If we are scrolling up... */
  ydest = 0;
  /*
   * Convert the slider's position (rows) to pixels.
   */
  ysrc =  (sliderpos - data->top) * data->fontheight;
  /*
   * Limit the source to the window height.
   */
  if(ysrc > data->canvas_height)
      ysrc = data -> canvas_height;
  /*
   * Fill in the points array with the bounding box
   * of the area that needs to be redrawn. This area cannot
   * be copied and must be redrawn.
   */
  points[1].y = points[0].y = data->canvas_height - ysrc;
  points[2].y = points[3].y = data->canvas_height;
}
/*
 * Set the top line of the text buffer.
 */
data->top = sliderpos;
/*
```

```
     * Copy the scrolled region to its new position.
     */
    XCopyArea(XtDisplay(data->canvas), XtWindow(data->canvas),
              XtWindow(data->canvas), data->gcread,
              xsrc, ysrc, data->canvas_width,
              data->canvas_height, xdest, ydest);
    /*
     * Clear the remaining area of any old text.
     */
    XClearArea(XtDisplay(w), XtWindow(data->canvas),
               points[0].x, points[0].y,
               0, points[2].y - points[0].y, 0);
    /*
     * Create a region from the points array, and call the
     * XtNexpose callback with the calculated region as
     * call_data.
     */
    region = XPolygonRegion(points, 4, EvenOddRule);
    XtCallCallbacks(data->canvas, XtNexpose, region);
    /*
     * Free the region.
     */
    XDestroyRegion(region);
  }
```

If the slider position is less than the top line in the window, then we need to scroll the window's contents down. The current contents of the window must be copied to the position determined by the difference between the old top and the new top of the window. Since the indexes are in terms of characters, we must multiply them by the font height to convert to pixel dimensions. The **points** array contains the coordinates of the rectangular region at the top of the window that must be redrawn. Scrolling down is done in a similar way, except that the **points** array contains the rectangular region at the bottom of the window that must be redrawn.

After calculating the coordinates of the regions to be moved and redrawn, **scroll_bar_moved()** sets **data->top** to its new value, and calls **XCopyArea()** to shift the bitmapped image in window to its new position. The remaining area of the window is cleared to remove the old text. Next, a region generated from the points array is used as the call_data argument to **XtCallCallbacks()**, which invokes the **handle_exposures()** callback function. Finally, we can free the region using **XDestroyRegion()**.

9.4 SUMMARY

This chapter discussed the Xlib functions used to display text in a window as well as the fonts X uses to represent characters. X draws text by performing a fill operation on a rectangular region using a bitmap representing a character as a mask. A font is a collection of bitmapped characters. X provides several functions for drawing strings in windows or pixmaps. Because X treats text the same as any graphics operation, application can combine Xlib text functions with clipping regions, graphics contexts, and raster operations.

The WorkSpace widget is useful when combining Xlib drawing functions with the widgets and architecture of the Xt Intrinsics. Using this widget, the programmer can let the Intrinsics handle the low-level details of the X protocol, but still directly control the contents of the widget's window.

The following chapter discusses the primitive graphics functions provided by Xlib and continues to explore graphics contexts, regions, and related functions.

10

USING THE X GRAPHICS PRIMITIVES

The previous chapters examined the X color model, graphics contexts, and regions. This chapter presents the graphics primitives provided by Xlib and uses some of these features in examples. Xlib provides a set of simple two-dimensional graphics functions for drawing points, lines, arcs and rectangles. These drawing functions use the same integer coordinate system as the functions that position windows. Applications that require more complex graphics functions for panning, scaling, or three-dimensional graphics must usually implement these as a layer above the Xlib graphics functions.[1] All graphics functions operate on a drawable, either a window or a pixmap.

10.1 DRAWING WITH POINTS

The simplest Xlib graphics function displays a single point in a drawable. The function

```
XDrawPoint(display, drawable, gc, x, y)
```

sets a single pixel at location x, y according to the specified GC. It is often more efficient to draw multiple points at once using the function

1. An extension to the X protocol, known as PEX, defines a PHIGS three-dimensional interface for X. This extension has not been implemented at the time this book is being written, but is being considered by the X Consortium as a standard. Some X vendors also provide their own sophisticated graphics packages as extensions to X.

```
XDrawPoints(display, drawable, gc, points, npoints, mode)
```

This function draws **npoints** points with a single server request. The **points** argument is an array of **XPoint** structures. The **mode** argument determines how the server interprets coordinates and must be one of the constants **CoordModeOrigin** or **CoordModePrevious**. If **CoordModeOrigin** is specified, the server interprets each coordinate relative to the origin of the drawable. The constant **CoordModePrevious** specifies that each coordinate is given relative to the preceding point. The server always interprets the first point relative to the drawable's origin.

Several attributes of the graphics context affect how points are drawn. These are:

```
GCFunction        GCPlaneMask GCForeground GCClipYOrigin
GCSubwindowMode   GCClipMask  GCBackground GCClipXOrigin
```

Let's look at a simple example that uses **XDrawPoint()** to illustrate the basic use of graphics functions in X. The program computes and displays a *fractal* image. Fractals are mathematical expressions based on complex numbers that produce interesting images from simple equations. This example displays a fractal image generated by repeatedly evaluating the expression

$$z = (z + k)^2$$

where both z and k are complex numbers. The value of z is initially set to $(0, 0)$, while k is initialized to the value of each (x, y) position in the window. After evaluating the expression some number of times for each point, we test the value of z to see how far it has moved from the (x, y) plane. If it is within some predetermined distance of the plane, the pixel is said to be part of the *Mandelbrot Set* and the color of the pixel is set to the same color as all other pixels in the Mandelbrot Set. Otherwise, some other color is chosen for the pixel. This example program bases the color on the distance of the point from the (x, y) plane.

The header file of this program includes the necessary X header files and defines a few data structures. The fractal program defines a **complex** structure to represent complex numbers, and also defines an **image_data** structure to store a graphics context, a pixmap (used to save the image once it is drawn), and some auxiliary data needed for the image calculation.

```
/*********************************************************
 * fractal.h: declarations for the fractal program
 *********************************************************/
#include <X11/StringDefs.h>
#include <X11/Intrinsic.h>
#include <Xw/Xw.h>
#include <Xw/WorkSpace.h>
#include <X11/Xutil.h>
#include "libXs.h"

void     resize();
```

```
void      redisplay();
void      create_image ();
/*
 * Structure to represent a complex number.
 */
typedef struct {
  float  real, imag;
} complex;
/*
 * Assorted information needed to generate and draw the image.
 */
typedef struct {
  int           depth, ncolors;
  float         range, max_distance;
  complex       origin;
  GC            gc;
  Pixmap        pix;
  Dimension     width, height;
} image_data, *image_data_ptr;
/*
 * Resource that affect the appearance of the fractal image.
 */
static XtResource resources[] = {
 {"depth", "Depth", XtRInt, sizeof (int),
   XtOffset(image_data_ptr, depth), XtRString, "20"          },
 {"real_origin", "RealOrigin", XtRFloat, sizeof (float),
   XtOffset(image_data_ptr, origin.real), XtRString, "-1.4" },
 {"imaginary_origin","ImaginaryOrigin",XtRFloat,sizeof(float),
   XtOffset(image_data_ptr, origin.imag), XtRString, "1.0"  },
 {"range", "Range", XtRFloat, sizeof(float),
   XtOffset(image_data_ptr,range), XtRString, "2.0"          },
 {"max_distance", "MaxDistance", XtRFloat, sizeof (float),
   XtOffset(image_data_ptr, max_distance),XtRString, "4.0"  }
 };
```

The header file also defines an **XtResources** array used by the resource manager to initialize some of the options in the **image_data** struct. The **depth** option determines how many times the fractal expression is evaluated for each pixel, while the **real_origin** and **imaginary_origin** allow the image to be *panned* to view different parts of the image. These are floating point coordinates because the example calculates the image in normalized floating coordinates. This allows us to generate the same image regardless of the size of the window that displays the image. The **range** parameter determines the width and height of the real coordinates of the image, and can be altered to *zoom* the image in and out, while the

max_distance parameter controls the *z* distance considered to be "close" to the *(x, y)* plane.

The main body of the program creates a Workspace widget used as a drawing canvas, and adds callbacks to handle **Expose** and **ConfigureNotify** events. The **CvtStringToFloat** type converter, which we wrote in Chapter 3, is installed before calling **XtGetApplicationResources()** to retrieve the data specified in the **resources** array. Before entering the main event loop, the function **resize()** is called to trigger the creation of the initial image.

```
/**********************************************
 * fractal.c: A simple fractal generator
 **********************************************/
#include "fractal.h"

main(argc, argv)
     int   argc;
     char *argv[];
{
  Widget     toplevel, canvas;
  image_data data;
  toplevel = XtInitialize(argv[0], "Mandelbrot", NULL, 0,
                           &argc, argv);
 /*
  *  Add the string to float type converter.
  */
 XtAddConverter(XtRString, XtRFloat,CvtStringToFloat,NULL, 0);
 XtGetApplicationResources(toplevel, &data, resources,
                           XtNumber(resources), NULL, 0);
 /*
  * Create the widget to display the fractal and register
  * callbacks for resize and refresh.
  */
 canvas = XtCreateManagedWidget("canvas",
                                XwworkSpaceWidgetClass,
                                toplevel, NULL, 0);
 init_data(canvas, &data);
 XtAddCallback(canvas, XtNexpose, redisplay, &data);
 XtAddCallback(canvas, XtNresize, resize, &data);
 XtRealizeWidget(toplevel);
 resize(canvas, &data, NULL);
 XtMainLoop();
}
```

The function **init_data()** creates a graphics context, determines how many colors are supported by the display, and initializes the **pixmap** member of the **image_data** structure to NULL.

```
init_data(w, data)
    Widget      w;
    image_data *data;
{
  int y;
  Arg wargs[2];
  /*
   * Get the size of the drawing area.
   */
  XtSetArg(wargs[0], XtNwidth,  &data->width);
  XtSetArg(wargs[1], XtNheight, &data->height);
  XtGetValues(w, wargs,2);
  /*
   * Find out how many colors we have to work with, and
   * create a default, writable, graphics context.
   */
  data->ncolors = XDisplayCells(XtDisplay(w),
                              XDefaultScreen(XtDisplay(w)));
  data->gc = XCreateGC(XtDisplay(w),
                     DefaultRootWindow(XtDisplay(w)),
                     NULL, NULL);
  /*
   *  Initialize the pixmap to NULL.
   */
  data->pix = NULL;
}
```

The fractal image is displayed when the window is exposed. However, the function **create_image()** actually generates the fractal. The function uses three nested **for** loops to evaluate the fractal expression. For each *(x, y)* coordinate, **create_image()** calculates the value of the expression repeatedly until either the maximum number of iterations are performed or until the *z* distance from the *(x, y)* plane exceeds the specified limit. If the point is still on the plane when all iterations are calculated, no point is drawn (which is equivalent to drawing the window's background color). If a point moves away from the plane before all iterations are calculated, the function draws a point on the screen. There are many ways to choose the color of each pixel. This example uses a straightforward method that achieves interesting results on color displays. The foreground color of the graphics context is determined by the z distance from the plane modulo the number of colors available.[2]

Notice that **create_image()** draws each point twice: once in the WorkSpace widget and once a pixmap. This creates a duplicate of the image in off-screen memory. Depending on the size of the window, this image can take considerable time to draw. Storing the image in off-screen memory allows us to use **XCopyArea()** to restore the image rather than recalculating the entire image each time the window is exposed.[3] However, we also have to be careful to draw the point in the window only if the widget has been realized. This is because **create_image()** is called from the widget's **XtNresize** callback list, and it is possible for this procedure to be called before the widget is realized.

```
void create_image (w, data)
     Widget          w;
     image_data     *data;
{
 int  x, y, iteration;
 /*
  * For each pixel on the window....
  */
 for (y = 0; y < data->height; y++) {
  for (x = 0; x < data->width; x++) {
    complex z, k;
   /*
    * Initialize K to the normalized, floating coordinate
    * in the x, y plane. Init Z to (0.0, 0.0).
    */
    z.real =  z.imag = 0.0;
    k.real =  data->origin.real + (float) x /
                 (float) data->width * data->range;
    k.imag =  data->origin.imag - (float) y /
                 (float) data->height * data->range;
   /*
    * Calculate z = (z + k) * (z + k) over and over.
    */
   for (iteration = 0; iteration < data->depth; iteration++){
```

2. This is not entirely portable to black and white displays. Although this program will work on a monochrome display, better results can be obtained by simply choosing the foreground color if the point is not on the plane and choosing the background color otherwise.

3. It isn't necessary to draw the point to the window at all. We could just store the image in the pixmap, then copy the image from the pixmap to the window. However, drawing the fractal image is time-consuming, and it is useful to provide some reassurance to the user that the program is making some progress by showing the preliminary image in the window as it is being created.

```
          float   distance, real_part, imag_part;

          real_part = z.real + k.real;
          imag_part = z.imag + k.imag;
          z.real = real_part * real_part - imag_part * imag_part;
          z.imag = 2 * real_part * imag_part;
          distance  = z.real * z.real + z.imag * z.imag;
         /*
          * If the z point has moved off the plane, set the
          * current foreground color to the distance (coerced to
          * an int and modulo the number of colors available),
          * and draw a point in both the window and the pixmap.
          */
         if (distance  >= data->max_distance){
           int color = (int) distance % data->ncolors;

           XSetForeground(XtDisplay(w), data->gc, color);
           XDrawPoint (XtDisplay(w), data->pix, data->gc, x, y);
           if(XtIsRealized(w))
            XDrawPoint (XtDisplay(w), XtWindow(w), data->gc,x,y);
           break;
         }
       }
     }
   }
 }
```

The callback function **redisplay()** handles **Expose** events by copying the image from a region in the pixmap to the window. This function uses **XClipBox()** to determine the smallest bounding that encloses the **Region** specified in the **call_data** parameter. Then it uses **XCopyArea()** to copy this rectangular area from the pixmap to the window. Copying an image between a pixmap and a window is normally much faster than recomputing the image. This program is a good example of an application that could benefit from a server that provides backing store to automatically maintain a window's contents. However, using a pixmap to maintain the image works even with X servers that do not support this feature.

```
void redisplay (w, data, region)
     Widget          w;
     image_data     *data;
     Region          region;
{
  XRectangle rect;
  /*
```

```
     * Extract the exposed area from the region and copy
     * from the saved pixmap to the window.
     */
    XClipBox(region, &rect);
    XCopyArea(XtDisplay(w), data->pix, XtWindow(w), data->gc,
              rect.x, rect.y,
              rect.width, rect.height,
              rect.x, rect.y);
}
```

The remaining function to be discussed is the **XtNresize** callback function **resize()**. This function frees the current pixmap, which no longer corresponds to the size of the window, and creates a new pixmap the same size as the window. It then calls **create_image()** to generate a new fractal based on the new window size. Fig. 10.1 shows the fractal generated by this program.

```
void resize(w, data, call_data)
     Widget          w;
     image_data     *data;
     caddr_t         call_data;
{
  Arg wargs[2];
  /*
   *  Get the new window size.
   */
  XtSetArg(wargs[0], XtNwidth,  &data->width);
  XtSetArg(wargs[1], XtNheight, &data->height);
  XtGetValues(w, wargs, 2);
  /*
   *  Free the old pixmap and create a new pixmap
   *  the size of the window.
   */
  if(data->pix)
     XFreePixmap(XtDisplay(w), data->pix);
  data->pix= XCreatePixmap(XtDisplay(w),
                           DefaultRootWindow(XtDisplay(w)),
                           data->width, data->height,
                           DefaultDepthOfScreen(XtScreen(w)));
  /*
   * Generate a new image.
   */
  create_image(w, data);
}
```

Figure 10.1 The fractal program.

Although using a pixmap to store the fractal image in off-screen memory partially alleviates the problem of handling **Expose** events for a graphics-intensive image application, the initial time required to compute and draw the image still leaves something to be desired. The calculation itself is time consuming, although there is little we can do about that because fractals are inherently expensive to compute. We can, however, optimize the drawing of the image by reducing the number of server requests. The function **XDrawPoints()** draws multiple points with a single server request. All points use the same graphics context, but do not have to be contiguous. Using **XDrawPoints()** to reduce the number of server requests greatly increases the speed of the fractal program. The only part of the fractal program that must change is the function **create_image()**.

```
void create_image (w, data)
     Widget         w;
     image_data          *data;
{
 int x, y, iteration;
 /*
  * We have to buffer all points of the same color, until
  * enough points are available to draw efficiently. Start
  * by zeroing all buffers.
```

```
  */
 init_buffer(data);
  /*
   * For each pixel on the window....
   */
 for (y = 0; y < data->height; y++) {
  for (x = 0; x < data->width; x++) {
   complex z, k;
   /*
    *  Initialize K to the normalized, floating coordinate in
    *  the x,y plane. Init Z to (0.0, 0.0).
    */
   z.real = z.imag = 0.0;
   k.real =  data->origin.real + (float) x /
                 (float) data->width * data->range;
   k.imag =  data->origin.imag - (float) y /
                (float) data->height * data->range;
   /*
    * Calculate z = (z + k) * (z + k) over and over.
    */
   for (iteration = 0; iteration < data->depth; iteration++){
    float distance, real_part, imag_part;
    real_part = z.real + k.real;
    imag_part = z.imag + k.imag;
    z.real    = real_part * real_part - imag_part * imag_part;
    z.imag    = 2 * real_part * imag_part;
    distance  = z.real * z.real + z.imag * z.imag;
    /*
     * If the z point has moved off the plane, buffer the
     * point using the integerized distance (modulo the
     * number of colors we have) as the color.
     */
    if (distance  >= data->max_distance){
      buffer_point(w, data, (int) distance % data->ncolors,
                  x, y);
      break;
    }
   }
  }
}
/*
 * Display all remaining points.
```

```
   */
   flush_buffer(w, data);
 }
```

The primary difference between this version of **create_image()** and the previous version is that instead of calling **XDrawPoint()** directly, **create_image()** calls the function **buffer_point()**. This function stores points until they can be drawn as a group using **XDrawPoints()**. The function **init_buffer()** must be called before beginning the calculations to initialize the data structures used by the buffer routines and **flush_buffer()** must also be called to flush the buffer after all points are generated.

The buffering routines use a global data structure containing a two-dimensional array of **XPoint** structures. The array holds **MAXPOINTS** number of points for **MAXCOLOR** possible colors. The **points** structure also contains an array of integers that indicates how many points are stored in each of the point arrays.

```
#define MAXPOINTS 500
#define MAXCOLOR 64
struct{
   XPoint   data[MAXCOLOR][MAXPOINTS];
   int      npoints[MAXCOLOR];
} points;
```

The function **init_buffer()** initializes the number of points of each color to zero.

```
init_buffer(data)
     image_data *data;
{
  int i;
  for(i=0;i<MAXCOLOR;i++)
    points.npoints[i] = 0;
}
```

The **buffer_point()** routine first checks how many points of the given color are already stored in the buffer. If this number is equal to the maximum number that can be buffered, it uses **XDrawPoints()** to draw all points stored in the buffer in both the window and the pixmap. Then, it resets the number of points for the given color to zero, and stores the current point in the buffer.

```
buffer_point(w, data, color, x , y)
     Widget       w;
     image_data *data;
     int          color, x,y;
{
  if(points.npoints[color] == MAXPOINTS - 1){
    /*
```

```
        * If the buffer is full, set the foreground color
        * of the graphics context and draw the points in both
        * the window and the pixmap.
        */
       XSetForeground(XtDisplay(w), data->gc, color);
       if(XtIsRealized(w))
         XDrawPoints (XtDisplay(w), XtWindow(w), data->gc,
                      points.data[color], points.npoints[color],
                      CoordModeOrigin);
       XDrawPoints (XtDisplay(w), data->pix, data->gc,
                    points.data[color], points.npoints[color],
                    CoordModeOrigin);
       /*
        * Reset the buffer.
        */
       points.npoints[color] = 0;
     }
     /*
      * Store the point in the buffer according to its color.
      */
     points.data[color][points.npoints[color]].x = x;
     points.data[color][points.npoints[color]].y = y;
     points.npoints[color] += 1;
   }
```

The function **flush_buffer()** must be called when the image calculation is finished to draw any points remaining in the buffer. This function loops through all colors, drawing the remaining points in both the window and the pixmap.

```
flush_buffer(w, data)
     Widget      w;
     image_data *data;
{
  int i;
  /*
   * Check each buffer.
   */
  for(i=0;i<data->ncolors;i++)
    /*
     * If there are any points in this buffer, display them
     * in the window and the pixmap.
     */
    if(points.npoints[i]){
```

```
            XSetForeground(XtDisplay(w), data->gc, i);
            if(XtIsRealized(w))
              XDrawPoints (XtDisplay(w), XtWindow(w), data->gc,
                           points.data[i], points.npoints[i],
                           CoordModeOrigin);
              XDrawPoints (XtDisplay(w), data->pix, data->gc,
                           points.data[i], points.npoints[i],
                           CoordModeOrigin);
            points.npoints[i] = 0;
          }
    }
```

Although the image calculation itself is still time consuming, buffering the points provides a significant speedup. In addition to reducing the time initially required to draw the image, buffering the drawing requests reduces the load on the server, which reduces the degree to which the fractal program interferes with other applications using the server. This buffering example was more complex than many applications because the Xlib functions for drawing multiple points and lines use only a single GC. A black and white version of this program would be much simpler.

10.2 DRAWING WITH LINES

The Xlib function

```
XDrawLine(display, drawable, gc, x1, y1, x2, y2)
```

draws a single line between two points. The way in which **XDrawLine()** draws lines is determined by the following attributes of the graphics context.

```
GCFunction          GCPlaneMask      GCLineWidth
GCLineStyle         GCCapStyle       GCFillStyle
GCSubwindowMode     GCClipXOrigin    GCClipYOrigin
GCClipMask
```

The function

```
XDrawSegments(display, drawable, gc, segments, nsegments)
```

draws multiple, discontiguous line segments with a single request. The line segments are specified by an array of type **XSegment**, which includes the members

```
short x1, y1, x2, y2;
```

Although the line segments do not need to be connected, **XDrawSegments()** draws all segments using the same graphics context. The function uses the same graphics context members as **XDrawLine()**.

The function

XDrawLines(display, drawable, gc, points, npoints, mode)

draws multiple connected lines. This function draws **npoints - 1** lines between the points in the point array. **XDrawLines()** draws all lines in the order in which the points appear in the array. The **mode** argument determines whether the points are interpreted relative to the origin of the drawable or relative to the last point drawn, and must be one of **CoordModeOrigin** or **CoordModePrevious**. **XDrawLines()** uses the **GCJoinStyle** attribute of the graphics context, in addition to the graphics context members used by **XDrawLine()**.

We can demonstrate **XDrawLine()** in a simple program that uses a technique known as *rubber banding*. A rubber band line is usually drawn interactively by the user. The user first sets an initial endpoint, usually by pressing a mouse button. A line is then drawn between this endpoint and the current position of the sprite. As the user moves the sprite, the line appears to stretch as if it were a rubber band connected between the sprite and the initial position. The rubber banding ends in response to some user action, typically when the mouse button is released. This technique is commonly used to allow the user to define a beginning and ending coordinate for drawing lines or other figures interactively.

The example program, named **rubberband** allows the user to draw rubber band lines in the window of a Workspace widget. The **rubberband** program begins by defining a data structure, **rubberband_data**, that contains information used by the event handlers that perform the rubber banding.

```
/**********************************************
 * rubberband.c: rubberband line example
 **********************************************/
#include <X11/StringDefs.h>
#include <X11/Intrinsic.h>
#include <X11/cursorfont.h>
#include <Xw/Xw.h>
#include <Xw/WorkSpace.h>

typedef struct {
    int start_x, start_y, last_x, last_y;
    GC  gc;
  } rubber_band_data;

void start_rubber_band();
void end_rubber_band();
void track_rubber_band();
```

The body of the program simply creates a Workspace widget and adds event handlers for **ButtonPress**, **ButtonRelease** and pointer motion events which work together to implement the rubber banding.

```
main(argc, argv)
 int   argc;
 char *argv[];
{
  Widget           toplevel, canvas;
  rubber_band_data data;

  toplevel = XtInitialize(argv[0], "Rubberband", NULL, 0,
                          &argc, argv);
  /*
   * Create a drawing surface, and add event handlers for
   * ButtonPress, ButtonRelease and MotionNotify events.
   */
  canvas = XtCreateManagedWidget("canvas",
                                 XwworkSpaceWidgetClass,
                                 toplevel, NULL, 0);
  XtAddEventHandler(canvas, ButtonPressMask, FALSE,
                    start_rubber_band, &data);
  XtAddEventHandler(canvas, ButtonMotionMask, FALSE,
                    track_rubber_band, &data);
  XtAddEventHandler(canvas, ButtonReleaseMask,
                    FALSE, end_rubber_band, &data);
  XtRealizeWidget(toplevel);
  /*
   * Establish a passive grab, for any button press.
   * Force the sprite to stay within the canvas window, and
   * change the sprite to a cross_hair.
   */
   XGrabButton(XtDisplay(canvas), AnyButton, AnyModifier,
               XtWindow(canvas), TRUE,
               ButtonPressMask | ButtonMotionMask |
               ButtonReleaseMask,
               GrabModeAsync, GrabModeAsync,
               XtWindow(canvas),
               XCreateFontCursor(XtDisplay(canvas),
                                 XC_crosshair));
  /*
   * Create the GC used by the rubber banding functions.
   */
  create_gc(canvas, &data);
  XtMainLoop();
}
```

This example introduces some new Xlib and Intrinsics functions. The function

```
XGrabButton(display, button, modifiers, grab_window,
            owner_events, event_mask, pointer_mode,
            keyboard_mode, confine_to, cursor)
```

establishes a *passive grab* on the sprite, or pointer. A passive grab takes effect automatically when the user presses the specified mouse button. Once the pointer is grabbed, the server reports all mouse events to the grabbing client, even if the sprite leaves the window. This allows the server to track pointer motion more efficiently. **XGrabButton()** also allows us to constrain the sprite to stay within a particular window while the grab is in effect. In this example, the sprite is constrained to the **canvas** window as long as the pointer grab is in effect. **XGrabButton()** also allows the programmer to specify the shape of the mouse cursor while the grab is in effect. In this example, the mouse cursor changes to a crosshair shape when the pointer is grabbed. The function

```
XCreateFontCursor(display, cursor_index)
```

retrieves a mouse cursor from a standard font. The file cursorfont.h defines a set of constants used to as indexes into the cursor font. When the user releases the mouse button, the grab automatically terminates and the mouse cursor returns to its previous shape.

The function **create_gc()** creates the graphics context used to draw the rubber band lines.

```
create_gc(w, data)
   Widget           w;
  rubber_band_data *data;
{
  XGCValues values;
  Arg       wargs[2];
  /*
   * Get the colors used by the widget.
   */
  XtSetArg(wargs[0], XtNforeground, &values.foreground);
  XtSetArg(wargs[1], XtNbackground, &values.background);
  XtGetValues(w, wargs,2);
  /*
   * Set the fg to the XOR of the fg and bg, so if it is
   * XOR'ed with bg, the result will be fg and vice-versa.
   * This effectively achieves inverse video for the line.
   */
  values.foreground = values.foreground ^ values.background;
  /*
   * Set the rubber band gc to use XOR mode and draw
   * a dashed line.
```

```
     */
    values.line_style = LineOnOffDash;
    values.function = GXxor;
    data->gc = XtGetGC(w, GCForeground | GCBackground |
                           GCFunction | GCLineStyle, &values);
}
```

The graphics context is created using the foreground and background colors obtained from the widget's resources. In addition, the line style is set to **LineOnOffDash** and the drawing function is set to XOR mode.

The task of drawing the rubber band line is performed by three cooperating event handlers. When the user presses a mouse button, the Intrinsics invokes the first event handler, **start_rubber_band()**. This function stores the position of the sprite when the **ButtonPress** event occurs as the initial position of the line, and also sets the last position of the line to the same point. The function **XDrawLine()** is called to draw the initial line, which is simply a point, because the start and end points are the same.

```
void start_rubber_band(w, data, event)
    Widget              w;
    rubber_band_data    *data;
    XEvent              *event;
{
    data->last_x  =  data->start_x = event->xbutton.x;
    data->last_y  =  data->start_y = event->xbutton.y;
     XDrawLine(XtDisplay(w), XtWindow(w),
               data->gc, data->start_x,
               data->start_y, data->last_x, data->last_y);
}
```

The function **track_rubber_band()** is called each time the sprite moves. It draws a line between the initial position at which the user pressed the mouse button and the current position of the sprite. Because the line is drawn in XOR mode, this erases the current line and restores the previous contents of the screen. The end points of the line are then updated to the current sprite position and the line is drawn again.

```
void track_rubber_band(w, data, event)
    Widget              w;
    rubber_band_data   *data;
    XEvent             *event;
{
    /*
     * Draw once to clear the previous line.
     */
    XDrawLine(XtDisplay(w), XtWindow(w), data->gc,
```

```
                   data->start_x,data->start_y,
                   data->last_x, data->last_y);
    /*
     * Update the endpoints.
     */
    data->last_x  =  event->xbutton.x;
    data->last_y  =  event->xbutton.y;
    /*
     * Draw the new line.
     */
    XDrawLine(XtDisplay(w), XtWindow(w), data->gc,
                   data->start_x, data->start_y,
                   data->last_x, data->last_y);
}
```

When the user releases the mouse button, the event handler **end_rubber_band()** is invoked. This function draws the line one last time in exclusive OR mode to erase the line. The function also stores the current position of the sprite in the client data structure where some other routine can retrieve it.

```
void end_rubber_band(w, data, event)
    Widget            w;
    rubber_band_data *data;
    XEvent           *event;
{
  /*
   * Clear the current line and update the endpoint info.
   */
   XDrawLine(XtDisplay(w), XtWindow(w), data->gc,
                  data->start_x, data->start_y,
                  data->last_x, data->last_y);
   data->last_x  =  event->xbutton.x;
   data->last_y  =  event->xbutton.y;
}
```

10.3 DRAWING POLYGONS AND ARCS

Xlib also provides functions for drawing more complex figures, including filled and unfilled polygons, arcs, and circles. The function

```
XDrawRectangle(display, drawable, gc, x, y, width, height)
```

draws the outline of a rectangle, while the function

```
XDrawRectangles(display, drawable, gc, rectangles,nrectangles)
```

draws multiple rectangles. The argument **rectangles** must be an array of type X**Rectangle**, which includes the members

```
short          x, y;
unsigned short width, height;
```

An arc can be drawn using the function

```
XDrawArc(display, drawable, gc, x, y, width, height,
         angle1, angle2)
```

This function draws an arc starting from angle1, relative to a three o'clock position, to angle2, within the bounding rectangle specified by the parameters **x**, **y**, **width**, **height**, as shown in Fig. 10.2. The angles are specified in units of *(degrees * 64)*. For example, this function can be used to draw a circle or ellipse by specifying a starting angle of zero degrees and an ending angle of *(64 * 360)* degrees. Angles greater than *(64 * 360)* degrees are truncated.

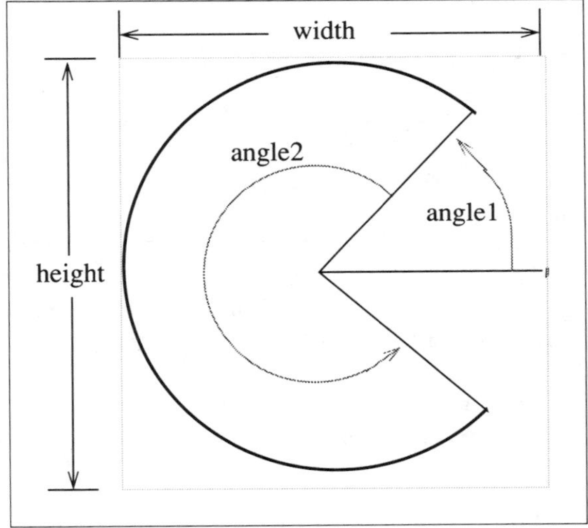

Figure 10.2 Dimensions of an Arc.

The function

```
XDrawArcs(display, drawable, gc, arcs, narcs)
```

draws multiple arcs with a single server request and uses an array of type **XArc** to define the parameters of each arc. The **XArc** structure contains the following members:

```
short          x, y;
unsigned short width, height;
short          angle1, angle2;
```

Xlib also provides functions for drawing polygons, rectangles, and arcs filled with a solid color or pattern. The function

```
XFillRectangle(display, drawable, gc, x, y, width, height)
```

draws a single rectangle filled as specified by the **GCForeground**, **GCBackground**, **GC-Tile**, and **GCStipple** attributes of the graphics context. The function

```
XFillRectangles(display, drawable, gc, rectangles,nrectangles)
```

draws multiple filled rectangles using an array of **XRectangle** structures. The function

```
XFillPolygon(display, drawable, gc, points, npoints,
             shape, mode)
```

draws a single polygon specified by an array of **XPoint** structures. If the path is not closed, **XFillPolygon()** automatically closes it before filling the figure. The shape parameter can be one of the constants **Complex**, **Convex**, or **Nonconvex**. The server can use this information to select the optimal drawing algorithm. The **mode** argument determines how the points are interpreted and must be one of the constants **CoordModeOrigin** or **CoordModePrevious**. The functions

```
XFillArc(display, drawable, gc, x, y, width, height,
         angle1, angle2)
```

and

```
XFillArcs(display, drawable, gc, arcs, narcs)
```

draw single and multiple filled arcs.

10.4 EXAMPLE: A SIMPLE DRAWING PROGRAM

This section concludes our discussion of the Xlib graphics functions by looking at a simple drawing program that uses many of the techniques and functions discussed in this chapter, as well as in the previous three chapters. The **draw** program shown in Fig. 10.3 allows the user to select shapes from a menu, and position them using the rubber banding techniques discussed in Section 10.2. The user can also select fill patterns from the tiles provided by the X Widget library for the shapes.

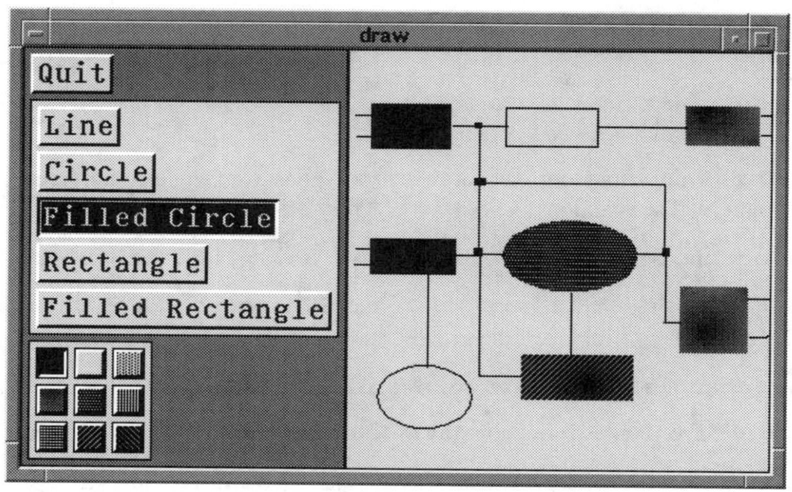

Figure 10.3 Using draw: A simple drawing program.

The header file, draw.h includes the X Widget header files used in this example, and also contains forward declarations of the callbacks and other procedures used in the program. The header file also includes definitions of three data structures used by the program. An array of type **GBUFFER** serves as a graphics buffer. Each position in the buffer stores a pair of *(x, y)* points, a graphics context and a pointer to a function that draws the object. The second data structure provides a central location for all client data used by the callback procedure. It is similar to the data structure used by the rubber banding function in Section 10.2, but is expanded to include a pointer to the graphics buffer and also a pointer to a function used to draw objects. The header also includes a declaration for an **XContext**. This is an identifier, used by the Xlib context manager, which we will discuss shortly.

```
/*********************************************
 * draw.h: declarations for the draw program
 *********************************************/
#include <X11/StringDefs.h>
#include <X11/cursorfont.h>
#include <X11/Intrinsic.h>
#include <X11/Xutil.h>
#include <Xw/Xw.h>
#include <Xw/WorkSpace.h>
#include <Xw/Form.h>
```

```
#include <Xw/RCManager.h>
#include <Xw/PButton.h>
#include <Xw/SRaster.h>

#define MAXOBJECTS 1000

typedef struct {
  int  x1, y1, x2, y2;
  int  (*func) ();
  GC   gc;
} GBUFFER;

typedef struct {
  int           start_x, start_y, last_x, last_y;
  GC            xorgc;
  GC            gc;
  int           (*current_func)();
  int           foreground, background;
  GBUFFER       buffer[MAXOBJECTS];
  int           next_pos;
} graphics_data;

void  draw_line();
void  draw_circle();
void  draw_rectangle();
void  draw_filled_circle();
void  draw_filled_rectangle();

void  activate();
void  refresh();
void  set_stipple();
void  start_rubber_band();
void  track_rubber_band();
void  end_rubber_band();
void  set_fill_pattern();
XContext  TileContext, FunctionContext;
```

The **draw** program uses a Form widget to manage a command pane built from a Row-Col widget and a drawing canvas (a Workspace widget). Fig. 10.4 shows the widget tree created by the graphics editor.

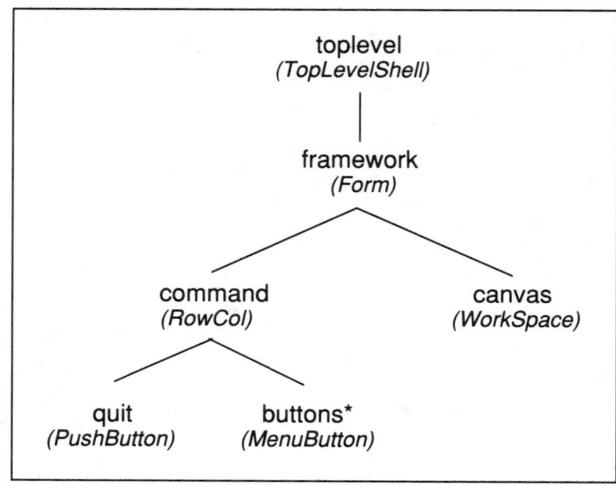

Figure 10.4 The draw widget tree.

The body of the program creates these widgets, initializes the graphics buffer and related data structures, and defines event handlers for the mouse buttons and pointer motion events.

```
/****************************************************
 * draw.c: a simple graphics drawing program.
 ****************************************************/
#include "draw.h"

main(argc, argv)
   int   argc;
   char *argv[];
{
  Widget toplevel, canvas, framework, command;
  graphics_data data;

  toplevel = XtInitialize(argv[0], "Draw", NULL, 0,
                          &argc, argv);
  framework = XtCreateManagedWidget("framework",
                                    XwformWidgetClass,
                                    toplevel, NULL, 0);
  /*
   * Create the column to hold the commands.
   */
```

```
command = XtCreateManagedWidget("command",
                                XwrowColWidgetClass,
                                framework, NULL, 0);
/*
 * Add a quit button.
 */
create_quit_button("Quit", command);
/*
 * Add the drawing command panel.
 */
create_drawing_commands(command, &data);
/*
 * Add a palette of fill patterns.
 */
create_fill_editor(command, &data);
/*
 * Create the drawing surface and add the
 * rubber banding callbacks.
 */
canvas = XtCreateManagedWidget("canvas",
                               XwworkSpaceWidgetClass,
                               framework, NULL, 0);
XtAddCallback(canvas, XtNexpose, refresh, &data);
XtAddEventHandler(canvas, ButtonPressMask, FALSE,
                  start_rubber_band, &data);
XtAddEventHandler(canvas, ButtonMotionMask, FALSE,
                  track_rubber_band, &data);
XtAddEventHandler(canvas, ButtonReleaseMask, FALSE,
                  end_rubber_band, &data);
XtRealizeWidget(toplevel);
/*
 * Establish a passive grab on the drawing canvas window.
 */
XGrabButton(XtDisplay(canvas), AnyButton, AnyModifier,
            XtWindow(canvas), TRUE,
            ButtonPressMask | ButtonMotionMask |
            ButtonReleaseMask,
            GrabModeAsync, GrabModeAsync,
            XtWindow(canvas),
            XCreateFontCursor(XtDisplay(canvas),
                              XC_crosshair));
/*
```

```
     * Initialize the  graphics buffer and other data.
     */
    init_data(canvas, &data);
    XtMainLoop();
  }
```

In addition to the quit button, the command panel contains a set of buttons used to issue drawing commands. The function **create_drawing_commands()** creates a RowCol widget containing a set of PushButton widgets, which the user can use to select the current drawing function. The selected function remains in effect until the user selects a new drawing function. Notice that each callback shares the **data** structure containing the graphics buffer through the callback functions' **client_data** argument.

```
create_drawing_commands(parent, data)
     Widget          parent;
     graphics_data *data;
{
  Widget w, commands;
  FunctionContext = XUniqueContext();
  /*
   * Group all commands in a column.
   */
  commands = XtCreateManagedWidget("commands",
                                   XwrowColWidgetClass,
                                   parent, NULL, 0);
  /*
   * Create a button for each drawing function.
   */
  w = XtCreateManagedWidget("Line", XwpushButtonWidgetClass,
                            commands, NULL, 0);
  XSaveContext(XtDisplay(w), w, FunctionContext, draw_line);
  XtAddCallback(w, XtNselect, activate, data);
  w = XtCreateManagedWidget("Circle",
                            XwpushButtonWidgetClass,
                           commands, NULL,0);
  XSaveContext(XtDisplay(w), w, FunctionContext, draw_circle);
  XtAddCallback(w, XtNselect, activate, data);
  w = XtCreateManagedWidget("Rectangle",
                            XwpushButtonWidgetClass,
                            commands, NULL,0);
  XSaveContext(XtDisplay(w), w, FunctionContext,
               draw_rectangle);
  XtAddCallback(w, XtNselect, activate, data);
```

```
    w = XtCreateManagedWidget("Filled Circle",
                              XwpushButtonWidgetClass,
                              commands, NULL,0);
    XSaveContext(XtDisplay(w), w, FunctionContext,
                 draw_filled_circle);
    XtAddCallback(w, XtNselect, activate, data);
    w = XtCreateManagedWidget("Filled Rectangle",
                              XwpushButtonWidgetClass,
                              commands, NULL,0);
    XSaveContext(XtDisplay(w), w, FunctionContext,
                 draw_filled_rectangle);
    XtAddCallback(w, XtNselect, activate, data);
}
```

Often, we can use the client data of callbacks and event handlers to associate a piece of data with a particular widget. However, only one piece of client data can be passed to any one function. In this example, we are using the client data to pass the data structure containing the graphics buffer between functions. However, in addition, the **activate()** function requires a pointer to a function to be installed as the current drawing function. Since the graphics buffer and its associated data is passed as client data, we must find some other way to associate a drawing function with a particular button.

One way to do this is to use Xlib's context manager. The context manager is intended to associate data with a window. It is basically a three dimensional sparse array. The first dimension is indexed by the display, the second by a window ID, and the third by a context type. Applications can create a unique context type with the function

```
XUniqueContext()
```

This function returns a unique ID. Data can be associated with a window using the function

```
XSaveContext(display, window, context, data)
```

The data is stored locally, in the same process space as the client, and not in the server. The data can be retrieved using

```
XFindContext(display, window, context, &data)
```

In this example, we are misusing the context manager slightly. Xlib documentation states that the first argument must be a pointer to a **Display** structure while the second argument is expected to be a window ID. However, the context manager really controls a simple three dimensional array, and the first three arguments to **XSaveContext()** and **XFindContext()** are simply used as indexes into the array. The window ID is eventually coerced into an **int**. Therefore, we can use a widget pointer just as well as a window ID for the second index.

So, **create_drawing_commands()** creates a unique context and uses it to associate the function **draw_line()** with the "Line" button, the function **draw_circle()** with the "Circle" button, and so on. We will see how this is used shortly.

The next section of the command panel contains a menu of patterns that can be used as fill patterns for rectangles and circles. The fill patterns are displayed in StaticRaster widgets, using the nine standard fill patterns provided by the X Widget library. The function **create_fill_editor()** creates a RowCol widget, and then calls **create_fill_button()** to add a button for each fill style. This function also creates a second context, which is used to associate a tile with each button.

```
create_fill_editor(parent, data)
     Widget         parent;
     graphics_data *data;
{
  Widget patterns;
  TileContext = XUniqueContext();

  patterns = XtCreateManagedWidget("patterns",
                                   XwrowColWidgetClass,
                                   parent, NULL, 0);
  create_fill_button(patterns, XwFOREGROUND,        data);
  create_fill_button(patterns, XwBACKGROUND,        data);
  create_fill_button(patterns, Xw25_FOREGROUND,     data);
  create_fill_button(patterns, Xw50_FOREGROUND,     data);
  create_fill_button(patterns, Xw75_FOREGROUND,     data);
  create_fill_button(patterns, XwVERTICAL_TILE,     data);
  create_fill_button(patterns, XwHORIZONTAL_TILE,   data);
  create_fill_button(patterns, XwSLANT_RIGHT,       data);
  create_fill_button(patterns, XwSLANT_LEFT,        data);
}
```

The function **create_fill_button()** creates the tile indicated by the **pattern** argument, converts it to a 16 by 16 bit **XImage** displayed by a StaticRaster widget. An **XtNselect** callback, **set_fill_pattern()**, is registered with each StaticRaster widget. When each button is selected, we need to retrieve the original tile pattern displayed by the widget. Here, we use the same approach we used earlier to associate a function with a widget, and store the tile in a context.

```
create_fill_button(parent, pattern, data)
     Widget         parent;
     int            pattern;
     graphics_data *data;
{
```

```
  Pixmap   tile, bitmap;
  Widget   button;
  XImage  *raster;
  Arg      wargs[1];
  Display *dpy = XtDisplay(parent);
  int      scr = DefaultScreen(dpy);
  /*
   * Get a tile corresponding to the given pattern.
   */
  tile = XwCreateTile (XtScreen(parent), WhitePixel(dpy, scr),
                       BlackPixel(dpy, scr), pattern);
  /*
   * Retrieve the XImage representing the tile pattern.
   */
  raster = XGetImage(dpy,tile,0,0,16,16, AllPlanes,XYPixmap);
  /*
   * Display the XImage in a StaticRaster widget.
   */
  XtSetArg(wargs[0], XtNsRimage,  raster);
  button =
        XtCreateManagedWidget("button", XwsrasterWidgetClass,
                              parent, wargs, 1);
  /*
   * Associate the tile with this button.
   */
  XSaveContext(XtDisplay(button), button, TileContext, tile);
  XtAddCallback(button, XtNselect, set_fill_pattern, data);
}
```

The **set_fill_pattern()** callback retrieves the tile from the context manager, and installs a new graphics context in the client data structure.

```
void set_fill_pattern(w, data, call_data)
    Widget         w;
    graphics_data *data;
    void          *call_data;
{
   Pixmap     tile;
   int        i;
   XGCValues  values;
   int        mask =  GCForeground | GCBackground |
                      GCTile | GCFillStyle;
   XFindContext(XtDisplay(w), w, TileContext, &tile);
```

```
    /*
     * Get a GC using this tile pattern
     */
    values.foreground = data->foreground;
    values.background = data->background;
    values.fill_style = FillTiled;
    values.tile       = tile;
    data->gc          = XtGetGC(w, mask, &values);
}
```

Now that we have seen how all the widgets used in this example are created, let's look at how the client data is initialized and used. The function **init_data()** initializes the current drawing function to NULL, sets the next available position in the graphics buffer to zero, and then creates two graphics contexts. One graphics context is used by the graphics objects, while the other graphics context is used by the rubber banding routines that position the objects.

```
init_data(w, data)
     Widget          w;
     graphics_data  *data;
{
  XGCValues values;
  Arg       wargs[5];
  data->current_func = NULL;
  data->next_pos     = 0;
  /*
   * Get the colors the user has set for the widget.
   */
  XtSetArg(wargs[0], XtNforeground, &data->foreground);
  XtSetArg(wargs[1], XtNbackground, &data->background);
  XtGetValues(w, wargs,2);
  /*
   * Fill in the values structure
   */
  values.foreground = data->foreground;
  values.background = data->background;
  values.fill_style = FillTiled;
  /*
   * Get the GC used for drawing.
   */
  data->gc= XtGetGC(w, GCForeground | GCBackground |
                       GCFillStyle, &values);
  /*
```

```
     * Get a second GC in XOR mode for rubber banding.
     */
    values.foreground = data->background ^ data->foreground;
    values.function   = GXxor;
    values.line_style = LineOnOffDash;
    data->xorgc = XtGetGC(w, GCFunction | GCForeground |
                             GCBackground | GCLineStyle,
                          &values);
}
```

The three event handlers in this example draw objects using a rubber banding approach similar to that described in Section 10.2. However, instead of a hard-coded Xlib drawing function, these routines use the **current_function** member of the shared client data to draw the figures. This allows the same rubber banding functions to draw all types of figures. The function **start_rubber_band()** sets the initial anchor point of the rubber band figure when the user presses a mouse button.

```
void start_rubber_band(w, data, event)
        Widget          w;
        graphics_data  *data;
        XEvent         *event;
{
  if(data->current_func){
    /*
     * Store the starting point and draw the initial figure.
     */
    data->last_x = data->start_x = event->xbutton.x;
    data->last_y = data->start_y = event->xbutton.y;
    (*(data->current_func))(w, data->xorgc,
                            data->start_x, data->start_y,
                            data->last_x, data->last_y);
  }
}
```

The function **track_rubber_band()** erases the previous figure by drawing it in XOR mode, updates the position, and redraws the figure each time the sprite moves.

```
void track_rubber_band(w, data, event)
        Widget          w;
        graphics_data  *data;
        XEvent         *event;
{
 if(data->current_func){
   /*
```

```
         * Erase the previous figure.
         */
        (*(data->current_func))(w, data->xorgc,
                                data->start_x, data->start_y,
                                data->last_x, data->last_y);
        /*
         * Update the last point.
         */
        data->last_x  =  event->xbutton.x;
        data->last_y  =  event->xbutton.y;
        /*
         * Draw the figure in the new position.
         */
        (*(data->current_func))(w, data->xorgc,
                                data->start_x, data->start_y,
                                data->last_x, data->last_y);
     }
   }
```

When the mouse button is released, the rubber banded figure is erased, and the figure is redrawn using the current graphics context. After updating the position information in data, the function **store_object()** is called to record the new object in the graphics buffer.

```
   void end_rubber_band(w, data, event)
           Widget          w;
           graphics_data  *data;
           XEvent         *event;
   {
     if(data->current_func){
        /*
         * Erase the XOR image.
         */
        (*(data->current_func))(w, data->xorgc,
                                data->start_x, data->start_y,
                                data->last_x, data->last_y);
        /*
         * Draw the figure using the normal GC.
         */
        (*(data->current_func))(w, data->gc,
                                data->start_x, data->start_y,
                                event->xbutton.x,
                                event->xbutton.y);

        /*
```

```
       * Update the data, and store the object in
       * the graphics buffer.
       */
      data->last_x  =  event->xbutton.x;
      data->last_y  =  event->xbutton.y;
      store_object(data);
    }
}
```

The key to using the same rubber band functions for all figures is to find a way to draw all figures using the same parameters. Although the various Xlib graphics functions are similar, they are not exactly the same. However, it is easy to define functions that require the same parameters. Each of the following functions takes a widget, a graphics context, and two *(x, y)* points. The function **draw_line()** draws a line between two points.

```
void draw_line(w, gc, x, y, x2, y2)
     Widget  w;
     GC      gc;
     int     x, y, x2, y2;
{
  Display *dpy = XtDisplay(w);
  Window   win = XtWindow(w);
  XDrawLine(dpy, win, gc, x, y, x2, y2);
}
```

The functions **draw_rectangle()** and **draw_filled_rectangle()** draw rectangles using the given points as the upper left and lower right corners of the rectangle. These functions are defined as

```
void draw_rectangle(w, gc, x, y, x2, y2)
     Widget w;
     GC     gc;
     int    x, y, x2, y2;
{
  Display *dpy = XtDisplay(w);
  Window   win = XtWindow(w);

  check_points(&x, &y, &x2, &y2);
  XDrawRectangle(dpy, win, gc,  x, y, x2 - x, y2 - y);
}

void draw_filled_rectangle(w, gc, x, y, x2, y2)
     Widget  w;
     GC      gc;
```

```
        int      x, y, x2, y2;
   {
     Display *dpy = XtDisplay(w);
     Window   win = XtWindow(w);

     check_points(&x, &y, &x2, &y2);
     XFillRectangle(dpy, win, gc, x, y, x2 - x, y2 - y);
   }
```

Some X servers do not draw polygonal figures correctly if the second point is less than the first in either direction. The auxiliary function **check_points()** checks for this case and reverses the coordinates if needed.

```
   check_points(x, y, x2, y2)
      int *x, *y, *x2, *y2;
   {
     if(*x2 < *x){ int tmp = *x; *x = *x2; *x2 = tmp;}
     if(*y2 < *y){ int tmp = *y; *y = *y2; *y2 = tmp;}
   }
```

The functions **draw_circle()** and **draw_filled_circle()** use the two points as the upper left and lower right corners of the bounding box of a circle. Theses functions are defined as

```
   void draw_circle(w, gc, x, y, x2, y2)
        Widget   w;
        GC       gc;
        int      x, y, x2, y2;
   {
     Display *dpy = XtDisplay(w);
     Window   win = XtWindow(w);

     check_points(&x, &y, &x2, &y2);
     XDrawArc(dpy, win, gc, x, y, x2 - x, y2 - y, 0, 64 * 360);
   }

   void draw_filled_circle(w, gc, x, y, x2, y2)
        Widget   w;
        GC       gc;
        int      x, y, x2, y2;
   {
     Display *dpy = XtDisplay(w);
     Window   win = XtWindow(w);
```

```
    check_points(&x, &y, &x2, &y2);
    XFillArc(dpy, win, gc, x, y, x2 - x, y2 - y, 0, 64 * 360);
  }
```

These functions must be installed as the current drawing function when the user selects one of the drawing commands. Each PushButton widget in the command pane has a callback function that activates the corresponding drawing function by setting the **current_func** member of the shared client data structure. This function is retrieved from the context manager, using **XFindContext()**. The **activate()** function is defined as

```
void activate(w, data, call_data)
     Widget          w;
     graphics_data  *data;
     void           *call_data;
{
  int (*func)();
  XFindContext(XtDisplay(w), w, FunctionContext, &func);
  data->current_func = func;
}
```

We must save each object in a graphics buffer so we can redraw the image when the WorkSpace widget is exposed. The function **store_object()** saves the size and location of the object, the graphics context, and a pointer to the function used to draw the object in the next available slot of the graphics buffer array. It then increments the **next_pos** counter. If the graphics buffer is full, the function returns without storing the object.

```
store_object(data)
     graphics_data *data;
{
  /*
   * Check for space.
   */
  if(data->next_pos >= MAXOBJECTS){
   printf("Warning: Graphics buffer is full\n");
   return;
  }
  /*
   * Save everything we need to draw this object again.
   */
  data->buffer[data->next_pos].x1 = data->start_x;
  data->buffer[data->next_pos].y1 = data->start_y;
  data->buffer[data->next_pos].x2 = data->last_x;
  data->buffer[data->next_pos].y2 = data->last_y;
  data->buffer[data->next_pos].func = data->current_func;
```

```
    data->buffer[data->next_pos].gc = data->gc;
    /*
     * Increment the next position index.
     */
    data->next_pos++;
  }
```

When the canvas widget is exposed, the Intrinsics invokes the callback functions on the **XtNexpose** callback list including the function **refresh()**. This function calls **XClearWindow()** and then loops through the graphics buffer, redrawing each object.

```
void refresh(w, data, call_data)
   Widget          w;
   caddr_t         call_data;
   graphics_data  *data;
{
  int i;
  XClearWindow(XtDisplay(w), XtWindow(w));
  for(i=0;i<data->next_pos;i++)
    (* (data->buffer[i].func))(w, data->buffer[i].gc,
                                 data->buffer[i].x1,
                                 data->buffer[i].y1,
                                 data->buffer[i].x2,
                                 data->buffer[i].y2);
}
```

The **draw** program's class resource file contains several useful customizations. The first set of resources defines the Form widget constraints for each widget. These constraints position the drawing canvas to the right of the command panel, and allow the canvas widget to be resized when the overall window is resized. The second part of the resource file sets the selection mode of the RowCol widgets to **one_of_many**, so that only one of the drawing commands and fill patterns are selected at once. The translations for these widgets are also redefined so that a **Button1Down** action selects a button, but **Button1Up** does nothing. Therefore, once a button is selected and highlighted, it remains highlighted until a new button is selected. Because the RowCol widget is in **one_of_many** mode, the RowCol widget calls the previous button's **XtNrelease** callback automatically when the user selects a new button.

```
#####################################################
# Draw: class resource file for the draw program
#####################################################
Draw*canvas.xRefName:                       command
Draw*canvas.xResizable:                     True
Draw*canvas.xAddWidth:                      True
```

```
Draw*canvas.yResizable:                  True
Draw*canvas.xAttachRight:                True
Draw*canvas.xAttachLeft:                 True
Draw*canvas.yAttachBottom:               True
Draw*canvas.yAttachTop:                  True
Draw*mode:                               one_of_many
Draw*commands*PushButton*translations:  <Btn1Down>:    select()
Draw*StaticRaster*translations:          <Btn1Down>:    select()
Draw*StaticRaster*showSelected:          True
```

10.5 SUMMARY

This chapter explored the graphics facilities provided by Xlib, and demonstrated how they can be used with the Xt Intrinsics and widgets. X provides simple two-dimensional graphics primitives although efforts are underway to provide more sophisticated three-dimensional capabilities. Various attributes of a graphics context control how the Xlib drawing functions affect a drawable and allow the programmer to create many special effects such as drawing rubber band lines, or manipulating plane masks to produce smooth animations.

Because each graphics operation makes a server request, complex images can be time consuming. It is often necessary to take extra steps to reduce the number of serve requests, by caching and combining requests, or by saving complete or partial renditions of images in off-screen pixmaps.

The following chapter leaves the topic of graphics operations and discusses ways to provide communication and data sharing between applications.

11

INTERCLIENT COMMUNICATION

X provides many facilities that allow applications to communicate with each other and to exchange and share data. Interclient communication involves the use of *atoms*, *properties*, and *client messages*. This chapter first describes atoms, and shows how atoms are used to identify names and types of properties. Then a short example demonstrates how properties can be used to store data in the server, where it can be shared by multiple clients. Next we discuss how applications can use client message events to communicate with each other, and finally we look at the X *selection* mechanism for exchanging typed data between applications.

11.1 ATOMS

An atom is a unique resource ID used to represent a string. The relationship is stored in the X server so that all clients connected to that server share the same ID for any particular string. Atoms are primarily used for efficiency; it is faster to compare two atoms (using ==) than to compare two strings (using **strcmp()**).

Creating an atom is referred to as *interning*. The function

```
XInternAtom(display, name, only_if_exists)
```

returns a unique atom corresponding to the string specified by name. When the boolean **only_if_exists** is **True**, **XInternAtom()** returns an atom ID if the atom already exists. If the atom does not exist, the function returns the constant **None**. When **only_if_exists** is **False**, **XInternAtom()** always returns an atom ID, creating a new atom unless the atom already exists. All applications that request an atom for the same string from the same server receive the same ID. The string must match exactly, including the case.

Applications can create new atoms to represent any arbitrary string. For example, the statement

```
Atom NEWATOM = XInternAtom(display, "A New Atom", False);
```

creates an atom, **NEWATOM**, representing the string

```
"A New Atom"
```

Once an atom is interned, it exists until the server is reset, even if the client that created the atom exits.

The function

```
XGetAtomName(display, atom)
```

returns the string corresponding to atom. Atoms are useful whenever a unique identifier that must be shared and recognized by multiple applications is required. For example, atoms are used to identify the type of data stored in a property. X predefines a small set of atoms to identify common data types such as **DRAWABLE**, **POINT**, **INTEGER**, **FONT**, and **PIXMAP**.

The symbols for all predefined atoms are preceded by the letters "**XA_**" to avoid name clashes between client-defined atoms. For example, the atom that identifies the type **INTEGER** is defined by the symbol **XA_INTEGER**. X also predefines atoms intended for other uses, including selection types, property names, and font properties. Applications that use predefined atoms must include the header file Xatom.h.

11.2 USING PROPERTIES

A property is a collection of named, typed data. Every property is associated with a window, and the data stored in the property is maintained by the server, where it can be accessed or altered by any client that has the window's ID and the name of the property. Properties are named and typed using atoms. The X server predefines some atoms commonly used as property names, including:

```
XA_CUT_BUFFER0        XA_RGB_RED_MAP           XA_WM_HINTS
XA_CUT_BUFFER1        XA_RESOURCE_MANAGER      XA_WM_ICON_NAME
XA_CUT_BUFFER2        XA_RGB_BEST_MAP          XA_WM_ICON_SIZE
XA_CUT_BUFFER3        XA_RGB_BLUE_MAP          XA_WM_NAME
XA_CUT_BUFFER4        XA_RGB_DEFAULT_MAP       XA_WM_NORMAL_HINTS
XA_CUT_BUFFER5        XA_RGB_GRAY_MAP          XA_WM_ZOOM_HINTS
XA_CUT_BUFFER6        XA_WM_CLASS              XA_WM_TRANSIENT_FOR
XA_CUT_BUFFER7        XA_WM_CLIENT_MACHINE
XA_RGB_GREEN_MAP      XA_WM_COMMAND
```

Although these property names are predefined by the server, the corresponding properties do not automatically exist nor do they necessarily contain any data. Xlib predefines property names as a convenience so clients can use these properties without explicitly interning the atoms. Like all predefined atoms, predefined property names begin with the letters "**XA_**". The data associated with a property is simply stored as a stream of bytes, and a second atom associated with the property identifies the type of the data. The server also predefines atoms to represent some common data types, including:

XA_ARC	**XA_ATOM**	**XA_BITMAP**
XA_CARDINAL	**XA_COLORMAP**	**XA_CURSOR**
XA_DRAWABLE	**XA_FONT**	**XA_INTEGER**
XA_PIXMAP	**XA_POINT**	**XA_RGB_COLOR_MAP**
XA_RECTANGLE	**XA_STRING**	**XA_VISUALID**
XA_WINDOW	**XA_WM_HINTS**	**XA_WM_SIZE_HINTS**

Applications can create new atoms to represent any data type, including client-defined structures. The server attaches no particular meaning to any atom.

The function

```
XChangeProperty(display, window, name, type,
                format, mode, &data, nelements)
```

stores the given data in a property of the window. The third and fourth arguments to **XChangeProperty()** must be atoms that specify the name and type of the property. The **format** argument specifies whether the data consists of multiples of 8, 16, or 32 bits. This information allows the server to do byte swapping, if necessary, when data is transferred between clients running on different machines. The **mode** argument specifies whether the data is to replace any data already stored in the property or be added to the beginning or the end of any existing contents, and must be one of the constants **PropModeReplace**, **PropModePrepend**, or **PropModeAppend**. The **data** argument specifies the address of the data to be stored while **nelement** specifies the length of the data in multiples of the unit specified by the **format** argument.

Window properties are normally used to share information with other clients. For example, most X window managers expect some basic properties to be stored in properties on every application's top level window. Programmers who use the Xt Intrinsics do not usually need to be aware of this, because the Intrinsics sets these properties automatically. One of these window manager properties, **XA_WM_NAME**, is expected to contain the name of a window. Xlib provides a convenient function

```
XStoreName(display, window, name)
```

which stores a string, specified by the argument name, in the **XA_WM_NAME** property of a window. This Xlib function provides an easy-to-use interface to **XChangeProperty()**, and is defined as

```
XStoreName (dpy, w, name)
    Display  *dpy;
    Window    w;
    char     *name;
{
 XChangeProperty(dpy, w, XA_WM_NAME, XA_STRING,
                 8, PropModeReplace,
                 (unsigned char *)name,
                 name ? strlen(name) : 0);
}
```

Many other Xlib functions, including **XSetStandardProperties()** and **XSetWM-Hints()**, are implemented similarly.

A property exists until the window with which it is associated is destroyed, or until a client explicitly deletes the property. The lifetime of a property is not determined by the lifetime of the client that stores the property. The function

```
XDeleteProperty(display, window, property)
```

deletes a property from a window's property list.

Clients can retrieve the data stored in a property with the Xlib function

```
XGetWindowProperty(display, window, name, offset, length,
                   delete, requested_type, &actual_type,
                   &actual_format, &nitems, &bytes_left,
                   &data);
```

This function returns the constant **Success**, defined in Xlib.h, if no error condition is encountered while executing the function. This does not imply that the property was found, or that any data was retrieved. The **name** argument must be an atom identifying the property containing the desired data. The **offset** argument specifies the starting point within the property from which data should be returned. The offset is measured in 32-bit quantities from the beginning of the stored data. The **length** argument specifies how many 32-bit multiples of the data should be returned. The boolean argument, **delete**, indicates whether or not the server should delete the data after it is retrieved. The **requested_type** must be either an atom identifying the desired type of the data or the constant **AnyPropertyType**. When **XGetWindowProperty()** returns, the argument **actual_type** is set to an atom representing the type of the data stored in the atom, while **actual_format** contains the format type of the data. If the property does not exist for the specified window, **actual_type** is set to **None**, and the **actual_format** is set to zero. The arguments **nitems** and **bytes_left** indicate the number of bytes retrieved and how many remaining bytes are stored in the property. This allows applications to retrieve large amounts of data by repeated calls to **XGetWindowProperty()**. If the function returns successfully, the **data** argument points to the bytes retrieved from the property. X allocates this data using

Xmalloc(), and applications should free the data using **Xfree()** when the data is no longer needed.

The Xlib function

```
XFetchName(display, window, name)
```

uses **XGetProperty()** to retrieve the name of a window, stored in the **XA_WM_NAME** property. This function is the counterpart to **XStoreName()** and is defined by Xlib as

```
Status XFetchName (dpy, w, name)
     Display *dpy;
     Window   w;
     char    **name;
{
  Atom              actual_type;
  int               actual_format;
  unsigned long  nitems;
  unsigned long  leftover;
  unsigned char *data = NULL;
  if (XGetWindowProperty(dpy, w, XA_WM_NAME, 0L, (long)BUFSIZ,
                              FALSE, XA_STRING, &actual_type,
                              &actual_format, &nitems,
                              &leftover, &data) != Success){
    *name = NULL;
    return (0);
  }
  if ((actual_type == XA_STRING) && (actual_format == 8)){
    *name = (char *)data;
     return (1);
  }
  if (data)
     Xfree ((char *)data);
 *name = NULL;
  return (0);
}
```

If the call to **XGetWindowProperty()** is unsuccessful, **XFetchName()** returns **False**, with **name** set to NULL. If the call was successful, **XGetWindowProperty()** returns **Success**, and **XFetchName()** checks whether the property type matches the requested type and also checks the format to ensure that the data is in 8-bit format. If these conditions are met, **XFetchName()** sets **name** to point to the retrieved data and returns a value of one. If the type and format of the data are incorrect, the function frees the retrieved data, using **Xfree()**, and returns zero.

11.2.1 Property Events

The X server notifies interested clients when any change occurs in a window's property list. The X server generates a **PropertyNotify** event when the data stored in a property changes, when a property is initially created, or when a property is deleted. Clients must request **PropertyNotify** events using the event mask **PropertyChangedMask**. The **PropertyNotify** event uses the **XPropertyEvent** structure. In addition to the basic members included in all events, this structure contains the following members

```
Atom        atom;
Time        time;
int         state;
```

The **atom** member contains the name of the modified property. The **state** member is set to the constant **NewValue** if the value of property has changed, or to **Deleted** if the property has been deleted. The **time** member is set to the server time when the property was modified.

11.2.2 Using Properties to Share Data

This section uses a simple example to demonstrate how properties and atoms can be used to allow two or more applications to share data. The first application, **controldata**, allows the user to control three parameters named **altitude**, **speed** and **direction**. The current values of these parameters are kept in a single data structure, stored in a property on the root window of the display. A second application, **monitordata**, displays the current value of this data. The monitoring application uses **PropertyNotify** events to detect changes in the data and update its display.

11.2.2.1 The controldata Program

First, let's examine the **controldata** program, which lets the user set some values using scroll bars. The program then stores these values in a property in the server.

Both applications use the same header file, data.h. This file includes the header files for the widgets used by both programs and also the definition of a data structure common to both programs. It also includes declarations of two new atoms used by both applications to identify a property and the data type stored in the property.

```
/*************************************************
 *  data.h: declarations for shared data example
 *************************************************/

#include <X11/StringDefs.h>
#include <X11/Intrinsic.h>
#include <Xw/Xw.h>
```

```
#include <Xw/ScrollBar.h>
#include <Xw/RCManager.h>
#include <Xw/PButton.h>
#include <Xw/SText.h>
#include "libXs.h"

/* Maximum settings */
#define MAX_SPEED 100
#define MAX_ANGLE 359
#define MAX_ALT   200
/*
 *  Data structure to be stored in a property
 */
typedef struct {
   int                speed;
   int                angle;
   float              altitude;
}  flight_data;
/*
 * Atoms representing the property name and data type.
 */
Atom         FLIGHT_DATA, FLIGHT_DATA_TYPE;
```

The **flight_data** structure contains three parameters shared by the two programs. The user can position a slider to set the value of each member of this structure between zero and the maximum value determined by corresponding constant: **MAX_ALT**, **MAX_ANGLE**, or **MAX_SPEED**.

The source file, controldata.c, includes the file data.h and globally defines the widgets used by the program. The main program initializes each member of the **flight_data** data structure to zero, and creates the ScrollBar widgets that control each parameter. A RowCol manager widget manages three columns, each containing a ScrollBar widget and StaticText widget. The StaticText widget displays a label for the scroll bar.

```
/************************************************
 *  controldata.c: The data controller
 ************************************************/

#include "data.h"

void        slider_moved();
Widget      speed_ctl, angle_ctl, temp_ctl;
Widget      create_control();
Widget      make_controller();
```

```
main(argc, argv)
     int           argc;
     char         *argv[];
{
  Widget          toplevel, row_col;
  flight_data     data;

  data.speed = data.angle = data.altitude = 0;
  toplevel = XtInitialize(argv[0], "Controller", NULL, 0,
                          &argc, argv);
  /*
   * Create the atoms to represent the properties
   * used to store the data.
   */
  create_atoms(toplevel);
  row_col = XtCreateManagedWidget("panel",
                                  XwrowColWidgetClass,
                                  toplevel, NULL, 0);
  /*
   *  Make three columns, each containing a label and a
   *  slider control to control: speed, direction,
   *  and altitude.
   */
  speed_ctl = make_controller("speed",     MAX_SPEED,
                              row_col, &data);
  angle_ctl = make_controller("direction", MAX_ANGLE,
                              row_col, &data);
  temp_ctl  = make_controller("altitude",  MAX_ALT,
                              row_col, &data);
  create_quit_button("quit", row_col);

  XtRealizeWidget(toplevel);
  XtMainLoop();
}
```

The function **create_atoms()** creates two new atoms. The first is the name of the property in which the data is stored and the other represents the type of the data.

```
create_atoms(w)
    Widget w;
{
 Display * dpy = XtDisplay(w);
```

```
 FLIGHT_DATA      = XInternAtom(dpy, "Flight Data",      0);
 FLIGHT_DATA_TYPE = XInternAtom(dpy, "Flight Data Type", 0);
}
```

The function **make_controller()** takes a name, a maximum value, a parent widget, and a pointer to some client data as arguments and creates a column containing a scroll bar and a label. It returns a pointer to the ScrollBar widget.

```
Widget make_controller(name, max, parent, data)
   char           *name;
   int             max;
   Widget          parent;
   flight_data   *data;
{
 Widget col, w;
 /*
  * Create a column to manage a single control and a label.
  */
 col = XtCreateManagedWidget(name, XwrowColWidgetClass,
                                  parent, NULL, 0);
 XtCreateManagedWidget("label", XwstatictextWidgetClass,
                             col, NULL, 0);
 w = create_control(col, "control", 0, max, data);

 return (w);
}
```

The function **create_control()** creates a ScrollBar widget, defines minimum and maximum values for the scroll bar, and registers the callbacks that are invoked when the user moves the scroll bar slider or selects an area of the scroll bar.

```
Widget create_control(parent, name, minimum, maximum, data)
     Widget         parent;
     char          *name;
     int            minimum, maximum;
     flight_data *data;
{
  int     n;
  Arg     wargs[2];
  Widget w;
  /*
   * Create a scroll bar with range minimum to maximum.
   */
  n = 0;
```

```
    XtSetArg(wargs[n], XtNsliderMin, minimum); n++;
    XtSetArg(wargs[n], XtNsliderMax, maximum); n++;
    w = XtCreateManagedWidget(name, XwscrollbarWidgetClass,
                              parent, wargs, n);
    /*
     * Register callback function for when the user moves the
     * scroll bar slider.
     */
    XtAddCallback(w, XtNsliderMoved, slider_moved, data);
    XtAddCallback(w, XtNareaSelected, slider_selected, data);
    return (w);
}
```

The **XtNsliderMoved** callback function **slider_selected()** is defined in libXs. (See Chapter 6). The callback function **slider_moved()** updates the member of the **flight_data** structure corresponding to the slider that moved, and then calls **XChangeProperty()** to store the data in the **FLIGHT_DATA** property of the default root window of the display.

```
void slider_moved(w, data, sliderpos)
     Widget        w;
     flight_data  *data;
     int           sliderpos;
{
  /*
   * Set the member of the flight_data corresponding to
   * the slider that invoked this callback.
   */
  if(w == angle_ctl)
     data->angle = sliderpos;
  else if(w == speed_ctl)
     data->speed = sliderpos;
  else if(w == temp_ctl)
     data->altitude = (float) sliderpos / 10.0;
  /*
   * Replace the previous contents of the property
   * with the new data.
   */
  XChangeProperty(XtDisplay(w),
                  DefaultRootWindow(XtDisplay(w)),
                  FLIGHT_DATA, FLIGHT_DATA_TYPE,
```

```
                          32,  PropModeReplace,
                          (unsigned char *) data, 4);
}
```

The class resource file contains the resources corresponding to the widget layout shown in Fig. 11.1.

```
####################################################
# Controller: Resource File for controller
####################################################
Controller*slideOrientation:              horizontal
Controller*panel*columns:                 3
Controller*panel*RowCol*columns:          1
Controller*speed*label*string:            Speed
Controller*direction*label*string:        Direction
Controller*altitude*label*string:         Altitude
```

11.2.2.2 The monitordata Program

The **controldata** program allows a user to control the values represented by a complex data structure, and stores this data structure in a property of the root window. This section examines the **monitordata** program, which uses **PropertyNotify** events to retrieve and display the current value of this data whenever the program detects changes in the **FLIGHT_DATA** property.

The program includes the header file data.h which contains the definition of the data structure used by both the **controldata** program and the **monitordata** program.

The first portion of the main program is similar to the **controldata** program, except that each of the three columns in the **monitordata** window consists of two StaticText widgets. One of these displays the current value of a member of the data structure, while the other is used as a label. The function **create_atoms()** is identical to the function used by the **controldata** program, and is not repeated here.

```
/**********************************************************
 *  monitordata.c: display the data set by controldata
 **********************************************************/
#include "data.h"

Widget    make_display();

main(argc, argv)
        int              argc;
        char            *argv[];
{
```

```
Widget      toplevel, rc, speed, direction,  altitude;
Window      root;
XEvent      event;
/*
 * Initialize the Intrinsics,saving the default root window.
 */
toplevel = XtInitialize(argv[0], "Monitordata", NULL, 0,
                        &argc, argv);
root =  DefaultRootWindow(XtDisplay(toplevel));
/*
 * Initialize the Atoms used for the properties.
 */
create_atoms(toplevel);
rc = XtCreateManagedWidget("panel", XwrowColWidgetClass,
                            toplevel,  NULL, 0);

/*
 * Create the display widgets.
 */
speed      = make_display("speed",     rc);
direction  = make_display("direction", rc);
altitude   = make_display("altitude",  rc);
create_quit_button("quit", rc);

XtRealizeWidget(toplevel);
/*
 * Request property change event for the ROOT window.
 */
XSelectInput(XtDisplay(toplevel), root, PropertyChangeMask);
/*
 *  Get the initial value of the data.
 */
update_data(speed, direction, altitude);
/*
 * We must use our own event loop to get properties
 * events for the ROOT window.
 */
while(TRUE){
  XtNextEvent(&event);
  /*
   * Check for property change events on the ROOT window
   * before dispatching the event through the Intrinsics.
   */
```

```
        switch (event.type){
          case PropertyNotify:
            if(event.xproperty.window == root &&
               event.xproperty.atom == FLIGHT_DATA)
             update_data(speed, direction, altitude);
            else
             XtDispatchEvent(&event);
            break;
          default:
             XtDispatchEvent(&event);
        }
      }
    }
```

The event loop for this program is quite different from previous examples. Because we stored the property on the root window of the display, we cannot use **XtMainLoop()**. The Xt Intrinsics event handler mechanism allows applications to register event handlers to be invoked when a event occurs relative to a specific *widget*, but **monitordata** needs to be notified when an event occurs relative to the root window. Since the root window is not a widget, we cannot use the Intrinsics' dispatch mechanism to handle the event. Therefore, we must write our own event loop to intercept the event before it reaches the event dispatcher. Before entering the event loop, the program uses the Xlib function **XSelectInput()** to request **PropertyNotify** events for the root window. The default root window of the display is specified as the event window and the event mask is given as **PropertyChangeMask**. This requests the X server to send **PropertyNotify** events to **monitordata** when any property of the root window changes. The event loop uses **XtNextEvent()** to remove each event from the event queue. A switch statement checks the type of each event to determine if it is a **PropertyNotify** event. If it is, and the **property** member of the event is the atom **FLIGHT_DATA**, **update_data()** is called to retrieve the data stored in the property and update the values displayed in each StaticText widget. Otherwise, the function **XtDispatchEvent()** is called to dispatch events to the appropriate widget. **XtDispatchEvent()** is also called for event types other that **PropertyNotify**.

The function **update_data()** uses **XGetWindowProperty()** to retrieve the contents of the **FLIGHT_DATA** property. The requested number of bytes is determined by the size of the **flight_data** structure. The length of the data actually retrieved is returned in the variable **nitems**, while **retdata** points to the contents of the property. If **XGetWindowProperty()** succeeds and the type of the property is **FLIGHT_DATA_TYPE**, the value of each field of the structure is converted to a string and displayed in the corresponding StaticText widget.

```
update_data(speed, direction, altitude)
     Widget speed, direction, altitude;
{
  int             type, format, nitems, left;
  flight_data    *retdata;
  char            str[100];
  Arg             wargs[1];
  /*
   * Retrieve the data from the root window property.
   */
  if(XGetWindowProperty(XtDisplay(speed),
                        DefaultRootWindow(XtDisplay(speed)),
                        FLIGHT_DATA, 0, sizeof(flight_data),
                        FALSE, FLIGHT_DATA_TYPE,
                        &type, &format, &nitems, &left,
                        &retdata) == Success &&
       type ==FLIGHT_DATA_TYPE){
    /*
     * If the data exists, display it.
     */
    sprintf(str, "%d", retdata->speed);
    XtSetArg(wargs[0], XtNstring, str);
    XtSetValues(speed, wargs, 1);

    sprintf(str, "%d", retdata->angle);
    XtSetArg(wargs[0], XtNstring, str);
    XtSetValues(direction, wargs, 1);

    sprintf(str, "%5.1f", retdata->altitude + 0.05);
    XtSetArg(wargs[0], XtNstring, str);
    XtSetValues(altitude, wargs, 1);
  }
}
```

The only **monitordata** function we have not discussed, **make_display()**, creates each column of StaticText widgets. One widget functions as a label for the data, while the other displays the value of the data.

```
Widget make_display(name, parent)
   char           *name;
   Widget          parent;
{
 Widget col, w;
```

```
/*
 * Create a row column widget containing two
 * StaticText widgets.
 */
col = XtCreateManagedWidget(name, XwrowColWidgetClass,
                            parent, NULL, 0);
XtCreateManagedWidget("label", XwstatictextWidgetClass,
                      col, NULL, 0);
w = XtCreateManagedWidget("display", XwstatictextWidgetClass,
                          col, NULL, 0);
return (w);
}
```

The class resource file, Monitordata, contains the resources corresponding to the widget layout shown in Fig. 11.1.

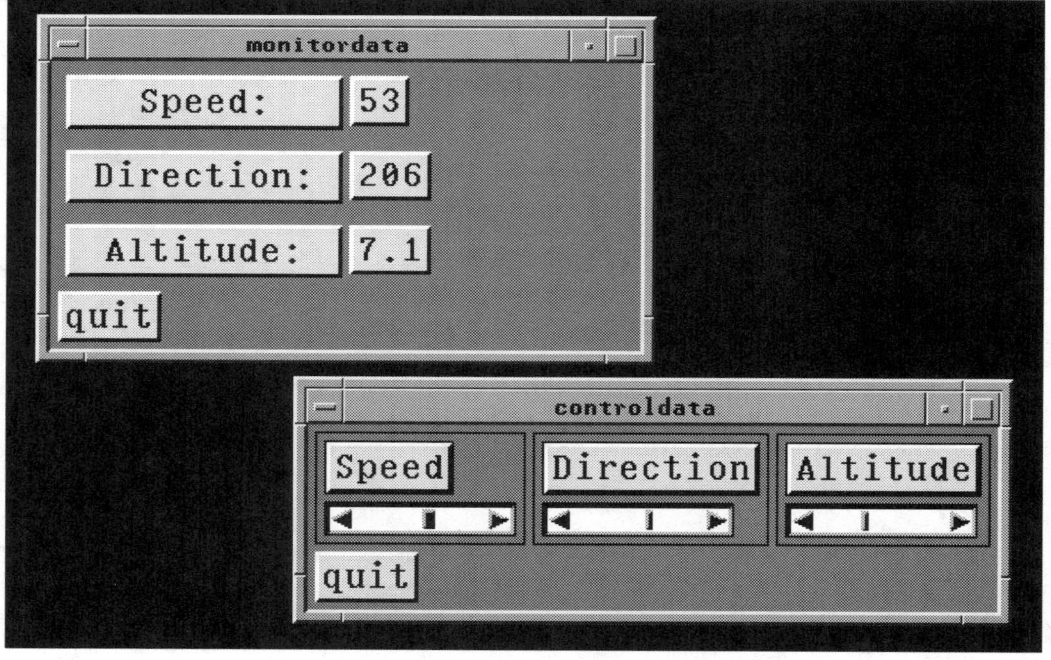

Figure 11.1 The monitordata and controldata programs.

```
##############################################################
# Monitordata: Resource file for monitordata program
#############################################################

Monitordata*RowCol*RowCol*columns:          2
Monitordata*RowCol*RowCol*BorderWidth:      0
Monitordata*StaticText.width:             150
Monitordata*StaticText.height:             30
Monitordata*speed*string:                  Speed:
Monitordata*direction*string:              Direction:
Monitordata*altitude*string:               Altitude:
```

This example illustrates how properties allow two separate applications to share data. **PropertyNotify** events allow multiple applications to be informed whenever a property changes. Properties and **PropertyNotify** events not only provide a way for applications to share data, but also provide a *trigger* mechanism that can be used to notify clients that data has changed and to synchronize multiple applications that use the data. Efficiency problems might arise if many applications use properties on the root window for such purposes, because **PropertyNotify** events cannot be requested for a particular property, only for all properties on a window's property list. However, the same effect can be achieved by having a set of related applications watch the properties on one common window instead of the root window.

The next section discusses a more direct way to provide communication between applications, using **ClientMessage** events.

11.3 COMMUNICATING WITH EVENTS

X allows applications to send events to any window. This feature can be used to forward events from one application to another, or to create and send new events. The function

```
XSendEvent(display, window, propagate, mask, &event)
```

sends an event to clients that have selected the event for the specified window. The window argument must be either a valid window ID on the given display, or the constant **PointerWindow**, in which case the event is sent to the window currently containing the sprite. The **window** argument can also be the constant **InputFocus**, requesting that the event be sent to the current focus window. If **InputFocus** is specified and the sprite is contained within the focus window, the event is sent to the smallest window or subwindow of the focus window containing the sprite. The boolean flag, **propagate**, determines whether the server should propagate the event to ancestors if the specified window has not selected the event type.

XSendEvent() can be used to send any valid X event type. The X server sends the event to all clients that have selected the events specified in the mask parameter for the given window. **XSendEvent()** returns a non-zero value if the function executes correctly. Successful execution does not imply that the intended window received the event, only that no error condition occurred.

11.3.1 Client Message Events

One common use of **XSendEvent()** is to send client messages. **ClientMessage** events are never generated by the server. They are used by applications to define new events and provide the basis for one form of interclient communication. **ClientMessage** events have no corresponding event mask and cannot be specifically selected. They are always received by the client that owns the window to which the event is sent.[1] The **XClientMessageEvent** structure is defined in Xlib.h as:

```
typedef struct {
     int           type;
     unsigned long serial;
     Bool          send_event;
     Display      *display;
     Window        window;
     Atom          message_type;
     int           format;
     union {
          char     b[20];
          short    s[10];
          long     l[5];
     } data;
} XClientMessageEvent;
```

In addition to the first five members that are common to all event types, the **ClientMessage** event structure contains a **message_type** field that identifies the subtype of the event. The subtype is specified by an atom whose meaning must be recognized by both the sending and receiving applications. The X server does not interpret the field. The **format** member specifies the data format of the bytes in the **data** field, and must be one of 8, 16, or 32. The **data** field consists of 20 bytes, declared as a union of bytes, shorts, and longs. Clients are free to use this data field for any purpose.

Because **ClientMessage** events are *non-maskable* events, applications must specify **NoEventMask** (or 0) as the event mask when registering event handlers for

1. The event is always received, in the sense that the server always places the event in the client's event queue. However, unless the client has defined an event handler for the event, it will be ignored.

ClientMessage events. For example, a function named **message_handler()** can be registered as an event handler for a widget with the statement

```
XtAddEventHandler(w, NoEventMask, TRUE, message_handler, NULL);
```

The argument following the event mask must be **True** to indicate that this is a non-maskable event.

11.3.2 An Example: xtalk

This section presents an example program that shows how **XSendEvent()** can be used to communicate between two applications. The program demonstrates **ClientMessage** events and also provides some additional examples of how properties and atoms can be used. The example, named **xtalk**, allows users on two different machines to communicate with each other, and is similar in spirit to the **talk** program found on most UNIX systems.

First, let's look at Fig. 11.2 and discuss how the program works from the user's viewpoint.

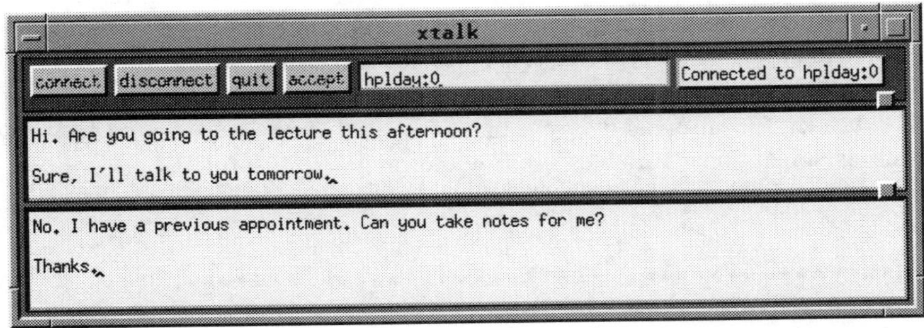

Figure 11.2 The xtalk program.

The main window of **xtalk** is divided into three primary areas: a command pane, and two message panes. The user types into the top message pane, while messages from a remote **xtalk** program appear in the bottom message pane. The user can request a connection to another **xtalk** user by typing the name of the other user's display into the text field in the upper left of the control pane, and then selecting the "connect" button. At this point, the message field on the right side of the command pane displays the message

```
Waiting for a response
```

Assuming there is an **xtalk** program running on the requested display, the remote **xtalk** displays a message

```
Connection requested from <machine>
```

where <machine> is the name of the first user's display.[2] If the user of the remote **xtalk** is willing to accept the **talk** request, he or she selects the "accept" button. Once a connection is established, the message field of each user's **xtalk** displays the message

```
Connected to <machine>
```

where <machine> is the name of the other user's machine. From this point on, until either user breaks the connection by selecting the disconnect button, everything typed in the top message pane of each **xtalk** is echoed in the bottom panel of the other **xtalk**.

The **xtalk** program uses **ClientMessage** events to make connection requests and to send "disconnect" and "accept" notifications between programs. In addition, the program uses **XSendEvent()** to forward each **KeyPress**, **ButtonPress**, and **MotionNotify** event that occurs in the top message pane of either **xtalk** to the lower text pane of the remote program. The **xtalk** program has several interesting aspects. First, the application must properly handle the atoms, properties, and window IDs on two different displays. Remembering when to use resources from the local display and when to use those of the remote display can be confusing, but interesting. This program also uses widget *sensitivity* to control what commands are available to the user at any given time, depending on the state of the program.[3] At any particular time, only the buttons that represent commands available to the user are sensitive to events. All other buttons are disabled and cannot be selected.

The header file for **xtalk** includes the header files for each widget class used by the program. The header file also defines several atoms used as subtypes of **ClientMessage** events as well as some global variables used by the program. The file defines some strings as constants to eliminate the possibility of spelling the words differently in different parts of the program.

```
/*************************************************
 *  xtalk.h: declarations used by xtalk
 *************************************************/

#include <stdio.h>
#include <X11/Intrinsic.h>
#include <X11/StringDefs.h>
#include <X11/Xatom.h>
#include <Xw/Xw.h>
#include <Xw/RCManager.h>
#include <Xw/VPW.h>
#include <Xw/TextEdit.h>
```

2. For this program to work, each user must be able to open the display of the other user. Security in X is handled by the xhost program or the file /usr/lib/X0.hosts. Consult your local user's documentation for details.

3. Every widget has a XtNsensitive resource that determines whether a widget responds to events. If a widget is insensitive, the Intrinsics does not dispatch device events for it or any of its children. Most widgets change their appearance, and are "grayed out" when they are in an insensitive state.

```
#include <Xw/SText.h>
#include <Xw/PButton.h>
#include "libXs.h"
/*
 *   Atoms used for communication
 */
Atom        XTALK_WINDOW, CONNECTION_REQUEST,
            CONNECTION_ACCEPT, DISCONNECT_NOTIFY;
Display    *remote_display = NULL;
Display    *my_display;
Window      remote_talker_window;
/*
 *  Various widgets
 */
Widget      name_field, msg_field,
            connect_button, disconnect_button,
            accept_button;
char       *othermachine[100];
char       *my_displayname;
int         connection_accepted = FALSE;
/*
 *  Define the strings used to create atoms
 */
#define XtNdisconnect          "Disconnect Notify"
#define XtNconnectionAccept    "Connection Accept"
#define XtNconnectionRequest   "Connection Request"
#define XtNtalkWindow          "XTalk Window"
/*
 * Declare the callbacks used in xtalk
 */
void     client_message_handler();
void     warn_wrong_pane();
void     accept_callback();
void     connect_callback();
void     disconnect_callback();
void     send_event();
void     send_to_other();
void     quit_callback();
void     desensitize();
```

The main body of the program uses **XtInitialize()** to initialize the toolkit and open the local X display, and then saves both the display and the name of the display for later use. Fig. 11.3 shows the widget tree created by **xtalk**. A VerticalPaned widget manages the three panes of the **xtalk** window. The top pane, created by the function **create_command_panel()**, contains a row of button widgets used to issue commands. The lower two panes each contain a TextEdit widget; The upper pane, referred to as the *talk* pane, allows the user to enter text. The lower pane, referred to as the *listen* pane, displays the text sent from remote **xtalk** programs. The event handler **send_to_other()**, registered for the talk pane, is invoked when a **KeyPress** event, any button event, or a **MotionNotify** event occurs in the talk pane. The listen pane has two event handlers defined, one for **KeyPress** events and the other for events with no event mask, which includes **ClientMessage** events. We will examine the purpose of these callbacks shortly.

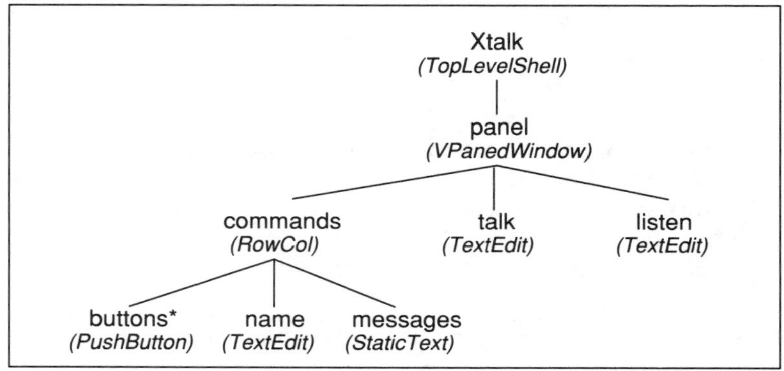

Figure 11.3 Widget tree for xtalk.

Finally, after realizing all widgets, the function **register_talker_window()** is called. This function stores the window ID of the listen pane in a property of the root window, where it can be accessed by other **xtalk** programs. This publicly announces the window ID to which remote **xtalk** programs can send connection requests. We cannot register the window ID until after the widget has been realized and the window actually exists.

```
/*********************************************
 *  xtalk.c
 *********************************************/
#include "xtalk.h"

main(argc, argv)
     int   argc;
     char *argv[];
{
  Widget toplevel, vpane, talk, listen;
  /*
```

```
     * Open display and save display and display name.
     */
    toplevel = XtInitialize(argv[0], "Xtalk", NULL, 0,
                            &argc, argv);

    my_display = XtDisplay(toplevel);
    my_displayname = XDisplayName(my_display);
    /*
     * Create a pane to hold all other widgets.
     */
    vpane = XtCreateManagedWidget("panel",
                                  XwvPanedWidgetClass,
                                  toplevel, NULL,0);
    create_command_panel(vpane);
    /*
     * Create the text panes used to talk.
     */
    talk = XtCreateManagedWidget("talk",
                                 XwtexteditWidgetClass,
                                 vpane, NULL, 0);
    XtAddEventHandler(talk, KeyPressMask |
                            ButtonPressMask |
                            ButtonReleaseMask |
                            PointerMotionMask,
                      FALSE, send_to_other, NULL);
    listen = XtCreateManagedWidget("listen",
                                   XwtexteditWidgetClass,
                                    vpane, NULL, 0);
    XtAddEventHandler(listen, KeyPressMask, FALSE,
                      warn_wrong_pane, NULL);
    XtAddEventHandler(listen, NoEventMask, TRUE,
                      client_message_handler, NULL);
    XtRealizeWidget(toplevel);
    /*
     * Store the listen window ID in a public place.
     */
    register_talker_window(listen);
    XtMainLoop();
}
```

The function **create_command_panel()** creates a row of buttons and text widgets in the top pane of the **xtalk** window. The buttons are initially disabled. The function adds a callback to each button's **XtNselect** callback list, and also adds a callback function,

desensitize(), to the **XtNrelease** callback list of the **disconnect_button** and **accept_button**. This callback function disables these buttons after they are selected. The **accept_button** is enabled when a connection request is received and disabled once a connection is accepted; the **disconnect_button** is enabled whenever a connection to another **xtalk** is established.

The **name_field** widget provides a place where the user can enter the name of a remote display. Finally, a StaticText widget serves as a status message area.

```
create_command_panel(parent)
   Widget parent;
{
  Widget  command, quit;
  Arg     wargs[3];
  int     n;
  /*
   * Create a row widget to hold the command buttons.
   */
  command = XtCreateManagedWidget("command",
                                  XwrowColWidgetClass,
                                  parent, NULL, 0);
  /*
   * Create the buttons.
   */
  connect_button = XtCreateManagedWidget("connect",
                                  XwpushButtonWidgetClass,
                                  command, NULL, 0);
  XtAddCallback(connect_button, XtNselect,
                connect_callback, NULL);
  disconnect_button = XtCreateManagedWidget("disconnect",
                                  XwpushButtonWidgetClass,
                                  command, NULL, 0);
  XtAddCallback(disconnect_button, XtNselect,
                disconnect_callback, NULL);
  XtAddCallback(disconnect_button, XtNrelease,
                desensitize, NULL);
  XtSetSensitive(disconnect_button, FALSE);
  quit = create_quit_button("quit", command);
  XtAddCallback(quit, XtNselect, quit_callback, NULL);
  accept_button = XtCreateManagedWidget("accept",
                                  XwpushButtonWidgetClass,
                                  command, NULL, 0);
  XtAddCallback(accept_button, XtNselect,
```

```
                     accept_callback, NULL);
  XtAddCallback(accept_button, XtNrelease, desensitize, NULL);
  XtSetSensitive(accept_button, FALSE);
  /*
   * Create a text field in which the user can
   * enter new machine names.
   */
  name_field =
       create_one_line_text_widget("name", command, NULL, 0);
  /*
   * Create the message area.
   */
  n = 0;
  XtSetArg(wargs[n], XtNstring, "No Current Connection"); n++;
  msg_field = XtCreateManagedWidget("messages",
                                    XwstatictextWidgetClass,
                                    command, wargs, n);
}
```

Before one **xtalk** program can send messages to another, it must have the window ID of the listen pane belonging to the other **xtalk**. The function **register_talker_window()** stores the window ID of the listen pane in a property of the root window, where it can be accessed by any other **xtalk** program. The function creates several atoms used by the program, and stores the listen window ID in the **XTALK_WINDOW** property.

```
register_talker_window(w)
     Widget w;
{
 Window   window = XtWindow(w);
 Display *dpy    = XtDisplay(w);
 /*
  * Intern the atoms used for communication.
  */
 XTALK_WINDOW       = XInternAtom(dpy, XtNtalkWindow, 0);
 CONNECTION_REQUEST = XInternAtom(dpy,XtNconnectionRequest,0);
 CONNECTION_ACCEPT  = XInternAtom(dpy, XtNconnectionAccept,0);
 DISCONNECT_NOTIFY  = XInternAtom(dpy, XtNdisconnect, 0);
  /*
   * Store the listen window ID on our root window.
   */
  XChangeProperty(dpy, DefaultRootWindow(dpy),
                  XTALK_WINDOW, XA_WINDOW,
```

```
                    32, PropModeReplace,
                    &window, 1);
}
```

To establish a connection with another **xtalk** program, the user must enter the name of a remote display in the **name_field** widget, and then select the **connect_button**. This action invokes the **connect_callback()** function, which attempts to open the display named by the string in the **name_field** widget. This function must make sure the string is not empty because **XOpenDisplay()** interprets an empty string as an instruction to open the display named by the environment variable **DISPLAY**, which is normally set to the local display. Therefore if the string is empty, **xtalk** would attempt to open a connection to itself. If the remote display is opened successfully, the function then retrieves the **XTALK_WINDOW** property from the remote display, and sends a connection request to the remote **xtalk** window.

```
void connect_callback(w, client_data, call_data)
   Widget   w;
   caddr_t  client_data, call_data;
{
  int         type, format, nitems, left, fail;
  Window     *retdata;
  Arg         wargs[2];
  char       *msg;
  Atom        REMOTE_XTALK_WINDOW;
  /*
   * Get the name of the display to connect to.
   */
  strcpy(othermachine, XwTextCopyBuffer(name_field));
  /*
   * Make sure the string isn't empty, so we don't connect
   * to ourselves.
   */
  if(strlen(othermachine) > 0){
    wprintf(msg_field, "%s", "Trying To Open Connection");
    /*
     * Attempt to open the remote display.
     */
    if((remote_display = XOpenDisplay(othermachine)) == NULL){
        wprintf(msg_field, "%s", "Connection Failed");
        return;
    }
    /*
     *  Get the REMOTE property containing THEIR listen ID.
```

```
         */
        REMOTE_XTALK_WINDOW  =
              XInternAtom(remote_display, XtNtalkWindow, 0);
        if(XGetWindowProperty(remote_display,
                              DefaultRootWindow(remote_display),
                              REMOTE_XTALK_WINDOW,
                              0, 4, FALSE, XA_WINDOW,
                              &type, &format, &nitems, &left,
                              &retdata) == Success &&
              type == XA_WINDOW){
          remote_talker_window = *retdata;
          /*
           *  If all went well, request a connection.
           */
          wprintf(msg_field, "Waiting for a response");
          send_talk_request();
        }
        /*
         *  If something went wrong, disconnect.
         */
        else
          XtCallCallbacks(disconnect_button, XtNselect, NULL);
      }
    }
```

Notice how atoms and properties on the remote display are accessed in this example. In previous sections we noted that an atom is a unique identifier for a string, shared by all applications. Here, we are connected to two servers, and there is no guarantee that any two servers use the same atom to represent the same string. The atom e depends on the order in which strings are interned, and are not based on the contents of the string. Therefore, we must obtain the **XTALK_WINDOW** atom defined by the remote server before retrieving the contents of the **XTALK_WINDOW** property from the remote display. Also notice that the first argument to **XGetWindowProperty()** refers to the *remote* display.

The function **send_talk_request()** sends a **ClientMessage** event requesting a connection to the remote **xtalk** program. First, this function determines the atom ID that represents the **XtNconnectionRequest** string on the remote display. Then it fills in the fields of an **XClientMessageEvent** structure with the remote display and the ID of the remote window. The atom **REMOTE_CONNECTION_REQUEST** is used as the subtype of the client message, and the display name of the local machine is copied into the data field. The function **XSendEvent()** sends the event to the remote **xtalk** window. Notice again that the display argument given to **XSendEvent()** refers to the *remote*, not the local, display. We cannot send the event using the local server, because the remote window does not exist on the local display. Also notice the **XFlush()** statement. **XFlush()** is an Xlib function that forces the server to process all requests in the calling client's request queue. This is seldom necessary, because **XtNextEvent()** flushes the queue each time it is called. However, **XtNextEvent()** flushes the local display, not the remote display. Without the call to **XFlush()**, the **ClientMessage** event would remain in the remote server's request queue until enough requests had accumulated to cause it to process the request. Explicitly flushing the remote request queue ensures that the remote server handles the **XSendEvent()** request in a timely manner.

```
send_talk_request()
{
  XClientMessageEvent   event;
  Atom REMOTE_CONNECTION_REQUEST;

  connection_accepted = FALSE;
  /*
   * Get the XtNconnectionRequest atom used
   * by the remote display.
   */
 REMOTE_CONNECTION_REQUEST =
         XInternAtom(remote_display, XtNconnectionRequest, 0);
  /*
   * Fill out the client message event structure.
   */
  event.display = remote_display;
  event.window  = remote_talker_window;
  event.type    = ClientMessage;
  event.format  = 32;
  event.message_type = REMOTE_CONNECTION_REQUEST;
  strcpy(event.data.b, my_displayname);
  /*
   *  Send the event.
   */
  XSendEvent(remote_display, remote_talker_window,
             True, XtAllEvents, &event);
  XFlush(remote_display);
}
```

When **xtalk** receives a client message, the Intrinsics invokes the event handler **client_message_handler()**, which looks at the subtype of the client message, and acts on those that it recognizes. Because the atoms used to identify subtypes are not constants, we cannot use a switch statement, and instead, we must check the subtype using a series of if statements.[4] If the subtype of the client message is **CONNECTION_REQUEST**, the **client_message_handler()** rings the terminal bell and displays a message to notify the user of the incoming connection request. It then saves a copy of the name of the machine making the connection request and enables the **accept_button** widget.

Other types of client messages are handled similarly. When a remote **xtalk** accepts a connection, it sends a client message of subtype **CONNECTION_ACCEPT**. After displaying a message for the user, the **client_message_handler()** disables the **disconnect_button** widget and enables the **connect_button** widget. The function also sets the global flag **connection_accepted** to **True**.

If the client message is of subtype **DISCONNECT_NOTIFY**, **xtalk** closes the display connection, resets various parameters and buttons to their initial state, and displays the message "Disconnected".

```
void client_message_handler(w, client_data, event)
   Widget       w;
   caddr_t      client_data;
   XEvent      *event;
{
  if(event->xclient.message_type == CONNECTION_REQUEST){
   /*
    * Notify the user of the incoming request and
    * enable the "accept" button.
    */
    XBell(XtDisplay(w), 0);
    strcpy(othermachine, event->xclient.data.b);
    wprintf(msg_field, "Connection Request from: %s",
            othermachine);
    XtSetSensitive(accept_button, TRUE);
  }
  else
    if(event->xclient.message_type == CONNECTION_ACCEPT){
      /*
       * Notify the user that the connection has
       * been accepted. Enable the "disconnect" button
       * and disable the "connect" button.
       */
      XBell(XtDisplay(w), 0);
      connection_accepted = TRUE;
      strcpy(othermachine, event->xclient.data.b);
      wprintf(msg_field, "Connected to %s", othermachine);
```

4. The atoms predefined by the X server are defined as constants, and so this restriction applies only to atoms that are created by an application.

```
          XtSetSensitive(connect_button, FALSE);
          XtSetSensitive(disconnect_button, TRUE);
        }
      else
        if(event->xclient.message_type == DISCONNECT_NOTIFY){
          /*
           * Close the remote display and reset
           * all command buttons to their initial state.
           */
          XBell(XtDisplay(w), 0);
          XCloseDisplay(remote_display);
          remote_display = NULL;
          connection_accepted = FALSE;
          othermachine[0] = '\0';
          wprintf(msg_field, "%s", "Disconnected");
          XtSetSensitive(connect_button, TRUE);
          XtSetSensitive(disconnect_button, FALSE);
        }
    }
```

When **xtalk** receives a connection request, the **accept_button** widget is enabled. If the user selects the **accept_button** widget, the **accept_callback()** function is invoked. This function attempts to open the remote display and retrieve the window ID of the remote **xtalk**'s listen pane. If successful, **send_talk_accept()** sends a client message indicating that the connection has been accepted. The function also disables the **connect_button** and enables the **disconnect_button**.

```
void accept_callback(w, client_data, call_data)
   Widget    w;
   caddr_t   client_data, call_data;
{
  int       type, format, nitems, left, fail;
  Window   *retdata;
  Atom      REMOTE_XTALK_WINDOW;
  /*
   * Make sure there really is another machine.
   */
  if(strlen(othermachine) > 0 ){
      /*
       * Attempt to open the remote display.
       */
    if((remote_display = XOpenDisplay(othermachine)) == NULL){
        wprintf(msg_field, "%s", "Connection Failed");
```

```
            return;
        }
        /*
         *  Get the window ID of the remote xtalk program.
         */
        REMOTE_XTALK_WINDOW  =
                    XInternAtom(remote_display, XtNtalkWindow, 0);
        if(XGetWindowProperty(remote_display,
                              DefaultRootWindow(remote_display),
                              REMOTE_XTALK_WINDOW,
                              0, 4, FALSE, XA_WINDOW,
                              &type, &format, &nitems, &left,
                              &retdata) == Success &&
                type ==  XA_WINDOW) {
          connection_accepted = TRUE;
          remote_talker_window = *retdata;
         /*
          * Notify the remote program that we accept connection.
          */
          send_talk_accept();
          wprintf(msg_field, "Connected to %s", othermachine);
          XtSetSensitive(connect_button, FALSE);
          XtSetSensitive(disconnect_button, TRUE);
        }
        else
          XtCallCallbacks(disconnect_button, XtNselect, NULL);
      }
    }
```

The function **send_talk_accept()** is similar to **send_talk_request()** except that the subtype of the client message is **REMOTE_CONNECTION_ACCEPT**. Notice that once again the atom is obtained from the remote display, so that the message can be recognized by the remote program.

```
send_talk_accept()
{
  XClientMessageEvent event;
  Atom REMOTE_CONNECTION_ACCEPT;
  /*
   * Get the XtNconnectionAccept atom used
   * by the remote display.
   */
  REMOTE_CONNECTION_ACCEPT = XInternAtom(remote_display,
```

```
                                          XtNconnectionAccept,
                                          FALSE);
    /*
     * Fill in the client message event structure.
     */
    event.display = remote_display;
    event.window  = remote_talker_window;
    event.type    = ClientMessage;
    event.format  = 8;
    event.message_type = REMOTE_CONNECTION_ACCEPT;
    strcpy(event.data.b, my_displayname);
    /*
     *  Send it.
     */
    XSendEvent(remote_display, remote_talker_window,
               True, XtAllEvents, &event);
    XFlush(remote_display);
  }
```

Once each program has established a connection to the other, each user can type into his or her talk pane. The event handler **send_to_other()** is invoked when any key or mouse event occurs in the talk pane. This function uses **XSendEvent()** to send the event to the remote **xtalk** program, where it is treated just as if the remote user had typed the text into the window. The result is that everything typed in the talk pane of the local **xtalk** program is also echoed in the listen pane of the remote **xtalk** program.

```
  void send_to_other(w, client_data, event)
     Widget     w;
     caddr_t    client_data;
     XEvent    *event;
  {
    /*
     * Make sure that we have a valid connection
     * before sending the event.
     */
    if(remote_display && remote_talker_window &&
         connection_accepted){
      event->xany.display = remote_display;
      event->xany.window  = remote_talker_window;
      XSendEvent(remote_display, remote_talker_window,
                 True, XtAllEvents, event);
```

```
        XFlush(remote_display);
      }
  }
```

The TextEdit widget does not provide a way to prevent the user from typing into the listen pane of the **xtalk** window. The TextEdit widget does not distinguish between events generated by the local keyboard and those sent by the remote **xtalk**. This could be confusing to the user, because text typed into the listen pane is echoed in the local listen pane, but is not sent to the remote **xtalk** program. Although we cannot intercept events generated by the keyboard, we can add an event handler that is called in addition to the one defined by the TextEdit widget. The event handler **warn_wrong_pane()** rings the terminal bell whenever the user types into the listen text pane to warn the user that he or she is using the wrong pane. This event handler examines the **send_event** member of each event to determine if the event was sent using **XSendEvent()**.

```
void warn_wrong_pane(w, client_data, event)
   Widget     w;
   caddr_t    client_data;
   XEvent     *event;
{
  /*
   * Just beep if the user types into the wrong pane.
   */
  if (!event->xany.send_event)
     XBell(XtDisplay(w), 0);
}
```

When a conversation has ended, either user can close the connection by selecting the **disconnect_button**, invoking the callback function **disconnect_callback()**. This callback resets the state of the buttons and variables used by the program, after calling the function **send_disconnect()** to notify the remote **xtalk** of the disconnection. Finally, **XCloseDisplay()** closes the connection to the remote display.

```
void disconnect_callback(w, client_data, call_data)
   Widget   w;
   caddr_t  client_data, call_data;
{
  /*
   * Send a disconnect notice and close the display.
   */
  if(remote_display){
    send_disconnect();
    XCloseDisplay(remote_display);
    wprintf(msg_field, "%s", "Disconnected");
```

```
        othermachine[0] = '\0';
        remote_display = NULL;
        XtSetSensitive(connect_button, TRUE);
      }
  }
```

The function **send_disconnect()** retrieves the remote display's **XtNdisconnect** atom, composes a client message of subtype **REMOTE_DISCONNECT_NOTIFY**, and sends the event.

```
send_disconnect()
{
 XClientMessageEvent event;
 Atom REMOTE_DISCONNECT_NOTIFY;
 /*
  * Get the XtNdisconnect atom used
  * by the remote display.
  */
 REMOTE_DISCONNECT_NOTIFY = XInternAtom(remote_display,
                                        XtNdisconnect,
                                        FALSE);
 connection_accepted = FALSE;
 /*
  * Fill out the client message event structure.
  */
 event.display = remote_display;
 event.window  = remote_talker_window;
 event.type    = ClientMessage;
 event.format  = 32;
 event.message_type = REMOTE_DISCONNECT_NOTIFY;
 /*
  * Send it.
  */
 XSendEvent(remote_display, remote_talker_window,
            True, XtAllEvents, &event);
 XFlush(remote_display);
}
```

The connection is also broken when either user exits the **xtalk** program. Therefore the **quit_callback()** function, invoked when the user selects the quit button, also calls **send_disconnect()** to notify the remote **xtalk** that the connection is about to be closed. This function also deletes the **XTALK_WINDOW** property, to prevent remote **xtalk**s from attempting to connect to a non-existent window. The program exits when the user releases the button, invoking the **quit()** callback function.

```
void quit_callback(w, client_data, call_data)
    Widget      w;
    caddr_t     client_data, call_data;
{
  Display *dpy = XtDisplay(w);
  /*
   * Inform the remote connection that we are shutting down.
   */
  if(remote_display && remote_talker_window)
    send_disconnect();
   /*
    * Clean up.
    */
   XDeleteProperty(dpy, DefaultRootWindow(dpy), XTALK_WINDOW);
}
```

The **xtalk** program attempts to enable and disable the command buttons to control the subset of commands available to the user at any given time. Sometimes buttons are enabled and disabled as a result of client messages, while at other times they are changed in response to a user's action. The last function used by **xtalk** is an **XtNrelease** callback defined for the buttons **connect_button**, **disconnect_button**, and **accept_button**. This callback disables each button after the user releases the button.[5]

```
void desensitize(w, client_data, call_data)
    Widget      w;
    caddr_t     client_data;
    caddr_t     call_data;
{
    XtSetSensitive(w, FALSE);
}
```

5. Notice that this callback is defined for the XtNrelease callback, so it is invoked when the button is released, rather than when the button is selected. This is important, because otherwise an interesting problem can occur. Suppose that this callback is defined for XtNselect. When a mouse button is pressed, the button typically changes to a highlighted (or inverse-video) mode. At the same time, the button's XtNsensitive resource is set to False by the callback. Now the button cannot receive any more events, including the ButtonRelease event that would return the button to its normal unhighlighted state. Not only does the button stay highlighted, but this can leave many widgets in the X Widget set in an unexpected state, because the pattern used to show that a widget is insensitive is based on its current color. We can avoid this problem by altering the sensitivity of the buttons only after the button is released.

11.4 THE X SELECTION MECHANISM

Most window systems support some mechanism for transferring information between windows. This is often referred to as "cut and paste," because the user deletes ("cuts") an object or section of text from one window and then transfers ("pastes") it into another window.[6] Because all X applications in the user's environment do not necessarily run on the same machine, X implements "cut and paste" via an interclient communication mechanism, using the X server as a central communications point.

The client messages discussed in the previous section allow applications to define their own communication protocols and provides a flexible way to exchange information. These facilities are useful when two or more programs need to define a particular style of communication, as demonstrated by the **xtalk** example. However, for this approach to work, every application involved must respond to the same types of client messages. Requiring every application to define and decipher client messages to do a simple "copy and paste" data transfer places an unacceptable burden on application programmers. On the other hand, a flexible facility that allows arbitrary data types to be copied between applications is highly desirable.

X provides several events and functions that work together to implement a flexible "copy and paste" mechanism. This section first discusses the basic concepts of this mechanism, and then demonstrates the concepts with two simple examples.

11.4.1 Basic Concepts

X supports data exchange between applications through the *selection* mechanism. Applications can define the contents of a selection and also request the contents of the selection from another application. Selections are owned and maintained by applications, but do not necessarily represent any existing data. Some applications may choose to generate the data represented by a selection only when another application requests a copy of the selection. Multiple selections can exist at once, each uniquely identified by different selection atoms. X predefines two selection atoms, **XA_PRIMARY**, and **XA_SECONDARY**; applications can also define additional selection atoms.

Any application can claim ownership of a selection by calling the Xlib function

```
XSetSelectionOwner(display, atom, window, time)
```

This function informs the X server that the specified window claims ownership of the selection corresponding to the given atom. The **time** argument is used to eliminate potential race conditions and should be set to the current server time. Applications can obtain the current server time from most X events. Since most applications grab ownership in response to a us-

---

6. A variation on this technique is often used. Instead of deleting the object from the first window, it is just copied. This should be referred to as "copy and paste," but often the phrase "cut and paste" is used loosely (although incorrectly) to apply to both techniques. This section actually describes "copy and paste."

er action, the timestamp in the corresponding event can be used to set the time. When an application claims ownership of a selection, the X server sends an **SelectionClear** event to the previous owner to notify it that it has lost the selection.

An application can ask for the ID of the window that currently owns a selection. The function

```
XGetSelectionOwner(display, atom)
```

returns the window ID of the current owner of the selection named by atom. Applications should call **XGetSelectionOwner()** after they request the selection to determine if they really own the selection. Once ownership of the selection is confirmed, an application should visually indicate the selection. Applications often indicate textual selections by displaying the region in inverse-video.

The function

```
XConvertSelection(display, atom, type, target_atom,
                  window, time)
```

allows applications to request the contents of a selection. This function requests that the selection corresponding to the argument **atom** be stored in a property specified by the **target_atom** on the given window. In addition, the **type** argument is an atom that specifies the desired form of the selection. For example, one application might request a selection as a string, while another might request the bitmap image of the region containing the selection. When **XConvertSelection()** is called, the server sends a **SelectionRequest** event to the current owner of the selection. The owner of the selection is responsible for converting the contents of the selection to the requested type, and storing the result in the given property of the requestor's window. Afterwards, the selection owner is expected to send a **SelectionNotify** event to the requesting application to inform it that the data has been stored. The requestor is expected to retrieve the data and then delete the property.

The server reports **SelectionRequest** events using a **XSelectionRequestEvent** structure, which, in addition to the information included in all events, includes the members

```
Window          owner;
Window          requestor;
Atom            selection;
Atom            target;
Atom            property;
Time            time;
```

The event contains the window ID of the owner of the selection and also the ID of the requestor. Three members of the event structure are atoms. The first, **selection**, identifies the name of the requested selection, while the second, **target**, specifies the data type desired by the requestor. The **property** atom contains the name of a property on the requestor's window where the data is to be stored.

After the owner of the selection converts the selection to the requested type and stores it on the given property of the requestor window, the selection owner is expected to send a **SelectionNotify** event back to the requestor. This event uses an **XSelectionEvent** structure, which includes the members

```
Window          requestor;
Atom            selection;
Atom            target;
Atom            property;
Time            time;
```

If the selection owner is able to provide the requested type of data, the owner sets the **target** atom to the requested data type. Otherwise the owner sets the atom to the constant **None**. The **selection** member indicates the name of the selection and the **property** specifies the name of the property in which the selection is stored.

When a client requests ownership of a selection, the X server sends the current owner a **SelectionClear** event to notify the application that it has lost the selection. This event uses the **XSelectionClearEvent** event structure, which includes the members

```
Atom            selection;
Time            time;
```

The **selection** atom indicates the name of the selection that has been lost, while **time** indicates the server time at which the event occurred.

We can summarize the X selection process by looking at the sequence of steps that occur in a typical exchange. Assume there are two windows, "Window A" and "Window B," and that "Window A" currently owns a selection. If "Window B" requests the value of that selection, the sequence shown in Fig. 11.4 takes place.

Window B:	Calls **XConvertSelection()** to ask for selection contents.
Window A:	Receives a **SelectionRequest** event.
Window A:	Converts the selection data to the type requested by Window B.
Window A:	Stores data on a property of Window B.
Window A:	Sends a **SelectionNotify** event to Window B
Window B:	Receives **SelectionNotify** event.
Window B:	Retrieves data from property.
Window B:	Deletes property.

Figure 11.4 Exchanging data using selections.

Now assume that Window B claims ownership of the selection. The sequence in Fig. 11.5 traces the steps that should occur when Window B calls **`XSetSelectionOwner()`**.[7]

Window B:	Calls **`XSetSelectionOwner()`** to grab the selection.
Window A:	Receives a **`SelectionClear`** event.
Window A:	Unhighlights selection.
Window B:	Calls **`XGetSelectionOwner()`**.
Window B:	Highlights selection if Window B is the owner.

Figure 11.5 Gaining ownership of a selection.

11.4.2 Selections With The Xt Intrinsics

The discussion in Section 11.4.1 is a little simplistic and ignores several issues. For example, to transfer large amounts of data efficiently, applications must break up the transfer into several smaller transfers. The complete selection mechanism is defined by the InterClient Communications Conventions Manual (ICCCM). Implementing the selection mechanism as described in this manual can be quite complex. Fortunately the Xt Intrinsics provides several functions that handle most of the details and allows applications to use a much simpler interface. In addition to being simpler to use, the Xt Intrinsics functions allow application to view all selection transfers as being atomic. The Intrinsics breaks up large data transfers into smaller ones automatically and transparently.

The Intrinsics defines three primary selection functions. The first of these is used to claim ownership of a selection:

```
XtOwnSelection(widget, selection, time, convert, lose, done)
```

The first argument to this function specifies the widget that claims ownership of the atom. The second argument is an atom that specifies the selection, usually **`XA_PRIMARY`** or **`XA_SECONDARY`**. The third argument is the current server time. As defined by the ICCCM, this time should not be the constant **`CurrentTime`**, but instead should be obtained from the user event responsible for claiming the selection. The last three argument specify procedures that must be defined by the application. The first specifies a procedure that the Intrinsics can call when another application requests the value of the selection. The second is a procedure to be called when the application loses the selection. The third is a procedure to be called when a requesting application has actually received the data from a request. This procedure is optional and can be given as NULL. **`XtOwnSelection()`** returns **`True`** if the caller owns the selection.

The **`convert`** procedure must have the form

7. The word *should* should be emphasized. This protocol depends on cooperation between all applications. Every application must follow the same procedures for this approach to work. At the time this book is being written, very few X applications follow this protocol or use the selection mechanism at all.

```
Boolean convert_proc(widget, selection, target,
                     type, value, length, format)
```

All parameters except the widget are pointers. the **selection** argument is a pointer to the requested selection atom. The **target** argument is a pointer to an atom that specifies the requested type, while **type** is a pointer to the type actually returned by this procedure. The **value** parameter is a pointer to the data returned by this procedure, while **length** and **format** indicate the size of the data pointed to by **value**. If the application registers a **done** procedure, the application owns the data in value, and should use the **done** procedure to free it, of needed. If the application does not register a **done** procedure it does not own the storage associated with value. The **convert_proc()** callback must return **True** if it successfully converted the selection and **False** if it could not fulfill the request.

The **lose** procedure must have the form

```
lose_proc(widget, selection)
```

where **widget** is the widget that lost the selection, and **selection** is an atom specifying the selection type.

The **done** procedure must have the form

```
done_proc(widget, selection, target)
```

where **widget** is the widget that owns the selection, **selection** is an atom indicating the selection, and **target** is an atom indicating the type of the transferred selection.

To request a selection, an application can call the function

```
XtGetSelectionValue(widget, selection, target, callback,
                    client_data, time)
```

Here, **widget** indicates the widget requesting the selection value, **selection** is an atom indicating the selection name, and **target** is an atom indicating the requested type of the data. The **callback** argument must specify a procedure defined by the application. The Intrinsics calls this function when it obtains the selection value. The form of this procedure must be

```
selection_callback(widget, client_data, selection, type,
value,
                    length, format)
```

The **client_data** parameter contains the client data specified by the application when registering the callback. The other parameters correspond to the data returned by the selection owner.

11.4.3 Adding Selection Capability to memo

The next two sections demonstrate the X selection mechanism using two simple programs. This section extends the **memo** program from Chapter 2 to grab ownership of the **XA_PRIMARY** selection when the user presses a mouse button in the message window. This version of memo uses a RowCol widget to manage the message window and a quit button. Like the earlier version, the message area is implemented using a StaticText widget. The application registers an event handler to claim ownership of the selection when a button is pressed in the message widget.

```
/**********************************************
 *  memo.c:  Current Selection Version
 **********************************************/
#include <X11/Intrinsic.h>
#include <X11/StringDefs.h>
#include <Xw/Xw.h>
#include <Xw/PButton.h>
#include <Xw/RCManager.h>
#include <Xw/SText.h>
#include <X11/Xatom.h>
#include "libXs.h"

void        grab_selection();
Boolean     convert_selection();
void        lose_selection();
char       *message;

main(argc, argv)
   int      argc;
   char    *argv[];
{
  Widget   toplevel, msg_widget, row_col;
  Arg      wargs[1];
  int      n;

  toplevel = XtInitialize(argv[0],"Memo",NULL,0, &argc, argv);
  /*
   *  Create a manager for the quit button and message window.
   */
  row_col = XtCreateManagedWidget("commands",
                                  XwrowColWidgetClass,
                                  toplevel, NULL, 0);
  create_quit_button("Quit", row_col);
```

```
  /*
   * Get the contents of the command line and display the
   * it in message window.
   */
  n = 0;
  if((message = concat_args(argc, argv)) != NULL){
    XtSetArg(wargs[n], XtNstring, message); n++;
  }
  msg_widget = XtCreateManagedWidget("text",
                                     XwstatictextWidgetClass,
                                     row_col, wargs, n);
   XtAddEventHandler(msg_widget, ButtonPress,
                     FALSE, grab_selection, NULL);
  /*
   * Realize all widgets and enter the event loop.
   */
  XtRealizeWidget(toplevel);
  XtMainLoop();
}
```

The **grab_selection()** event handler claims ownership of the **XA_PRIMARY** selection by calling **XtOwnSelection()**. It then confirms that it owns the selection before calling **invert_widget()** to highlight the selected text. Because the **invert_widget()** function toggles the highlighting of the selection, we must ensure that the selection is not accidently unhighlighted while we still own the selection. Therefore, we must also set the widget sensitivity to **False**, to prevent the user from selecting the widget again.

```
void grab_selection(w, client_data, event)
     Widget    w;
     void     *client_data;
     XEvent   *event;
{
  /*
   * Claim ownership of the PRIMARY selection.
   */
  if(XtOwnSelection(w, XA_PRIMARY,
                    event->xbutton.time, convert_selection,
                    lose_selection, NULL)){
    invert_widget(w);
    XtSetSensitive(w, FALSE);
  }
}
```

The function **invert_widget()** retrieves the current foreground and background colors of a widget and reverses them. This is a generally useful function that we can place in the libXs library.

```
/**********************************************************
 * invert.c: utility function for inverting a widget's color.
 **********************************************************/
#include <X11/Intrinsic.h>
#include <X11/StringDefs.h>
#include <Xw/Xw.h>

invert_widget(w)
     Widget  w;
{
  Arg  wargs[3];
  int  fg, bg;
  /*
   * Get the widget's current colors.
   */
  XtSetArg(wargs[0], XtNforeground, &fg);
  XtSetArg(wargs[1], XtNbackground, &bg);
  XtGetValues(w, wargs, 2);
  /*
   * Reverse them and set the new colors.
   */
  XtSetArg(wargs[0], XtNforeground, bg);
  XtSetArg(wargs[1], XtNbackground, fg);
  XtSetValues(w, wargs, 2);
}
```

The Intrinsics calls the callback function **convert_selection()** whenever **memo** receives a request for the value of the selection. This callback function checks the requested type to be sure it is a type it can handle. In this example, **memo** can only handle requests for type **XA_STRING**. More sophisticated programs might convert to other data types before returning. If the request type is **XA_STRING**, this callback function sets the return parameters to the values corresponding to the selection and returns **True**. Otherwise it returns **False**.

```
static Boolean convert_selection(w, selection, target,
                                 type, value, length, format)
    Widget         w;
    Atom           *selection, *target, *type;
    caddr_t        *value;
    unsigned long *length;
```

```
    int             *format;
{
  if (*target == XA_STRING) {
        *type = XA_STRING;
        *value = message;
        *length = strlen(message);
        *format = 8;
        return TRUE;
     }
   else
     return FALSE;
}
```

The Intrinsics calls the callback function **lose_selection()** when the message widget loses the selection. This function simply inverts the widget to its normal state and then restores the message widget's sensitivity.

```
static void lose_selection(w, selection)
  Widget    w;
  Atom     *selection;
{
  invert_widget(w);
  XtSetSensitive(w, TRUE);
}
```

We can use this version of **memo** to see how the selection mechanism allows applications to take ownership of a selection. Try running several instances of **memo** at once and click the mouse in each of the windows. As you select each window, the message changes to inverse-video, while the previously selected window reverts to normal video.

11.4.4 A Simple Clipboard

The second part of the selection example is a program named **clipboard** that copies and displays the value of the current **PRIMARY** selection upon request. A clipboard provides a temporary place to save data. The user can select the contents of the clipboard, in the same way as the **memo** program, to allow the data in the clipboard to be transferred to another client. The main portion of the program is similar to **memo**, but rather than extracting the message from the command line, the string displayed by the clipboard is obtained from the owner of the current selection. Like **memo** from the previous section, this program creates a RowCol widget that manages the message window and a quit button. The user copies the contents of the current selection to the clipboard by selecting a second PushButton widget.

```
/*************************************************************
 * clipboard.c: A simple clipboard using X selections
 *************************************************************/
#include <X11/Intrinsic.h>
#include <X11/StringDefs.h>
#include <Xw/Xw.h>
#include <Xw/PButton.h>
#include <Xw/RCManager.h>
#include <Xw/SText.h>
#include <X11/Xatom.h>
#include "libXs.h"

void      grab_selection();
void      request_selection();
Boolean   convert_selection();
void      lose_selection();
void      show_selection();
char     *message;

main(argc, argv)
    int     argc;
    char   *argv[];
{
  Widget   toplevel, selection, request, row_col;

  toplevel = XtInitialize(argv[0], "Clipboard", NULL,
                          0, &argc, argv);
  row_col = XtCreateManagedWidget("commands",
                                  XwrowColWidgetClass,
                                  toplevel, NULL, 0);
  create_quit_button("Quit", row_col);
  /*
   * Create a button used to request the selection and
   * a text widget to display it.
   */
  request = XtCreateManagedWidget("getselection",
                                  XwpushButtonWidgetClass,
                                  row_col, NULL, 0);
  selection = XtCreateManagedWidget("currentselection",
                                    XwstatictextWidgetClass,
                                    row_col, NULL, 0);
  XtAddEventHandler(request, ButtonPress, FALSE,
```

```
                        request_selection, selection);
  XtAddEventHandler(selection, ButtonPress, FALSE,
                        grab_selection, NULL);

  XtRealizeWidget(toplevel);
  XtMainLoop();
}
```

This example defines two event handlers. The **grab_button()** function, defined as an **ButtonPress** event handler for the **selection** widget, is identical to the function defined for **memo** in the previous section. The function **grab_button()** also calls the functions **lose_selection()** and **convert_selection()**, also identical to those described in the previous section. Together, these functions claim ownership of the selection for the selection widget and handle converting selection requests

The **request_selection()** event handler requests the value of the **XA_PRIMARY** selection when the user presses the mouse in the request widget. This function simply calls **XtGetSelectionValue()** and is defined as

```
void request_selection(w, client_data, event)
     Widget    w;
     void     *client_data;
     XEvent   *event;
{
  XtGetSelectionValue(w, XA_PRIMARY, XA_STRING,
                         show_selection, client_data,
                         event->xbutton.time);
}
```

Notice that the **time** argument to **XtGetSelectionValue()** is obtained from the event that caused this handler to be called.

XtGetSelectionValue() registers a callback function, **show_selection()**, to be called when the Intrinsics obtains the value of the requested selection. It checks the type of the requested selection, and if it is a string, uses **XtSetValues()** to display it in the **selection** widget. Notice that the **selection** widget is passed as client data.

```
static void show_selection(w, client_data, selection, type,
                           value, length, format)
    Widget          w;
    caddr_t         client_data;
    Atom           *selection, *type;
    caddr_t         value;
    unsigned long  *length;
    int            *format;
{
```

```
    Arg wargs[2];
    if (*type == XA_STRING){
      XtSetArg(wargs[0],XtNstring, value);
      XtSetValues(client_data, wargs, 1);
      message = value;
    }
}
```

Now we can combine the clipboard program with the memo example to experiment with transferring selections between applications. Fig. 11.6 shows several instances of **memo**, and a **clipboard**. Clicking on any **memo** window causes that application to grab ownership of the selection. Selecting the clipboard's "getselection" button retrieves and displays the contents of the selection. The contents of the clipboard can also be selected and transferred to other clipboards or any other X client that uses the selection mechanism.

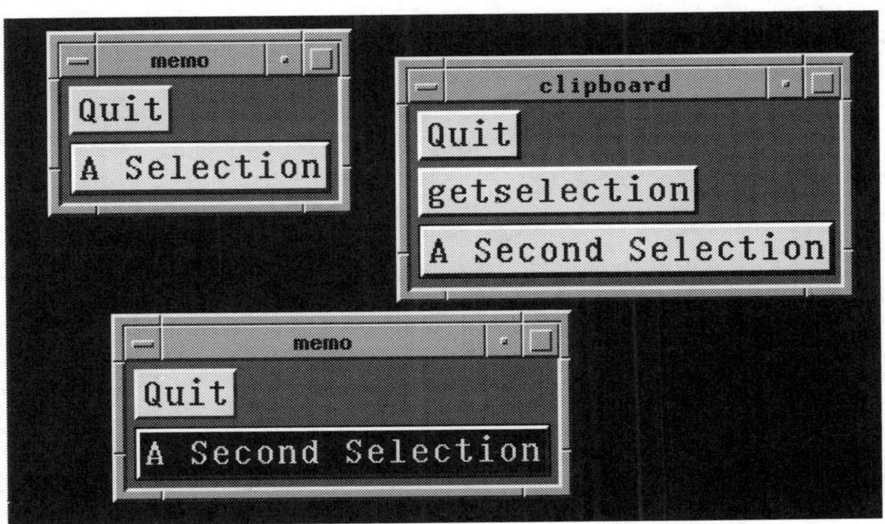

Figure 11.6 Retrieving a selection.

11.5 SUMMARY

This chapter discussed several features of X that allow applications to communicate with each other. Atoms provide an efficient way to compare strings between applications. The server assigns an identifier to a string, which is shared by applications that use the same server. Among other things, atoms can be used to identify properties, property types, and types of client message.

Properties are collections of data, stored in the server. Every property has a name and also stores an atom that identifies the type of the data stored in the property. The X server does not interpret the data in a property, allowing applications to store and retrieve any series of bytes. Because properties are stored in the server, applications can retrieve data stored by other clients. This provides one way to shared typed data between applications.

Client messages allow applications to define new event types, which applications use to communicate directly with other applications. Client messages are typed using atoms, and applications that use client messages must agree on the format and meaning of the messages.

X also provides support for exchanging typed data, using selections. Applications can claim ownership of a selection or request the owner to convert the selection to a particular type and transfer it. The server automatically handles notifications between the owner of the selection and applications requesting its contents, or applications seeking to become the owner of the selection.

12

CREATING NEW WIDGETS

Earlier chapters discussed ways to build user interfaces by combining suitable widgets from the X Widget set, defining a few callbacks and event handlers, and occasionally using Xlib functions. However, many programmers eventually find that they need a component not supplied by any existing widget set. In this case, the programmer can use the architecture defined by the Xt Intrinsics to create a new widget class.

After a brief overview of the internal architecture of a widget, this chapter presents some examples that illustrate how to create new widget classes. Widgets fall into three major categories. This chapter examines the simplest type of widget: those that can have no children. Chapter 13 presents an example of a composite widget that manages other widgets, and Chapter 14 discusses constraint widgets that control the geometry of their children according to additional information associated with each child.

12.1 THE ARCHITECTURE OF A WIDGET

The Xt Intrinsics defines the basic architecture of a widget. This architecture allows widgets built by different programmers to work together smoothly. For example, the programs in this book mix the basic widgets provided by the Xt Intrinsics and the X Widget set. These widgets can coexist peacefully in a single application because they share the same architecture. For the same reason, it is usually possible to mix widgets from other widget sets as well.[1]

The Xt Intrinsics defines an object-oriented architecture that organizes widgets into classes. From a widget programmer's viewpoint, a class consists of some private data structures and a set of procedures that operate on those procedures. Using object-oriented terminology, these procedures are referred to as *methods*.

Every widget consists of two basic components, a *class part* and an *instance-specific part*. Each of these components is implemented as a C structure containing data and pointers to methods. The Intrinsics defines the organization of each structure. All widgets belonging to the same class share a single copy of the data and methods in the class part, while each individual widget has its own copy of the data in the instance-specific part. The structure that contains the class part of a widget is known as the *class record*, while the structure that contains the instance-specific part is referred to as the *instance record*. A widget's class record is usually allocated and initialized statically at compile time, while a unique copy of the instance record is created at run time for each individual widget. The following sections discuss the organization and purpose of each of these widget components.

12.1.1 The Widget Class Record

A widget's class record contains data and methods that are common to all widgets of the class. Since all widgets belonging to the same class share the same class record, the class record must contain only static data that does not relate directly to the state of an individual widget. For example, every widget's class record includes a field containing the widget's class name. The class record also contains methods that define the appearance and behavior of all widgets in the class. Although most of these methods operate on the data in the widget's instance record, the methods themselves are shared by all widgets in a class.

All widget classes are subclasses of the Core widget class. This means, among other things, that the components of the Core widget's class record and instance record are included in the corresponding records of all other widget classes. The Core widget's class record is defined as

```
typedef struct{
    CoreClassPart   core_class;
} WidgetClassRec, *WidgetClass;
```

where **CoreClassPart** is a structure defining the class data provided by the Core widget class. The widget class for Core is declared as a pointer to the Core widget's class record,

---

1. Although this is true in theory, conflicts may arise in practice because each widget set defines its own user interface style and policy. Although the programmer may be able to mix different widget sets without many *programmatic* problems, inconsistencies in the interaction style and appearance between widget sets may cause a problem for the user. Many widget sets, including the X Widget set, attempt to define a particular style of user interface. Programmers should be aware of the human factors involved in designing a good user interface and mix widgets from different widget sets with caution.

```
WidgetClass widgetClass;
```

This is the widget class that applications use as the **class** argument to **XtCreateWidget()** when creating a Core widget.

The Core widget's class record contains a single field, **core_class**, which is also a structure, **CoreClassPart**. The Core widget defines this structure as

```
typedef struct _CoreClassPart {
    WidgetClass         superclass;
    String              class_name;
    Cardinal            widget_size;
    XtProc              class_initialize;
    XtWidgetClassProc   class_part_initialize;
    Boolean             class_inited;
    XtInitProc          initialize;
    XtArgsProc          initialize_hook;
    XtRealizeProc       realize;
    XtActionList        actions;
    Cardinal            num_actions;
    XtResourceList      resources;
    Cardinal            num_resources;
    XrmClass            xrm_class;
    Boolean             compress_motion;
    Boolean             compress_exposure;
    Boolean             compress_enterleave;
    Boolean             visible_interest;
    XtWidgetProc        destroy;
    XtWidgetProc        resize;
    XtExposeProc        expose;
    XtSetValuesFunc     set_values;
    XtArgsFunc          set_values_hook;
    XtAlmostProc        set_values_almost;
    XtArgsProc          get_values_hook;
    XtWidgetProc        accept_focus;
    XtVersionType       version;
    _XtOffsetList      *callback_private;
    String              tm_table;
    XtGeometryHandler   query_geometry;
    XtStringProc        display_accelerator;
    caddr_t             extension;
  } CoreClassPart;
```

We can divide the fields in this structure into two basic categories: class data and pointers to methods. The data fields include:

- **superclass**. A pointer to the class record belonging to widget's *superclass*.
- **class_name**. A string indicating the name of this class, used by the resource manager when retrieving a widget's resources. For the Core widget class, the **class_name** is "Core".
- **widget_size**. The size of the widget's instance record structure. This is usually determined using **sizeof()**.
- **class_inited**. A boolean that indicates whether this class structure has been initialized. A widget's class structure is initialized only once. The widget programmer must always initialize this flag to **False**.
- **actions**. A list of actions supported by this widget class, used by the translation manager.
- **num_actions**. The length of the **actions** list.
- **resources**. The list of resources used by all widgets of this class. The resource manager uses this list to initialize each widget's instance record at run time.
- **num_resources**. The length of the resource list.
- **xrm_class**. A private data field containing a representation of the widget's class name is used by the resource manager.
- **compress_motion**. A boolean that indicates whether the Intrinsics should compress mouse motion events for this widget.
- **compress_exposure**. A boolean that indicates whether the Intrinsics should compress **Expose** events for this widget.
- **compress_enterleave**. A boolean value indicating whether **EnterNotify** and **LeaveNotify** events should be reported to this widget if there are no other events between them.
- **visible_interest**. A boolean value that indicates whether the widget wants to know when it is visible.
- **version**. The version of the Xt Intrinsics. This is usually set to the constant **XtVersion**. The Intrinsics checks this field at run time to ensure that the widget's and the Intrinsics' versions match. Widget writers who are sure their widgets will work with multiple versions of the Intrinsics can set this field to **XtVersionDontCheck**.

Section 12.2.3 discusses the initialization of the data in this structure in more detail, as we discuss the implementation of an example widget. The remaining members of the Core class record are pointers to the methods that determine the behavior of the Core widget class. These members include:

```
class_initialize          class_part_initialize
initialize                initialize_hook
realize                   destroy
```

```
resize                      expose
set_values                  set_values_hook
set_values_almost           get_values_hook
accept_focus                query_geometry
```

Every widget class must define these methods in one way or another. They are often inherited from the widget's superclass, and some may also be specified as NULL if the widget class does not require the particular method. We will discuss each of these methods in Section 12.2.3 as we build a simple widget.

12.1.2 The Instance Record

Each individual widget has its own copy of a structure known as an instance record. The instance record contains the current state of the widget. For example, every widget's instance record contains the window ID of the widget's window, and also the size and location of the window. The instance record also contains a pointer to the widget's class record. Fig 12.1 illustrates this architecture, showing the relationship between the class record and instance records of several widgets belonging to the Core widget class.

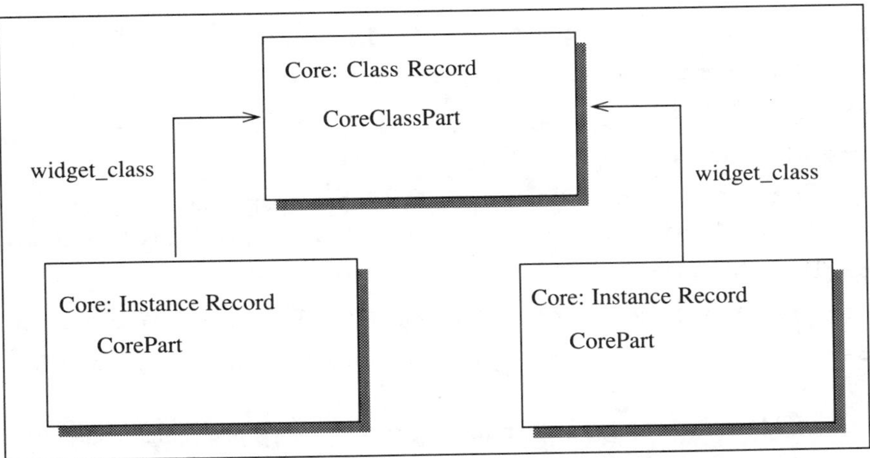

Figure 12.1 Class architecture of a widget.

The Core widget's instance record is defined as

```
typedef struct{
     CorePart core;
} WidgetRec, *Widget;
```

From this definition, we might guess that when an application declares a variable of type **Widget**, it is declaring the variable as a pointer to the widget's instance record. Actually, the **Widget** type used by applications is not defined as a pointer to this structure, because the Intrinsics uses the data abstraction techniques discussed in Section 12.1.4. The **Widget** type used by applications is declared as a pointer to an empty structure:

```
typedef struct _WidgetRec *Widget;
```

The function **XtCreateWidget()** returns a pointer to a block of memory allocated based on the **widget_size** field of the class record. The Core widget's instance record contains one member, a **CorePart**. Every widget contains a copy of this **CorePart** data structure in its instance record. In addition to general information needed by the Intrinsics to manipulate the widget, this structure caches some information about the widget's window, to reduce the need to query the server for this information. The information in the **CorePart** structure includes:

- **self**. A pointer to this instance record. The **self** member is of type **Widget**.
- **widget_class**. A pointer to the class record for this widget class.
- **parent**. A pointer to the instance record of this widget's parent.
- **name**. A string containing the name of this particular widget.
- **screen**. The **Screen** structure used by this widget.
- **colormap**. The ID of the colormap associated with the widget's window.
- **window**. The ID of the X window used by the widget.
- **x, y, width, height.** The position and dimensions of the widget's window. The type of **x** and **y** is **Position**, while the type of **width** and **height** is **Dimension.**
- **depth**. The depth of the window.
- **border_width**. The width of the window's border, declared as type **Dimension**.
- **border_pixel** and **border_pixmap**. The pixel index and pattern used for the window border.
- **background_pixel** and **background_pixmap**. The pixel index and pattern used for the window background.
- **event_table**. A private structure used to maintain the event mask and event handlers used by the window.
- **constraints**. A pointer to a constraints structure. This field is NULL unless the widget is a child of a constraint widget. If so, the definition of the **constraints** structure is defined by the widget's parent. (See Chapter 14).
- **visible**. If the **visible_interest** member of the widget's class record is set to **True**, this flag is guaranteed to be **True** when the widget's window is visible. The flag may be **False** if the window is not visible, but this is not guaranteed.

- **sensitive**. If this flag is **True**, the widget responds to events (i.e., the Intrinsics invokes its event handlers). If it is **False**, device events are ignored, although **Expose**, **ConfigureNotify** and some other events are still processed.
- **ancestor_sensitive**. **True** if the widget's parent is sensitive to events. If a widget is insensitive, its children are also insensitive.
- **managed**. **True** if the widget is managed by another widget.
- **mapped_when_managed**. If this flag is **True**, the Intrinsics automatically maps the widget's window whenever the widget is managed and unmaps it when it is unmanaged.
- **being_destroyed**. Widgets are destroyed in two phases. The first phase sets the **being_destroyed** flag to prevent other functions from operating on the widget while it is being destroyed.
- **destroy_callbacks**. A pointer to a list of callbacks to be invoked when the widget is destroyed.
- **popup_list**. The Xt Intrinsics allows popups to be attached to any widget. If a widget has a popup associated with it, the popup widget is listed here.
- **num_popups**. The length of the **popup_list**.

12.1.3 Inheritance

Inheritance is a powerful feature of many object-oriented systems, including the Xt Intrinsics. Inheritance allows new classes to be created that automatically have most or all the characteristics of another class, but with a few additional or different features. Inheritance allows a programmer to create a new widget class without having to program every detail of the new widget. Often, a widget programmer can design a new widget class by specifying only how the new class differs from its superclass.

Many object-oriented languages provide inheritance as a language construct. However, the Xt Intrinsics is written in the C language, which does not directly support object-oriented programming. In the Xt Intrinsics, inheritance is implemented by including the components of the class record and the instance record from each of the widget's superclasses in the new widget's class and instance records. Each widget class in the inheritance hierarchy contributes one component to these structures.

For example, suppose we want to create a new widget class whose class name is Basic. Assume that we would like this new Basic widget class to be identical to the Core widget class except that we need the Basic widget class to support a foreground pixel and a graphics context, neither of which are provided by the Core widget class. To create this new widget class, we must first define a class record for the new widget class.

```
typedef struct{
     CoreClassPart    core_class;
     BasicClassPart   basic_class;
} BasicClassRec, *BasicWidgetClass;
```

The new widget class record contains two members. The first is the same **CoreClassPart** structure used by the Core widget class. The second is the additional class part for the new widget class. The Basic widget class doesn't require an additional class resources and therefore the structure **BasicClassPart** is defined as an dummy structure:

```
typedef struct{
      int    ignore;
} BasicClassPart;
```

Next, we can define the Basic widget's class pointer as

```
BasicWidgetClass basicWidgetClass;
```

The Basic widget's instance record consists of the **CorePart** structure defined by the Core widget class, followed by a structure defined by the Basic widget. The instance record is defined as

```
typedef struct{
    CorePart    core;
    BasicPart   basic;
} BasicRec, *BasicWidget;
```

The structure **BasicPart** defines the new instance-specific resources needed by the Basic widget

```
typedef struct{
   int    foreground;
   GC     gc;
} BasicPart;
```

Internally, the Basic widget's methods can refer to the **foreground** and **gc** members by accessing the **basic** field of the widget's instance record. For example,

```
w->basic.foreground
```

These methods can also access the resources defined by the Core widget class, through the **core** member of the instance record. For example,

```
w->core.background_pixel
```

Fig. 12.2 shows the architecture of the new Basic Widget class, including the superclass pointer to the Core widget class.

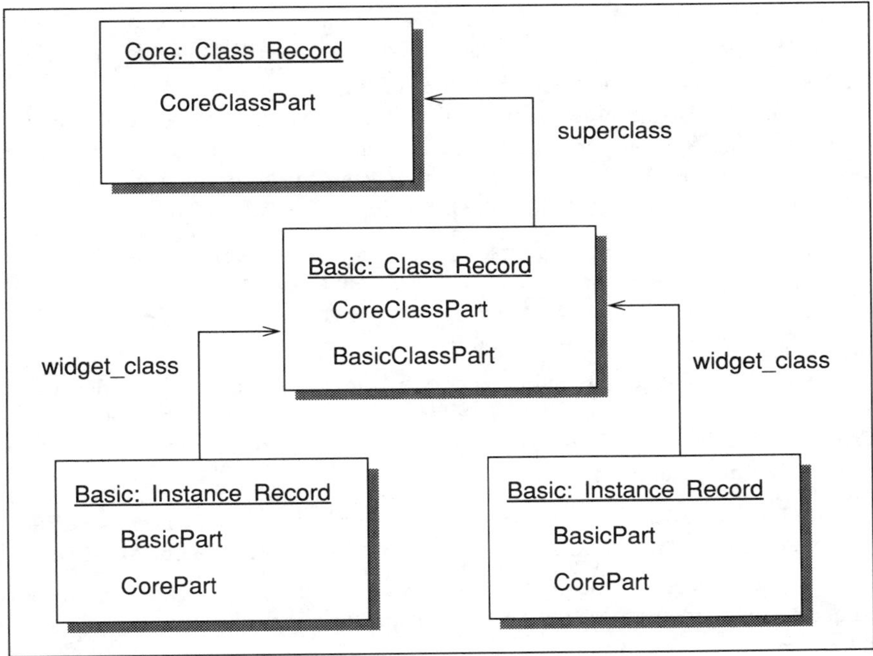

Figure 12.2 Inheriting from the Core widget class.

New widget classes inherit the resources defined by their superclass by specifically including the definition of the superclass structure in the definition of the new class. However, the Xt Intrinsics also provides a mechanism for inheriting the methods defined by a superclass. This is done in two ways. The first mechanism is referred to as *chaining*. When a method is chained, the Intrinsics invokes the method defined by each of the widget's superclass first, before invoking the widget's method. This allows a widget to inherit part of the behavior of its superclass. The Core widget methods that are chained are:

```
ClassInitialize()          ClassPartInitialize()
InitializeHook()           SetValuesHook()
GetValuesHook()            Initialize()
SetValues()
```

For example, if an application were to create an instance of the Basic widget described in the previous section, the Intrinsics would invoke the Core widget's **Initialize()** method first, and then the Basic widget's **Initialize()** method. If needed, the Basic widget's **Initialize()** method can override any of the resources in the **CorePart** set by the Core widget's **Initialize()** method. If the Basic widget class requires no initialization in addition to that done by the Core **Initialize()** method, the widget programmer can set the **initialize** field of its class record to NULL. In this example, the Basic widget's **Initialize()** method must create a graphics context based on the foreground color in the **BasicPart** structure and the background color found in the CorePart structure.

The Xt Intrinsics also provides a mechanism for inheriting methods that are not chained. This is done by using special symbols to specify the methods in the widget's class record. Each symbol is defined by the superclass that added the method to the widget's class record. For example, the Core widget class defines the following symbols for its methods

XtInheritTranslations	**XtInheritRealize**
XtInheritResize	**XtInheritExpose**
XtInheritSetValuesAlmost	**XtInheritAcceptFocus**
XtInheritQueryGeometry	

These symbols can be used by any subclass of the Core widget class. They do not have to be redefined by each widget class. Only those classes that contribute new methods to the class record need to define new symbols. For example, the Composite widget class defines symbols for its new methods, including

XtInheritGeometryManager	**XtInheritChangeManaged**
XtInheritInsertChild	**XtInheritDeleteChild**

When a widget class specifies one of these symbols in the class record, the Intrinsics copies the corresponding method used by the widget's superclass into the widget's class structure at class initialization time.

12.1.4 Data Abstraction

The Xt Intrinsics uses a data abstraction technique to hide the implementation of a widget from applications that use the widget. This technique involves maintaining both a private, complete definition of each widget structure, and a public, incomplete definition. Applications that use a widget see only the incomplete definition of the widget, and therefore cannot directly access fields in the widget structure. Applications declare all widgets as type **Widget**, which is known as an *opaque type*. This means the application has a pointer to the widget structure, but does not have access to the real definition of the data that it represents. Therefore it cannot access the contents of the data structure.[2]

To implement this style of data abstraction, the widget programmer must organize the widget implementation into several different files. Each widget implementation consists of one or more private header files, a public header file, and one or more C source files. The private header file contains the real definitions used internally by the widget, while the public header file contains only those definitions required by applications that use the widget.

---

2. To say that the contents of the structure cannot be accessed is really wishful thinking. In C, it is always possible to compromise the integrity of such schemes using pointer arithmetic.

12.1.4.1 The Private Header File

Every widget class has at least one private header file containing the complete definitions of the widget class record and instance record. Most widget classes have only a single private header file whose name, by convention, ends with the letter "P". For example, the name of the Core widget's private header file is CoreP.h. This file contains the true definitions of the **CoreClassPart** structure and the **CorePart** structure. Finally, the private header file can contain definitions of any other private data structures or variables used by the widget.

It is customary to enclose widget header files within pairs of **#ifdef** statements to prevent problems if the header file is included in an application more than once. Using this convention, the Basic widget's private header file would have the form

```
#ifndef BASICP_H
#define BASICP_H

/* Declarations go here */

#endif BASICP_H
```

12.1.4.2 The Public Header File

The public header file for most widget classes is very simple and declares any public information exported by the widget. At a minimum, it contains an external declaration of a pointer to the widget class record, used by applications as an argument to **XtCreateWidget()**. For example, the Core widget class's public file, Core.h, contains only the declaration of a pointer to the widget class

```
extern WidgetClass widgetClass;
```

The public header also often contains definitions of resource strings used by the program. Like the private header file, a widget's public header should also be enclosed within **#ifdef** statements to prevent multiple definitions. By convention, the Basic widget's public header file would have the form

```
#ifndef BASIC_H
#define BASIC_H

/* Declarations go here */

#endif BASIC_H
```

12.1.4.3 The Widget Source File

The source files for most widgets have a similar structure. Each file includes both the widget class's public and private header files as well as the public and private Intrinsic header files.

The file then declares forward references to the methods and other internal functions used by the widget, followed by a resource list used by the resource manager to initialize the widget's resources and a list of the actions used by the translation manager. Next, the widget's class record is statically initialized, and then the widget's methods are defined. These methods are usually declared as static so that they are not visible to applications.

12.2 A BASIC WIDGET: THE DIAL WIDGET

Although at first exposure the widget architecture may seem to be complex and confusing, it is simple to use in practice. This section provides a practical look at the widget architecture by creating a new widget class, which we will name the Dial widget class. A Dial widget displays a rotary dial, similar in appearance to an analog clock, that can be used as a gauge or valuator. An indicator, similar to a clock hand, indicates the relative value displayed by the dial. The Dial widget can display information between a range specified by any two integers. The Dial widget defines resources that allow users and applications to control the number of markers between the minimum and maximum values, and also the position of the indicator. The Dial widget also defines a callback list that allows an application to register a function which the widget invokes when the user selects the widget. Fig. 12.3 shows the physical appearance of a Dial widget.

The widgets described in this and the following chapters are simple examples of typical widgets, designed specifically for this book. They are not part of the X Widget set nor any vendor's widget set. To avoid confusion, the names of all widgets presented in Chapter 12, 13, and 14 begin with the prefix "Xs" to indicate the X-sample widget set. Otherwise, the naming and capitalization used in the examples follow the conventions normally used by the Xt Intrinsics and X Widgets, as described in Chapter 2. Following widget conventions, names of widget methods have the same names as the corresponding member of the widget class record, except that the method name uses mixed case. For example, the method corresponding to the **`set_values`** member of a widget's core part is usually named **`SetValues()`**.

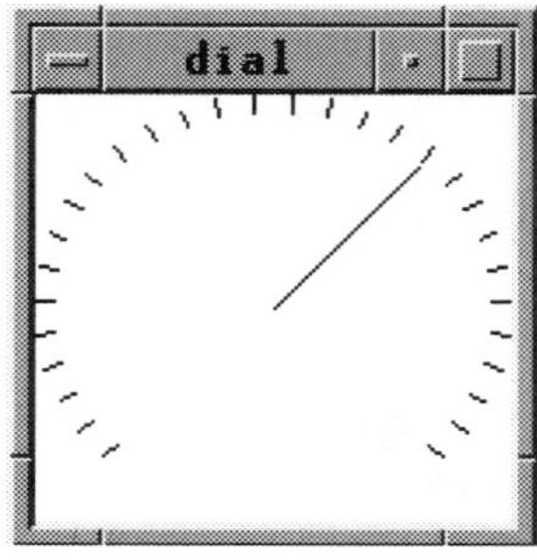

Figure 12.3 A Dial widget.

12.2.1 The Private Header File: DialP.h

We will begin the discussion of the Dial widget class by examining the contents of the private header file, DialP.h. We must first define a structure containing the Dial widget's contribution to the class record.

```
typedef struct _XsDialClassPart{
       int ignore;
} XsDialClassPart;
```

Even when a widget class has nothing significant to add to the class record, each widget class is expected to add a member to the class record. The Dial widget inherits directly from the Core widget class. Therefore, we can define the Dial widget's full class record as

```
typedef struct _XsDialClassRec{
   CoreClassPart    core_class;
   XsDialClassPart  dial_class;
} XsDialClassRec;

extern XsDialClassRec XsdialClassRec;
```

The resources used by the Dial widget class are defined in the instance record. The structure **XsDialPart** defines the resources added by the Dial widget.

```
typedef struct _XsDialPart {
   Pixel     indicator_color;  /* Color of the            */
   Pixel     foreground;       /*  indicator and markers */
   int       minimum;          /* minimum value           */
   int       maximum;          /* maximum value           */
   int       markers;          /* number of marks         */
   Dimension marker_length;    /* in pixels               */
   Position  position;         /* indicator position      */
   Position  indicator_x;      /* x,y position of tip     */
   Position  indicator_y;      /*     of the indicator    */
   Position  center_x;         /* coordinates of the      */
   Position  center_y;         /*     dial center         */
   GC        dial_GC;          /* assorted gc's           */
   GC        indicator_GC;
   GC        inverse_GC;
   XPoint    segments[MAXSEGMENTS];
   XtCallbackList select;    /* callback list           */
 } XsDialPart;
```

This structure maintains the current state of each Dial widget, and includes such things as the relative position of the indicator and the color of the markers. Some of the members of this structure (the maximum and minimum dial settings, for example) can be accessed by an application using the Intrinsics functions **XtSetValues()** and **XtGetValues()**. The widget programmer must define corresponding resources in the widget's resource list. Other fields in the **XsDialPart** are strictly for internal use. The widget's **Initialize()** method derives some of these fields from other resource values. For example, the graphics contexts are derived from the widget's foreground and background colors. The segments member is an array of points that define the line segments used to draw the face of the dial. The size of this array must be defined earlier in the file.

```
#define MAXSEGMENTS 200
```

Having defined the **XsDialPart** data structure, we can define the Dial widget's instance record by combining the **CorePart** structure defined by the Core widget class and the **XsDialPart**.

```
typedef struct _XsDialRec {
   CorePart          core;
   XsDialPart        dial;
} XsDialRec;
```

This completes the Dial widget class's private header file.

12.2.2 The Public Header File: Dial.h

The Dial widget's public header file defines the Dial widget's class pointer and also defines some strings used to specify resources. Widgets that define new resource names should make these names available to applications by including them in the public header file.

```
/******************************************************
 * Dial.h: Public header file for Dial Widget Class
 ******************************************************/
#ifndef  DIAL_H
#define  DIAL_H

extern WidgetClass XsdialWidgetClass;
typedef struct _XsDialClassRec * XsDialWidgetClass;
typedef struct _XsDialRec      * XsDialWidget;
/*
 * Define resource strings for the Dial widget.
 */
#define XtNselect          "select"
#define XtNmarkers         "markers"
#define XtNminimum         "minimum"
#define XtNmaximum         "maximum"
#define XtNindicatorColor "indicatorColor"
```

```
#define XtNposition          "position"
#define XtNmarkerLength      "markerLength"

#define XtCMarkers           "Markers"
#define XtCMin               "Min"
#define XtCMax               "Max"
#endif DIAL_H
```

12.2.3 The Dial Widget Source File: Dial.c

The file Dial.c contains the declaration and static initialization of the Dial widget's class record, and also contains the widget's methods. Dial.c begins by including the Intrinsics's private header file, IntrinsicsP.h, the private header file of the Dial widget's superclass, CoreP.h, and the Dial widget's public and private header files. In addition, the first part of the file defines several convenient macros used by the widget, and declares the widget's methods. Notice that these methods are declared as static, making them private to this file and effectively hiding them from applications that use the widget.

```
/*********************************************************
 * Dial.c: The Dial Widget Methods
 *********************************************************/
#include <stdio.h>
#include <math.h>
#include <X11/IntrinsicP.h>
#include <X11/Intrinsic.h>
#include <X11/StringDefs.h>
#include <X11/CoreP.h>
#include "DialP.h"
#include "Dial.h"

#define  RADIANS(x)   (M_PI * 2.0 * (x) / 360.0)
#define  DEGREES(x)   ((x) / (M_PI * 2.0) * 360.0)
#define  MIN_ANGLE    225.0
#define  MAX_ANGLE    270.0

static void    select_dial ();
static void    Initialize();
static void    Redisplay();
static void    Resize();
static void    Destroy();
static Boolean SetValues();
```

The next section of the source file defines an action list and a translations list used by the translation manager to map between a user action and a method that is invoked when the action occurs. These statements specify that, by default, the "**select()**" action is invoked in response to a **<Btn1Down>** action. An array of type **XtActionsRec** maps the "**select()**" action to a function, **select_dial()**, defined later in the file.

```
static char defaultTranslations[] = "<Btn1Down>: select()";

static XtActionsRec actionsList[] = {
  { "select",    (XtActionProc) select_dial},
};
```

Next, we must define a resource list used by the resource manager to initialize the widget's instance record when an application creates a Dial widget. The resources are automatically stored in the appropriate fields of the instance record. The Dial widget's resource list is defined as

```
static XtResource resources[] = {
  {XtNmarkers, XtCMarkers, XtRInt, sizeof (int),
    XtOffset(XsDialWidget, dial.markers), XtRString, "10"  },
  {XtNminimum, XtCMin, XtRInt, sizeof (int),
    XtOffset(XsDialWidget, dial.minimum), XtRString, "0"   },
  {XtNmaximum, XtCMax, XtRInt, sizeof (int),
    XtOffset(XsDialWidget, dial.maximum), XtRString, "100" },
  {XtNindicatorColor, XtCColor, XtRPixel, sizeof (Pixel),
    XtOffset(XsDialWidget, dial.indicator_color),
    XtRString, "Black"                                     },
  {XtNposition, XtCPosition, XtRPosition, sizeof (Position),
    XtOffset(XsDialWidget, dial.position), XtRString, "0"  },
  {XtNmarkerLength,XtCLength,XtRDimension,sizeof (Dimension),
    XtOffset(XsDialWidget, dial.marker_length),
    XtRString, "5"                                         },
  {XtNforeground, XtCForeground, XtRPixel, sizeof (Pixel),
    XtOffset(XsDialWidget, dial.foreground),
    XtRString, "Black"                                     },
  {XtNselect, XtCCallback, XtRCallback, sizeof(caddr_t),
    XtOffset (XsDialWidget, dial.select),
    XtRCallback, NULL                                      },
 };
```

Notice that only new resources added by the Dial widget class are included in this list. The Dial widget also inherits the resources defined by the **CorePart** of the widget's instance record from the Core widget class. The resource manager initializes the resources inherited from the Core widget class before retrieving the resources defined by the Dial widget. A widget can override the default values for resources defined by its superclass if necessary. However, the Dial widget does not need to override any Core resources.

12.2.3.1 The Class Record

The next step is to define the contents of the Dial widget's class record, which is initialized at compile time by declaring the contents of the structure statically in the source code.

```
XsDialClassRec  XsdialClassRec = {
     /* CoreClassPart */
   {
    (WidgetClass) &widgetClassRec,    /* superclass              */
    "Dial",                           /* class_name              */
    sizeof(XsDialRec),                /* widget_size             */
    NULL,                             /* class_initialize        */
    NULL,                             /* class_part_initialize */
    FALSE,                            /* class_inited            */
    Initialize,                       /* initialize              */
    NULL,                             /* initialize_hook         */
    XtInheritRealize,                 /* realize                 */
    actionsList,                      /* actions                 */
    XtNumber(actionsList),            /* num_actions             */
    resources,                        /* resources               */
    XtNumber(resources),              /* num_resources           */
    NULLQUARK,                        /* xrm_class               */
    TRUE,                             /* compress_motion         */
    TRUE,                             /* compress_exposure       */
    TRUE,                             /* compress_enterleave     */
    TRUE,                             /* visible_interest        */
    Destroy,                          /* destroy                 */
    Resize,                           /* resize                  */
    Redisplay,                        /* expose                  */
    SetValues,                        /* set_values              */
    NULL,                             /* set_values_hook         */
    XtInheritSetValuesAlmost,         /* set_values_almost       */
    NULL,                             /* get_values_hook         */
    NULL,                             /* accept_focus            */
    XtVersion,                        /* version                 */
    NULL,                             /* callback private        */
    defaultTranslations,              /* tm_table                */
    NULL,                             /* query_geometry          */
    NULL,                             /* display_accelerator     */
    NULL,                             /* extension               */
```

```
      },
         /* Dial class fields */
     {
      0,                                 /* ignore                    */
      }
   };

   WidgetClass XsdialWidgetClass = (WidgetClass) &XsdialClassRec;
```

Writing a new widget primarily consists of filling in this structure with appropriate values and then writing the methods that define the semantics of the widget. The following section examines the purpose of each member of the class record in the context of the Dial example, and discusses each of the Dial widget's methods.

The structure of the first part of the Dial class record is inherited from the Core widget class. However, the Dial widget is responsible for initializing this data. The first line indicates that the Dial widget inherits from the Core widget class by specifying a pointer to the Core class record. The next line specifies the class name of the widget, "Dial". **XtCreateWidget()** uses the **widget_size** member of the class record to allocate a new instance of the widget. The **widget_size** member must be set to the size, in bytes, of the Dial widget's instance record.

In addition to the static initialization of the class record, some classes must be initialized dynamically when the first widget belonging to the class is created. The **class_initialize()** and **class_part_initialize()** members allow the widget programmer to define methods to initialize the widget's class record at run time. Because the Dial widget's class record requires no run-time initialization, these members are set to NULL. Regardless of whether or not the widget requires dynamic initialization, every widget must initialize the **class_inited** field to **False**.

The next member of the Dial class structure points to the widget's actions list, followed by the length of the actions list. If the widget adds no actions to those defined by its superclasses, the **actions** member can be set to NULL, and the **num_actions** field can be set to zero.

Similarly, the **resource** member points to the widget's resource list, if the widget has one, and **num_resource** indicates the length of the list. The translation manager merges the actions list and the resources of a widget with those supplied by its superclasses.

The next four fields of the class structure define how the widget wishes to have events reported to it. The Dial widget specifies that the Intrinsics should compress all events.

The Dial widget must compute the location of the indicator on the face of the dial and draw the indicator whenever its position changes. It is therefore useful to know if the widget is visible, to avoid redrawing the indicator unnecessarily. Therefore we will set the **visible_interest** field to **True**, requesting the Intrinsics to keep the **visible** member of the Dial widget's instance record up to date.

The Dial widget does not use the **dial** part of the class record and initializes its dummy member to NULL.

12.2.3.2 Methods

A widget's methods determine its behavior. All methods are private to the Dial widget, and the application programmer can not invoke them directly. Instead, the Intrinsics invokes a widget's methods when events occur or when an application calls the interface functions provided by the Intrinsics. For example, applications use the function **XtCreateWidget()** to create a Dial widget, the function **XtRealizeWidget()** to realize the widget, **XtManageWidget()** and **XtUnmanageWidget()** to manage and unmanage the widget, and so on. Users can also customize the Dial widget using the resource manager, and applications can use the functions **XtSetValues()** and **XtGetValues()** to set and retrieve the widget's resources. These Intrinsics functions call the appropriate methods based on the class of each particular widget.

Not every widget class defines every method in the class structure. For example, the Dial widget does not define several methods in the class record, including

ClassInitialize()	**ClassPartInitialize()**
InitializeHook()	**SetValuesHook()**
GetValuesHook()	**QueryGeometry()**

The Dial widget initializes the members of the class record corresponding to these methods to NULL.

The Dial widget class inherits the **Realize()** and **SetValuesAlmost()** methods from its superclass by specifying **XtInheritRealize** and **XtInheritSetValues-Almost** for these methods. The remaining methods are defined by the Dial widget class. These methods are

Initialize()	**Destroy()**
Resize()	**Redisplay() (expose)**
SetValues()	

The following sections present each of the methods defined by the Dial widget.

The Initialize() Method

While the class record of most widgets can be initialized at compile time, the instance record of each widget must be initialized at run time. When a new widget is created, the Intrinsics invokes the widget's **Initialize()** method specified in the widget's class record. This method has two parameters, each of which are versions of the widget's instance record. Every **Initialize()** method has the form

```
static void Initialize (request, new)
    Widget request, new;
```

Each resource in the **request** widget is set to the original value obtained from defaults in the widgets resource list, taken from values specified by the application when creating the widget, or taken from the user's resource files. The **new** argument contains a copy of the same widget structure. However, by the time this method is called, the new structure has already been modified by each of the widget's superclasses' **Initialize()** methods. In this case, the Intrinsics calls the Core widget's **Initialize()** method before it calls the Dial widget's **Initialize()** method. A widget's **Initialize()** method may therefore rely on the widget's superclasses to initialize the inherited resources in the instance record. Each widget class needs to initialize only those resources it adds. The **Initialize()** method can also check any of the resources defined by its superclasses that it cares about and recalculate them if necessary. For example, the **new** parameter contains the size and location of the widget, as determined by the Core widget class. The Dial widget's **Initialize()** checks these fields and resets them if they are not acceptable. Unless the application or the user sets the size of the widget's window, it will have zero height and width at this point. The X server will generate an error if a widget attempts to create a zero width or height window, so every widget should make sure the window has acceptable dimensions.

When changing values set by a superclass, the widget must consider both the values in new widget structure and the original values provided by the resource manager, found in the request parameter, and resolve any differences. All changes must be made to the **new** structure.

The Dial widget's **Initialize()** method is defined as

```
static void Initialize (request, new)
    XsDialWidget request, new;
{
  XGCValues values;
  XtGCMask  valueMask;
  /*
   * Make sure the window size is not zero. The Core
   * Initialize() method doesn't do this.
   */
  if (request->core.width == 0)
    new->core.width = 100;
  if (request->core.height == 0)
    new->core.height = 100;
  /*
   * Make sure the min and max dial settings are valid.
   */
  if (new->dial.minimum >= new->dial.maximum) {
    XtWarning ("Maximum must be greater than the Minimum");
    new->dial.minimum = 0;
    new->dial.maximum = 100;
```

```
    }
    if (new->dial.position > new->dial.maximum) {
      XtWarning ("Position exceeds the Dial Maximum");
      new->dial.position =  new->dial.maximum;
    }
    if (new->dial.position < new->dial.minimum) {
      XtWarning ("Position is less than the Minimum");
      new->dial.position =  new->dial.minimum;
    }
    /*
     * Allow only MAXSEGMENTS / 2 markers
     */
    if(new->dial.markers > MAXSEGMENTS / 2){
      XtWarning ("Too many markers");
      new->dial.markers = MAXSEGMENTS / 2;
    }
    /*
     * Create the graphics contexts used for the dial face
     * and the indicator.
     */
    valueMask = GCForeground | GCBackground;
    values.foreground = new->dial.foreground;
    values.background = new->core.background_pixel;
    new->dial.dial_GC = XtGetGC (new, valueMask, &values);

    values.foreground = new->dial.indicator_color;
    new->dial.indicator_GC = XtGetGC (new,valueMask,&values);

    valueMask = GCForeground | GCBackground;
    values.foreground = new->core.background_pixel;
    values.background = new->dial.indicator_color;
    new->dial.inverse_GC = XtGetGC (new, valueMask, &values);

    Resize (new);
}
```

This method begins by checking the size of the widget's window. If the user or the application specifies a size, the resource manager sets the window size before this method is called. Otherwise, we must ensure that the window width and height are greater than zero. The **Initialize()** method also checks the value of other parameters, such as the maximum and minimum dial settings, to be sure they are reasonable, and initializes derived data fields, such as the graphics contexts used by the widget. The resource manager initializes the widget structure, using the widget's resource list, before the **Initialize()** method is called. Therefore, we can base the graphics contexts on the foreground color in the **dial_part** of the instance record, and the background color in the **core_part** of the instance record. The Dial widget's **Initialize()** method also calls the widget's **Resize()** method, which calculates the initial position of the dial markers and indicator.

The Realize() Method

The function **XtRealizeWidget()** invokes a widget's **Realize()** method, which is responsible for creating the window used by the widget. Since this method is almost always the same for each widget class, most widget classes inherit their superclass's **Realize()** method. Unlike the **Initialize()** method, the **Realize()** method is not chained. The Dial widget inherits its superclass's **Realize()** method by specifying the symbol **XtInheritRealize** in the class record. The **realize** field of the widget's class record cannot be set to NULL unless the widget class is never realized. Realizing a widget whose **Realize()** method is NULL generates a fatal error.

The Destroy() Method

Before a widget is destroyed, the Intrinsics invokes the widget's **Destroy()** method. This method is chained, although the calling order is reversed with respect to other chained methods. The function **XtDestroyWidget()** calls each widget's **Destroy()** method before its superclass's **Destroy()** method. Each widget class is expected to clean up the resources it has created. For example, the Dial widget class creates three graphics contexts and also defines a callback list that should be removed before the widget is destroyed. A widget's **Destroy()** method must not free the widget structure itself; this is done by the Intrinsics. The Dial widget's **Destroy()** method is defined as

```
static void Destroy (w)
     XsDialWidget w;
{
  XtDestroyGC (w->dial.indicator_GC);
  XtDestroyGC (w->dial.inverse_GC);
  XtDestroyGC (w->dial.dial_GC);
  XtRemoveAllCallbacks (w, XtNselect, w -> dial.select);
}
```

The Resize() Method

The Intrinsics invokes a widget's **Resize()** method whenever the widget's window is reconfigured in any way. The **Resize()** method should examine the members of the widget structure and recalculate any derived data that is dependent on the configuration of the widget's window. The Dial widget must recalculate the center of the window, the size of the indicator, and the line segments used to draw the face of the dial. Because the X server generates an **Expose** event if the contents of a window are lost because of resize, the **Resize()** method only updates the data needed to allow the **Redisplay()** method to redraw the widget correctly and does not actually redraw the window. This method generates a set of line segments that defines the circular face of the dial, centered in the widget window. The Dial widget's **Resize()** method is defined as

```
static void Resize (w)
    XsDialWidget w;
{
  double     angle, cosine, sine, increment;
  int        i;
  Position   start_x, start_y;
  XPoint    *ptr;
  /*
   * Get the address of the first line segment.
   */
  ptr = w->dial.segments;
  /*
   * calculate the center of the widget
   */
  w->dial.center_x = w->core.width/2;
  w->dial.center_y = w->core.height/2;
  /*
   *  Generate the segment array containing the
   *  face of the dial.
   */
  increment = RADIANS(MAX_ANGLE) /(float)(w->dial.markers -1);
  start_x = w->dial.center_x - w->dial.marker_length;
  start_y = w->dial.center_y - w->dial.marker_length;
  angle = RADIANS(MIN_ANGLE);
  for (i = 0; i < w->dial.markers;i++){
   cosine = cos(angle);
   sine   = sin(angle);
   ptr->x    = w->dial.center_x + w->dial.center_x * sine;
   ptr++->y = w->dial.center_y - w->dial.center_y * cosine;
   ptr->x    = w->dial.center_x + start_x * sine;
   ptr++->y = w->dial.center_y - start_y * cosine;
   angle += increment;
  }
 calculate_indicator_pos(w);
}
```

The auxiliary function **calculate_indicator_pos()** calculates the coordinates of the end point of the indicator, based on the indicator position and the size of the window. It is defined as

```
static calculate_indicator_pos(w)
     XsDialWidget w;
{
  double   normalized_pos, angle;
  Position end_x, end_y;
  /*
   * Make the indicator two pixels shorter than the
   * inner edge of the markers.
   */
  end_x = w->dial.center_x - w->dial.marker_length - 2;
  end_y = w->dial.center_y - w->dial.marker_length - 2;
   /*
    * Normalize the indicator position to lie between zero
    * and 1, and then convert it to an angle.
    */
  normalized_pos = (w->dial.position - w->dial.minimum)/
                (float)(w->dial.maximum - w->dial.minimum);
  angle = RADIANS(MIN_ANGLE + MAX_ANGLE   * normalized_pos);
   /*
    * Find the x,y coordinates of the tip of the indicator.
    */
  w->dial.indicator_x = w->dial.center_x + end_x * sin(angle);
  w->dial.indicator_y = w->dial.center_y - end_y * cos(angle);
}
```

The Redisplay() Method

A widget's **Redisplay()** method is responsible for redrawing any information in the widget's window when an **Expose** event occurs.[3] A widget's **expose** member can be set to NULL if the widget does not need to display anything. The Dial widget's **Redisplay()** method draws the face of the dial, using the line segments calculated by the **Resize()** method, and draws the dial indicator at its current position. The **Redisplay()** method is invoked with three parameters: the widget instance to be redisplayed, a pointer to an **Expose** event, and a **Region**. If the **compress_exposures** member of the widget's

3. Notice that this is one case where we cannot simply use a mixed case version of the name of the class record member as the method name. The symbol Expose is defined in X.h as an event type, using a C #define statement:

    #define Expose 12

Therefore, the C pre-processor would replace any method named Expose() by 12().

class structure is **True**, the **region** contains the sum of the rectangles reported in all **Expose** events, and the **event** parameter contains the bounding box of the region. If **compress_exposures** is **False**, the **region** parameter is NULL. The Dial widget requests that **Expose** events be compressed, so we can use the **region** argument as a clip mask for the graphics contexts to eliminate redrawing the dial face unnecessarily. Notice that the **Redisplay()** checks the **visible** member of the **CorePart** of the widget's instance record and redraws the dial face only if the widget is visible.

```
static void Redisplay (w, event, region)
     XsDialWidget  w;
     XEvent       *event;
     Region        region;
{
  if(w->core.visible){
    /*
     * Set the clip masks in all graphics contexts.
     */
    XSetRegion(XtDisplay(w), w->dial.dial_GC, region);
    XSetRegion(XtDisplay(w), w->dial.indicator_GC, region);
    /*
     * Draw the markers used for the dial face.
     */
    XDrawSegments(XtDisplay(w), XtWindow(w),
                  w->dial.dial_GC,
                  w->dial.segments,
                  w->dial.markers);
    /*
     * Draw the indicator at its current position.
     */
    XDrawLine(XtDisplay(w), XtWindow(w),
              w->dial.indicator_GC,
              w->dial.center_x,
              w->dial.center_y,
              w->dial.indicator_x,
              w->dial.indicator_y);
   }
 }
```

The SetValues() Method

The **SetValues()** method allows a widget to be notified when one of its resources is set or changed. This can occur when the resource manager initializes the widget's resources, or when an application calls **XtSetValues()**. The **SetValues()** methods are chained, and are invoked in superclass to subclass order.

The **SetValues()** method takes three arguments, each a version of the widget's instance record. The form of every **SetValues()** method is

```
static Boolean SetValues (current, request, new)
     Widget current, request, new;
```

The **current** parameter contains the current unaltered state of the widget. The **request** parameter contains the values requested for the widget by a combination of the user's resource files, the widget default resources and the application. The **new** parameter contains the state of the widget after all superclass **SetValues()** methods have been called. Like the **Initialize()** method, the **SetValues()** method must resolve any differences between these parameters and may override any values that it wishes. All changes must be made to the **new** widget. Notice that at this point the Intrinsics layer has already changed the requested values in the **new** widget. The **SetValues()** method's primary task is to generate any data derived from parameters that have changed and check that all requested values are acceptable.

The **SetValues()** method returns a boolean value indicating whether the widget should be redrawn. If this value is **True**, the Intrinsics causes an **Expose** event to be generated for the entire window. Because the **SetValues()** method can be invoked at any time, it must not assume that the widget is realized. Therefore, this method must not perform any graphics operations on the widget's window (which might not exist yet) unless the widget is realized.

The Dial widget's **SetValues()** method checks the minimum and maximum values of the dial to ensure that they are reasonable, and resets the values if they are out of range. If the foreground or background colors have changed, we must create new graphics contexts. Last, if the dial position has changed, the method calls the auxiliary function **calculate_indicator_pos()** to calculate the new position of the indicator. If only the position of the indicator has changed, and the redraw flag is still **False**, the old indicator is erased by drawing it with the inverse GC, and then displayed at the new position by drawing it with the normal GC. Notice that when erasing the indicator both the old position and the old graphics context are obtained from the current widget, in case the indicator moves and changes color at the same time.

The Dial widget's **SetValues()** method is defined as

```
static Boolean SetValues (current, request, new)
     XsDialWidget current, request, new;
{
  XGCValues   values;
  XtGCMask    valueMask;
  Boolean     redraw = FALSE;
```

```
Boolean    redraw_indicator = FALSE;
/*
 * Make sure the new dial values are reasonable.
 */
if (new->dial.minimum >= new->dial.maximum) {
  XtWarning ("Minimum must be less than Maximum");
  new->dial.minimum = 0;
  new->dial.maximum = 100;
}
if (new->dial.position > new->dial.maximum) {
  XtWarning("Dial position is greater than the Maximum");
  new->dial.position =  new->dial.maximum;
}
if (new->dial.position < new->dial.minimum) {
  XtWarning("Dial position is less than the Minimum");
  new->dial.position =  new->dial.minimum;
}
/*
 * If the indicator color or background color
 * has changed, generate the GC's.
 */
if(new->dial.indicator_color!=current->dial.indicator_color||
 new->core.background_pixel !=current->core.background_pixel){
   valueMask = GCForeground | GCBackground;
   values.foreground = new->dial.indicator_color;
   values.background = new->core.background_pixel;
   new->dial.indicator_GC = XtGetGC(new, valueMask,&values);
   values.foreground = new->core.background_pixel;
   values.background = new->dial.indicator_color;
   new->dial.inverse_GC = XtGetGC(new, valueMask, &values);
   redraw_indicator = TRUE;
 }
 /*
  * If the marker color has changed, generate the GC.
  */
 if (new->dial.foreground != current->dial.foreground){
   valueMask = GCForeground | GCBackground;
   values.foreground = new->dial.foreground;
   values.background = new->core.background_pixel;
   new->dial.dial_GC = XtGetGC (new, valueMask, &values);
   redraw = TRUE;
 }
```

```
  /*
   * If the indicator position has changed, or if the min/max
   * values have changed, recompute the indicator coordinates.
   */
  if (new->dial.position != current->dial.position ||
      new->dial.minimum != current->dial.minimum ||
      new->dial.maximum != current->dial.maximum){
    calculate_indicator_pos(new);
    redraw_indicator = TRUE;
  }
  /*
   * If only the indicator needs to be redrawn and
   * the widget is realized, erase the current indicator
   * and draw the new one.
   */
  if(redraw_indicator && ! redraw &&
     XtIsRealized(new) && new->core.visible){
    XDrawLine(XtDisplay(current), XtWindow(current),
              current->dial.inverse_GC,
              current->dial.center_x,
              current->dial.center_y,
             current->dial.indicator_x,
              current->dial.indicator_y);
    XDrawLine(XtDisplay(new), XtWindow(new),
              new->dial.indicator_GC,
              new->dial.center_x,
              new->dial.center_y,
              new->dial.indicator_x,
              new->dial.indicator_y);
      }
  return (redraw);
}
```

12.2.3.3 Defining Action Procedures.

The last procedure defined by the Dial widget is not a method, but is specified in the list of actions defined at the beginning of the file. This list associates an action named "**select()**" with a function **select_dial()**. By default, the "**select()**" action is bound to the user event <**Btn1Down**>. The actions provided by a widget are entirely up to the widget programmer. The Dial widget assumes that the "**select()**" action is the result of a mouse button event, and calculates the position of the indicator based on the coordinates of the mouse event. The position is then used as the **call_data** argument to the

XtNselect callback list. This callback list is defined in the Dial widget's instance record. The **select_dial()** procedure uses **XtCallCallbacks()** to invoke any **XtNselect** callback functions registered by the application programmer. The **select_dial()** function is defined as

```
static void select_dial (w, event)
     XsDialWidget        w;
     XEvent             *event;
{
  Position    pos;
  double      angle;

  pos = w->dial.position;
  if(event->type == ButtonPress ||
         event->type == MotionNotify){
    /*
     * Get the angle in radians.
     */
   angle=atan2((double)(event->xbutton.y - w->dial.center_y),
               (double)(event->xbutton.x - w->dial.center_x));
   /*
    * Convert to degrees from the MIN_ANGLE.
    */
   angle = DEGREES(angle) - (MIN_ANGLE - 90.0);
   if (angle < 0)
     angle = 360.0 + angle;
   /*
    * Convert the angle to a position.
    */
   pos = w->dial.minimum + (angle /
             MAX_ANGLE * (w->dial.maximum - w->dial.minimum));
  }
  /*
   * Use the position as the call_data to the callback list.
   */
  XtCallCallbacks (w, XtNselect, pos);
}
```

This concludes the implementation of our first widget. Because the Dial widget uses the architecture and follows the basic conventions of the Xt Intrinsics, it can be combined freely with other widgets in applications. The following section looks at an example program using the Dial widget.

12.2.4 Using The Dial Widget

In this section, we will look at an application of the Dial widget described in the previous section. This simple example creates a single Dial widget and defines a callback that moves the dial indicator to the position of the sprite when the user clicks the mouse within the Dial window.

Every application that uses the Dial widget must include the Intrinsic.h header file and also the Dial widget's public header file, Dial.h. After initializing the Intrinsics, the program creates a Dial widget using **XtCreateManagedWidget()**, and adds a function to the widget's XtNselect callback list. After realizing the toplevel widget, the application enters the main event loop. At this point, a single Dial widget, similar to the image in Fig. 12.3, should appear on the screen.

```
/******************************************************
 * dial.c : test the Dial widget class
 ******************************************************/

#include <X11/Intrinsic.h>
#include "Dial.h"

void select_callback();

main(argc, argv)
  int   argc;
  char *argv[];
{
  Widget toplevel, dial;
  /*
   * Initialize the Intrinsics.
   */
  toplevel = XtInitialize(argv[0], "DialTest", NULL,
                          0, &argc, argv);
  /*
   * Create a dial widget and add a select callback.
   */
  dial = XtCreateManagedWidget("dial", XsdialWidgetClass,
                               toplevel, NULL, 0);
  XtAddCallback(dial, XtNselect, select_callback, NULL);
  XtRealizeWidget(toplevel);
  XtMainLoop();
}
```

The callback function **select_callback()** uses **XtSetValues()** to reposition the dial indicator. The Dial widget's **XtNSelect** callback provides the position of the indicator corresponding to the location of the sprite in the **call_data** argument. We can use **XtSetValues()** to move the Dial widget's indicator to the new position. The callback is defined as

```
void select_callback(w, client_data, position)
  Widget     w;
  caddr_t    client_data;
  int        position;
{
  Arg wargs[1];

  XtSetArg(wargs[0], XtNposition, position);
  XtSetValues(w, wargs, 1);
}
```

12.2.5 Compiling the Dial Widget Example

Since we may want to use the Dial widget in many applications, it is useful to place the widget in the libXs library where it can be linked with applications that use it. We can add the Dial widget to the library in the same way as any other functions.

```
cc -c Dial.c ar ruv libXs.a Dial.o
```

Then the dial can be compiled and linked with the command

```
cc -o dial dial.c -lXs -lXt -lX11 -lm
```

Note that the Dial widget is based on the R3 version of the Xt Intrinsics. Therefore, it *must* be linked with an R3 or later version of the Intrinsics.

12.3 USING INHERITANCE: THE SQUAREDIAL WIDGET

Programmers often find that they need a widget similar to, but not exactly like, an existing widget. In this case, it is often easiest to create a new widget class by inheriting from the existing, similar widget class. We used inheritance in the previous section (the Dial widget class inherits from the Core widget class), but it is possible to go further and inherit from any widget that meets our needs, not just the basic classes provided by the Intrinsics.

Let's illustrate this with a simple example. Suppose the Dial example of this chapter is almost what we need, except that we would like markers on the dial face to be square instead of round. We could, of course, write a whole new widget class that creates the square dial face. This new class would also have to duplicate everything the Dial class already does.

It is much faster and simpler to inherit from the Dial class and reuse some of the work we did in the Dial widget. Fig. 12.4 shows the inheritance tree and the architecture of the Square-Dial widget class, described in the following sections.

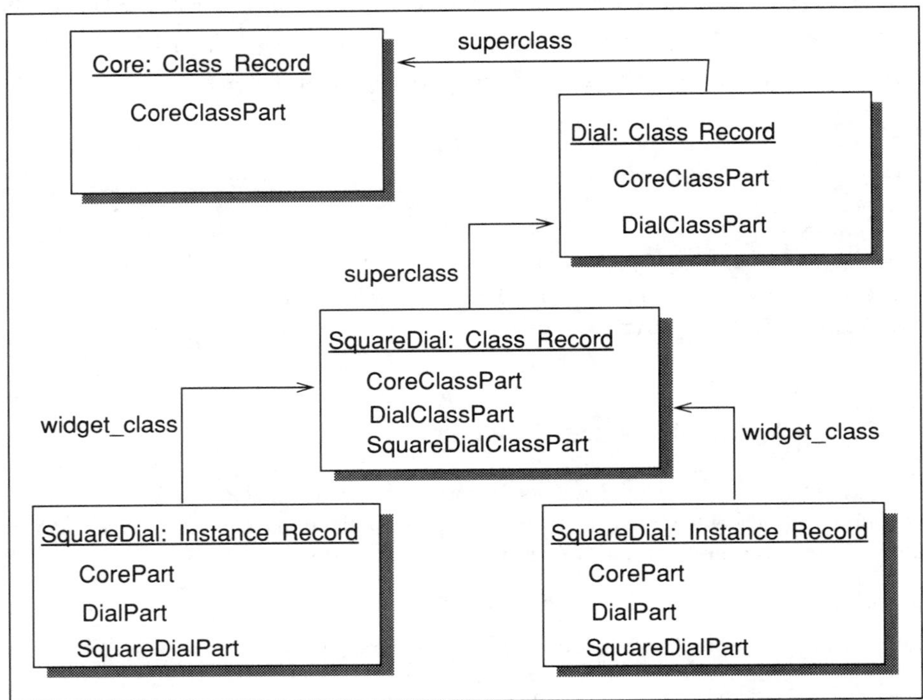

Figure 12.4 Architecture of the SquareDial widget class.

12.3.1 The Private Header File: SquareDialP.h

As with any widget class we must create a new private header file containing the definition of the SquareDial widget's class record and instance record. The file SquareDialP.h defines a dummy SquareDial class part.

```
typedef struct _XsSquareDialClassPart{
   int ignore;
} XsSquareDialClassPart;
```

The class record for the new class is defined by adding the SquareDial class part to the Core and Dial widget class parts.

```
typedef struct _XsSquareDialClassRec {
   CoreClassPart              core_class;
   XsDialClassPart            dial_class;
   XsSquareDialClassPart      square_dial_class;
} XsSquareDialClassRec;

extern XsSquareDialClassRec XssquareDialClassRec;
```

The SquareDial widget class's contribution to the instance record is also a dummy structure, because we are only going to change the way the new widget displays information, and no new resources are required. This dummy structure is added to the instance record after the Dial widget's contribution to the instance record.

```
typedef struct _XsSquareDialPart{
  int ignore;
} XsSquareDialPart;

typedef struct _XsSquareDialRec{
   CorePart           core;
   XsDialPart         dial;
   XsSquareDialPart   squaredial;
} XsSquareDialRec;
```

12.3.2 The Public Header File: SquareDial.h

The public header file contains the public declarations of the SquareDial widget class, and defines the same strings used by the Dial widget class. If we were creating a entire set of widgets, we could define these resources in a header file shared by all widgets in the set. For now, it is easier to just duplicate them.

```
/*********************************************************
 * SquareDial.h:The SquareDial widget public header file.
 *********************************************************/
#ifndef  SQUAREDIAL_H
#define  SQUAREDIAL_H

extern WidgetClass XssquareDialWidgetClass;

typedef struct _XsSquareDialClassRec * XsSquareDialWidgetClass;
typedef struct _XsSquareDialRec      * XsSquareDialWidget;

#define XtNselect            "select"
#define XtNmarkers           "markers"
```

```
#define XtNminimum        "minimum"
#define XtNmaximum        "maximum"
#define XtNindicatorColor "indicatorColor"
#define XtNposition       "position"
#define XtNmarkerLength   "markerLength"
#define XtCMarkers        "Markers"
#define XtCMin            "Min"
#define XtCMax            "Max"
#endif  SQUAREDIAL_H
```

12.3.3 The Source File: SquareDial.c

The source file of the new widget class must initialize the class record of the new widget class and define any new methods used by the widget. The SquareDial widget class only defines two methods, the **Initialize()**, and **Resize()** methods. The **Initialize()** method is called in addition to the Dial widget's **Initialize()** method, while the Resize method is called instead of the Dial widget's **Resize()** method. The SquareDial class inherits the Dial widget class's **Redisplay()** method and also its translations. Notice that SquareDial.c includes the Dial widget's private header file. The initial declarations and class initialization of the SquareDial widget class is done as follows:

```
/*****************************************************
 * SquareDial.c: A subclass of the Dial widget class
 *****************************************************/

#include <stdio.h>
#include <X11/IntrinsicP.h>
#include <X11/Intrinsic.h>
#include <X11/StringDefs.h>
#include "CoreP.h"
#include "DialP.h"
#include "Dial.h"
#include "SquareDialP.h"
#include "SquareDial.h"

static void Resize();
static void Initialize();

XsSquareDialClassRec  XssquareDialClassRec = {
/* CoreClassPart */
  {
   (WidgetClass) &XsdialClassRec,  /* superclass              */
```

```
    "SquareDial",                    /* class_name              */
    sizeof(XsSquareDialRec),         /* widget_size             */
    NULL,                            /* class_initialize        */
    NULL,                            /* class_part_initialize   */
    FALSE,                           /* class_inited            */
    (XtWidgetProc) Initialize,       /* initialize              */
    NULL,                            /* initialize_hook         */
    XtInheritRealize,                /* realize                 */
    NULL,                            /* actions                 */
    0,                               /* num_actions             */
    NULL,                            /* resources               */
    0,                               /* num_resources           */
    NULLQUARK,                       /* xrm_class               */
    TRUE,                            /* compress_motion         */
    TRUE,                            /* compress_exposure       */
    TRUE,                            /* compress_enterleave     */
    TRUE,                            /* visible_interest        */
    NULL,                            /* destroy                 */
    (XtWidgetProc) Resize,           /* resize                  */
    XtInheritExpose,                 /* expose                  */
    NULL,                            /* set_values              */
    NULL,                            /* set_values_hook         */
    XtInheritSetValuesAlmost,        /* set_values_almost       */
    NULL,                            /* get_values_hook         */
    XtInheritAcceptFocus,            /* accept_focus            */
    XtVersion,                       /* version                 */
    NULL,                            /* callback private        */
    XtInheritTranslations,           /* tm_table                */
    NULL,                            /* query_geometry          */
    NULL,                            /* display_accelerator     */
    NULL                             /* extension               */
    },
      /* Dial class fields */
   {
    0,                               /* ignore                  */
    },
      /* Square Dial class fields */
   {
    0,                               /* ignore                  */
    }
};
```

```
WidgetClass XssquareDialWidgetClass =
         (WidgetClass) &XssquareDialClassRec;
```

The SquareDial **Initialize()** method simply calls the SquareDial widget's **Resize()** method to override some of the calculations done by the Dial widget class's **Initialize()** method.

```
static void Initialize(request, new)
  XsDialWidget    request, new;
{
  Resize(new);
}
```

Finally, the SquareDial defines its own **Resize()** method. **Resize()** recomputes the line segments that represent the face of the dial as a square rather than a circle. We can rely on the inherited **Redisplay()** method to actually draw the segments.

```
static void Resize(w)
  XsSquareDialWidget    w;
{
  int      marks_per_side, h_increment, v_increment, i;
  XPoint  *ptr;
  /*
   * Get the address of the segment array.
   */
  ptr = w->dial.segments;
  /*
   * Calculate the center of the window.
   */
  w->dial.center_x = w->core.width / 2;
  w->dial.center_y = w->core.height / 2;
  /*
   * Position the marks up the left side, across the top,
   * and down the right side of the window.
   */
   marks_per_side = w->dial.markers/ 3;
   h_increment = w->core.width / marks_per_side;
   v_increment = w->core.height / marks_per_side;
  /*
   * Do the left side.
   */
  for(i=0;i<marks_per_side;i++){
     ptr->x   = 0;
```

```
      ptr++->y = i * v_increment;
       ptr->x   = w->dial.marker_length;
      ptr++->y = i * v_increment;
     }
   /*
    * Do the top.
    */
    for(i=0;i<marks_per_side;i++){
      ptr->x   = i * h_increment;
      ptr++->y = 0;
      ptr->x   = i * h_increment;
      ptr++->y = w->dial.marker_length;
   }
    /*
     * Do the right side.
     */
    for(i=0;i<marks_per_side;i++){
      ptr->x   = w->core.width - w->dial.marker_length;
      ptr++->y = i * v_increment;
      ptr->x   = w->core.width;
      ptr++->y = i * v_increment;
   }
  }
```

This completes the implementation of the SquareDial widget class. By inheriting the behavior of the Dial class, we were able to create the new SquareDial class by writing fewer lines of code than if we had designed the new widget class from scratch. The Dial widget class consists of 308 uncommented lines of code, while the SquareDial widget class required only 116. In addition, it is not necessary (in theory) to have access to the Dial widget's source code in order to inherit from it. In practice, we were able to create a new class easily because we had detailed information about how the Dial class works. Because we know how the dial face was drawn, and that the line segments used for the dial are computed in the Dial widget's **Resize()** method, we were able to make the desired changes by redefining only that method. This would be more difficult without access to the source code.

12.3.4 Using The SquareDial Widget Class

The new SquareDial class is used in exactly the same way as the Dial widget class. We can simply change the header file and the widget class specified to **XtCreateWidget()** in the dial test program we used earlier to produce the file sqdial.c.

```
/*******************************************************
 * sqdial.c : Test of the Square Dial widget class
 *******************************************************/
#include <X11/Intrinsic.h>
#include "SquareDial.h"

void select_callback();

main(argc, argv)
    int   argc;
    char *argv[];
  {
    Widget toplevel, dial;
    /*
     * Initialize the Intrinsics.
     */
    toplevel = XtInitialize(argv[0], "DialTest", NULL,
                            0, &argc, argv);
    /*
     * Create a square dial widget and assign a callback.
     */
    dial = XtCreateManagedWidget("dial",
                                 XssquareDialWidgetClass,
                                 toplevel, NULL, 0);
    XtAddCallback(dial, XtNselect, select_callback, NULL);
    XtRealizeWidget(toplevel);
    XtMainLoop();
}
```

The callback function, **select_callback()**, is defined exactly as in the earlier example. This program produces the display shown in Fig. 12.5.

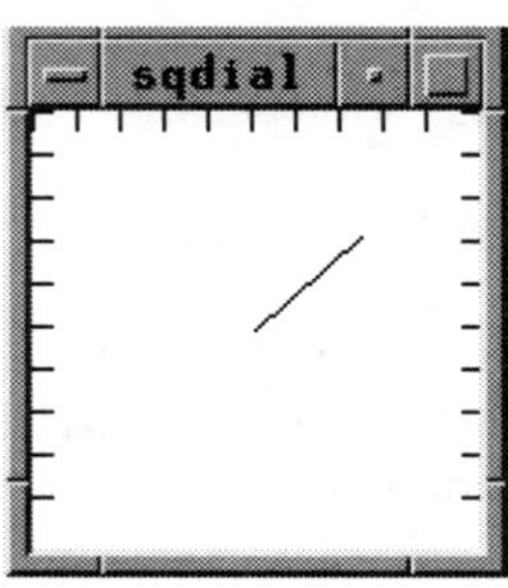

Figure 12.5 A SquareDial widget.

12.4 META-CLASSES

In the previous section we saw how inheritance can simplify the task of writing a new widget. Often this task can be made even easier by carefully structuring new widget classes. It is often possible to extract some general functionality from two or more new widget classes and create a meta-class. Remember that in the Xt Intrinsics a meta-class is a class that is not intended to be instantiated directly, but serves as a superclass for other similar widgets. For example, in addition to the two types of dials discussed in this chapter, we can probably think of other types of dials or gauges that share some of the characteristics of the Dial and SquareDial widget classes. Therefore, we might consider restructuring the widget classes in this chapter by defining a Gauge meta-class that includes those components common to all dials and gauges. This meta-class might include the creation of graphics contexts, the management of minimum and maximum values, and so on. Using this approach, the two widget classes discussed in this chapter might become the RoundDial and SquareDial classes, which could both be subclasses of the Gauge widget class. Fig. 12.6 shows how this widget hierarchy might look.

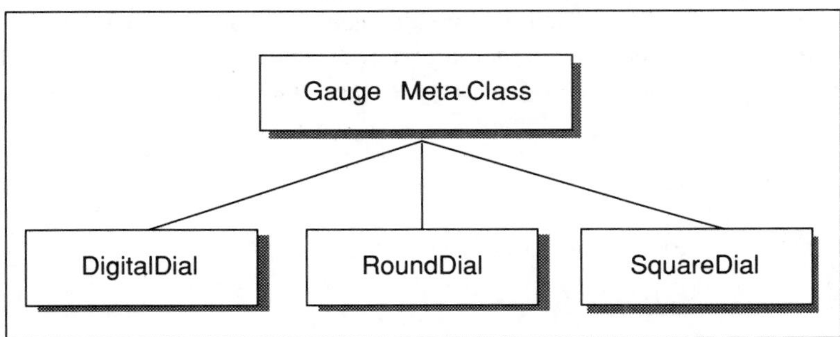

Figure 12.6 Organization of a Gauge meta-class.

When creating a complete new widget set, it is often useful to create a hierarchy of meta-classes. With this approach, the top meta-class in the hierarchy defines elements that all widget classes in the set have in common, while each subclass becomes more and more specialized. Such an organization allows the widget programmer to create new widget classes with the least amount of effort, although there is some extra initial effort required to design and create the meta classes. For example, this approach is used by the X Widget set, where most basic widgets inherit from the Primitive meta-class and most composite widgets inherit from the Manager widget class. Had we chosen to make the Dial widget a subclass of the Primitive widget class, basic resources such as the foreground color and the **XtNselect** callback list would have been provided for us automatically.

12.5 SUMMARY

This chapter discussed the architecture of a widget class and created a simple widget class that inherits from the Core widget class. Widgets consist of two basic parts, a class record and an instance record. The class record contains components shared by all widgets of a class, for example, the widget's class name, resource list and methods. Methods are private procedures that operate on the data in the widget's instance record. Each widget has its own copy of the instance record. This structure records the state of the specific widget: the size and position of the widget's window, the colors it uses, and so on.

The implementation of a widget uses a data abstraction technique that uses a private header file containing the true definition of the widget and a public file containing an incomplete definition. Applications see only the incomplete definition, and use Intrinsics functions to create and manipulate the widget.

When creating a new widget, programmers can often reuse parts of a similar widget by inheriting from that widget. To do this, the programmer includes the superclass's class record and instance record in the new widgets definition. Special symbols also allow the programmer to specify that the Intrinsics should copy some of the superclass's methods into the new widget's class record. Other methods are chained, so that the superclass's methods are called first. This provides another way to inherit part of the behavior of another widget.

The following chapters discuss how to design widgets that manage other widgets.

13

CREATING COMPOSITE WIDGETS

In the previous chapter, we built some simple widgets that defined their own appearance and style of interaction. This chapter presents a more complex type of widget known as a composite widget. These widgets are subclasses of the Composite meta-class, which is defined by the Xt Intrinsics and is a subclass of the Core widget class. The Composite class inherits all the characteristics of the Core widget class, and adds the ability to manage child widgets. Widgets belonging to subclasses of the Composite widget class are referred to as composite widgets. Composite widgets are used primarily as containers for other widgets and are responsible for managing the geometry of their children. A managed widget is never permitted to resize or move itself directly. Instead, it must request its parent to make the changes. The parent widget considers the request and allows the change, disallows the change, or suggests a compromise, depending on its management policy. Although they do not usually have display semantics, composite widgets are an important part of any widget set because they allow the application programmer to combine other widgets to create a complete user interface.

This chapter discusses the general architecture of the Composite widget class, and then presents an example of a composite widget.

13.1 ARCHITECTURE OF A COMPOSITE WIDGET

The Composite widget class, along with the Xt Intrinsics, defines the basic mechanism for managing children. Every composite widget's class record contains the methods that implement each widget's management policy, while its instance record maintains a list of managed children.

The first two members of every composite widget's class record includes both the Core widget class's **CoreClassPart** structure and a new **CompositeClassPart** structure. For example, the Composite widget class's class record is defined as

```
typedef struct _CompositeClassRec {
    CoreClassPart       core_class;
    CompositeClassPart  composite_class;
} CompositeClassRec;
```

The **CompositeClassPart** structure contains pointers to the methods that manage children. This structure is defined as

```
typedef struct _CompositeClassPart {
    XtGeometryHandler geometry_manager;
    XtWidgetProc      change_managed;
    XtArgsProc        insert_child;
    XtWidgetProc      delete_child;
    caddr_t           extension;
} CompositeClassPart;
```

Each composite widget class must supply these methods in one form or another. Section 13.2.3 discusses each of these methods in the context of an example composite widget.

Each composite widget's instance record includes the **CorePart** structure defined by the Core widget class, followed by a **CompositePart** structure. The Composite widget class's instance record is defined as

```
typedef struct _CompositeRec {
    CorePart      core;
    CompositePart composite;
} CompositeRec;
```

The **CompositePart** structure is defined in the Composite widget's private header file as

```
typedef struct _CompositePart {
    WidgetList   children;
    Cardinal     num_children;
    Cardinal     num_slots;
    XtOrderProc  insert_position;
} CompositePart;
```

The first member of this structure, **children**, is a list of all widgets managed by the composite widget, while the second member, **num_children**, indicates the number of children on this list. The field **num_slots** is set to the maximum size of the list, and is used by the widget to alter the size of the children list dynamically. The last member of the **CompositePart** structure is a pointer to a method that must return an integer index to the **children** array. This index determines the position in the **children** list where the next child is to be inserted. Most widget classes inherit this method from the Composite widget class, but they can choose to redefine this method to control the order of the widgets on their list of children.

13.2 A COMPOSITE WIDGET: THE ROW WIDGET

The easiest way to understand how a composite widget works is to look at an example. This section creates a new composite widget class, which we will name the Row widget class.

Every composite widget implements its own management policy that determines how its children are positioned. The Row widget's management policy is simple. It places all managed children in a single row, evenly separated by any remaining space. The Row widget determines the position of each child widget; children may not move themselves. The Row widget honors all resize requests from children as long as there is enough room or the Row widget itself can grow to accommodate the request. The Row widget serves only as a container for other widgets and therefore has no display semantics itself. Fig. 13.1 shows a Row widget managing several button widgets.

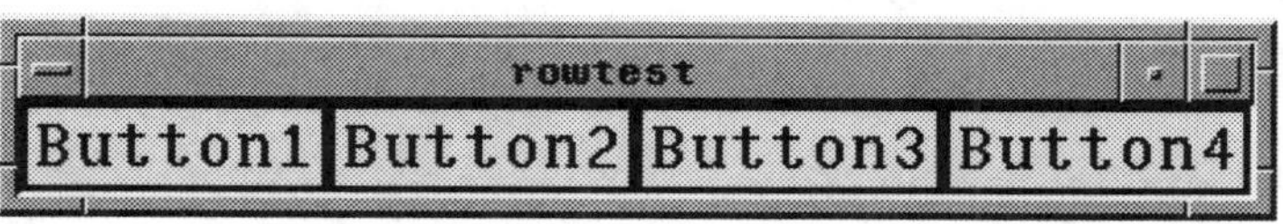

Figure 13.1 The Row widget.

Like all widgets, composite widgets consist of private header files, a public header file, and one or more source files. The following sections describe the contents of each of the Row widget's files.

13.2.1 The Private Header File: RowP.h

The Row widget's private header file contains the definitions of the Row widget's class record and the instance record. The Row widget inherits directly from the Composite widget class. It defines its class record by adding its own class part structure to the class parts defined by the Core and Composite widget classes. Because the Row widget uses no additional class data, its class part is a dummy structure.

```
typedef struct _XsRowClassPart {
          int    empty;
} XsRowClassPart;
```

The Row widget's complete class record can be defined as

```
typedef struct _XsRowClassRec {
    CoreClassPart       core_class;
    CompositeClassPart  composite_class;
    XsRowClassPart      row_class;
} XsRowClassRec;

extern XsRowClassRec XsrowClassRec;
```

The next step in creating a widget is to define the instance record. The Row widget requires no additional data in its instance record, so its contribution to the instance record is also a dummy structure, defined as

```
typedef struct {
     int empty;
} XsRowPart;
```

The Row widget's complete instance record is defined as

```
typedef struct _XsRowRec {
    CorePart        core;
    CompositePart   composite;
    XsRowPart       row;
}  XsRowRec;
```

13.2.2 The Private Header File: Row.h

The Row widget's public header file is similar to the public header file for all widgets and consists of only a few public definitions:

```
extern WidgetClass XsrowWidgetClass;
typedef struct _XsRowClassRec *XsRowWidgetClass;
typedef struct _XsRowRec      *XsRowWidget;
```

Applications use the class pointer, **XsrowWidgetClass**, as an argument to **XtCreateWidget()** to create a Row widget.

13.2.3 The Source File: Row.c

The file Row.c contains the static definition of the Row widget class record, as well as the Row widget's methods. The source file includes the Composite widget class's header files in addition to the private and public Intrinsic header files. It also includes the private and public Row widget header files.

```
/**********************************************
 * Row.c: Methods for the Row widget
 **********************************************/

#include     <X11/IntrinsicP.h>
#include     <X11/Intrinsic.h>
#include     <X11/Composite.h>
#include     <X11/CompositeP.h>
#include     "RowP.h"
#include     "Row.h"
```

Next, the methods and other functions used by the Row widget are declared as static, making these functions private to the file. **MAX()** and **MIN()** are useful macros that determine the larger and smaller of two numbers, respectively.

```
#define MAX(a,b)  ((a) > (b) ? (a) : (b))
#define MIN(a,b)  ((a) < (b) ? (a) : (b))

static void                 Initialize();
static void                 Resize();
static void                 ChangeManaged();
static Boolean              SetValues();
static XtGeometryResult     GeometryManager();
static XtGeometryResult     PreferredSize();
static XtGeometryResult     try_layout();
```

13.2.3.1 The Class Record

The Row widget's class record is initialized entirely at compile time. Because the Row widget has no display semantics of its own and provides no actions or resources, it does not use many of the methods defined by the Core class part. For example, there is no need for a **SetValues()** method or an **Expose()** method. However, we must define several new methods that allow the Row widget to manage its children.

```
XsRowClassRec XsrowClassRec = {
  {
    /* core_class members       */
    (WidgetClass) &compositeClassRec, /* superclass          */
    "Row",                            /* class_name          */
    sizeof(XsRowRec),                 /* widget_size         */
    NULL,                             /* class_initialize    */
    NULL,                             /* class_part_init     */
    FALSE,                            /* class_inited        */
    Initialize,                       /* initialize          */
```

```
    NULL,                          /* initialize_hook    */
    XtInheritRealize,              /* realize            */
    NULL,                          /* actions            */
    0,                             /* num_actions        */
    NULL,                          /* resources          */
    0,                             /* num_resources      */
    NULLQUARK,                     /* xrm_class          */
    TRUE,                          /* compress_motion    */
    TRUE,                          /* compress_exposure  */
    TRUE,                          /* compress_enterleave*/
    FALSE,                         /* visible_interest   */
    NULL,                          /* destroy            */
    Resize,                        /* resize             */
    NULL,                          /* expose             */
    NULL,                          /* set_values         */
    NULL,                          /* set_values_hook    */
    XtInheritSetValuesAlmost,      /* set_values_almost  */
    NULL,                          /* get_values_hook    */
    NULL,                          /* accept_focus       */
    XtVersion,                     /* version            */
    NULL,                          /* callback_private   */
    NULL,                          /* tm_table           */
    PreferredSize,                 /* query_geometry     */
    NULL,                          /* display_accelerator*/
    NULL,                          /* extension          */
  },
  {
    /* composite_class members */
    GeometryManager,               /* geometry_manager   */
    ChangeManaged,                 /* change_managed     */
    XtInheritInsertChild,          /* insert_child       */
    XtInheritDeleteChild,          /* delete_child       */
    NULL,                          /* extension          */
  },
  {
    /* Row class members */
    0,                             /* empty              */
  }
};
WidgetClass XsrowWidgetClass = (WidgetClass) &XsrowClassRec;
```

The superclass member of the class record specifies a pointer to **compositeClassRec**, the Composite widget class's class structure. The Row widget requires no run time initialization of the class structure, so the members **class_initialize** and **class_part_initialize** are set to NULL. Because there are no actions or settable resources, the **actions** and **resource** members are also set to NULL. The Row widget sets the **visible_interest** member of the class record to **False** because it does not display anything itself, and does not care if it is visible.

13.2.3.2 Methods

The Row widget defines three core part methods similar to those defined by the simple Dial widget in Chapter 12. However, the most interesting aspect of any composite widget class is the way it manages its children. The Row widget defines several methods and auxiliary functions that allow the Row widget to control the geometry of its children and also negotiate the geometry of the Row widget with its parent. The following sections discuss each of the Row widget's methods, beginning with the basic methods that all widget classes must provide before discussing the methods added by the Composite widget class.

The Initialize() Method

Because the Row widget defines no additional resources of its own, the Row widget's **Initialize()** method is simple. Every widget's **Initialize()** method should check that the width and height of its window are greater than zero. The **Initialize()** method is defined as

```
static void Initialize(request, new)
    XsRowWidget request, new;
{
  if (request -> core.width <= 0)
    new -> core.width = 5;
  if (request -> core.height <= 0)
    new -> core.height = 5;
}
```

The Realize() Method

Like most widgets, the Row widget class inherits the basic method defined by the Core widget class to create its window. The Row widget sets the **realize** member of its class record to the symbol **XtInheritRealize** to inherit the **Realize()** method used by the Composite widget class. In turn, the Composite widget class inherits its **Realize()** method from the Core widget class.

The InsertChild() Method

Every composite widget must have an **InsertChild()** method that is responsible for adding new child widgets to the composite widget's list of children. **XtCreateWidget()**

calls this method when it creates a widget as a child of a composite widget. Most composite widgets inherit the basic method defined by the Composite widget by specifying the symbol **XtInheritInsertChild** for the **insert_child** member of the class record. The Composite widget's **InsertChild()** method adds new children to the children list, enlarging the list using **XtRealloc()**, if needed. It calls the widget's **InsertPosition()** method to determine the next available position in the **children** array. The Row widget also inherits its **InsertPosition()** method from the Composite widget class. The Composite widget's **InsertPosition()** method always returns the position at the end of the list. The list of children contains all widgets created as a child of the composite widget, regardless of whether or not they are currently managed. A composite widget can discover whether a particular child widget is managed by examining the managed field of the child's core part.

The DeleteChild() Method

Every composite widget must provide a method to remove a child from its list of children. Most widgets, including the Row widget, inherit this method from the Composite class, by setting the **delete_child** member of the class record to the symbol **XtInheritDeleteChild**.

The Resize() Method

The Row widget bases the layout of its children on its own size. When a widget's size changes, the Intrinsics invokes its **Resize()** method. The Row widget's **Resize()** method simply calls an auxiliary function, **do_layout()**, to recalculate the layout of its children.

```
static void Resize(w)
     XsRowWidget    w;
{
  do_layout(w);
}
```

The function **do_layout()** determines the position of each managed child. It iterates twice over the list of children found in the composite part of the instance record. On the first pass it computes the sum of the widths of all managed children, to determine how much space, if any, it can place between each widget. The second pass positions each managed child evenly separated in a single row.

```
do_layout(parent)
     XsRowWidget parent;
{
  Widget      child;
  int         i;
  Dimension   childwidth = 0;
  Position    xpos = 0;
```

```
    Dimension  pad = 0;
    int    n_managed_children = 0;
   /*
    * Compute the total width of all managed children and
    * determine how many children are managed.
    */
    for (i = 0; i < parent -> composite.num_children; i++){
      child = parent -> composite.children[i];
      if(child->core.managed){
        n_managed_children++;
        childwidth += child->core.width +
                                child->core.border_width * 2;

      }
    }
    /*
     *  Divide any remaining space by the number
     *  of children.
     */
    if((n_managed_children > 1) &&
            (parent->core.width > childwidth))
      pad = (parent->core.width - childwidth) /
                                     (n_managed_children - 1);

    for (i = 0; i < parent -> composite.num_children; i++){
      child = parent -> composite.children[i];
      if(child->core.managed){
         XtMoveWidget (child, xpos, 0);
         xpos += pad + child->core.width +
                                   child->core.border_width * 2;

       }
    }
  }
```

The QueryGeometry() Method

Managing the geometry of a widget's children often requires a series of negotiations between the composite widget, its parent and its children. While a composite widget has complete control over the geometry of its children, it has no control over its own geometry. Often, a widget that manages the layout of multiple children must alter the size or position of one or more widgets to fulfill its particular layout policy within the constraints mandated by its own size. In this situation, it is often useful for the widget to be able to determine the preferred size of each of its children.

Every widget contains a pointer to a **QueryGeometry()** method in its core class part. This method is invoked by the Intrinsics function

```
XtQueryGeometry(widget, &intended, &preferred)
```

A composite widget that intends to change the size or position of one of its children can call this function to determine the child's preferred geometry. The **intended** and **preferred** parameters are structures of type **XtWidgetGeometry**, which contains the members

```
XtGeometryMask mask;
Position       x, y;
Dimension      width, height;
Widget         sibling;
int            stack_mode;
```

The **mask** member of this structure indicates which members of the structure contain valid information and must be set any combination of the masks:

CWX	**CWY**	**CWWidth**
CWHeight	**CWBorderWidth**	**CWSibling**
CWStackMode		

Before calling **XtQueryGeometry()**, the parent widget indicates the changes it plans to make in an **XtWidgetGeometry** structure and uses it as the **intended** argument. If the child widget has no **QueryGeometry()** method, **XtQueryGeometry()** fills in the **preferred** geometry structure with the child widget's current geometry. Otherwise it invokes the child's **QueryGeometry()** method. If the proposed changes are acceptable to the child widget, its **QueryGeometry()** method should return the constant **XtGeometryYes**. If the changes are unacceptable, or if they are identical to the child's current geometry, the method should return **XtGeometryNo**. If some of the proposed changes are acceptable, but others are not, the method can fill in the preferred structure with its preferred geometry and return the constant **XtGeometryAlmost**.

A parent widget is under no obligation to a child to maintain the child's preferred geometry, and may choose to ignore the information returned by **XtQueryGeometry()**. The Row widget bases its preferred geometry on the maximum height and the total width of its managed children. Although this is simple in principle, the method that computes the Row widget's preferred geometry is a bit long because there are many cases to test. The Row widget's **QueryGeometry()** method is defined as

```
static XtGeometryResult PreferredSize(w, request, preferred)
    XsRowWidget w;
    XtWidgetGeometry *request, *preferred;
{
  Widget child;
```

```
int i;
/*
 * If no changes are being made to width or
 * height, just agree.
 */
if(!(request->request_mode & CWWidth) &&
   !(request->request_mode & CWHeight))
  return (XtGeometryYes);
/*
 * Calculate our minimum size.
 */
preferred->width = 0;
preferred->height = 0;
for (i = 0; i < w -> composite.num_children; i++){
  child = w -> composite.children[i];
  if(child->core.managed){
     preferred->width += child->core.width +
                          child->core.border_width * 2;
     if(preferred->height < child->core.height +
              child->core.border_width * 2)
        preferred->height = child->core.height +
                          child->core.border_width * 2;
   }
}
preferred->request_mode = CWWidth | CWHeight;
/*
 * If both width and height are requested.
 */
if((request->request_mode & CWWidth) &&
   (request->request_mode & CWHeight)){
  /*
   * If we are to be the same or bigger, say ok.
   */
  if(preferred->width >= request->width &&
          preferred->height >= request->height){
    preferred->width = request->width;
    preferred->height = request->height;
    return (XtGeometryYes);
  }
  /*
   * If both dimensions are unacceptable, say no.
   */
```

```
      else
        if(preferred->width < request->width &&
           preferred->height < request->height)
         return (XtGeometryNo);
      /*
       * Otherwise one must be right, so say almost.
       */
        else
           return (XtGeometryAlmost);
    }
    /*
     * If only the width is requested, either it's
     * OK or it isn't.
     */
    else
      if(request->request_mode & CWWidth){
        if(preferred->width >= request->width){
           preferred->width = request->width;
           return (XtGeometryYes);
        }
        else
          return (XtGeometryNo);
      }
    /*
     * If only the height is requested, it's
     * all or nothing.
     */
    else
      if(request->request_mode & CWHeight){
        if(preferred->height >= request->height){
           preferred->height = request->height;
           return (XtGeometryYes);
        }
        else
          return (XtGeometryNo);
      }
      return (XtGeometryYes);
  }
```

Notice that this method does not help the Row widget manage its children, but rather assists the parent of a Row widget in managing the Row widget itself. Ideally, every widget should define this method to make it easier for its parent to manage the widget's geometry. Geometry management of multiple widgets is a process of negotiation that requires some give and take between all widgets involved. This negotiation is more likely to succeed if every widget defines a **QueryGeometry()** method that provides accurate information about the best size of the widget. Widgets that always claim that their current geometry is the preferred geometry (by specifying the **query_geometry** member as NULL) do little to help the negotiation process.

The GeometryManager() Method

As mentioned previously, a widget should never attempt to alter its size or location directly, because the geometry of every widget is the responsibility of the widget's parent. Geometry requests are made using the function

```
XtMakeGeometryRequest(widget, &request, &reply)
```

This function takes a **XtWidgetGeometry** structure as an argument and returns one of the constants

XtGeometryYes	**XtGeometryNo**
XtGeometryAlmost	**XtGeometryDone**

XtMakeGeometryRequest() invokes the parent's **GeometryManager()** method. If the parent allows the request, this method returns the constant **XtGeometryYes**, and **XtMakeGeometryRequest()** makes the requested changes. If the **GeometryManager()** method fulfills the request itself, it should return **XtGeometryDone**. The parent's **GeometryManager()** method can also disallow the request by returning **XtGeometryNo** or suggest a compromise by returning **XtGeometryAlmost**.

The Row widget's **GeometryManager()** method begins by checking for and rejecting any changes to the position of a child widget. If the request involves a change in width or height, the method saves the child widget's original size and temporarily sets the widget to the requested size. Next, the Row widget's **GeometryManager()** method calls the auxiliary function **try_layout()** to determine if the new size is acceptable. The **try_layout()** function returns a result of type **XtGeometryResult**, and also a mask containing information about which dimension, if any, is unacceptable. If the result of **try_layout()** is **XtGeometryNo**, the **GeometryManager()** method restores the widget's original dimensions and returns **XtGeometryNo**. If the result is **XtGeometryAlmost**, **GeometryManager()** restores the original values for the unacceptable dimensions and returns **XtGeometryAlmost**. In this case, the child widget can choose to use the compromise suggested by the Row widget and call **XtMakeGeometryRequest()** a second time using the suggested values, or it can abort the request and keep its original geometry. Finally, if **try_layout()** returns **XtGeometryYes**, **GeometryManager()** calls **do_layout()** to reposition the children before returning the value **XtGeometryYes**.

```
static XtGeometryResult GeometryManager(w, request, reply)
    Widget              w;
    XtWidgetGeometry    *request;
    XtWidgetGeometry    *reply;
{
  XsRowWidget       rw = (XsRowWidget) w -> core.parent;
  Mask              mask;
  XtGeometryResult  result;
  Dimension         wdelta, hdelta;
  /*
   * Say no.  We control the vertical....
   */
  if ((request->request_mode & CWX &&
                    request->x != w->core.x)||
      (request->request_mode & CWY &&
                    request->y != w->core.y))
    return (XtGeometryNo);
  /*
   *  Otherwise, grant all requests if they fit.
   */
  if (request->request_mode &
                    (CWWidth | CWHeight | CWBorderWidth)){
    /*
     * Save the original widget size, and set the
     * corresponding widget fields to the requested sizes.
     */
    Dimension savewidth       = w->core.width;
    Dimension saveheight      = w->core.height;
    Dimension saveborderwidth = w->core.border_width;

    if (request->request_mode & CWWidth)
      w->core.width  = request->width;
    if (request->request_mode & CWHeight)
      w->core.height = request->height;
    if (request->request_mode & CWBorderWidth)
      w->core.border_width = request->border_width;
    /*
     * See if we can still handle all the children
     * if the request is granted.
     */
    result = try_layout(rw, &mask, &wdelta, &hdelta);
    /*
```

```
         * If the children won't fit, restore the widget to its
         * original size, and return no.
         */
        if(result == XtGeometryNo){
          w->core.width  = savewidth;
          w->core.height = saveheight;
          w->core.border_width = saveborderwidth;
          return (XtGeometryNo);
        }
        /*
         * If only one dimension fits, restore the one that
         * doesn't fit and return "almost".
         */
        if(result == XtGeometryAlmost){
          reply->request_mode = request->request_mode;
          if(!(mask & CWWidth)){
           reply->width = w->core.width = savewidth;
           reply->border_width  = saveborderwidth;
           w->core.border_width = saveborderwidth;
          }
          if(!(mask & CWHeight))
            reply->height = w->core.height = saveheight;

          return (XtGeometryAlmost);
        }
        /*
         *  If we got here, everything must fit, so reposition
         *  all children based on the new size, and return "yes".
         */
        do_layout(rw);
        return (XtGeometryYes);
      }
      return (XtGeometryYes);
    }
```

The function **try_layout()** calculates the Row widget's minimum width and height, based on the current size of its managed children. If all children fit, the function returns **XtGeometryYes**. Otherwise, the Row widget issues a resize request to its parent in an attempt to accommodate the new size of its children. In this case, **try_layout()** returns the value returned by the request. If the Row widget's parent suggests a compromise geometry, **do_layout()** sets the **mask** argument to indicate the dimension that changed and calculates the difference between the requested width and height and the allowed width and height. This information is used by the **ChangeManaged()** method described in the next section.

```
static XtGeometryResult
try_layout(parent, mask, w_delta, h_delta)
     XsRowWidget parent;
     Mask        *mask;
     Dimension   *w_delta, *h_delta;
{
  int  i;
  Dimension total_width = 0, max_height = 0;
  /*
   * Get the bounding width and height of all children.
   */
  for (i = 0; i < parent -> composite.num_children; i++){
   Widget    child;
   Dimension width, height;

  child  = parent -> composite.children[i];
  if(child->core.managed){
    height =child->core.height + child->core.border_width * 2;
    width  =child->core.width + child->core.border_width * 2;
    total_width += width;
    max_height = MAX(max_height, height);
  }
 }
 /*
  *  If everyone doesn't fit, ask if we can grow. Return the
  *  result, after setting the mask to indicate which (if
  *  any) dimension is ok.
  */
 if(total_width > parent->core.width ||
     max_height > parent->core.height){
   XtGeometryResult result;
   Dimension replyWidth, replyHeight;
   Dimension width  =  MAX(total_width, parent->core.width);
   Dimension height = MAX(max_height, parent->core.height);

   result = XtMakeResizeRequest (parent, width, height,
                                     &replyWidth, &replyHeight);
   *mask = NULL;
   if(total_width == replyWidth)
     *mask  = CWWidth;
```

```
    if(max_height == replyHeight)
     *mask  |= CWHeight;

    if(result == XtGeometryAlmost)
      XtMakeResizeRequest (parent, replyWidth, replyHeight,
                                NULL, NULL);
    *w_delta = total_width - parent->core.width;
    *h_delta = max_height - parent->core.height;
    return (result);
  }
  /*
   * If everybody fits, just return yes.
   */
  *mask = CWWidth | CWHeight;
  return (XtGeometryYes);
}
```

These two functions, **GeometryManager()** and **try_layout()**, illustrate several aspects of the process of negotiating geometry. The Row widget completely controls the geometry of its children and tries its best to accommodate their preferred sizes. However, the Row widget cannot control its own size; that is controlled by its parent. The Row bases its preferred size on the sum of its children's sizes, and attempts to grow if necessary to contain its managed children. If all widgets cooperate, this negotiation process works smoothly. However, this process fails if any widget in an application's widget tree does not negotiate.

The ChangeManaged() Method

A composite widget's **ChangeManaged()** method is invoked whenever one of its children changes between being managed or unmanaged. Composite widgets generally use this method to recalculate the layout of their children when the set of managed widgets changes. The Row widget's **ChangeManaged()** method first calls **try_layout()** to determine whether all children still fit. Remember that **try_layout()** attempts to increase the size of the Row widget if all children do not fit. If **try_layout()** fails, it returns a delta indicating the difference between the size of the Row widget and the size needed to contain all the children. In this case, **ChangeManaged()** reduces the width of each widget by its share of the width delta, and reduces each widget's height to at least the height of the Row widget. Once the children's sizes have been adjusted, **ChangeManaged()** calls **do_layout()** to position each child.

```
static void ChangeManaged(w)
     XsRowWidget w;
{
  XtGeometryResult result;
```

```
    Dimension         width, height, delta, i;
    Mask              mask;
    Widget            child;
    /*
     * See if all children fit.
     */
    result = try_layout(w, &mask, &width, &height);
    /*
     * If they don't, resize all children to be smaller.
     */
    if(result != XtGeometryYes){
      if(w->composite.num_children > 0){
       delta = width / w->composite.num_children;
       for(i=0;i<w->composite.num_children;i++){
         child = w->composite.children[i];
         height = MIN(child->core.height,
                      w->core.height -child->core.border_width);
         if(child->core.managed)
           XtResizeWidget(child,
                          child->core.width - delta,
                          height,
                          child->core.border_width);
       }
     }
    }
    /*
     * Move all children to their new positions.
     */
    do_layout(w);
}
```

Notice that this method resizes all children equally if the total size of all managed children exceeds the available space. This method could be improved by adding calls to **XtQueryGeometry()** to check each child's preferred geometry, in case one child is more willing than others to have its size reduced.

13.2.4 USING THE ROW WIDGET

This section describes a simple program, **rowtest**, that tests the Row widget's management capabilities. The program uses a Row widget to manage four button widgets. Several callbacks allow the buttons to request size changes, and also to add and delete buttons.

```
/*********************************************
 * rowtest.c: Program to test the Row widget
 *********************************************/

#include <X11/StringDefs.h>
#include <X11/Intrinsic.h>
#include <Xw/Xw.h>
#include <Xw/PButton.h>
#include "Row.h"

void   make_big();
void   unmanage();
void   manage();

char *names[] = {"Button1", "Button2", "Button3", "Button4"};

main(argc, argv)
  int    argc;
  char  *argv[];
{
  Widget toplevel, row, buttons[4];
  Arg    wargs[2];
  int    i;
  /*
   * Initialize the Intrinsics.
   */
  toplevel = XtInitialize(argv[0], "RowTest", NULL,
                          0, &argc, argv);
  /*
   * Create a Row widget.
   */
  row = XtCreateManagedWidget("row", XsrowWidgetClass,
                              toplevel, NULL, 0);
  /*
   * Add children to the Row widget.
   */
  for(i=0;i<XtNumber(names);i++)
    buttons[i] = XtCreateWidget(names[i],
                                XwpushButtonWidgetClass,
                                row, NULL, 0);

  XtAddCallback(buttons[0], XtNrelease, make_big, NULL);
```

```
    XtAddCallback(buttons[1], XtNrelease, unmanage, NULL);
    XtAddCallback(buttons[2], XtNrelease, manage, buttons[1]);
    XtAddCallback(buttons[3], XtNrelease, make_big, NULL);

    XtManageChildren(buttons, XtNumber(buttons));
    XtRealizeWidget(toplevel);
    XtMainLoop();
  }
```

Fig. 13.1 in Section 13.2 shows the initial layout of the buttons produced by this program.

The **rowtest** program defines three callback functions that demonstrate and test the Row widget's geometry manager. The first callback, **make_big()**, is registered as a **XtNselect** callback function for the widgets **Button1** and **Button4**. Each time the user selects one of these buttons, this callback function requests the Row widget to increase the width and height of the button by 10 pixels.

```
  void make_big(w, button, call_data)
    Widget      w;
    Widget      button;
    caddr_t     call_data;
  {
    Arg         wargs[2];
    Dimension   width, height;
    /*
     *  Get the current width and height of the widget.
     */
    XtSetArg(wargs[0], XtNwidth,  &width);
    XtSetArg(wargs[1], XtNheight, &height);
    XtGetValues(w, wargs, 2);
    /*
     * Increment the width and height by 10 pixels.
     */
    width +=10;
    height +=10;
    /*
     * Set the new sizes.
     */
    XtSetArg(wargs[0], XtNwidth, width);
    XtSetArg(wargs[1], XtNheight, height);
    XtSetValues(w, wargs, 2);
    }
```

Fig. 13.2 shows the layout of the **rowtest** example after this function has been called several times.

Figure 13.2 Handling resize requests.

A second **XtNselect** callback function is registered for **Button2**. The **unmanage()** function calls **XtUnmanageChild()**, and causes the Row widget's **ChangeManaged()** method to be invoked to recompute the widget layout. This function is defined as

```
void unmanage(w, client_data, call_data)
   Widget      w;
   caddr_t     client_data;
   caddr_t     call_data;
{
  XtUnmanageChild(w);
}
```

The last callback function is registered with **Button3**. This function calls **XtManageChild()** to add **Button2** back to the Row widget's managed list.

```
void manage(w, button, call_data)
   Widget      w;
   Widget      button;
   caddr_t     call_data;
{
  XtManageChild(button);
}
```

Fig. 13.3 shows the how the Row widget adjusts the layout when **Button2** is unmanaged.

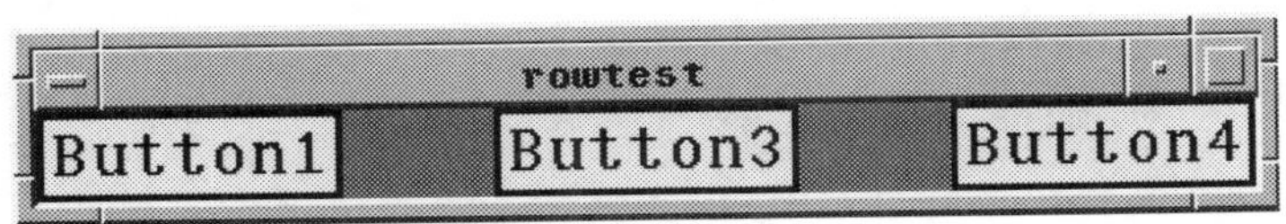

Figure 13.3 Row widget after unmanaging Button2.

13.3 SUMMARY

This chapter introduced the architecture of a composite widget. All composite widgets are subclasses of the Composite widget class. The distinguishing feature of a composite widget is that it can manage other widgets, known as its children. Composite widgets are responsible for managing the geometry of its children. Widgets can never resize or move themselves directly; instead, they must request their parent to do it for them. Composite widgets define several methods solely for the purpose of managing children.

An understanding of how composite widgets are implemented and how they negotiate and control widget geometries can help an application programmer to choose the best widget for a given task. This chapter explored composite widgets by building a simple example, the Row widget class. We can see from this example that the widget programmer has a large amount of latitude in determining the management policy of its children. The layout policy used by the Row widget is completely arbitrary, and others can easily be imagined. For example, instead of denying resize requests when no more room is available, the Row widget could allow the request, but reduce the size of all other children to create the extra space. Different policies regarding spacing between children are also possible. Many manager widgets provide resources that allow the application programmer to alter the layout policy of a composite widget. This makes the widget much more flexible, but increases the complexity of the widget and can make the widget's behavior less predictable.

The next chapter discusses the Constraint widget class, a powerful subclass of the Composite widget class.

14

CREATING CONSTRAINT WIDGETS

In the last chapter, we saw how composite widgets manage the layout of other widgets. Composite widgets usually apply their management policy uniformly without regard to any special characteristics of their children. The Constraint widget class is a subclass of the Composite widget class that manages its children based on additional information associated with each child. The class name comes from the fact that this information often takes the form of some constraint. For example, one might like to impose the constraint, "The ScrollBar widget must always be to the left of the TextEdit widget."

A constraint widget has all the responsibilities of a composite widget, but must also manage the constraints imposed on each widget. This chapter discusses the Constraint widget class and presents an example of a constraint widget whose children represent a tree-structured graph.

14.1 ARCHITECTURE OF CONSTRAINT WIDGETS

The Constraint widget class's architecture is similar to that of the Composite widget class. However, the Constraint widget class adds methods and resources used to handle constraints. Every constraint widget includes the **`CoreClassPart`**, the **`CompositeClassPart`**, and the **`ConstraintClassPart`** as the first components of its class record.

```
typedef struct _ConstraintClassRec {
    CoreClassPart       core_class;
    CompositeClassPart  composite_class;
    ConstraintClassPart constraint_class;
 } ConstraintClassRec;
```

The **ConstraintClassPart** structure contains information and methods used by every constraint widget.

```
typedef struct _ConstraintClassPart {
    XtResourceList  resources;
    Cardinal        num_resources;
    Cardinal        constraint_size;
    XtInitProc      initialize;
    XtWidgetProc    destroy;
    XtSetValuesFunc set_values;
    caddr_t         extension;
} ConstraintClassPart;
```

In addition to the basic resource list contained in the Core part of every widget class, the **ConstraintClassPart** of a constraint widget's class record contains a constraint resource list. The resource manager uses this resource list to initialize the constraints structure attached to each child widget. Every widget has a pointer to a constraint structure in the **CorePart** of its instance record (See Chapter 12). This pointer is set to **NULL** unless the child is managed by a constraint widget.

When a widget is managed by a constraint widget, the Intrinsics allocates space for a constraint structure. The **constraint_size** member of the parent's **ConstraintClassPart** specifies the size of the constraint structure and also contains pointers to three new methods that initialize and manage the constraints of the composite widget's children.

The Constraint widget class's instance record is defined as

```
typedef struct _ConstraintRec {
    CorePart       core;
    CompositePart  composite;
    ConstraintPart constraint;
} ConstraintRec, *ConstraintWidget;
```

The Constraint widget class requires no additional fields in its instance record, so **ConstraintPart** is defined as a dummy structure.

```
typedef struct _ConstraintPart {
    int    *empty;
} ConstraintPart;
```

Each constraint widget must also define the constraint structure attached to each of its children. This structure is specific to each particular type of constraint widget and the policy it supports. The example in the following section shows how this is done.

14.2 A CONSTRAINT WIDGET: THE TREE WIDGET

The easiest way to understand the Constraint widget class is by looking at an example. The rest of this chapter presents an example of a constraint widget, the Tree widget class. A Tree widget organizes its children as a hierarchical graph according to a constraint that specifies each child widget's position in the tree.[1] Applications can use the resource manager to specify this constraint when the widget is created. The following sections look at the public and private header files used by the Tree widget and then discuss the Tree widget's methods.

14.2.1 The Tree Private Header File: TreeP.h

The Tree widget's private header file defines the class record, the instance record, and the constraint record attached to each widget managed by the Tree widget. The Tree widget does not require any additional resources in the class record, so its contribution is a dummy structure.

```
typedef struct _XsTreeClassPart {
    int          ignore;
} XsTreeClassPart;
```

The Tree widget's complete class record is defined as

```
typedef struct _XsTreeClassRec {
    CoreClassPart        core_class;
    CompositeClassPart   composite_class;
    ConstraintClassPart  constraint_class;
    XsTreeClassPart      tree_class;
} XsTreeClassRec;

extern XsTreeClassRec XstreeClassRec;
```

The Tree widget's instance record contains auxiliary information used to lay out the nodes in the tree. This information includes the minimum and maximum spacing between nodes of the tree, the foreground color and graphics context used to draw lines connecting the nodes, and some auxiliary data used by the methods that calculate the position of each widget. The instance record also includes a member that points to a widget used as the root of the tree. The tree widget creates this **tree_root** widget to guarantee that every child

1. We have already used many of the terms associated with trees to refer to the X window and widget hierarchies, as well as the inheritance relationship between widget classes. Therefore, in the following discussion each element of the tree is referred to as a node. Each node, except for the root of the tree, has a super node and can also have subnodes.

widget has a super node. This simplifies the tree layout calculations. The **XsTreePart** structure is defined as

```
typedef struct {
    Dimension      h_min_space;
    Dimension      v_min_space;
    Pixel          foreground;
    GC             gc;
    TreeOffsetPtr  horizontal;
    TreeOffsetPtr  vertical;
    Widget         tree_root;
} XsTreePart;
```

The type **TreeOffsetPtr** is a pointer to an auxiliary structure used by the functions that compute the tree layout. This structure is defined as

```
typedef struct {
    Dimension  *array;
    int         size;
  }  TreeOffset, *TreeOffsetPtr;
```

The Tree widget's complete instance record is defined as

```
typedef struct _XsTreeRec {
    CorePart         core;
    CompositePart    composite;
    ConstraintPart   constraint;
    XsTreePart       tree;
}  XsTreeRec;
```

We must also define the constraint structure that the Tree widget attaches to its children. This structure is defined as

```
typedef struct _TreeConstraintsRec {
      Widget       super_node;
      WidgetList   sub_nodes;
      long         n_sub_nodes;
      long         max_sub_nodes;
      Position     x, y;
} TreeConstraintsRec, *TreeConstraints;
```

This structure contains the child's super node, a list of the child's subnodes, and also records the current length and maximum size of the subnode list. The tree layout algorithm uses the **x** and **y** members when calculating each widget's position.

14.2.2 The Tree Public Header File: Tree.h

The Tree widget's public header file is straightforward and similar to the examples in previous chapters. In addition to the type declarations, the header file defines the resource strings that refer to resources defined by the Tree widget.

```
/****************************************************
 * Tree.h: Public header file for the Tree widget
 ****************************************************/

extern WidgetClass  XstreeWidgetClass;

typedef struct _XsTreeClassRec *XsTreeWidgetClass;
typedef struct _XsTreeRec      *XsTreeWidget;

#define XtNhorizontalSpace      "horizontalSpace"
#define XtNverticalSpace        "verticalSpace"
#define XtCPad                  "Pad"
#define XtNsuperNode            "superNode"
#define XtCSuperNode            "SuperNode"
```

14.2.3 The Tree Widget Source File: Tree.c

The file Tree.c contains the declaration of the class record and the Tree widget's private methods. The file begins by including the Xt Intrinsics private header file, the Core, Composite, and Constraint widget's private header files, and also the public and private Tree widget header files.

```
/*************************************************
 * Tree.c: The Tree Widget Source File
 *************************************************/

#include  <X11/Intrinsic.h>
#include  <X11/IntrinsicP.h>
#include  <X11/StringDefs.h>
#include  <X11/CoreP.h>
#include  <X11/CompositeP.h>
#include  <X11/ConstrainP.h>
#include  "Tree.h"
#include  "TreeP.h"
#define   MAX(a,b) ((a) > (b) ? (a) : (b))
```

Forward declarations of the methods and other functions used by the Tree widget come next, followed by the Tree widget's resource lists. This resource list allows applications and users to use the resource manager to control the minimum horizontal and vertical space between nodes and also the foreground color used to draw lines between nodes.

```
static void                Initialize();
static void                ConstraintInitialize();
static Boolean             ConstraintSetValues();
static void                Resize();
static Boolean             SetValues();
static XtGeometryResult GeometryManager();
static void                ChangeManaged();
static void                insert_new_node();
static void                delete_node();
static void                new_layout();
static void                Redisplay();
static TreeOffsetPtr       create_offset();
static int                 compute_positions();
static void                shift_subtree();
static void                set_positions();
static void                reset();
static Position            current_position();
static void                set_current_position();
static Position            sum_of_positions();

static XtResource resources[] = {
 {XtNhorizontalSpace,XtCSpace,XtRDimension,sizeof(Dimension),
   XtOffset(XsTreeWidget, tree.h_min_space), XtRString,"15" },
 {XtNverticalSpace,XtCSpace, XtRDimension,sizeof (Dimension),
   XtOffset(XsTreeWidget, tree.v_min_space), XtRString,"5"  },
 {XtNforeground, XtCForeground, XtRPixel, sizeof (Pixel),
  XtOffset(XsTreeWidget, tree.foreground), XtRString,"Black"},
};
```

Constraint widgets usually specify an additional resource list used by the resource manager to set the values in the constraint part of each child widget. The Tree widget's constraint resource list allows applications to use **XtSetValues()** to specify each widget's super node.

```
static XtResource treeConstraintResources[] = {
 {XtNsuperNode, XtCSuperNode, XtRPointer, sizeof(Widget),
   XtOffset(TreeConstraints, super_node), XtRPointer, NULL},
};
```

14.2.3.1 The Class Record

Like each of the examples in previous chapters, the class record for the Tree widget class is initialized entirely at compile time.

```
XsTreeClassRec XstreeClassRec = {
  {
    /* core_class fields  */
    (WidgetClass) &constraintClassRec,/* superclass         */
    "Tree",                           /* class_name         */
    sizeof(XsTreeRec),                /* widget_size        */
    NULL,                             /* class_init         */
    NULL,                             /* class_part_init    */
    FALSE,                            /* class_inited       */
    Initialize,                       /* initialize         */
    NULL,                             /* initialize_hook    */
    XtInheritRealize,                 /* realize            */
    NULL,                             /* actions            */
    0,                                /* num_actions        */
    resources,                        /* resources          */
    XtNumber(resources),              /* num_resources      */
    NULLQUARK,                        /* xrm_class          */
    TRUE,                             /* compress_motion    */
    TRUE,                             /* compress_exposure  */
    TRUE,                             /* compress_enterleave*/
    TRUE,                             /* visible_interest   */
    NULL,                             /* destroy            */
    NULL,                             /* resize             */
    Redisplay,                        /* expose             */
    SetValues,                        /* set_values         */
    NULL,                             /* set_values_hook    */
    XtInheritSetValuesAlmost,         /* set_values_almost  */
    NULL,                             /* get_values_hook    */
    NULL,                             /* accept_focus       */
    XtVersion,                        /* version            */
    NULL,                             /* callback_private   */
    NULL,                             /* tm_table           */
    NULL,                             /* query_geometry     */
    NULL,                             /* display_accelerator*/
    NULL,                             /* extension          */
  },
  {
    /* composite_class fields */
```

```
        GeometryManager,                      /* geometry_manager     */
        ChangeManaged,                        /* change_managed       */
        XtInheritInsertChild,                 /* insert_child         */
        XtInheritDeleteChild,                 /* delete_child         */
        NULL,                                 /* extension            */
      },
      {
        /* constraint_class fields */
       treeConstraintResources,              /* subresources         */
       XtNumber(treeConstraintResources),/* subresource_count    */
       sizeof(TreeConstraintsRec),           /* constraint_size      */
       ConstraintInitialize,                 /* initialize           */
       NULL,                                 /* destroy              */
       ConstraintSetValues,                  /* set_values           */
       NULL,                                 /* extension            */
       },
      {
        /* Tree class fields */
        0,                                    /* ignore               */
      }
    };
```

The Tree class pointer is declared internally as a pointer to this **XstreeClassRec** structure.

```
    WidgetClass XstreeWidgetClass = (WidgetClass) &XstreeClassRec;
```

14.2.3.2 Methods

The primary difference between a constraint widget and a composite widget is the additional methods that initialize and set values in each child widget's constraint record. The **Initialize()** and **SetValues()** methods manage the constraint widget's resources, while the **ConstraintInitialize()** and **ConstraintSetValues()** methods manage the constraints attached to each child widget.

The Initialize() Method

The Intrinsics invokes the Tree widget's **Initialize()** method when the Tree widget is created. The **Initialize()** method first checks that the width and height of the widget are greater than zero, and then creates a graphics context used to draw the lines connecting the nodes of the tree. Next it creates a widget that serves as the root of the tree. This widget is created, but never managed. It is not visible to the user and only exists to simplify the tree layout calculations. Finally, the horizontal and vertical fields of the Tree widget's instance record are initialized. We will discuss the use of these fields and the function **create_offset()** along with the tree layout algorithm.

```
static void Initialize(request, new)
    XsTreeWidget request, new;
{
  Arg        wargs[2];
  XGCValues values;
  XtGCMask  valueMask;
  /*
   * Make sure the widget's width and height are
   * greater than zero.
   */
  if (request->core.width <= 0)
    new->core.width = 5;
  if (request->core.height <= 0)
    new->core.height = 5;
  /*
   * Create a graphics context for the connecting lines.
   */
  valueMask = GCForeground | GCBackground;
  values.foreground = new->tree.foreground;
  values.background = new->core.background_pixel;
  new->tree.gc = XtGetGC (new, valueMask, &values);
  /*
   * Create the "fake" root widget.
   */
  new->tree.tree_root = (Widget) NULL;
  XtSetArg(wargs[0], XtNwidth, 1);
  XtSetArg(wargs[1], XtNheight, 1);
  new->tree.tree_root =
          XtCreateWidget("root", widgetClass, new, wargs, 2);
  /*
   * Allocate the tables used by the layout
   * algorithm.
   */
  new->tree.horizontal = create_offset(10);
  new->tree.vertical   = create_offset(10);
}
```

The ConstraintInitialize() Method

Every constraint widget also has a **ConstraintInitialize()** method. The Intrinsics invokes this method each time a child of the Tree widget is created, to initialize the child's constraint record. The arguments **request** and **new** are versions of a child of the Tree widget, not the Tree widget itself. The **request** parameter is copy of the widget with all resources as originally requested by a combination of command line arguments, the contents of the resource database and widget defaults. The **new** parameter is the widget after it has been processed by all superclasses's **ConstraintInitialize()** methods. The Tree widget's **ConstraintInitialize()** method sets the **n_sub_nodes** and **sub_nodes** members of each child's constraint record to NULL and checks to see if the widget has a super node. If so, the child widget is added to the super node widget's list of subnodes. Otherwise, the widget becomes a subnode of the **tree_root** widget created by the Tree widget. Notice the test to determine whether the **tree_root** widget exists. This prevents the **tree_root** widget from attempting to add itself recursively to its own list of subnodes when it is created.

```
static void ConstraintInitialize(request, new)
     Widget request, new;
{
  TreeConstraints tree_const =
            (TreeConstraints) new->core.constraints;
  XsTreeWidget tw = (XsTreeWidget) new->core.parent;
  /*
   * Initialize the widget to have no subnodes.
   */
  tree_const->n_sub_nodes = tree_const->max_sub_nodes = 0;
  tree_const->sub_nodes   = (WidgetList) NULL;
  tree_const->x = tree_const->y = 0;
  /*
   * If this widget has a super node, add it to that
   * widget' subnodes list. Otherwise make it a subnode of
   * the tree_root widget.
   */
  if(tree_const->super_node)
    insert_new_node(tree_const->super_node, new);
  else
    if(tw->tree.tree_root)
      insert_new_node(tw->tree.tree_root, new);
}
```

In many constraint widget's methods, a child's constraint records are accessed by coercing the **constraint** member of the child's **core** part to the proper type. We can also retrieve the Tree widget structure by coercing the **parent** member of the child's **core** part to a **XsTreeWidget** structure.

The SetValues() Method

The **SetValues()** method is called when a Tree widget resource is altered. The Tree widget's **SetValues()** method must check the values of three resources. If the Tree widget's foreground color is altered, a new graphics context is created and the **redraw** flag is set to **True**. If either of the horizontal or vertical space resources is modified, **SetValues()** calls the auxiliary functions **new_layout()** to reposition all children. Finally, **SetValues()** returns the value of the **redraw** flag that indicates whether or not the Intrinsics should force the window to be redrawn.

```
static Boolean SetValues(current, request, new)
    XsTreeWidget current, request, new;
{
 int         redraw = FALSE;
 XGCValues values;
 XtGCMask  valueMask;
 /*
  * If the foreground color has changed, redo the GC's
  * and indicate a redraw.
  */
 if (new->tree.foreground != current->tree.foreground ||
     new->core.background_pixel !=
                           current->core.background_pixel){
   valueMask          = GCForeground | GCBackground;
   values.foreground = new->tree.foreground;
   values.background = new->core.background_pixel;
   new->tree.gc     = XtGetGC (new, valueMask, &values);
   redraw = TRUE;
 }
 /*
  * If the minimum spacing has changed, recalculate the
  * tree layout. new_layout() does a redraw, so we don't
  * need SetValues to do another one.
  */
 if (new->tree.v_min_space != current->tree.v_min_space ||
     new->tree.h_min_space != current->tree.h_min_space){
   new_layout(new);
   redraw = FALSE;
```

```
  }
  return (redraw);
}
```

The ConstraintSetValues() Method

The Intrinsics invokes the **ConstraintSetValues()** method when a child's constraint resource is altered. The only resource in the Tree widget's constraint resource list is the **XtNsuperNode** resource. If this resource has changed, the Tree widget calls the function **delete_node()** to remove the affected child widget from the subnode list of the widget's current super node. Then the method **insert_node()** is called to add the widget to the new super node's list of subnodes. Notice that the **new** widget structure is passed to both of these methods. This is important because each of these methods stores a pointer to the widget in a list. The new structure is the actual widget. The other arguments are temporary copies of the widget's instance record, created by the Intrinsics before calling the **ConstraintSetValues()** method. Finally, if the Tree widget is realized, **ConstraintSetValues()** calls the auxiliary function **new_layout()** to recalculate the position of each child widget.

```
static Boolean ConstraintSetValues(current, request, new)
    Widget current, request, new;
{
  TreeConstraints newconst =
                       (TreeConstraints) new->core.constraints;
  TreeConstraints current_const =
                     (TreeConstraints) current->core.constraints;
  XsTreeWidget tw = (XsTreeWidget) new->core.parent;
  /*
   * If the super_node field has changed, remove the widget
   * from the old widget's sub_nodes list and add it to the
   * new one.
   */
   if(current_const->super_node != newconst->super_node){
    if(current_const->super_node)
      delete_node(current_const->super_node, new);
    if(newconst->super_node)
      insert_new_node(newconst->super_node, new);
    /*
     * If the Tree widget has been realized,
     * compute new layout.
     */
    if(XtIsRealized(tw))
```

```
      new_layout(tw);
  }
  return (False);
}
```

The auxiliary functions **insert_node()** and **delete_node()** are responsible for managing the **sub_nodes** list in each child's constraint record. Each time a new subnode is added, the **insert_node()** function checks whether the list is large enough to contain another widget. If not, the list must be enlarged using **XtRealloc()**. Then the function adds the widget to the end of the list and increments the **n_sub_nodes** index.

```
static void insert_new_node(super_node, node)
     Widget super_node, node;
{
  TreeConstraints super_const =
                (TreeConstraints)super_node->core.constraints;
  TreeConstraints node_const =
                  (TreeConstraints) node->core.constraints;
  int index = super_const->n_sub_nodes;

  node_const->super_node = super_node;
  /*
   * If there is now more room in the sub_nodes array,
   * allocate additional space.
   */
  if (super_const->n_sub_nodes == super_const->max_sub_nodes){
   super_const->max_sub_nodes +=
                     (super_const->max_sub_nodes / 2) + 2;
   super_const->sub_nodes =
        (WidgetList) XtRealloc(super_const->sub_nodes,
                              (super_const->max_sub_nodes) *
                               sizeof(Widget));
  }
  /*
   * Add the sub_node in the next available slot and
   * increment the counter.
   */
  super_const->sub_nodes[index] = node;
  super_const->n_sub_nodes++;
}
```

The function **delete_node()** performs the opposite operation, removing a widget from the list of subnodes, closing any gap in the list caused by the removal of an entry, and decrementing the **n_sub_nodes** counter.

```
static void delete_node(super_node, node)
    Widget  super_node, node;
{
  TreeConstraints node_const =
                     (TreeConstraints) node->core.constraints;
  TreeConstraints super_const;
  int             pos, i;
  /*
   * Make sure the super_node exists.
   */
  if(!super_node) return;

  super_const =(TreeConstraints) super_node->core.constraints;
  /*
   * Find the sub_node on its super_node's list.
   */
  for (pos = 0; pos < super_const->n_sub_nodes; pos++)
    if (super_const->sub_nodes[pos] == node)
      break;
  if (pos == super_const->n_sub_nodes) return;
  /*
   * Decrement the number of sub_nodes
   */
  super_const->n_sub_nodes--;
  /*
   * Fill in the gap left by the sub_node.
   * Zero the last slot for good luck.
   */
  for (i = pos; i < super_const->n_sub_nodes; i++)
    super_const->sub_nodes[i] = super_const->sub_nodes[i+1];
  super_const->sub_nodes[super_const->n_sub_nodes] = 0;
}
```

The Constraint Tree

Now that we have introduced the functions used to initialize and modify the constraint records of the Tree widget's children, let's pause and look closer at the structure created by these constraints. The following small code segment creates a Tree widget that manages three children.

```
tree = XtCreateManagedWidget("TreeTest", XstreeWidgetClass,
                              toplevel, NULL, 0);
widg1 =  XtCreateManagedWidget("One", widgetClass,
                              tree, NULL, 0);
XtSetArg(wargs[0], XtNsuperNode, widg1);
widg2 =  XtCreateManagedWidget("Two", widgetClass,
                              tree, wargs, 1);
XtSetArg(wargs[0], XtNsuperNode, widg1);
widg3 =  XtCreateManagedWidget("Three", widgetClass,
                              tree, wargs, 1);
```

Let's consider the contents of the constraint record of each of these widgets and also the dummy **tree_root** widget created by the Tree widget at the point after **widg3** has been created. The **tree_root** widget's **super_node** field is NULL, and its **sub_nodes** list contains a single widget, **widg1**. The **super_node** field of **widg2**'s constraint record contains a pointer to the **tree_root** widget, and its **sub_nodes** list contains two widgets, **widg2**, and **widg3**. The **sub_nodes** fields of **widg2** and **widg3** contain a pointer to **widg1**, and their **sub_nodes** list is empty. Fig. 14.1 shows how these pointers create a hierarchical graph.

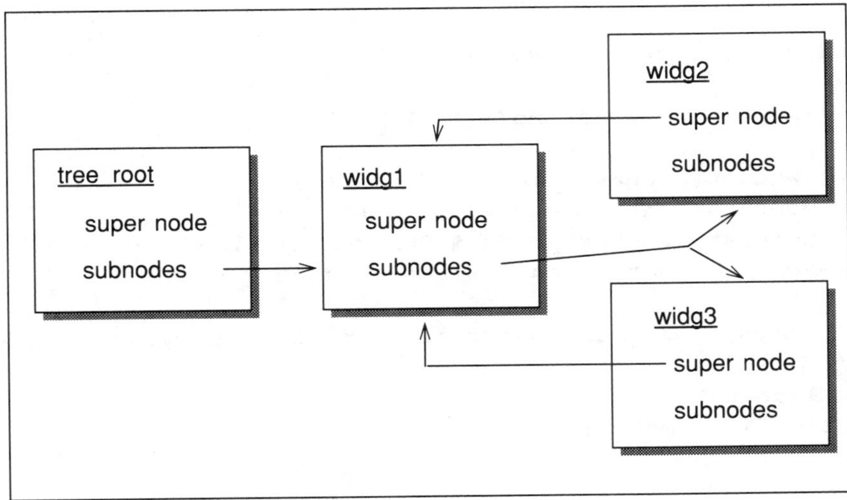

Figure 14.1 A hierarchical constraints structure.

The GeometryManager() Method

The Intrinsics invokes the Tree widget's **GeometryManager()** method when a child of the Tree widget makes a geometry request. The Tree widget's management policy does not allow a child to change its position, because the tree layout algorithm determines the position of every widget. However, the geometry manager grants all size requests without question. **GeometryManager()** calls **the auxiliary function**, **new_layout()**, to recompute and redraw the tree layout before returning **XtGeometryYes**.

```
static XtGeometryResult GeometryManager(w, request, reply)
    Widget              w;
    XtWidgetGeometry    *request;
    XtWidgetGeometry    *reply;
{
  XsTreeWidget tw = (XsTreeWidget) w->core.parent;
  /*
   * No position changes allowed!.
   */
 if((request->request_mode & CWX && request->x != w->core.x)||
    (request->request_mode & CWY && request->y != w->core.y))
   return (XtGeometryNo);
 /*
  * Allow all resize requests.
  */
 if (request->request_mode & CWWidth)
   w->core.width = request->width;
 if (request->request_mode & CWHeight)
   w->core.height = request->height;
 if (request->request_mode & CWBorderWidth)
   w->core.border_width = request->border_width;
 /*
  *  Compute the new layout based on the new widget sizes;
  */
 new_layout(tw);
 return (XtGeometryYes);
}
```

The ChangeManaged() Method

The Intrinsics invokes the Tree widget's **ChangeManaged()** method whenever the Tree widget's set of managed children changes. **ChangeManaged()** simply calls **new_layout()** to calculate the desired position of all children.[2]

```
static void ChangeManaged(tw)
    XsTreeWidget tw;
{
  new_layout(tw);
}
```

The Redisplay() Method

The **Redisplay()** method is called whenever an **Expose** event occurs and is also called by other Tree widget methods to redraw the lines connecting the nodes of the tree. This method ignores the arguments event and region to allow other Tree widget methods to call it with NULL event and/or region arguments. This method loops through each child on the Tree widget's list of children, drawing a line from the right edge to the left edge of each of the widget's subnodes.

```
static void Redisplay (w, event, region)
     XsTreeWidget    w;
     XEvent         *event;
     Region          region;
{
 int                i, j;
 TreeConstraints tree_const;
 Widget            child;
 /*
  * If the Tree widget is visible, visit each managed child.
  */
 if(w->core.visible)
   for (i = 0; i < w->composite.num_children; i++){
     child = w->composite.children[i];
     tree_const = (TreeConstraints) child->core.constraints;
     /*
      * Draw a line between the right edge of each widget
      * and the left edge of each of its sub_nodes. Don't
```

2. In most constraint widgets, this method should also update the constraint records of all affected widgets when a widget is managed or unmanaged. However, this brings up several sticky issues in the Tree widget (for example, what should be done with a widget's subnodes when the widget is unmanaged, but the subnodes are still managed?), and complicates the Tree widget example beyond the scope of this book. Therefore, this example treats managed and unmanaged children in exactly the same way.

```
         * draw lines from the fake tree_root.
         */
         if(child != w->tree.tree_root &&
            tree_const->n_sub_nodes)
          for (j = 0; j < tree_const->n_sub_nodes; j++)
            XDrawLine(XtDisplay(w), XtWindow(w),
                      w->tree.gc,
                      child->core.x + child->core.width,
                      child->core.y + child->core.height / 2,
                      tree_const->sub_nodes[j]->core.x,
                      tree_const->sub_nodes[j]->core.y +
                      tree_const->sub_nodes[j]->core.height/ 2);
      }
   }
```

14.2.3.3 The Tree Layout Procedures

The previous sections presented each of the Tree widget's methods. The remaining functions are auxiliary functions used to determine the position of each child widget. The layout algorithm uses a few simple rules of thumb intended to produce an aesthetically pleasing tree layout. The basic rules, worded to apply to trees that are laid out horizontally, are:

- A tree should be as narrow as possible.
- Each node should be placed as close as possible to its siblings.
- Each node should be centered to the left of its subnodes.
- Nodes at the same level should begin at the same horizontal position.
- The shape of any given subtree should be independent of its position in the tree.

The concept of the tree layout algorithm is simple. The first node of each level is initially positioned at *y* coordinate 0, and each successive node on the same level is placed below its neighbor. After the positions of all nodes within a particular branch are determined, the super node of the branch is centered to the left of its subnodes. If this position is less than the next available position on the super node's level, we must shift the entire subtree. The offset necessary to move the super node to the next available position at its level is calculated and the entire sub-tree is shifted. This function establishes the *y* coordinate of each widget. To determine the *x* position of each widget, we store the maximum width of all nodes at each level. Once the *y* position of each widget has been computed, this information is used to determine the final *x* position of each widget.

The function **new_layout()** provides the top-level interface to the layout algorithm. The function resets the auxiliary tables used to store temporary information then calls other functions to do the real work.

```
static void new_layout(tw)
     XsTreeWidget   tw;
{
  /*
   *  Reset the auxiliary tables.
   */
  reset(tw->tree.vertical);
  reset(tw->tree.horizontal);
  /*
   * Compute each widget's x,y position
   */
  compute_positions(tw, tw->tree.tree_root, 0);
  /*
   * Move each widget into place.
   */
  set_positions(tw, tw->tree.tree_root, 0, 0);
  /*
   * Redisplay the lines connecting nodes.
   */
  if(XtIsRealized(tw)){
    XClearWindow(XtDisplay(tw), XtWindow(tw));
    Redisplay (tw, NULL, NULL);
  }
}
```

The function **reset()** initializes two data structures that store the next available position in the vertical direction and the maximum width of the widgets on each level in the horizontal direction. We will look at this data structure and its related functions shortly.

The main portion of the tree layout algorithm is handled by the function **compute_positions()**.

```
static int compute_positions(tw, w, level)
    XsTreeWidget tw;
    Widget       w;
    long         level;
{
  Position        current_hpos, current_vpos;
  int              i, depth = 0;
  TreeConstraints tree_const =
                         (TreeConstraints) w->core.constraints;
  /*
   * Get the current positions for this level.
   */
```

```
current_hpos = current_position(tw->tree.horizontal, level);
current_vpos = current_position(tw->tree.vertical, level);
/*
 * Set the current horizontal width to the max widths of all
 * widgets at this level.
 */
set_current_position(tw->tree.horizontal, level,
                     MAX(current_hpos, w->core.width));
/*
 * If the node has no sub_nodes, just set the vertical
 * position to the next available space.
 */
if(tree_const->n_sub_nodes == 0){
  tree_const->y = current_vpos;
}
else {
   Widget           first_kid, last_kid;
   TreeConstraints const1, const2;
   Position         top, bottom;
  /*
   * If the node has sub_nodes, recursively figure the
   * positions of each sub_node.
   */
  for(i = 0; i < tree_const->n_sub_nodes; i++)
    depth = compute_positions(tw, tree_const->sub_nodes[i],
                                   level + 1);
  /*
   * Now that the vertical positions of all children are
   * known, find the vertical extent of all sub_nodes.
   */
  first_kid= tree_const->sub_nodes[0];
  last_kid=tree_const->sub_nodes[tree_const->n_sub_nodes-1];
  const1   = (TreeConstraints) first_kid->core.constraints;
  const2   = (TreeConstraints) last_kid->core.constraints;
  top      = const1->y + first_kid->core.height / 2;
  bottom   = const2->y + last_kid->core.height / 2;
  /*
   * Set the node's position to the center of its sub_nodes.
   */
  tree_const->y = (top + bottom) / 2 - (w->core.height / 2);
  /*
   * If this position is less than the next available
```

```
     * position, correct it to be the next available position,
     * calculate the amount by which all sub_nodes must be
     * shifted, and shift the entire sub-tree.
     */
     if(tree_const->y < current_vpos){
       Dimension offset = current_vpos - tree_const->y;
       for(i = 0; i < tree_const->n_sub_nodes; i++)
         shift_subtree(tree_const->sub_nodes[i], offset);
       /*
        * Adjust the next available space at all levels below
        * the current level.
        */
       for(i = level + 1; i <= depth; i++){
        Position pos = current_position(tw->tree.vertical,i);
        set_current_position(tw->tree.vertical, i,pos+offset);
       }
       tree_const->y = current_vpos;
    }
  }
  /*
   * Record the current vertical position at this level.
   */
  set_current_position(tw->tree.vertical, level,
                       tw->tree.v_min_space +
                       tree_const->y + w->core.height);
  return (MAX(depth, level));
}
```

The function **shift_subtree()** moves the entire subtree below the given widget by an integer offset.

```
static void shift_subtree(w, offset)
     Widget     w;
     Dimension  offset;
{
  int               i;
  TreeConstraints tree_const =
                         (TreeConstraints) w->core.constraints;
  /*
   * Shift the node by the offset.
   */
  tree_const->y += offset;
  /*
```

```
     * Shift each subnode into place.
     */
    for(i=0; i< tree_const->n_sub_nodes; i++)
      shift_subtree(tree_const->sub_nodes[i], offset);
}
```

Once the layout of all widgets has been determined, the function **set_positions()** sets the *x* position of each widget and calls **XtMoveWidget()** to move each widget into place. If all children don't fit in the Tree widget, this function makes a geometry request to the Tree widget's parent to attempt to enlarge the Tree widget.

```
static void set_positions(tw, w, level)
     XsTreeWidget tw;
     Widget       w;
     int          level;
{
  int                  i;
  Dimension            replyWidth = 0, replyHeight = 0;
  XtGeometryResult     result;

  if(w){
    TreeConstraints tree_const =
                       (TreeConstraints) w->core.constraints;
    /*
     * Add up the sum of the width's of all nodes to this
     * depth, and use it as the x position.
     */
    tree_const->x = (level * tw->tree.h_min_space) +
                 sum_of_positions(tw->tree.horizontal, level);
    /*
     * Move the widget into position.
     */
    XtMoveWidget (w, tree_const->x, tree_const->y);
    /*
     * If the widget position plus its width or height doesn't
     * fit in the tree, ask if the tree can be resized.
     */
    if(tw->core.width < tree_const->x + w->core.width ||
       tw->core.height < tree_const->y + w->core.height){
     result =
       XtMakeResizeRequest(tw,
                           MAX(tw->core.width,
                               tree_const->x + w->core.width),
```

```
                                MAX(tw->core.height,
                                    tree_const->y +w->core.height),
                                    &replyWidth, &replyHeight);
        /*
         * Accept any compromise.
         */
        if (result == XtGeometryAlmost)
          XtMakeResizeRequest (tw, replyWidth, replyHeight,
                               NULL, NULL);
      }
      /*
       * Set the positions of all sub_nodes.
       */
      for(i=0; i< tree_const->n_sub_nodes;i++)
        set_positions(tw, tree_const->sub_nodes[i], level + 1);
    }
}
```

The remaining functions store and retrieve a value from a dynamically resizable array. The layout functions use these functions to store the next available position and the maximum width of each level. These functions are straightforward. The function **create_offset()** allocates an array of the given size.

```
static TreeOffsetPtr create_offset(size)
   long size;
{
 TreeOffsetPtr  offset =
                   (TreeOffsetPtr) XtMalloc(sizeof(TreeOffset));
 offset->size = size;
 offset->array =
             (Dimension *) XtMalloc(size * sizeof(Dimension));
 return (offset);
}
```

The **reset()** function zeroes all entries in a table.

```
static void reset(offset)
   TreeOffsetPtr offset;
{
  long i;
  for(i=0; i< offset->size; i++)
    offset->array[i] = 0;
}
```

The function **current_position()** returns the value in an given position in a table. If the requested position is greater than the size of the table, the function returns zero.

```
static Position current_position(offset, position)
   TreeOffsetPtr  offset;
   long           position;
{
  if(position >= offset->size)
    return (0);
  return (offset->array[position]);
 }
```

The function **set_current_position()** stores a value in a table at a given index position. If index is larger than the size of the table, the table is enlarged using **XtRealloc()**.

```
static void set_current_position(offset, index, value)
   TreeOffsetPtr offset;
   int           index;
   Dimension     value;
{
 if(index >= offset->size){
   offset->size = index + index / 2;
   offset->array =
     (Dimension *) XtRealloc(offset->array,
                        offset->size * sizeof(Dimension));
 }
 offset->array[index] = value;
}
```

The **sum_of_positions()** function returns the sum of all values in a table up to the given position.

```
static Position sum_of_positions(offset, index)
   TreeOffsetPtr  offset;
   long           index;
{
  int    i;

  Position  sum  = 0;
  long    stop = index;
  if(index > offset->size)
    stop = offset->size;
  for (i=0;i < stop; i++)
```

```
      sum += offset->array[i];
    return (sum);
  }
```

This completes the implementation of the Tree widget. The next section discusses an example using the Tree widget.

14.2.4 Using The Tree Widget

This section shows how an application can use the Tree widget to display a tree. In this example, the Tree widget is managed by a ScrolledWindow widget to allow the tree to display an area larger than the screen if necessary. The program, named **sort**, reads a list of integers from standard input and displays them in a binary sort tree.[3] A binary sort tree is a tree in which the value of the key in each left subnode is less than the value of its super node's key, and the value of the key in each right subnode is greater than its super node's key. The header includes the various header files and defines a structure used to store the sorted tree.

```
/***********************************************************
 * sort.c: Display a binary sort tree using the tree widget.
 ***********************************************************/

#include <stdio.h>
#include <X11/StringDefs.h>
#include <X11/Intrinsic.h>
#include <Xw/Xw.h>
#include <Xw/SText.h>
#include <Xw/SWindow.h>
#include "Tree.h"
/*
 * Define the structure for a node in the binary sort tree.
 */
typedef struct _node {
  int            key;
  struct _node  *left;
  struct _node  *right;
} node;

extern node *insert_node();
extern node *make_node();
```

3. Notice that although this example uses the Tree widget to display a binary tree, the Tree widget is not limited to binary trees.

The body of the program creates the Tree widget, and then inserts numbers read from standard input into a binary sorted tree of **node** structures. Once the tree is built, the function **show_tree()** creates a widget for each node of the tree.

```
main(argc, argv)
    int argc;
    char **argv;
{
  Widget     toplevel, sw, tree;
  int        i;
  node       *head = NULL;
  int         digit;
  toplevel = XtInitialize(argv[0], "Sort", NULL, 0,
                                   &argc, argv);
  /*
   * Put the tree in a scrolled window, to handle
   * large trees.
   */
   sw = XtCreateManagedWidget("swindow",
                                      XwswindowWidgetClass,
                                      toplevel, NULL, 0);
   /*
    * Create the tree widget.
    */
   tree = XtCreateManagedWidget("tree", XstreeWidgetClass,
                                      sw, NULL, 0);
   /*
    * Create a binary sort tree from data read from stdin.
    */
   while(scanf("%d", &digit) != EOF)
      head = insert_node(digit, head);
   /*
    * Create the widgets representing the tree.
    */
   show_tree(tree, head, NULL);

   XtRealizeWidget(toplevel);
   XtMainLoop();
}
```

The function **insert_node()** inserts an integer into the appropriate node of a tree. If the tree doesn't exist, an initial node is allocated and the given key becomes the root of the sort tree. Otherwise, this function follows the branches of the tree until a leaf is found. The new key is inserted at the leaf. At each node, the branch that is followed depends on whether the key in that node is less than or greater than the new key.

```
node *insert_node(key, head)
     int   key;
     node *head;
{
  node *prev, *ptr  = head;
  /*
   * If the tree doesn't exist, just create and
   * return a new node.
   */
  if(!head)
    return (make_node(key));
  /*
   * Otherwise, find a leaf node, always following the
   * left branches if the key is less than the value in each
   * node, and the right branch otherwise.
   */
  while(ptr != NULL){
    prev = ptr;
    ptr = (key < ptr->key) ? ptr->left : ptr->right;
  }
  /*
   * Make a new node and attach it to the appropriate branch.
   */
  if (key < prev->key)
    prev->left = make_node(key);
  else
    prev->right = make_node(key);
   return (head);
}
```

The function **make_node()** creates a new node structure, stores the integer key, and initializes the node's subnode pointers to NULL.

```
node *make_node(key)
     int   key;
{
  node  *ptr = (node *) malloc(sizeof(node));

  ptr->key  = key;
  ptr->left = ptr->right = NULL;
```

```
    return (ptr);
  }
```

Once the tree has been sorted, the function **show_tree()** performs a pre-order traversal of the nodes, and creates widgets for each node. The function also sets the **XtNsuperNode** constraint for each widget to the widget previously created for the super node in the binary tree.

```
show_tree(parent, branch, super_node)
     Widget   parent;
     node    *branch;
     Widget   super_node;
{
  Widget   w;
  char    *name[100];
  Arg      wargs[3];
  int      n = 0;
  /*
   * If we've hit a leaf, return.
   */
  if(!branch) return;
  /*
   * Create a widget for the node, specifying the
   * given super_node constraint.
   */
  sprintf(name, "%d", branch->key);
  XtSetArg(wargs[n], XtNsuperNode, super_node); n++;
  XtSetArg(wargs[n], XtNstring, name); n++;
  w = XtCreateManagedWidget(name, XwstatictextWidgetClass,
                                    parent, wargs, n);
  /*
   * Recursively create the subnodes, giving this node's
   * widget as the super_node.
   */
  show_tree(parent, branch->left,  w);
  show_tree(parent, branch->right, w);
}
```

We can try this program by creating a sample data file containing some numbers.

```
% cat tree.data
50 21 72 10 15 17 19 11 14 80 60
90 83 91 65 52 79 25 67 63 68 66
```

Then we can run the sort program to produce the tree in Fig. 14.2.

```
% sort < tree.data
```

The window shown in Fig. 14.2 was produced by setting the StaticText widget's **XtNborderWidth** resource to zero.

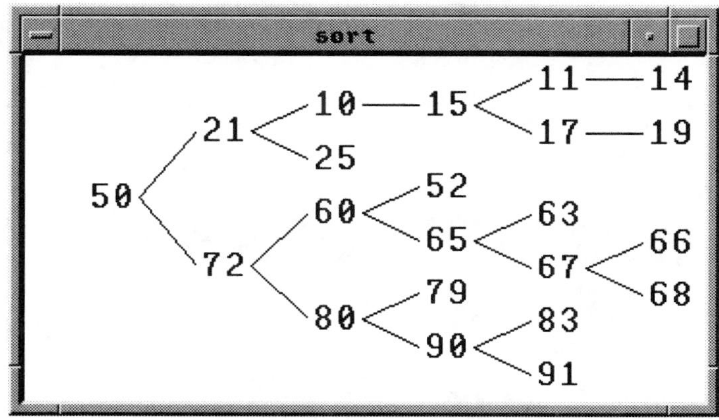

Figure 14.2 A binary sort tree.

14.3 SUMMARY

This chapter presented the architecture and construction of a Constraint widget. The Constraint widget class is a subclass of the Composite widget class that uses additional information attached to its children to determine how the children are managed. Each constraint widget attaches a constraint record to its children to store this additional information, and often provides additional resources for the child widget. The constraint resources allow the application programmer or the user to specify the corresponding values in the constraint record, and influence the layout of each individual widget. Constraint widgets define additional methods to initialize and manage changes to its children's constraint record.

The Tree widget presented in this chapter provides one example of the type of constraint information that can be attached to a widget. Each widget position is constrained by its hierarchical relationship to other widgets in a tree-structured graph. The actual positions are determined by heuristics that specify the desirable shape of a tree.

APPENDIX A

THE X WIDGET CLASS TREE

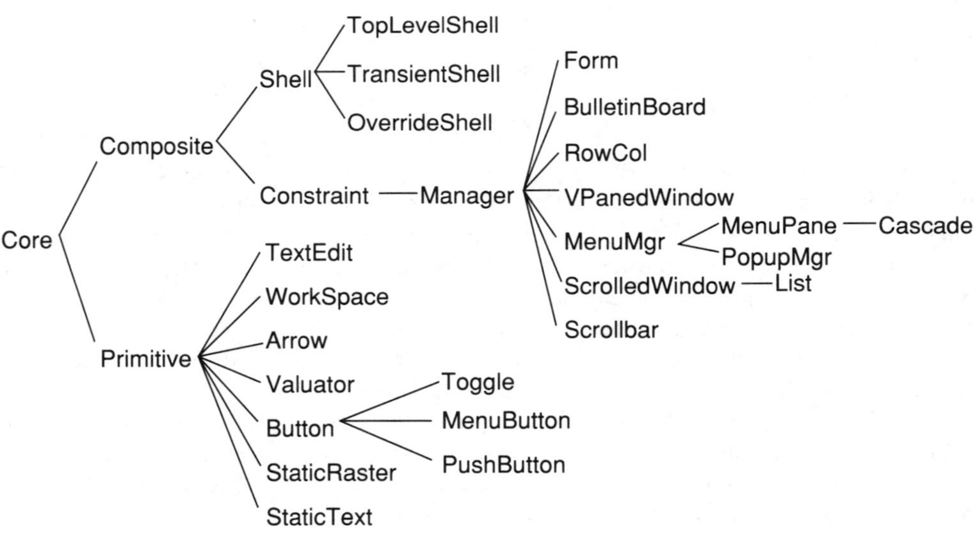

APPENDIX B

QUICK WIDGET REFERENCE

This appendix is a mini-reference guide to the widget classes in the X Toolkit Intrinsics and the X Widget set. Each entry briefly describes the widget class, listing its class and class name, and its superclasses. Each entry also lists the resources added by the widget class. To determine the complete list of resources used by each widget class, refer to the resources defined by each of the widget's superclasses. For more information, or examples of how the widget is used, refer to the chapter and section listed in each entry.

Each entry contains a table listing the resources recognized by the widget class. The first entry lists the resource name. To set this resource in a resource file, strip of the initial **XtN**. The second column shows the default value of the resource, while the third and fourth columns list the possible values of the resource from a programmer's and a user's view, respectively. When a resource can be set to any of a range of values, the type of that value is shown in brackets. For example, the Core widget's **XtNborderWidth** resource can be set to any integer value, so it is given as **<Integer>**. Other resources expect specific strings or constants. These are listed explicitly. For example, the user can set the Arrow widget's **XtNarrowDirection** resource to one of **arrow_up**, **arrow_down**, **arrow_left**, or **arrow_right**, while the programmer can use one of **XwARROW_UP**, **XwARROW_DOWN**, **XwARROW_LEFT**, or **XwARROW_RIGHT**.

CORE INTRINSICS WIDGETS

COMPOSITE

Class: `compositeWidgetClass`
Class Name: `Composite`
Superclasses: `Core`
Description:

The Composite widget class is a meta-class defined by the X Toolkit Intrinsics. Composite widgets are used as containers for other widgets.

Refer To: Section 4.3.2, 13.2

CONSTRAINT

Class: `constraintWidgetClass`
Class Name: `Constraint`
Superclasses: `Core`, `Composite`
Description:

The Constraint widget class is a meta-class defined by the Xt Intrinsics. A constraint widget attaches additional resources to its children. The constraint widget normally uses these constraints to manage the geometry of its children.

Refer To: Section 4.3.3, 14.1

CORE

Class: `widgetClass`
Class Name: `Core`
Superclasses: `None`
Description:

The Core widget class is a meta-class provided by the X Toolkit Intrinsics. It serves as the superclass of all widgets.

Refer To: Section 4.3.1, 12.1
Resources:

Resource	Default	Programmer	User
XtNancestorSensitive	TRUE	<Boolean>	<Boolean>
XtNx	0	<Integer>	<Integer>
XtNy	0	<Integer>	<Integer>
XtNwidth	0	<Integer>	<Integer>
XtNheight	0	<Integer>	<Integer>
XtNdepth	0	<Integer>	<Integer>
XtNbackground	1	<Pixel>	<Pixel>

XtNbackgroundPixmap	None	<Pixmap>	-
XtNborderWidth	1	<Integer>	<Integer>
XtNborderColor	0	<Integer>	<Integer>
XtNborderPixmap	None	<Pixmap>	-
XtNsensitive	TRUE	<Boolean>	<Boolean>
XtNmappedWhenManaged	TRUE	<Boolean>	<Boolean>
XtNtranslations	NULL	<Translation list>	

Callbacks:

Callback List	Call Data Type
XtNdestroy	NULL

SHELL

Class: shellWidgetClass
Class Name: Shell
Superclasses: Core, Composite
Description:

The Shell widget class is defined by the Xt Intrinsics and provides an interface between applications and the window manager. Every application uses a Shell widget or a subclass of Shell as its top level widget.

Refer To: Section 4.3.4, 4.5
Resources:

Resource	Default	Programmer	User
XtNallowShellResize	False	<Boolean>	<Boolean>
XtNgeometry	NULL	<String>	<String>
XtNcreatePopupChildProc	NULL	<Function>	-
XtNsaveUnder	FALSE	<Boolean>	<Boolean>
XtNoverrideRedirect	FALSE	<Boolean>	<Boolean>

THE X WIDGET SET

ARROW

Class: XwarrowWidgetClass
Class Name: Arrow
Superclasses: Core, Primitive
Description:

The Arrow widget displays a selectable arrow.

Refer To: Section 4.4.4

Resources:

Resource	Default	Programmer	User
XtNarrowDirection	arrow_up	XwARROW_UP	arrow_up
		XwARROW_DOWN	arrow_down
		XwARROW_LEFT	arrow_left
		XwARROW_RIGHT	arrow_right

Actions:

Action	Default Binding
enter()	EnterWindow
leave()	LeaveWindow
select()	Btn1Down
release()	Btn1Up
select()	<KeyDown>Select
release()	<KeyUp>Select

Callbacks:

Callback List	Call Data Type
XtNselect	NULL
XtNrelease	NULL

BULLETIN BOARD

Class: XwBulletinWidgetClass
Class Name: BulletinBoard
Superclasses: Core, Composite, Constraint, Manager
Description:

The BulletinBoard widget is a composite widget which does not enforce any ordering on its children. Applications and/or users can use the resource manager to specify the location of all children of the Bulletin Board widget.

Refer To: Section 4.4.6

BUTTON

Class: XwbuttonWidgetClass
Class Name: Button
Superclasses: Core, Primitive
Description:

The Button widget class is a meta-class that serves as a superclass for all other button classes in the X Widget set.

Refer To: Section 4.4.5

Resources:

Resource	Default	Programmer	User
XtNfont	Fixed	<XFontStruct>	<Font Name>
XtNlabel	NULL	<String>	<String>
XtNlabelLocation	right	XwLEFT	left
		XwRIGHT	right
		XwCENTER	center
XtNvSpace	2	<Integer>	<Integer>
XtNhSpace	2	<Integer>	<Integer>
XtNset	False	<Boolean>	<Boolean>
XtNsensitiveTile	75_FOREGROUND	<XwTILE Type>	<XwTILE Type>
XtNborderWidth	0	<Integer>	<Integer>

CASCADE

Class: XwcascadeWidgetClass
Class Name: Cascade
Superclasses: MenuPane
Description:

A cascading menu pane.

Refer To: Section 4.4.7
Resources:

Resource	Default	Programmer	User
XtNtitlePosition	top	XwTOP	top
		XwBOTTOM	bottom

Actions:

Action	Default Binding
select()	<Btn1Down>:
visible()	<Visible>
unmap()	<Unmap>
leave()	<LeaveWindow>

Callbacks:

Callback List	Call Data Type
XtNselect	NULL

FORM

Class: XwformWidgetClass
Class Name: Form
Superclasses: Core, Composite, Constraint, Manager

Description:

The Form widget class is a constraint widget that uses a set of layout rules to determine the spatial relationship between its managed children.

Refer To: Section 4.4.6.3

Constraint Resources:

Resource	Default	Programmer	User
XtNxRefName	NULL	<Widget Name>	<Widget Name>
XtNxRefWidget	NULL	<Widget>	-
XtNxOffset	0	<Integer>	<Integer>
XtNxAddWidth	False	<Boolean>	<Boolean>
XtNxVaryOffset	False	<Boolean>	<Boolean>
XtNxResizable	False	<Boolean>	<Boolean>
XtNxAttachRight	False	<Boolean>	<Boolean>
XtNxAttachOffset	0	<Integer>	<Integer>
XtNyRefName	NULL	<Widget Name>	
XtNyRefWidget	NULL	<Widget>	-
XtNyOffset	0	<Integer>	<Integer>
XtNyAddHeight	False	<Boolean>	<Boolean>
XtNyVaryOffset	False	<Boolean>	<Boolean>
XtNyResizable	False	<Boolean>	<Boolean>
XtNyAttachBottom	False	<Boolean>	<Boolean>
XtNyAttachOffset	0	<Integer>	<Integer>

LIST

Class: XwlistWidgetClass

Class Name: List

Superclasses: Core, Composite, Constraint, Manager, ScrolledWindow

Description:

The List widget class is a composite widget that displays its children in scrollable rows and columns.

Resources:

Resource	Default	Programmer	User
XtNnumColumns	1	<Integer>	<Integer>
XtNselectionMethod	single	XwSINGLE	single
		XwMULTIPLE	multiple
XtNselectionStyle	instant	XwINSTANT	instant
		XwSTICKY	sticky
XtNelementHighlight	border	XwBORDER	border
		XwINVERT	invert
XtNselectionBias	no_Bias	XwNO_BIAS	no_bias
		XwCOL_BIAS	col_bias

		XwROW_BIAS	row_bias
XtNcolumnWidth	0	<Integer>	<Integer>
XtNelementHeight	0	<Integer>	<Integer>
XtNselectedElements	NULL	<WidgetList Pointer>	-
XtNdestroyMode	shrink_column	XwNO_SHRINK	no_shrink
		XwSHRINK_COLUMN	shrink_column
		XwSHRINK_ALL	shrink_all
XtNnumSelectedElements	0	<Integer>	-

Constraint Resources:

Resource	Default	Programmer	User
XtNrowPosition	-1	<Integer>	<Integer>
XtNcolumnPosition	-1	<Integer>	<Integer>

Actions:

Action	Default Binding
enter()	EnterWindow
leave()	LeaveWindow

Callbacks:

Callback List	Call Data Type
XtNSelect	NULL
XtNdoubleClick	<Widget>

MANAGER

Class: XwmanagerWidgetClass

Class Name: Manager

Superclasses: Core, Composite, Constraint

Description:

The Manager widget class is a meta-class that serves as a superclass for most composite and constraint widget classes in the X Widget set.

Resources:

Resource	Default	Programmer	User
XtNforeground	Black	<Pixel>	<Color Name>
XtNbackgroundTile	background	Any XwTILE	
XtNhighlightThickness	0	<Integer>	<Integer>
XtNtraversalOn	False	<Boolean>	<Boolean>
XtNlayout	minimize	XwIGNORE	ignore
		XwMINIMIZE	minimize
		XwMAXIMIZE	maximize

Actions:

Action	Default Binding
`enter()`	`EnterWindow`
`leave()`	`LeaveWindow`
`visible()`	`<Visible>`
`focusIn()`	`<FocusIn>`

MENU

Class: `XwmenumgrWidgetClass`
Class Name: `MenuMgr`
Superclasses: `Core`, `Composite`, `Constraint`, `Manager`
Description:

The MenuMgr widget class is a meta-class that supports other menu manager subclasses.

Refer To: Section 4.4.7
Resources:

Resource	Default	Programmer	User
`XtNassociateChildren`	`TRUE`	`<Boolean>`	`<Boolean>`
`XtNmenuPost`	`Btn3Down`	`<Any Valid Translation>`	
`XtNmenuSelect`	`Btn1Down`	`<Any Valid Translation>`	
`XtNmenuUnpost`	`NULL`	`<Any Valid Translation>`	
`XtNkbdSelect`	`<Key>Select`	`<Any Valid Translation>`	

MENU BUTTON

Class: `XwmenubuttonWidgetClass`
Class Name: `MenuButton`
Superclasses: `Core`, `Primitive`, `Button`
Description:

The MenuButton widget class provides a single selectable element of a menu. It can also be used as a general button widget.

Refer To: Section 4.4.7
Resources:

Resource	Default	Programmer	User
`XtNborderWidth`	`0`	`<Integer>`	`<Integer>`
`XtNlabelType`	`<String>`	`Xw<String>`	`<String>`
		`XwIMAGE`	`image`
`XtNlabelImage`	`NULL`	`<XImage>`	-
`XtNcascadeImage`	`NULL`	`<XImage>`	-
`XtNmarkImage`	`NULL`	`<XImage>`	-

XtNsetMark	FALSE	<Boolean>	<Boolean>
XtNcascadeOn	NULL	<Widget>	-
XtNkbdAccelerator	NULL	<Any Translation>	
XtNmgrOverrideMnemonic	FALSE	<Boolean>	<Boolean>
XtNmnemonic	NULL	<Any Translation>	
XtNhighlightStyle	widget_defined	XwPATTERN_BORDER XwWIDGET_DEFINED	pattern_border widget_defined
XtNinvertOnEnter	True	<Boolean>	<Boolean>
XtNmenuMgrId	NULL	<Widget>	-

Actions:

Action	Default Binding
enter()	EnterWindow
leave()	LeaveWindow
moved()	Pointer Motion
select()	Btn1Down
release()	Btn1Up
traverseLeft()	TraverseLeft
traverseRight()	TraverseRight
traverseNext()	TraverseNext
traversePrev()	TraversePrev
traverseHome()	TraverseHome
traverseUp()	TraverseUp
traverseDown()	TraverseDown
traverseNextTop()	TraverseNextTop

Callbacks:

Callback List	Call Data TypePurpose
XtNselect	NULL
XtNcascadeUnselect	<XwunselectParams>
XtNcascadeSelect	NULL

MENU PANE

Class: XwmenupaneWidgetClass
Class Name: MenuPane
Superclasses: Core, Composite, Constraint, Manager, MenuMgr
Description:

The MenuPane widget class is a meta-class that provides basic resources used by its subclasses.

Refer To: Section 4.4.7
Resources:

Resource	Default	Programmer	User
XtNfont	fixed	<XFontStruct>	<Font Name>

XtNtitle<String>	NULL	<String>	<String>
XtNtitleImage	NULL	<XImage>	-
XtNtitleShowing	TRUE	<Boolean>	<Boolean>
XtNattachTo	NULL	<Widget Name>	<Widget Name>
XtNmgrTitleOverride	FALSE	<Boolean>	<Boolean>
XtNtitleType	<String>	Xw<String>	<String>
		XwIMAGE	image
XtNmnemonic	NULL	<Any Translation>	

POPUP MENU MANAGER

Class: XwpopupmgrWidgetClass
Class Name: PopupMgr
Superclasses: Core, Composite, Constraint, Manager, MenuMgr
Description:

The PopupMgr widget class is a composite widget that manages one or more popup menu panes.

Refer To: Section 4.4.7
Resources:

Resource	Default	Programmer	User
XtNstickyMenus	FALSE	<Boolean>	<Boolean>
XtNpostAccelerator	NULL	<Any Translation>	

PRIMITIVE

Class: XwprimitiveWidgetClass
Class Name: Primitive
Superclasses: Core
Description:

Primitve is a meta-class for all non-composite widgets in the X widget set.

Resources:

Resource	Default	Programmer	User
XtNforeground	Black	<Pixel>	<Color Name>
XtNbackgroundTile	background	<XwTILE>	<XwTILE>
XtNtraversalType	highlight_off	XwHIGHLIGHT_OFF	highlight_off
		XwHIGHLIGHT_ENTER	
			highlight_enter
		XwHIGHLIGHT_TRAVERSAL	
			highlight_traversal
XtNhighlightThickness	0	<Integer>	<Integer>
XtNhighlightStyle	pattern_border	XwPATTERN_BORDER	pattern_border
		XwWIDGET_DEFINED	widget_defined
XtNhighlightColor	Black	<Pixel>	<Color Name>

XtNhighlightTile	50_foreground	<XwTILE>	<XwTILE>
XtNrecomputeSize	TRUE	<Boolean>	<Boolean>

PUSH BUTTON

Class: XwpushButtonwidgetClass

Class Name: PushButton

Superclasses: Core, Primitive, Button

Description:

The PushButton widget class provides a style of button that normally inverts when selected and returns to its normal state when released. This behavior can be modified by setting appropriate resources.

Refer To: Section 4.4.5

Resources:

Resource	Default	Programmer	User
XtNtoggle	False	<Boolean>	<Boolean>

Actions:

Action	Default Binding
enter()	EnterWindow
leave()	LeaveWindow
select()	Btn1Down
unselect()	Btn1Up

Callbacks:

Callback List	Call Data TypePurpose
XtNselect	NULL
XtNrelease	NULL

ROWCOL

Class: XwrowColWidgetClass

Class Name: RowCol

Superclasses: Core, Composite, Constraint, Manager

Description:

The RowCol widget class is a manager widget that arranges its managed children into rows and columns.

Refer To: Section 4.4.6.2

Resources:

Resource	Default	Programmer	User
XtNhSpace	4	<Integer>	<Integer>
XtNvSpace	4	<Integer>	<Integer>

XtNlayoutType	requested_columns	XwREQUESTED_COLUMNS	requested_columns
		XwMAXIMUM_COLUMNS	maximum_columns
		XwMAXIMUM_UNALIGNED	maximum_unaligned
XtNcolumns	1	<Integer>	<Integer>
XtNforceSize	False	<Boolean>	<Boolean>
XtNsingleRow	False	<Boolean>	<Boolean>
XtNmode	n_of_many	XwN_OF_MANY	n_of_many
		XwONE_OF_MANY	one_of_many

SCROLL BAR

Class: XwscrollbarWidgetClass
Class Name: ScrollBar
Superclasses: Core, Composite, Constraint, Manager
Description:

The ScrollBar widget class combines a Valuator widget with two Arrow widgets to produce a complete scroll bar.

Refer To: Section 4.4.4
Resources:

Resource	Default	Programmer	User
XtNsliderMin	0	<Integer>	<Integer>
XtNsliderMax	100	<Integer>	<Integer>
XtNsliderOrigin	0	<Integer>	<Integer>
XtNsliderExtent	10	<Integer>	<Integer>
XtNslideOrientation	vertical	XwVERTICAL	vertical
		XwHORIZONTAL	horizontal
XtNinitialDelay	500	<Integer>	<Integer>
XtNrepeatRate	100	<Integer>	<Integer>
XtNgranularity	2	<Integer>	<Integer>

Callbacks:

Callback List	Call Data TypePurpose
XtNareaSelected	intslider position
XtNsliderMoved	intslider position
XtNsliderReleased	intslider position

SCROLLED WINDOW

Class: XwswindowWidgetClass
Class Name: ScrolledWindow

Superclasses: **Core, Composite, Constraint, Manager, ScrolledWindow**
Description:

The ScrolledWindow widget class combines a Bulletin Board widget with vertical and horizontal scrollbars to provide general scrolling functionality.

Refer To: Section 14.2.4
Resources:

Resource	Default	Programmer	User
XtNvsbX	-1	<Integer>	<Integer>
XtNvsbY	-1	<Integer>	<Integer>
XtNvsbWidth	20	<Integer>	<Integer>
XtNvsbHeight	0	<Integer>	<Integer>
XtNhsbX	-1	<Integer>	<Integer>
XtNhsbY	-1	<Integer>	<Integer>
XtNhsbWidth	0	<Integer>	<Integer>
XtNhsbHeight	20	<Integer>	<Integer>
XtNinitialDelay	500	<Integer>	<Integer>
XtNforceHorizontalSB	FALSE	<Boolean>	<Boolean>
XtNforceVerticalSB	FALSE	<Boolean>	<Boolean>
XtNinitialX	0	<Integer>	<Integer>
XtNinitialY	0	<Integer>	<Integer>
XtNborderPad	4	<Integer>	<Integer>

Actions:

Action	Default Binding
enter()	EnterWindow
leave()	LeaveWindow

Callbacks:

Callback List	Call Data Type
XtNvScrollEvent	intslider position
XtNhScrollEvent	intslider position

STATIC RASTER

Class: **XwstaticrasterWidgetClass**
Class Name: **StaticRaster**
Superclasses: **Core, Primitive**
Description:

The StaticRaster widget display an uneditable XImage structure.

Refer To: Section 7.5.2

Resources:

Resource	Default	Programmer	User
XtNsRimage	NULL	<XImage>	-
XtNinvertOnSelect	True	<Boolean>	<Boolean>
XtNshowSelected	True	<Boolean>	<Boolean>
XtNset	False	<Boolean>	<Boolean>

Actions:

Action	Default Binding
enter()	EnterWindow
leave()	LeaveWindow
select()	Btn1Down
release()	Btn1Up

Callbacks:

Callback List	Call Data Type
XtNselect	XEvent
XtNrelease	XEvent

STATIC TEXT

Class: XwstatictextWidgetClass
Class Name: StaticText
Superclasses: Core, Primitive
Description:

The StaticText widget displays an uneditable <String>.

Refer To: Section 4.4.2, 2.4
Resources:

Resource	Default	Programmer	User
XtNhSpace	2	<Integer>	<Integer>
XtNvSpace	2	<Integer>	<Integer>
XtNalignment	left	XwALIGN_LEFT	left
		XwALIGN_CENTER	center
		XwALIGN_RIGHT	right
XtNgravity	CenterGravity	CenterGravity	CenterGravity
		NorthGravity	NorthGravity
		NorthEastGravity	NorthEastGravity
		NorthWestGravity	NorthWestGravity
		EastGravity	EastGravity
		SouthGravity	SouthGravity
		SouthEastGravity	SouthEastGravity
		SouthWestGravity	SouthWestGravity
		WestGravity	WestGravity

XtNwrap	TRUE	<Boolean>	<Boolean>
XtNstrip	TRUE	<Boolean>	<Boolean>
XtNlineSpace	0	<Integer>	<Integer>
XtNfont	Fixed	<XFontStruct>	<Font Name>
XtNString	NULL	<String>	<String>

Actions:

Action	Default Binding
enter()	EnterWindow
leave()	LeaveWindow
select()	Btn1Down
release()	Btn1Up

Callbacks:

Callback List	Call Data Type
XtNselect	XEvent
XtNrelease	XEvent

TEXT EDIT

Class: XwtexteditWidgetClass
Class Name: TextEdit
Superclasses: Core, Primitive
Description:

The TextEdit widget provides a customizable multiple line text editor. The TextEdit widget is designed to separate the components that store and manipulate the text from the mechanism that displays it. The text is stored in a component known as the Source. Applications programmers may define new Source components if needed. The TextEdit widget defines actions for each editing operation it provides. The default translations provide EMACS style editing commands.

Refer To: Section 4.4.3
Resources:

Resource	Default	Programmer	User
XtNheight	200	<Integer>	<Integer>
XtNwidth	200	<Integer>	<Integer>
XtNdisplayPosition	0	<Integer>	<Integer>
XtNinsertPosition	0	<Integer>	<Integer>
XtNleftMargin	2	<Integer>	<Integer>
XtNrightMargin	2	<Integer>	<Integer>
XtNtopMargin	2	<Integer>	<Integer>
XtNbottomMargin	2	<Integer>	<Integer>
XtNsourceType	Stringsrc	XwStringSrc	Stringsrc

		XwdiskSrc	**discsrc**
		XwprogDefinedSrc	**progdefinedsrc**
XtNwrap	**softwrap**	**XwWrapOff**	**wrapoff**
		XwSoftWrap	**softwrap**
		XwHardWrap	**hardwrap**
XtNwrapForm	**sourceform**	**XwSourceForm**	**sourceform**
		XwDisplayForm	**displayform**
XtNwrapBreak	**wrapwhitespace**	**XwWrapAny**	**wrapany**
		XwWrapWhiteSpace	**wrapwhitespace**
XtNscroll	**autoscrolloff**	**XwAutoScrollOff**	**autoscrolloff**
		XwAutoScrollVertical	**autoscrollvertical**
		XwAutoScrollHorizontal	**autoscrollhorizontal**
		XwAutoScrollBoth	**autoscrollboth**
XtNgrow	**growoff**	**XwGrowOff**	**growoff**
		XwGrowHorizontal	**growhorizontal**
		XwGrowVertical	**growvertical**
		XwGrowBoth	**growboth**
XtNfont	**Fixed**	**<XFontStruct>**	**<Font Name>**
XtNforeground	**Black**	**<Pixel>**	**<Color Name>**

Actions:

Action	Default Binding
forward-character()	**Ctrl<Key>F**
traverse-right()	**Ctrl<Key>Right**
forward-character()	**<Key>Right**
backward-character()	**Ctrl<Key>B**
traverse-left()	**Ctrl<Key>Left**
backward-character()	**<Key>Left**
forward-word()	**Meta<Key>F**
backward-word()	**Meta<Key>B**
forward-paragraph()	**Meta<Key>]**
backward-paragraph()	**Ctrl<Key>[**
beginning-of-line()	**Ctrl<Key>A**
end-of-line()	**Ctrl<Key>E**
next-line()	**Ctrl<Key>N**
traverse-down()	**Ctrl<Key>Down**
next-line()	**<Key>Down**
previous-line()	**Ctrl<Key>P**

```
traverse-up()                       Ctrl<Key>Up
previous-line()                     <Key>Up
next-page()                         Ctrl<Key>V
traverse-next()                     Ctrl<Key>Next
next-page()                         <Key>Next
previous-page()                     Meta<Key>V
traverse-prev()                     Ctrl<Key>Prior
previous-page()                     <Key>Prior
beginning-of-file()                 Meta<Key>\\<
end-of-file()                       Meta<Key>\\>
traverse-home()                     Ctrl<Key>Home
end-of-file()                       Shift<Key>Home
beginning-of-file()                 <Key>Home
scroll-one-line-up()                Ctrl<Key>Z
scroll-one-line-down()              Meta<Key>Z
delete-next-character()             Ctrl<Key>D
delete-next-character()             <Key>DeleteChar
delete-previous-character()         <Key>BackSpace
delete-previous-character()         Ctrl<Key>H
delete-next-word()                  Meta<Key>D
delete-previous-word()              Meta<Key>H
kill-word()                         Shift Meta<Key>D
backward-kill-word()                Shift Meta<Key>H
kill-selection()                    Ctrl<Key>W
kill-to-end-of-line()               Ctrl<Key>K
kill-to-end-of-paragraph()          Meta<Key>K
unkill()                            Ctrl<Key>Y
stuff()                             Meta<Key>Y
newline-and-indent()                Ctrl<Key>J
newline-and-backup()                Ctrl<Key>O
newline()                           Ctrl<Key>M
newline()                           <Key>Return
newline-and-indent()                <Key>InsertLine
redraw-display()                    Ctrl<Key>L
focus-in()                          <FocusIn>
focus-out()                         <FocusOut>
select-start()                      <Btn1Down>
extend-adjust()                     Button1<PtrMoved>
extend-end()                        <Btn1Up>
stuff()                             <Btn2Down>
extend-start()                      <Btn3Down>
extend-adjust()                     Button3<PtrMoved>
extend-end()                        <Btn3Up>
execute()                           <Key>Execute
insert-char()                       <Key>
insert-char()                       Shift<Key>
```

```
          enter()                           <EnterWindow>
          leave()                           <LeaveWindow>
```

Public Functions:

```
     XwTextClearBuffer(w)
          Widget w;

     XwTextCopySelection(w)
          Widget w;

     XwTextUnsetSelection(w)
          Widget w;

     XwTextInsert(w, string)
          Widget  w;
          char   string;

     XwTextSetInsertPos(w, pos)
          Widget         w;
          XwTextPosition pos;

     XwTextGetInsertPos(w, pos)
          Widget w;

     XwTextSetSelection(w, left, right)
          Widget         w;
          XwTexTposition left, right;


     XwTextGetSelection(w, left, right)
          Widget         w;
          XwTextPosition left, right;

     XwTextReplace(w, startPos, endPos, text)
          Widget         w;
          XwTextPosition startPos, endPos;
          char           text;

     XwTextRedraw(w)
          Widget w;

     XwTextUpdate(w, status)
          Widget  w;
```

```
     <Boolean> status;

XwTextGetLastPos(w, lastPos)
     Widget         w;
     XwTextPosition lastPos;

XwTextSetSource(w, source, startPos)
     Widget          w;
     XwTextSourcePtr source;
     XwTextPosition  startPos;

XwTextReadSubString(w, startpos, endpos,
                    target, targetsize, targetused)
     Widget          w;
     XwTextPosition  startpos, endpos;
     unsigned char  target;
     int             targetsize, targetused;
```

Callbacks:

Callback List	Call Data Type
XtNmotionVerification	XwTextVerifyPtr
XtNmodifyVerification	XwTextVerifyPtr
XtNleaveVerification	XwTextVerifyPtr
XtNexecute	NULL

```
typedef struct {
  XEvent           xevent;
  XwVerifyOpType    operation;
  <Boolean>         doit;
  XwTextPosition    currInsert, newInsert;
  XwTextPosition    startPos, endPos;
  XwTextBlock      text;
} XwTextVerifyCD, XwTextVerifyPtr;
```

TILES

Description:

A set of tiles and utility functions.

Refer To: Section 7.4

VALUATOR

Class: `XwvaluatorWidgetClass`

Class Name: `Valuator`
Superclasses: `Core, Primitive`
Description:

The Valuator widget provides a slider within a horizontal or vertical window. The position of the slider may be controlled programmatically from an application or interactively by the user.

Refer To: Section 4.4.4
Resources:

Resource	Default	Programmer	User
XtNsliderMin	0	<Integer>	<Integer>
XtNsliderMax	100	<Integer>	<Integer>
XtNsliderOrigin	0	<Integer>	<Integer>
XtNsliderExtent	10	<Integer>	<Integer>
XtNslideOrientation	vertical	XwVERTICAL	vertical
		XwHorizontal	horizontal
XtNsliderTile	foreground	<XwTILE>	<XwTILE>

Actions:

Action	Default Binding
enter()	EnterWindow
move()	Button1 PtrMoved
leave()	LeaveWindow
select()	Btn1Down
release()	Btn1Up

VERTICAL PANED WINDOW

Class: `XwvPanedWidgetClass`
Class Name: `VPanedWindow`
Superclasses: `Core, Composite, Constraint, Manager`
Description:

The VPanedWindow widget class is a composite class that arranges its children in vertical tiles. The user can adjust the size of each pane interactively.

Refer To: Section 5.4.1
Resources:

Resource	Default	Programmer	User
XtNsashIndent	-10	<Integer>	<Integer>
XtNborderFrame	1	<Integer>	<Integer>
XtNpadding	3	<Integer>	<Integer>
XtNframed	TRUE	<Boolean>	<Boolean>
XtNrefigureMode	TRUE	<Boolean>	<Boolean>

WORKSPACE

Class: `XwworkspaceWidgetClass`

Class Name: `WorkSpace`

Superclasses: `Core, Primitive`

Description:

The WorkSpace widget class provides an empty widget that can be used by applications as a destination for graphics operations.

Refer To: Section 9.3, 10.1

Actions:

Action	Default Binding
`keydown()`	`KeyDown`
`enter()`	`EnterWindow`
`leave()`	`LeaveWindow`
`select()`	`Btn1Down`
`release()`	`Btn1Up`

Callbacks:

Callback List	Call Data Type
`XtNexpose`	NULL
`XtNresize`	NULL
`XtNkeyDown`	NULL

APPENDIX C

SELECTED Xt INTRINSICS FUNCTIONS

XtAddActions()

Add new actions to an action list.

Syntax:

```
void XtAddActions(action, num_actions)
      XtActionList action;
      Cardinal     num_actions;
```

Refer To: Section 2.4.5

See Also:

```
XtOverrideTranslations()
XtAugmentTranslations()
```

XtAddCallback()

Adds a function to one of a widget's callback lists.

Syntax:

```
void XtAddCallback(w, callback_kind, callback, client_data)
      Widget          w;
      XtCallbackKind callback_kind;
      XtCallbackProc callback;
      void           *client_data;
```

Refer To: Section 2.4.4

See Also:

```
XtRemoveCallback()
XtRemoveCallbacks()
```

XtAddCallbacks()

Adds a list of callback procedures to a widget's callback list.

Syntax:

```
void XtAddCallbacks (widget, callback_name, callbacks);
      Widget              widget;
      String              callback_name;
      XtCallbackList      callbacks;
```

Refer To:

```
XtAddCallback()
XtRemoveCallback()
XtRemoveCallbacks()
```

XtAddConverter()

Registers a new type converter with the Intrinscs resource manager facilities.

Syntax:

```
void XtAddConverter(from, to, converter, args, nargs)
  String             from, to;
  XtConverter        converter;
  XtConvertArgList   args;
  Cardinal           nargs;
```

Refer To: Section 3.3.4

XtAddEventHandler()

Adds an event handler function, **proc**. When any event specified by **event_mask** occurs within the widget **w**, the event handler will be invoked with the widget, the event, and the specified **client_data** as arguments.

Syntax:

```
void XtAddEventHandler(w, event_mask, nonmaskable, proc,
client_data)
      Widget          w;
      XtEventMask     event_mask;
```

```
        Boolean        nonmaskable;
        XtEventHandler proc;
        void          *client_data;
```

Refer To: Section 2.4.3

See Also:

XtAddRawEventHandler()
XtRemoveEventHandler()
XtRemoveRawEventHandler()

XtAddInput()

Adds a file descriptor as an input source and returns a unique ID. When the specified condition occurs on the source, the function proc will be called with the ID, the source file descriptor, and client_data as arguments.

Syntax:

```
XtInputId XtAddInput(source, condition, proc, client_data)
      int                    source;
      void                  *condition;
      XtInputCallbackProc proc;
      void                  *client_data;
```

Refer To: Section 5.8

See Also:

XtRemoveInput()

XtAddRawEventHandler()

Adds an event handler to a widget without selecting the event for the widget's window.

Syntax:

```
void XtAddRawEventHandler(widget, eventMask, nonmaskable,
                                  proc, client_data)
     Widget           widget;
     EventMask        eventMask;
     Boolean          nonmaskable;
     XtEventHandler   proc;
     void            *client_data ;
```

See Also:

XtAddEventHandler()
XtRemoveEventHandler()
XtRemoveRawEventHandler()

XtAddTimeOut()

Registers a callback function to be called in interval milliseconds. The callback is removed once it has been invoked.

Syntax:

```
XtIntervalId XtAddTimeOut(interval, proc, client_data)
      unsigned long        interval;
      XtTimerCallbackProc proc
      void                *client_data;
```

Refer To: Section 5.6

See Also:

`XtRemoveTimeout()`

XtAugmentTranslations()

Merges a translation table with a widget's existing translation table.

Syntax:

```
void XtAugmentTranslations(widget, new)
     Widget          widget;
     XtTranslations new;
```

Refer To: Section 2.4.5

See Also:

`XtAddActions()`
`XtOverrideTranslations()`

XtCallCallbacks()

Invokes all procedures on the named callback list.

Syntax:

```
void XtCallCallbacks(w, callback_kind, call_data)
      Widget          w;
      XtCallbackKind  callback_kind;
      void           *call_data;
```

Refer To: Section 12.2.2.3

See Also:

`XtAddCallbacks()`

XtCalloc()

Calls `calloc()` and issues an error message if allocation fails.

Syntax:

```
char *XtCalloc(num, size);
      Cardinal num;
      Cardinal size;
```

Refer To:

```
XtMalloc()
XtFree()
XtRealloc()
```

XtCheckSubclass()

Similar to **XtIsSubclass()**, except that an error message is generated if the widget is not a subclass of the named widget class.

Syntax:

```
void XtCheckSubclass(w, widget_class, message)
      Widget      w;
      WidgetClass widget_class;
      String      message;
```

See Also:

```
XtIsSubclass()
```

XtClass()

A macro that accesses a pointer to the class record of a widget

Syntax:

```
WidgetClass XtClass(w)
      Widget w;
```

Refer To: Section 5.7

See Also:

```
XtSuperClass()
```

XtCreateApplicationShell()

Creates a top level shell widget that provides an interface between the application and the window manager.

Syntax:

```
Widget XtCreateApplicationShell (name, widget_class,
                                  args, num_args);
        String      name;
```

```
        WidgetClass  widget_class;
        ArgList      args;
        Cardinal     num_args;
```

Refer To: Section 2.5, 4.3.4

See Also:

```
XtCreatePopupShell()
XtInitialize()
XtCreateWidget()
```

XtCreateManagedWidget()

A convenience function that creates a widget and issues a manage child request.

Syntax:

```
Widget XtCreateManagedWidget (name, widget_class, parent,
                                    args, num_args);
     String       name;
     WidgetClass  widget_class;
     Widget       parent;
     ArgList      args;
     Cardinal     num_args;
```

Refer To: Section 2.2.3

See Also:

```
XtCreateWidget()
XtManageChild()
```

XtCreatePopupShell()

Creates a popup shell widget.

Syntax:

```
Widget XtCreatePopupShell(name, class, parent,
                                args, num_args)
        String       name;
        WidgetClass  class;
        Widget       parent;
        ArgList      args;
        Cardinal     num_args;
```

Refer To: Section 4.4.7.1

See Also:

```
XtCreateApplicationShell()
```

XtCreateWidget()

Creates and returns a new instance of the given widget class.

Syntax:

```
Widget XtCreateWidget(name, class, parent, args, num_args)
      String       name;
      WidgetClass  class;
      Widget       parent;
      ArgList      args;
      Cardinal     num_args;
```

Refer To: Section 2.2.2

See Also:

```
XtCreateManagedWidget()
XtCreateApplicationShell()
```

XtDestroyGC()

Decrements a reference counter for this graphics context. If the count is zero, the graphics context is freed.

Syntax:

```
void XtDestroyGC(gc)
      GC gc;
```

See Also:

```
XtGetGC()
```

XtDestroyWidget()

Destroys a widget and all children of the widget.

Syntax:

```
void XtDestroyWidget(w)
      Widget w;
```

See Also:

```
XtCreateWidget()
```

XtDispatchEvent()

This function looks up the widget associated with the event window in an event structure, and invokes the widget's event handlers for that event.

Syntax:

```
void XtDispatchEvent(event)
   XEvent *event;
```

See Also:

```
XtMainLoop()
XtNextEvent()
```

XtDisplay()

A macro that returns the display associated with a widget.

Syntax:

```
Display *XtDisplay(w)
       Widget w;
```

Refer To: Section 2.2.2
See Also:

```
XtScreen()
```

XtError()

Reports an error message and exit.

Syntax:

```
void XtError(message)
       String message;
```

See Also:

```
XtSetErrorFunction()
XtWarning()
```

XtFree()

Frees memory allocated by **XtMalloc()**, **XtCalloc()**, or **XtRealloc()**.

Syntax:

```
void XtFree(ptr);
   char *ptr;
```

See Also:

```
XtMalloc()
XtCalloc()
XtRealloc()
```

XtFreeTranslations()

Deallocates a translation table.

Syntax:

```
void XtFreeTranslations(stateTable)
     XtTranslations stateTable;
```

See Also:

```
XtParseTranslations()
```

XtGetGC()

Returns a read-only graphics context for use with the given widget. The graphics contexts are cached for efficiency and may be shared with other widgets.

Syntax:

```
GC XtGetGC(w, value_mask, values)
      Widget     w;
      XtGCMask   value_mask;
      XGCValues *values;
```

Refer To: Section 8.1

See Also:

```
XtFreeGC()
```

XtGetValues()

Retrieves the current value of the resources specified in the args array.

Syntax:

```
void XtGetValues(w, args, num_args)
      Widget   w;
      ArgList  args;
      Cardinal num_args;
```

Refer To: Section 2.2.5

See Also:

```
XtSetValues()
```

XtInitialize()

Performs essential initialization of the X Toolkit intrinsics. Also opens the X display and loads the user's resource data base. Must be called by every X Toolkit application before other X Toolkit functions are called.

Syntax:

```
Widget XtInitialize(name, class_name, options, num_options,
                    argc, argv)
      String            name;
      String            class_name;
      XrmOptionDescRec  options;
      Cardinal          num_options;
      Cardinal         *argc;
      char             *argv[];
```

Refer To: 2.2.1

XtInput Masks()

These masks are used as argument masks to **XtAddInput()**.

Syntax:

```
#define XtInputNoneMask       0L
#define XtInputReadMask       (1L<<0)
#define XtInputWriteMask      (1L<<1)
#define XtInputExceptMask     (1L<<2)
```

Refer To: Section 5.8.1

See Also:

XtAddInput()

XtIsComposite()

Returns **True** if the widget is a subclass of the Composite widget class.

Syntax:

```
void XtIsComposite(w)
      Widget w;
```

See Also:

XtClass()
XtIsSubclass()

XtIsRealized()

A macro that returns **True** if the widget has been realized.

Syntax:

```
Boolean XtIsRealized(w)
      Widget w;
```

See Also:

XtRealizeWidget()

XtIsSubclass()

Returns **True** if the widget is a subclass of the given widget class.

Syntax:

```
Boolean XtIsSubclass(w, widget_class)
      Widget      w;
      WidgetClass widget_class;
```

See Also:

```
XtClass()
```

XtMainLoop()

A convenience function that calls **XtNextEvent()** and **XtDispatchEvent()** in an infinite loop.

Syntax:

```
void XtMainLoop()
```

Refer To: Section 2.2.4

See Also:

```
XtNextEvent()
XtDispatchEvent()
```

XtMakeGeometryRequest()

Used internally by a widget to request a configuration change. If the widget's parent suggests a compromise, the **reply** structure contains the compromise geometry.

Syntax:

```
XtGeometryResult XtMakeGeometryRequest(w, request, reply)
      Widget             w;
      XtWidgetGeometry *request;
      XtWidgetGeometry *reply;
```

Refer To: Section 13.2.3.2

See Also:

```
XtMakeResizeRequest()
```

XtMakeResizeRequest()

Provides a simpler interface to **XtMakeGeometryRequest()** when only changes to a widget's width and height are desired.

Syntax:

```
XtGeometryResult XtMakeResizeRequest(w, width, height,
                                     replyWidth,
replyHeight)
        Widget     w;
        Dimension  width, height;
        Dimension *replyWidth, *replyHeight
```

See Also:

```
XtMakeGeometryRequest
```

XtMalloc()

Calls **malloc()** and issues an error message if allocation fails.

Syntax:

```
char *XtMalloc(size);
        Cardinal size;
```

See Also:

```
XtCalloc()
XtRealloc()
XtFree()
```

XtManageChild()

Adds a single widget to its parent's managed set.

Syntax:

```
void XtManageChild(child)
        Widget child;
```

Refer To: Section 2.2.3

See Also:

```
XtUnmanageChild()
XtManageChildren()
```

XtManageChildren()

Adds a list of widgets to their parents' managed set.

Syntax:

```
void XtManageChildren(children, num_children)
        WidgetList children;
        Cardinal   num_children;
```

Refer To: Section 2.2.3

See Also:

XtUnmanageChildren()
XtManageChild()

XtMoveWidget()

Moves a widget to the specified (*x*, *y*) position. Normally, only a widget's parent may use this function.

Syntax:

```
void XtMoveWidget(w, x, y)
        Widget   w;
        Position x;
        Position y;
```

Refer To: Section 13.2.3.2

See Also:

XtMakeResizeRequest()

XtNameToWidget()

Returns the widget structure for a named widget, within the widget tree of the reference widget. The names argument may be a list of names separated by dots (".").

Syntax:

```
Widget XtNameToWidget(reference, names);
        Widget reference;
        String names;
```

See Also:

XtWindowToWidget()

XtNextEvent()

If there is an event in the X event queue, **XtNextEvent()** removes it and returns. Otherwise, it waits until an event is available.

Syntax:

```
void XtNextEvent(event)
        XEvent *event;
```

Refer To: Section 2.2.4

See Also:

XtMainLoop()

XtNumber()

A macro that determines the number of elements in a fixed-size array.

Syntax:

```
Cardinal XtNumber(array)
      ArrayVariable array;
```

Refer To: Section 2.2.5

XtOffset()

A macro used to calculate the byte offset of a field within a structure.

Syntax:

```
Cardinal XtOffset(pointer_type, field_name)
      Type  pointer_type;
      Field field_name;
```

Refer To: Section 3.3.2

XtOverrideTranslations()

Installs a new translation table in a widget instance, overriding the existing translation table.

Syntax:

```
void XtOverrideTranslations(widget, new)
     Widget         widget;
     XtTranslations new;
```

Refer To: Section 2.4.5

See Also:

```
XtAugmentTranslations()
XtFreeTranslations()
XtParseTranslationTable()
```

XtParseTranslationTable()

Parses a string of translations and returns a translation table.

Syntax:

```
XtTranslations XtParseTranslationTable(source)
      String *source;
```

Refer To: Section 2.4.5

See Also:

```
XtAugmentTranslations()
XtFreeTranslations()
XtOverrideTranslations()
```

XtPeekEvent()

Returns the event at the head of the event queue, without removing it from the queue.

Syntax:

```
void XtPeekEvent(event)
        XEvent *event;
```

Refer To: Section 5.5

See Also:

```
XtNextEvent()
XtPending()
```

XtPending()

Returns the number of events pending in the X event queue.

Syntax:

```
Boolean XtPending()
```

Refer To: Section 5.5

See Also:

```
XtNextEvent()
XtPeekEvent()
```

XtPopdown()

Pops down a widget popped up with **XtPopup()**.

Syntax:

```
void XtPopdown(widget)
    Widget  widget;
```

Refer To: Section 4.5

See Also:

```
XtPopup()
XtCreatePopupShell()
```

XtPopup()

Pops up a popup shell widget.

Syntax:

```
void XtPopup(widget, grab_kind)
    Widget       widget;
    XtGrabKind  grab_kind;
```

Refer To: Section 2.2.2

See Also:

```
XtPopdown()
XtCreatePopupShell()
```

XtRealizeWidget()

Calls a widget's **realize** procedure, which normally creates an X window for the widget.

Syntax:

```
void XtRealizeWidget(w)
    Widget  w;
```

See Also:

```
XtIsRealized()
```

XtRealloc()

Calls **realloc()** and issues an error message if allocation fails.

Syntax:

```
char *XtRealloc(ptr, num);
    char    *ptr;
    Cardinal num;
```

See Also:

```
XtMalloc()
XtCalloc()
XtFree()
```

XtRemoveAllCallbacks()

Removes all functions from the callback list.

Syntax:

```
void XtRemoveAllCallbacks(w, callback_kind)
    Widget          w;
    XtCallbackKind  callback_kind;
```

Refer To: Section 12.2.3.2

```
XtRemoveCallback()
XtAddCallback()
```

XtRemoveCallback()

Removes a function from a callback list.

Syntax:

```
void XtRemoveCallback(w, callback_kind, callback,
client_data)
    Widget          w;
    XtCallbackKind callback_kind;
    XtCallbackProc callback;
    void           *client_data;
```

See Also:

```
XtRemoveAllCallbacks()
XtAddCallback()
```

XtRemoveCallbacks()

Removes a list of callback procedures from a callback list.

Syntax:

```
void XtRemoveCallbacks (widget, callback_name, callbacks);
   Widget            widget;
   String            callback_name;
   XtCallbackList    callbacks;
```

See Also:

```
XtAddCallback()
XtRemoveAllCallbacks()
XtRemoveCallbacks()
```

XtRemoveEventHandler()

Removes the specified function, **proc**, from a widget's list of event handlers.

Syntax:

```
void XtRemoveEventHandler(w, event_mask, nonmaskable,
                          proc, client_data)
    Widget          w;
    XtEventMask     event_mask;
```

```
        Boolean          nonmaskable;
        XtEventHandler proc;
        void            *client_data;
```

Refer To: Section 5.6.1

See Also:

`XtAddEventHandler()`

XtRemoveInput()

Removes the input source associated with an **XtInputId**.

Syntax:

```
void XtRemoveInput(id)
    XtInputId id;
```

See Also:

`XtAddInput()`

XtRemoveRawEventHandler()

Removes an event handler added using **XtAddRawEventHandler()**.

Syntax:

```
void XtRemoveRawEventHandler(widget, eventMask,
nonmaskable,
                              proc, client_data)
    Widget           widget;
    EventMask        eventMask;
    Boolean          nonmaskable;
    XtEventHandler   proc;
    void            *client_data ;
```

See Also:

`XtRemoveEventHandler()`
`XtAddRawEventHandler()`

XtRemoveTimeOut()

Removes the callback associated with the timeout ID.

Syntax:

```
void XtRemoveTimeOut(id)
    XtIntervalId id;
```

Refer To: Section 5.6.1

See Also:

```
XtAddTimeOut()
```

XtResizeWidget()

Resizes a widget. Normally, only a widget's parent may use this function.

Syntax:

```
void XtResizeWidget(w, width, height, border_width)
    Widget    w;
    Dimension width;
    Dimension height;
    Dimension border_width;
```

See Also:

```
XtMoveWidget()
XtMakeResizeRequest()
```

XtResource

The structure used to define each entry in a resource list.

Syntax:

```
typedef struct _XtResource {
  String    resource_name; /* Resource name         */
  String    resource_class;/* Resource class        */
  String    resource_type;/* desired representation*/
  Cardinal  resource_size;/* Size in bytes         */
  Cardinal  resource_offset;/* Offset from base    */
  String    default_type; /* default representation*/
  void     *default_addr; /* default resource      */
} XtResource;
```

Refer To: Section 3.3.2

See Also:

```
XtGetApplicationResources()
```

XtScreen()

A macro that returns the Screen structure associated with a widget.

Syntax:

```
Screen *XtScreen(w)
      Widget w;
```

Refer To: Section 2.2.2

See Also:

```
XtDisplay()
```

XtSetArg()

A macro used to set the contents of an **Arg** structure.

Syntax:

```
#define XtSetArg(arg, n, d) \
    ( (arg).name = (n), (arg).value = (XtArgVal)(d) )
```

Refer To: Section 2.2.5

See Also:

```
XtSetValues()
XtGetValues()
```

XtSetErrorHandler()

Register an application-defined function to be called when an error occurs.

Syntax:

```
void XtSetErrorHandler(errorProc)
    (*errorProc)(String);
```

See Also:

```
XtError()
```

XtSetMappedWhenManaged()

Sets a widget's **XtNmapWhenManaged** resource. If **True**, the widget window will be mapped whenever the widget is managed.

Syntax:

```
void XtSetMappedWhenManaged(w, map_when_managed)
     Widget  w;
     Boolean map_when_managed;
```

See Also:

```
XtManageChild()
```

XtSetSensitive()

Sets the sensitive state of a widget. Widgets that are insensitive do not respond to events and often take on a different appearance.

Syntax:

```
void XtSetSensitive(w, sensitive)
     Widget   w;
     Boolean  sensitive;
```

Refer To: Section 11.3.2

XtSetValues()

Modifies the current value of a resource associated with a widget.

Syntax:

```
void XtSetValues(w, args, num_args)
     Widget   w;
     ArgList  args;
     Cardinal num_args;
```

Refer To: Section 2.2.5

See Also:

```
XtGetValues()
XtSetArg()
```

XtSetWarningHandler()

Registers an application-defined function to be called when a warning is issued.

Syntax:

```
void XtSetWarningHandler(errorProc)
    (*errorProc)(String);
```

See Also:

```
XtWarning()
```

XtSuperclass()

A macro that returns a pointer to the clas structure of a widget's superclass.

Syntax:

```
WidgetClass XtSuperclass(w)
    Widget w;
```

See Also:

```
XtClass()
```

XtTransformCoords()

Converts a *(x, y)* location in the coordinates of a widget to the coordinates of the root window.

Syntax:

```
void XtTransformCoords(w, x, y, rootx, rooty);
    Widget    w;
    Position  x, y;
    Position *rootx, *rooty;
```

XtUnmanageChild()

Removes a single widget from its parent's managed set.

Syntax:

```
void XtUnmanageChild(child)
    Widget child;
```

See Also:

```
XtManageChild()
XtUnmanageChildren()
```

XtUnmanageChildren()

Removes a list of widgets from their parents' managed set.

Syntax:

```
void XtUnmanageChildren(children, num_children)
    WidgetList children;
    Cardinal   num_children;
```

Refer To: Section 13.2.4

See Also:

```
XtUnmanageChild()
XtManageChildren()
```

XtWarning()

Issues a non-fatal warning message.

Syntax:

```
void XtWarning(message);
    String message;
```

See Also:

```
XtSetWarningHandler()
XtError()
```

XtWidgetGeometry

A structure used by **XtMakeGeometryRequest()** to make widget geometry requests.

Syntax:

```
typedef struct {
    XtGeometryMask request_mode;
    Position       x, y;
    Dimension      width, height, border_width;
    Widget         sibling;
    int            stack_mode;
} XtWidgetGeometry;
```

The member **stack_mode** may be one of **Above**, **Below**, **TopIf**, **BottomIf**, or **Opposite**.

Refer To: Section 13.2.3.1

See Also:

```
XtMakeGeometryRequest()
XtMakeResizeRequest()
```

XtWidgetResult

An enumerated type returned by geometry functions.

Syntax:

```
typedef enum  {
    XtGeometryYes,    /* Request accepted.          */
    XtGeometryNo,     /* Request denied.            */
    XtGeometryAlmost, /* Compromise suggested.      */
    XtGeometryDone    /* Request accepted and done.*/
} XtGeometryResult;
```

Refer To: Section 13.2.3.1

See Also:

```
XtMakeGeometryRequest()
XtMakeResizeRequest()
```

XtWindow()

A macro that returns the X window ID used by the widget.

Syntax:

```
Window XtWindow(w)
     Widget  w;
```

Refer To: Section 2.2.2

See Also:

```
XtWindowToWidget()
```

XtWindowToWidget(

Returns the widget structure associated with a window ID.

Syntax:

```
Widget XtWindowToWidget(display, window);
     Display *display;
     Window   window;
```

See Also:

```
XtWindow()
```

APPENDIX D

WHERE TO GET X

The complete X11 distribution is available from many sources. The complete R3 distribution is quite large (around 90 Megabytes) and includes X servers for many machines, various X-based toolkits, and assorted contributed software. The R2 Xt Intrinsics and the R2-based HP X Widget set are also included in the R3 distribution. You can get X on a 9 track, 1600bpi tape directly from MIT by sending a check for $200 (US dollars) to:

MIT Software Distribution Center
MIT E32-300
77 Mass. Ave.
Cambridge, MA 02139
(617) 253 6966

Those with access to ARPAnet can get the complete X system free via anonymous ftp from a number of sources. At publication time, the following machines were among those making the X11R3 release available.

Machine	Net Address	X directory
gatekeeper.dec.com	128.45.9.52	pub/X.V11R3/
mordred.cs.purdue.edu	192.5.48.2	pub/X11/Release3/
giza.cis.ohio-state.edu	128.146.6.150	pub/X.V11R3/
nic.mr.net	192.12.250.5	pub/X.V11R3/
uunet.uu.net	192.12.141.129	X/X.V11R3/
expo.lcs.mit.edu	18.30.0.212	pub/R3/

There are several electronic mailing lists and bulletin boards that pertain to X. The primary electronic mailing list is

xpert@athena.mit.edu

Those with access to ARPA-net can subscribe to the comp.windows.x bulletin board. There may be other local bulletin boards as well. For example, X users in the San Francisco area can subscribe to ba.windows.x.

X user groups can also be a good source of information. The largest group is the X User's Group (XUG). This national organization publishes a newsletter containing news and technical articles related to X. They can be reached by mail at

XUG
c/o Integrated Computer Solutions
163 Harvard Street
Cambridge, MA 02139

or via electronic mail at xug@expo.lcs.mit .edu. Local chapters of XUG have been formed in many areas as well.

As this is being written, an R3 version of the HP Widget set that works for the examples in this book could be obtained by applying a set of patches to the R2 widget set. The patches are available via anonymous ftp from expo.lcs.mit.edu. The patches are in a file called Xw.patch.works.tar.Z. Of course, this information is subject to change.

Many vendors also sell supported versions of X. The following list shows the members of the X Consortium at the time of this writing. Many of these companies have or will have X-based products.

X Consortium Members

Apollo Computer, Inc.	Apple Computer, Inc.
AT&T	Bull
CalComp	Control Data Corporation
Data General Corporation	Digital Equipment Corporation
Eastman Kodak Company	Fujitsu
Hewlett Packard	IBM
NEC Corporation	NCR Corporation
Prime Computer, Inc.	Rich, Inc
Sequent Computer Systems Inc.	Siemans AG
Silicon Graphics, Inc.	Sony Corporation
Sun Microsystems, Inc.	Tektronix, Inc.
Texas Instruments	Unisys Corporation
Wang Laboratories	Xerox Corporation

X Consortium Affiliates

Acer Copunterpoint
Ardent Computer
CETIA
GfxBase
Interactive Systems Corporation
Integrated Computer Solutions
Locus Computing
MIPS Computer Systems
Nova Graphics International
O'Reilly & Associates
Software Productivity Consortium
Stellar Computer Inc.
Visual Technology Inc.
Adobe Systems
Carnegie Mellon University
Evans & Sutherland
Integrated Solutions
Interactive Development Environments
University of Kent at Canterbury
Megatek Corporation
Network Computing Devices
Open Software Foundation
PCS Computer Systeme GmbH
Solbourne Computer Inc.
UNICAD, Inc.
Xpi, Inc
SGIP - Societe de Gestion et d'Informatique Publicis
INESC - Instituto de Engenharia de Sistemas e Computadores

APPENDIX E

X EVENTS AND EVENT MASKS

The following table lists the event mask, its associated event type or types, and the structure name associated with the event type. Some of these structures actually are typedefs to a generic structure that is shared between two event types. Note that N.A. appears in columns for which the information is not applicable.

Event Mask	Event Type	Structure
ButtonMotionMask	MotionNotify	XPointerMovedEvent
Button1MotionMask		
Button2MotionMask		
Button3MotionMask		
Button4MotionMask		
Button5MotionMask		
ButtonPressMask	ButtonPress	XButtonPressedEvent
ButtonReleaseMask	ButtonRelease	XButtonReleasedEvent
ColormapChangeMask	ColormapNotify	XColormapEvent
EnterWindowMask	EnterNotify	XEnterWindowEvent
LeaveWindowMask	LeaveNotify	XLeaveWindowEvent
ExposureMask	Expose	XExposeEvent
GCGraphicsExposures	GraphicsExpose	XGraphicsExposeEvent
	NoExpose	XNoExposeEvent
FocusChangeMask	FocusIn	XFocusInEvent
	FocusOut	XFocusOutEvent
KeymapStateMask	KeymapNotify	XKeymapEvent

KeyPressMask	KeyPress	XKeyPressedEvent
KeyReleaseMask	KeyRelease	XKeyReleasedEvent
OwnerGrabButtonMask	N.A.	N.A.
PointerMotionMask	MotionNotify	XPointerMovedEvent
PointerMotionHintMask	N.A.	N.A.
PropertyChangeMask	PropertyNotify	XPropertyEvent
ResizeRedirectMask	ResizeRequest	XResizeRequestEvent
StructureNotifyMask	CirculateNotify	XCirculateEvent
	ConfigureNotify	XConfigureEvent
	DestroyNotify	XDestroyWindowEvent
	GravityNotify	XGravityEvent
	MapNotify	XMapEvent
	ReparentNotify	XReparentEvent
	UnmapNotify	XUnmapEvent
SubstructureNotifyMask	CirculateNotify	XCirculateEvent
	ConfigureNotify	XConfigureEvent
	CreateNotify	XCreateWindowEvent
	DestroyNotify	XDestroyWindowEvent
	GravityNotify	XGravityEvent
	MapNotify	XMapEvent
	ReparentNotify	XReparentEvent
	UnmapNotify	XUnmapEvent
SubstructureRedirectMask	CirculateRequest	XCirculateRequestEvent
	ConfigureRequest	XConfigureRequestEvent
	MapRequest	XMapRequestEvent
N.A.	ClientMessage	XClientMessageEvent
N.A.	MappingNotify	XMappingEvent
N.A.	SelectionClear	XSelectionClearEvent
N.A.	SelectionNotify	XSelectionEvent
N.A.	SelectionRequest	XSelectionRequestEvent
VisibilityChangeMask	VisibilityNotify	XVisibilityEvent

APPENDIX F

COMPLETE LibXs SOURCE LISTING

The following pages contain a complete listing of the libXs utility functions used throughout this book. All of these are described at the point at which they are introduced, but it may be useful to see them gathered together in one place.

```
/****************************************************
 *  libXs.h: declarations for the X-sample library
 ****************************************************/
#define FONTHEIGHT(f)  ((f)->max_bounds.ascent + \
                        (f)->max_bounds.descent)
#define XtRFloat "Float"

typedef struct {
   char*       name;
   void        (*func)();
   caddr_t     data;
} menu_struct;

extern Widget create_quit_button();
extern Widget create_menu_manager();
extern Widget create_menu_pane();
extern void   invert_widget();
extern Widget create_one_line_text_widget();
```

```
extern char  *concat_args();
extern void   CvtStringToFloat();
extern void   slider_selected();

/**************************************************
 * concat.c: utility function to concatenate
 *           command-line arguments into a string.
 **************************************************/
#include <stdio.h>

char * concat_args(n, words)
    int   n;
    char *words[];
{
  char *buffer;
  int   i, len = 0;
  /*
   * If there are no arguments other than the program
   * name, just return an empty string.
   */
  if (n <= 1)
    return ("");
  /*
   * Figure out the total length of the string.  We
   * need to include one space between each word too.
   */
  for (i = 1; i < n; i++)
    len += strlen(words[i]);
  len += (n - 1);    /* One space between each word */
  /*
   * Allocate the buffer and initialize.  Die if
   * memory is not available.
   */
  buffer = (char *) malloc(len + 1);/* For the NULL*/
  if (buffer == NULL) {
    fprintf(stderr, "Out of memory in concat_args()\n");
    exit(1);
  }
  buffer[0] = '\0';
  /*
   * Put each word in the buffer, putting a
   * space between each one.
```

```
   */
  for (i = 1; i < n; i++)  {
    if (i > 1)
      strcat(buffer, " ");
    strcat (buffer, words[i]);
  }
  return (buffer);
}

/**************************************************
 * str2flt.c: Convert a string to a float.
 **************************************************/
#include <X11/Intrinsic.h>
#include <X11/StringDefs.h>

void CvtStringToFloat(args, nargs, fromVal, toVal)
     XrmValuePtr args, fromVal, toVal;
     int         *nargs;
{
  static float result;
  /*
   * Make sure the number of args is correct.
   */
  if (*nargs != 0)
   XtWarning("String to Float conversion needs no arguments");
  /*
   * Convert the string in the fromVal to a floating pt.
   */
  if (sscanf((char *)fromVal->addr, "%f", &result) == 1) {
    /*
     * Make the toVal point to the result.
     */
    toVal->size = sizeof (float);
    toVal->addr = (caddr_t) &result;
  }
  else
  /*
   * If sscanf fails, issue a warning that something is wrong.
   */
   XtStringConversionWarning((char *) fromVal->addr, "Float");
}
```

```
/**************************************************************
* oneline.c: Create a single line editable text field
**************************************************************/
#include <X11/StringDefs.h>
#include <X11/Intrinsic.h>
#include <Xw/Xw.h>
#include <Xw/TextEdit.h>
#include "libXs.h"
/*
 * Just ring the terminal bell.
 */
static void beep(w, event, params, num_params)
     Widget w;
     XEvent *event;
     String *params;
     int     num_params;
{
  XBell(XtDisplay(w), 100);
}
/*
 * Associate the action "beep" with the function.
 */
static XtActionsRec actionsTable [] = {
  {"beep",   beep},
};
/*
 * Override all translations that enter a newline.
 */
static char defaultTranslations[] =
  "Ctrl<Key>J:          beep() \n\
   Ctrl<Key>O:          beep() \n\
   Ctrl<Key>M:          beep() \n\
   <Key> Return:        beep()";

Widget create_one_line_text_widget(name, parent, args, nargs)
     char   *name;
     Widget parent;
     Arg    args[];
     int    nargs;
{
  XFontStruct   *font;
  Widget         w;
```

```
  Arg            wargs[1];
  XtTranslations trans_table;
  /*
   * Add the actions and compile the translations.
   */
  XtAddActions(actionsTable, XtNumber(actionsTable));
  trans_table = XtParseTranslationTable(defaultTranslations);
  /*
   * Create a TextEdit widget.
   */
  w = XtCreateManagedWidget(name, XwtexteditWidgetClass,
                            parent, args, nargs);
  /*
   * Install our translations.
   */
  XtOverrideTranslations(w, trans_table);
  /*
   * Get the font used by the widget.
   */
  XtSetArg(wargs[0], XtNfont, &font);
  XtGetValues(w, wargs, 1);
  /*
   * Set the widget height according to the font height.
   */
  XtSetArg(wargs[0], XtNheight, FONTHEIGHT(font) + 6 );
  XtSetValues(w, wargs, 1);
  return (w);
}

/*********************************************************
 * quit.c: A utility function that adds a quit button
 *********************************************************/
#include <X11/Intrinsic.h>
#include <X11/StringDefs.h>
#include <Xw/Xw.h>
#include <Xw/PButton.h>
/*
 * Define a callback to exit(). Make it static - no need
 * to make it known outside this file.
 */
static void quit_callback(w, client_data, call_data)
     Widget    w;
```

```
     caddr_t    client_data;
     caddr_t    call_data;
{
   exit(0);
}
/*
 * Function to add a quit button to any composite widget.
 */
Widget create_quit_button(label, parent)
     char   *label;
     Widget  parent;
{
  Arg    wargs[1];
  Widget w;
  XtSetArg(wargs[0], XtNlabel, label);
  w = XtCreateManagedWidget("quit", XwpushButtonWidgetClass,
                            parent, wargs, 1);
  /*
   * Quit on the release (button up), so the application can
   * do something on the select (button down) if needed.
   */
  XtAddCallback(w, XtNrelease, quit_callback, NULL);
  return (w);
}

/**********************************************************
 * menus.c: Simple menu package
 **********************************************************/
#include <X11/StringDefs.h>
#include <X11/Intrinsic.h>
#include <X11/Shell.h>
#include <Xw/Xw.h>
#include <Xw/MenuBtn.h>
#include <Xw/Cascade.h>
#include <Xw/PopupMgr.h>
#include "libXs.h"
Widget create_menu_manager(parent, mgrname)
   Widget  parent;
   char   *mgrname;
{
  Widget shell = XtCreatePopupShell(mgrname, shellWidgetClass,
                                    parent, NULL, 0);
```

```
 Widget menu_mgr =XtCreateManagedWidget(mgrname,
                                        XwpopupmgrWidgetClass,
                                        shell, NULL, 0);

  return (menu_mgr);
}

create_pane(mgr, mgrname, name, menulist, nitems)
     Widget       mgr;
     char        *name, *mgrname;
     menu_struct *menulist;
     int          nitems;
{
  Arg         wargs[1];
  Widget      menupane, pane_shell;
  int         i;
  WidgetList buttons;
  /*
   * Allocate a widget list to hold all
   * button widgets.
   */
  buttons = (WidgetList) XtMalloc(nitems * sizeof(Widget));
  /*
   * Create a popup shell to hold this pane.
   */
 pane_shell=XtCreatePopupShell("pane_shell", shellWidgetClass,
                                  mgr, NULL, 0);

  /*
   * Create a Cascade menu pane, and attach
   * it to the given menu manager.
   */
  XtSetArg(wargs[0], XtNattachTo, (XtArgVal) mgrname);
  menupane = XtCreateManagedWidget(name, XwcascadeWidgetClass,
                                     pane_shell, wargs, 1);

  /*
   * Create a menu button for each item in the menu.
   */
  for(i=0;i<nitems;i++){
    buttons[i] = XtCreateWidget(menulist[i].name,
                                XwmenubuttonWidgetClass,
                                menupane, NULL, 0);
    XtAddCallback (buttons[i], XtNselect,
                   menulist[i].func, menulist[i].data);
```

```
  }
  /*
   * Manage all button widgets.
   */
  XtManageChildren(buttons, nitems);
}

/*****************************************************
 * slider.c: utility to make slider move to the sprite
 *           location when clicking the background of
 *           a scrollbar widget.
 *****************************************************/
#include <X11/Intrinsic.h>
#include <Xw/Xw.h>
#include <Xw/ScrollBar.h>

void slider_selected(w, ignore, sliderpos)
     Widget   w;
     caddr_t  ignore;
     int      sliderpos;
{
  Arg wargs[1];
  /*
   * Move the slider bar to the selected point.
   */
  XtSetArg(wargs[0], XtNsliderOrigin, sliderpos);
  XtSetValues(w, wargs, 1);
  /*
   * Call the callback list for XtNsliderMoved to
   * alter the colors appropriately.
   */
  XtCallCallbacks(w, XtNsliderMoved, sliderpos);
}

/**********************************************************
 * invert.c: invert a widget's color.
 **********************************************************/
#include <X11/Intrinsic.h>
#include <X11/StringDefs.h>
#include <Xw/Xw.h>

invert_widget(w)
```

```
     Widget w;
{
  Arg wargs[3];
  int fg, bg;
  /*
   * Get the widget's current colors.
   */
  XtSetArg(wargs[0], XtNforeground, &fg);
  XtSetArg(wargs[1], XtNbackground, &bg);
  XtGetValues(w, wargs, 2);
  /*
   * Reverse them and set the new colors.
   */
  XtSetArg(wargs[0], XtNforeground, bg);
  XtSetArg(wargs[1], XtNbackground, fg);
  XtSetValues(w, wargs, 2);
}

/*******************************************************
 * talkto.c: set up two way pipes
 *******************************************************/
#include<stdio.h>
void
talkto(cmd)
    char   *cmd;
{
  int   to_child[2],  /* pipe descriptors from parent->child*/
        to_parent[2]; /* pipe descriptors from child->parent*/
  int   pid;

  pipe(to_child);
  pipe(to_parent);
  if (pid = fork(), pid == 0){      /* in the child   */
     close(0);                      /* redirect stdin */
     dup(to_child[0]);
     close(1);                      /* redirect stdout*/
     dup(to_parent[1]);

     close(to_child[0]);            /* close pipes    */
     close(to_child[1]);
     close(to_parent[0]);
     close(to_parent[1]);
```

```
     execlp(cmd, cmd, NULL);        /* exec the new cmd  */
   }
   else if (pid > 0){               /* in the parent     */
      close(0);                     /* redirect stdin    */
      dup(to_parent[0]);

      close(1);                     /* redirect stdout   */
      dup(to_child[1]);

      setbuf(stdout, NULL);         /* no buffered output */

      close(to_child[0]);           /* close pipes */
      close(to_child[1]);
      close(to_parent[0]);
      close(to_parent[1]);
    }
    else {                          /* error!       */
      fprintf(stderr,"Couldn't fork process %s\n", cmd);
      exit(1);
    }
}

/**********************************************************
 * wprintf.c: fprintf-like function for StaticText
 **********************************************************/
#include <varargs.h>
#include <stdio.h>
#include <X11/Intrinsic.h>
#include <X11/StringDefs.h>
#include <Xw/Xw.h>
#include <Xw/SText.h>

void wprintf(va_alist)
     va_dcl
{
  Widget w;
  char *format;
  va_list args;
  char str[1000];
  Arg  wargs[1];
  /*
```

```
    * Init the variable length args list.
    */
  va_start(args);
  /*
   * Extract the destination widget.
   * Make sure it is a StaticText widget.
   */
  w = va_arg(args, Widget);
  if(XtClass(w) != XwstatictextWidgetClass)
  XtError("wprintf() requires a Static Text Widget");
   /*
   * Extract the format to be used.
   */
  format = va_arg(args, char *);
  /*
   * Use vsprintf to format the string to be displayed
   * in the StaticText widget.
   */
  vsprintf(str, format, args);
  XtSetArg(wargs[0], XtNstring, str);
  XtSetValues(w, wargs, 1);
  va_end(args);
}
```

APPENDIX G

USING THIS BOOK WITH X11R2

Most of the examples in this book work correctly with either X11 Release 2 or X11 Release 3. In cases where there is a difference, the text describes R3. To avoid any confusion, this appendix lists the sections that are R3 dependent. Some sections also assume that you have a version of the HP X Widget set for R3. (See Appendix D.) The examples in all other sections have been used succesfully with both R2 and R3 widgets and matching versions of the Xt Intrinsics.

- Section 2.5.

  The R2 Intrinsics does not support application contexts, nor multiple displays.

- Section 3.2

  The R2 resource manager requires the top level shell to be included in all resource specifications. For example, the complete name and class lists on page 45 would have to be given as

  ```
  draw.draw.panel.commands.button1.foreground
  Draw.TopLevelShell.BulletinBoard.RowCol.PushButton.Foreground
  ```

  Of course, an asterisk can be always used as a wild card, so incomplete specifications can be done as described in Chapter 3.

- Section 5.7

  The R2 Intrinscs does not implement WorkProcs, so this entire example does not apply to R2.

- Section 9.3

The fileviewer requires a slight change to work correctly with R2 widgets. The lines

```
Dimension      canvas_height;      /* canvas dimensions     */
Dimension      canvas_width;
```

in the declaration of the text_data struct on page 201 must be changed to

```
int    canvas_height;      /* canvas dimensions     */
int    canvas_width;
```

- Section 11.4

  The R2 Intrinsics does not implement the selection mechanisms described in this chapter. The basic Xlib facilities can be used to implement similar applications.

- Section 12.2 and 12.3

  The Dial widget will work with the R2 Intrinsics with only a minor change. The **display_accelerator** and **extensions** members of the **CoreClassPart** were added with R3. If these are removed, both the Dial and SquareDial widgets will compile with the R2 Intrinsics.

- Section 13.2

  The Row widget will also work with R2 if the **display_accelerator** and **extensions** members of the **CoreClassPart** are removed. The **extensions** member of the **CompositeClassPart** must also be removed.

- Chapter 14, Section 14.2

  This widget is more difficult to modify for R2. First, the The **display_accelerator** and **extensions** members of the **CoreClassPart** must be removed, along with the **extensions** members of the **CompositeClassPart** and **ConstraintClassPart**. In addition, the **ConstraintSetValues()** procedure changed in R3. In R2, the **current** argument contained the address of the "real" widget, while in R3 the **new** parameter is the real widget. Therefore, in R2, the **ConstraintSetValues()** procedure, which requires the address of the widget, must be changed to the following:

```
static Boolean ConstraintSetValues(current, request, new)
    Widget current, request, new;
{
  TreeConstraints newconst =
                    (TreeConstraints) new->core.constraints;
  TreeConstraints current_const =
                  (TreeConstraints) current->core.constraints;
  XsTreeWidget tw = (XsTreeWidget) new->core.parent;
  /*
```

```
     * If the super_node field has changed, remove the widget
     * from the old widget's sub_nodes list and add it to the
     * new one.
     */
    if(current_const->super_node != newconst->super_node){
     if(current_const->super_node)
       delete_node(current_const->super_node, current);
     if(newconst->super_node)
       insert_new_node(newconst->super_node, current);
     /*
      * If the Tree widget has been realized,
      * compute new layout.
      */
     if(XtIsRealized(tw))
       new_layout(tw);
   }
   return (False);
 }
```

BIBLIOGRAPHY

C and UNIX Programming

[Kern78] Kernigham, B. W. and R. Pike, *The Unix Programming Environment*, Prentice Hall, 1978.

[Kern78] Kerningham, B. W. and D. M. Ritchie, *The C Programming Language*, Prentice Hall, 1978.

[Roch85] Rochkind, M., *Advanced Unix Programming*, Prentice Hall, 1985.

Graphics

[Foley82] Foley, J. D. and A. van Dam, *Fundamentals of Interactive Computer Graphics*, Addison-Wesley, 1983.

[Mand83] Mandelbrot, B., *The Fractal Geometry of Nature*, W. H. Freeman, 1983.

Object-Oriented Programming

[Cox86] Cox, Brad, *Object-Oriented Programming, An Evolutionary Approach*, Addison-Wesley, 1986.

[Goldb83] Goldberg, Adele and David Robson, *Smalltalk-80: The Language and its Implementation*, Addison-Wesley, 1983.

[Mayer88] Mayer, Bertrand, *Object-Oriented Software Construction*, Prentice Hall, 1988.

[Stroust86] Stroustrup, Bjarne, *The C++ Programming Language*, Addison-Wesley, 1986.

User Interfaces

[Schneid87] Shneiderman, Ben , *Designing the User Interface*, Addison-Wesley, 1987.

[Smith89] Smith, Wanda, *Using Computer Color Effectively*, Prentice-Hall, 1989.

Window Systems

[Hopgood86] Hopgood, F. R. A., *Methodology of Window Management*, Springer-Verlag, New York, 1986.

[Myers88] Myers, Brad A., "Window Interfaces: A Taxonomy of Window Manager User Interfaces," *IEEE Computer Graphics & Applications*, vol. 8, no. 5, pp. 65-84, September, 1988.

[Pike88] Pike, Rob, "Window Systems Should Be Transparent," *USENIX Computing Systems*, vol. 1, no. 3, pp. 279-296, Summer, 1988.

The X Window System

[Asente88] Asente, Paul, "Simplicity and Productivity," *UNIX Review*, vol. 6, no. 9, pp. 57-63.

[Gancarz86] Gancarz, M., "UWM: A User Interface for X Windows," in *Proceedings of the Summer, 1986 USENIX Conference*, pp. 429-440.

[Gettys88] Gettys, Jim, "Flexibility Is Key To Meet Requirements For X Window System Design," *Computer Technology Review*, pp. 87-89, Summer, 1988.

[Gettys86] Gettys, Jim, "Problems Implementing Window Systems in UNIX," in *Proceedings of the Winter, 1986 USENIX Conference*, pp. 89-97.

[Jones89] Jones, Oliver, *Introduction to the X Window System*, Prentice-Hall, 1989.

[Lee88] Lee, Ed, "Window of Opportunity," *UNIX Review*, vol. 6, no. 6, pp 47-61.

[Lemke89] Lemke, David and S. H. Rosenthall, "Visualizing X11 Clients", in *Proceedings of the Winter, 1989 USENIX Conference*, pp. 125-138.

[Linton89] Linton, Mark A., John M. Vlissides, and Paul R. Calder, "Composing User Interfaces with InterViews", *IEEE Computer*, vol. 22, no. 2, pp. 65-84, February, 1989.

[McCorm88] McCormack, Joel and Paul Asente, "Using the X Toolkit or How to Write a Widget," in *Proceedings of the Summer, 1988 USENIX Conference*, pp. 1-13.

[McCorm88] McCormack, Joel and Paul Asente, "An Overview of the X Toolkit," in *Proceedings of the ACM SIGGRAPH Symposium on User Interface Software*, pp. 46-55, October, 1988.

[Nadeau88] Nadeau, David R., "High-Performance 3-D Graphics In A Window Environment," *Computer Technology Review*, pp. 89-93, Fall,1988.

[Nye88] Nye, Adrian, *The Xlib Programming Manul*, O'Reilly and Associates, 1988.

[Nye88] Nye, Adrian, *The Xlib Reference Manul*, O'Reilly and Associates, 1988.

[O'Reilly89] O'Reilly, Tim, "The Toolkits (and Politics) of X Windows," *UNIX World*, vol. 6, no. 2, pp. 66-73, February, 1989.

[Probst86] Probst, Richard, "OPEN LOOK Toolkits," *SunTechnology*, vol. 1, no. 4, pp. 76-86, Autumn, 1986.

[Rao87] Rao, R. and S. Wallace, "The X Toolkit," in *Proceedings of the Summer, 1987 USENIX Conference*.

[Roch89] Rochkind, Marc. "XVTL: A Virtual Toolkit for Portability Between Window Systems," in *Proceedings of the Winter, 1989 USENIX Conference*, pp. 151-163.

[Rosen88] Rosenthal, David S., "A Simple X.11 Client Program, or, How Hard Can It Really Be to Write 'Hello, World'?," in *Proceedings of the Winter, 1988 USENIX Conference*, pp. 229-235.

[Rosen88] Rosenthal, David S., "Going For Baroque," *UNIX Review*, vol. 6, no. 6, pp. 71-79.

[Rost88] Rost, Randi J., "Adding a Dimension to X," *UNIX Review*, vol. 6, no. 10, pp. 51-59.

[Schaufler88] Schaufler, Robin, "X11/NeWS Design Overview," in *Proceedings of the Summer, 1988 USENIX Conference*, pp. 23-35.

[Scheifler88] Scheifler, Robert W., James Gettys, and Ron Newman, *X Window System*, DEC Press, 1988.

[Scheifler86] Scheifler, Robert W. and Jim Gettys, "The X Window System," *ACM Transactions on Graphics*, vol. 5, no. 2, pp. 79-109, April, 1986.

[Swick88] Swick, Ralph R. and Mark S. Ackerman, "The X Toolkit: More Bricks for Building User Interfaces," in *Proceedings of the Winter, 1988 USENIX Conference*, pp. 221-233.

INDEX

D

E

F

G

H

I

P

R

S

T

U

V

W

X

Y